Pro Spring Dynamic Modules for OSGi™ Service Platforms

Daniel Rubio

Apress®

Pro Spring Dynamic Modules for OSGi™ Service Platforms

ISBN-13 (pbk): 978-1-4302-1612-4

ISBN-13 (electronic): 978-1-4302-1613-1

9 8 7 6 5 4 3 2 1

Lead Editors: Steve Anglin, Tom Welsh
Technical Reviewer: Gerd Wütherich
Editorial Board: Clay Andres, Steve Anglin, Mark Beckner, Ewan Buckingham, Tony Campbell, Gary Cornell, Jonathan Gennick, Jonathan Hassell, Michelle Lowman, Matthew Moodie, Duncan Parkes, Jeffrey Pepper, Frank Pohlmann, Ben Renow-Clarke, Dominic Shakeshaft, Matt Wade, Tom Welsh
Project Manager: Kylie Johnston
Copy Editor: Ami Knox
Associate Production Director: Kari Brooks-Copony
Production Editor: Laura Cheu
Compositor: Susan Glinert Stevens
Proofreader: Liz Welch
Indexer: Brenda Miller
Artist: April Milne
Cover Designer: Kurt Krames
Manufacturing Director: Tom Debolski

Distributed to the book trade worldwide by Springer-Verlag New York, Inc., 233 Spring Street, 6th Floor, New York, NY 10013. Phone 1-800-SPRINGER, fax 201-348-4505, e-mail orders-ny@springer-sbm.com, or visit http://www.springeronline.com.

For information on translations, please contact Apress directly at 2855 Telegraph Avenue, Suite 600, Berkeley, CA 94705. Phone 510-549-5930, fax 510-549-5939, e-mail info@apress.com, or visit http://www.apress.com.

Apress and friends of ED books may be purchased in bulk for academic, corporate, or promotional use. eBook versions and licenses are also available for most titles. For more information, reference our Special Bulk Sales–eBook Licensing web page at http://www.apress.com/info/bulksales.

The source code for this book is available to readers at http://www.apress.com.

To my family and friends. The ones who put up with the many instances of "I can't today . . . " and "I can't tommorrow . . . " that brought about this book.

Contents at a Glance

Contents

About the Author

DANIEL RUBIO is a consultant with over 10 years of experience in enterprise and web technologies. Specializing in web-based architectures that integrate with back-end systems such as relational databases, ERPs, and CICS, he's relied on Java, CORBA, and .NET technology throughout his career to deliver cost-effective solutions to the financial and manufacturing industries.

Additionally, he writes articles on emerging technologies for various content networks in this same space, which include TheServerSide.com, Oracle Technology Network, SearchSOA.com, and his own blog, WebForefront.com. Currently, Daniel is founder and technical lead at MashupSoft.com.

About the Technical Reviewer

GERD WÜTHERICH is a consultant and software architect living in Hamburg, Germany. His main area of expertise is in building modular enterprise application systems utilizing OSGi technology, especially in combination with the Spring Framework. He is the author of the German OSGi book *Die OSGi Service Platform* and a frequent speaker at international conferences. More information is available at `http://www.gerd-wuetherich.de`.

Acknowledgments

Even with prior writing experience, I never thought writing a book would be such a massive undertaking. I was accustomed to a fast loop between myself and an editor with three or four e-mail exchanges from proposal to finished article. If it took over a thousand exchanges simply to help me shape the content of this book, I wouldn't be surprised.

First off I'd like to acknowledge everyone at Apress. The people involved at the initial stages of the book—when it was just an idea: Steve Anglin, Dominic Shakeshaft, and Joohn Choe. The people with whom I interacted once the book got underway all the way to its end: Kylie Johnston, Tom Welsh, and Matthew Moodie. And the people involved toward the final stages of this project: Ami Knox, Laura Cheu, and Stephanie Parker. And of course, every other person at Apress who had a role in this book with whom I didn't have the opportunity to interact directly.

For helping me to keep the content accurate on the technical front, special thanks go to Gerd Wütherich, who served as the book's technical reviewer, as well as Colin Yates, who initially took part in the technical review process.

In addition, the book would not have been possible without many articles, documents, and blog posts by the people who shape OSGi, Spring, and Spring-DM technology, including Adrian Colyer, Alex Blewitt, Costin Leau, Eric Newcomer, Neil Bartlett, Martin Lippert, Peter Kriens, Rob Harrop, and Rod Johnson. And of course, the many other people active in these areas who surely influenced my thought processes, but whom I unfortunately can't credit individually due to space constraints and the limitations of memory.

And finally, I thank my family and friends. Although did I evoke long blank stares after I tried to explain this book's purpose in layman's terms, but (in what is perhaps the best morale support one could ask for), these same people kept asking me about this project's progress. I would need too much space to do it individually, so to everyone who asked, thank you. I consider you a part of this effort for providing face-to-face moral support.

Introduction

This book is about OSGi's role in enterprise Java and how the Spring Dynamic Modules for OSGi (Spring-DM) fulfills this role.

I first learned about OSGi when the Eclipse IDE started using it in its plug-in architecture. At the time, the versioning and modularity features seemed nicer "for an IDE" than what was available using stand-alone Java. However, OSGi still seemed something reserved to the internal workings of an IDE.

Next, I read about Java SE initiatives to incorporate similar modularity features, with OSGi being a leading contender. Competing in this space were JSR-277, "Java Module System," and JSR-291, "Dynamic Component Support for Java," the latter based on OSGi principles. Knowing that OSGi might very well influence the Java language itself—via Java SE—raised my interest in OSGi and how it could be applied to scenarios in the enterprise Java space.

It didn't take much research to find out that some Java EE application server vendors had relied on those same OSGi features to design their products. But in much the same way as the Eclipse IDE, OSGi still seemed reserved to the internal workings of a product. So I was still left with a big question: could OSGi influence enterprise Java applications in some other way? When I discovered Spring-DM, the answer became clear: yes.

OSGi along with Spring-DM will make you rethink the way you design Java applications. Support for runtime versioning is probably one of the biggest changes you will appreciate. Running multiple versions of the same class in a JVM instance is a difficult task in stand-alone Java, requiring the use of custom class loaders.

With OSGi this is not the case. No longer will you need to check your `CLASSPATH` variable to avoid running multiple JARs with the same name that may contain conflicting classes. OSGi eliminates this burden, letting you install and run as many different JAR versions as required in a single JVM instance.

This same approach will also play a part in your enterprise Java applications. The typical enterprise Java application is packaged as a Web Archive (WAR) or Enterprise Archive (EAR), monolithic formats containing every dependency used by an application. While these formats are warranted due to the way in which Java EE application servers (containers) operate—providing class isolation for each application—OSGi will make these heavyweight formats look irrelevant, since it can manage versioning and class isolation at a another level.

Additionally, WARs and EARs often contain the same staple JARs, such as logging, Java frameworks, or special libraries, leading to multiple instances of the same JAR taking up valuable memory resources in application servers. By avoiding WARs and EARs, OSGi can manage a single JAR, with different versions, that is shared across various applications.

As a consequence of applying OSGi principles to enterprise Java applications, the deployment infrastructure—Java EE application servers—will also reveal some weaknesses. That is why you also need to learn about SpringSource dm Server, a new breed of Java EE application server designed to accommodate the special features of OSGi and Spring-DM.

Once you've got a feel for OSGi's packaging approach and the benefits it brings in terms of runtime versioning and class isolation, you can start to think about OSGi services. Though not a prerequisite for using OSGi's other features, OSGi services will allow your applications to expose and consume business logic in more manageable pieces.

Instead of having application JARs expose and access Java classes available in other JARs, as is typically done, OSGi allows you to expose and consume prebuilt services contained in JARs. This allows business logic to become more manageable, since you don't have to access individual classes, but rather just query an OSGi service to obtain an end result more quickly.

Still, don't think you need to rely on the entire Spring Framework as a prerequisite to use OSGi in your enterprise Java applications. Spring-DM simply makes it easier to use OSGi in your applications employing the principles set forth by this framework. The purpose of Spring-DM is that you won't have to learn or deal with the OSGi API directly, but rather rely on dependency injection and descriptors—tenets of the Spring Framework—to work with OSGi.

As a technologist, you may well ask yourself whether OSGi and Spring-DM are the future, or just alternatives to other approaches that are likely to surpass them. I can point you to various sources that indicate that both OSGi's and Spring-DM's futures are solid.

Project Jigsaw is one of the catalysts that makes OSGi a frontrunner in the race for incorporating a module system into Java SE. For more details on this project, I will point you to a post from Mark Reinhold, Principal Engineer at Sun Microsystems for JavaSE, on the subject and its relation to OSGi: `http://blogs.sun.com/mr/entry/jigsaw`.

As far as Spring-DM is concerned, its principles now form part of RFC-124, "A Component Model for OSGi," which itself forms part of OSGi's 4.2 release, so its relevance is more than assured in the OSGi ecosystem. For more details on this last initiative, I can point you to two sources, one by Eric Newcomer, Chief Technology Officer at IONA, `http://blogs.iona.com/newcomer/archives/000578.html`, and another by Adrian Colyer, Chief Technology Officer at SpringSource, `http://blog.springsource.com/2008/09/01/early-draft-of-osgi-service-platform-release-42-specification-now-available/`.

To what extent OSGi and Spring-DM will form part of your day-to-day tasks as a Java developer is still questionable, but that they will steadily gain influence should be without question. You need not look as far as the previous resources to observe the traction both technologies are gaining in terms of standardization—explore the contents of this book to discover for yourself the benefits they bring to Java development.

Who This Book Is For

Java developers who use the Spring Framework and are looking to take advantage of OSGi features as well as Java developers in general looking to explore OSGi's role on server-side development will benefit.

How This Book Is Structured

Chapter 1 provides an introduction to OSGi. It includes a detailed look at the concepts and benefits of using OSGi with Java. It also contains a sample application to help you familiarize yourself with how OSGi applications are structured and deployed.

Chapter 2 provides an introduction to the Spring Framework. It includes a detailed look at the core concepts that have made this framework so popular in enterprise Java applications. It also contains a comprehensive application that illustrates various areas covered by the framework, such as persistence through Relational Database Management Systems (RDBMS), Model-View-Controller (MVC) design, integration testing, and deployment to a web container. Though anyone familiar with the Spring Framework should be able to skip this chapter, I recommend that you take a look at the sample application, since future chapters involve redesigned versions of this same application.

Chapter 3 provides an introduction to integrating Spring and OSGi. It includes a detailed look at the various layers—as they relate to enterprise Java applications—that need to be contemplated in order to integrate Spring and OSGi. In addition, it also contains a sample application that illustrates how Spring-DM is used in the overall design of an application.

Chapter 4 covers Spring-DM in depth. It includes an overview of fragments and extenders—OSGi concepts—and how they relate to Spring-DM. It also covers the various Spring-DM elements used inside Spring-type descriptors for registering and looking up OSGi services.

Chapter 5 provides an introduction to the SpringSource dm Server. It includes a detailed look at why this software eases the deployment of OSGi and Spring-DM applications, as well as the concepts you need to familiarize yourself with in order to use it. In addition, it contains a sample application that illustrates how to design and deploy an application using an RDBMS. (This is a version of the application introduced in Chapter 2.)

Chapter 6 covers OSGi versioning. It includes a series of case scenarios and the entire spectrum of OSGi versioning behaviors, which includes package versioning, bundle versioning, fragment versioning, and versioning cases applicable to Spring-DM and the SpringSource dm Server. A discussion on OSGi split packages is also included.

Chapter 7 covers data access and bundle management without the SpringSource dm Server. It takes a detailed look at deploying full-fledged applications without the provisions of the SpringSource dm Server. This includes a detailed look at RDBMS access in the context of OSGi, bundle dependency management using Apache Ivy, and using BND to transform JARs into OSGi-compliant bundles. It also contains a sample application ported from Chapter 5.

Chapter 8 covers web applications in the context of Spring-DM. It zooms in on how web applications are delegated and processed by an OSGi'fied web container. It also contains application samples for enabling Secure Socket Layer (SSL) or https:// web sites, working with Flex applications, and using the Jetty web server, all in the context of Spring-DM. These last applications are ported from the application presented in Chapter 7.

Chapter 9 covers Spring-DM testing. It includes a detailed look at the Spring-DM testing framework and how it facilitates the creation of tests in the context of Spring-DM. In addition, it provides working tests for the applications designed in earlier chapters.

Prerequisites

The book requires working knowledge of the Java programming language.

Downloading the Code

The source code for this book is available to readers at `http://www.apress.com` in the Source Code section of this book's home page. Please feel free to visit the Apress web site and download all the code there. You can also check for errata and find related titles from Apress.

Contacting the Author

You can contact me at `osgi@webforefront.com`.

CHAPTER 1

Introducing OSGi

OSGi—originally an acronym for Open Services Gateway Initiative—emerged in 1999 to address the needs of the embedded device market. Close to 30 companies, many of which were already invested in the language of the time, Java, worked to develop this initiative, designed to use that language to target the embedded device market for the home.[1]

1999 was a crazy year in the technology sector, with everything under the sun showing some type of promise in the whirlwind dot-com mania that ensued. It was a time to dream big, be ambitious, and think outside the box more than ever, and the architects behind OSGi did just that, envisioning a set of features missing in the Java platform at the time.

Chaotic though its time of inception was, OSGi's design has proved resilient and has helped it to expand into many markets that employ Java software. Let's take a 100,000-foot view of OSGi's primary feature set before we zoom in on the details of its working parts.

Hot-pluggability was one feature envisioned by the OSGi expert group, a technical term referring to a system capable of being altered without interrupting its ongoing operation.

Today high-end disk arrays are perhaps the most common hot-pluggable item in the IT sector, allowing any disk failure to be corrected without the need for a system to be shut down, thus guaranteeing 24-hour availability.

In the embedded device for the home circa 1999, hot-pluggability was not common. So you need only imagine the ripple effect a device failure could have on a networked home or the angst of rebooting this type of system if any one device needed to be repaired or reinstalled.

Another target pursued by OSGi members was that of *autodiscovery*, whereby one device is capable of reusing software present in another device. Here again, in retrospect to the year 1999, embedded devices were severely limited in terms of memory and storage resources, so that a device autodiscovering and reusing software present in another device was a highly desirable trait.

If you were to draw OSGi's focus areas in terms of bull's-eyes, hot-pluggability and autodiscovery would likely be the most visible features from 100,000 feet, with a common pattern of *dynamic behavior* emerging between the two.

1. Peter Kriens, "How OSGi Changed My Life," *ACM Queue* Vol. 5, No. 8 (January/February 2008)

When a damaged disk is replaced on a hot-pluggable disk array, it is said to have been *dynamically* configured, since no system shutdown ever takes places. Similarly, an autodiscovery process by its very definition is something that takes place dynamically; since no intervention takes places, dependencies are simply autodiscovered.

So if you attempted to summarize the essence behind hot-pluggability and autodiscoverability, you would likely agree that all this entails *dynamic behavior*, which is why OSGi defines itself as a *dynamic module system for Java*.[2]

So it is that today you can see OSGi's feature set influencing the Java ecosystem, arising from its origins in the embedded market and spreading to the automotive sector, smart phones, development tools, and more recently, Java's de facto standard for server-side platforms, Java Enterprise Edition (EE).

Armed with this brief overview, let's dig deeper into where these concepts are applied in the architecture of a Java application, and what new concepts you need to familiarize yourself with in order to put OSGi's feature set to work.

OSGi Concepts and Architecture

Let's begin the same way most maps illustrating travel routes start out, using a "you are here" point of reference to illustrate how a non-OSGi Java application evolves into one using OSGi.

Java's Virtual Machine, Java Classes, and the CLASSPATH Variable

Class files made up of bytecode—it doesn't get any more basic than that for a Java application, no matter what operating system you are targeting or whether you're using 32 bits or 64 bits, have 64KB or 4GB of memory, or are using the oldest or latest Java version. The architecture imposed by Java itself forces any application to use class files made up of bytecode to deliver on Java's mantra, "write once, run everywhere," via the Java Virtual Machine (JVM).

Well, this is excellent for all the benefits of using the JVM, but let's examine how it is these class files made up of bytecode interact with the JVM. I will start by mentioning that a JVM requires precise instructions on where to locate class files needed by the applications running on it, a process that is achieved using the `CLASSPATH` variable.

The `CLASSPATH` variable is a colon- or semicolon-separated list—the former for Unix, the latter for Windows—containing the location of each class file needed to properly execute an application running on a JVM. Though individually declaring class files inside the `CLASSPATH` variable is possible, declaring groups of classes as a unit is far more typical.

2. OSGi Alliance, "OSGi Technology—The Solution," `http://www.osgi.org/About/Technology#Solution`

The unit format used for the purpose of grouping Java classes is the *JAR* format, or Java Archive, which is nothing more than a zipped file containing associated class files.

So it is that once a JVM is started, its bootstrapping classes go on to form part of the JVM's memory footprint, with the remaining classes declared in the `CLASSPATH` variable being loaded into memory as they are needed by applications.

The mechanism is simple, so simple in fact, that besides the special flag—`Xbootclasspath`, which allows the JVM to load certain class files or JAR files before the core Java classes (a.k.a. bootstrapping classes)—there is no way to add more sophisticated behaviors to the way the `CLASSPATH` variable and Java classes interact. In this case, simplicity gives the following characteristics to your JVM and the applications executing on it:

- **One class name and version per class loader (a JVM uses one class loader by default)**: Classes are accessible on a last declared–last loaded basis. This means that if for some reason the same class or multiple JARs containing the same class are declared, it will be the bytecode contained in the last declared class that is considered valid for that particular JVM instance. This can have the most serious repercussions when deploying multiple classes or JAR files, each dependent on different versions of the same class, as only one class by name can form part of a JVM instance. Class loaders are an exception to this rule; see the sidebar "Class Loaders: Custom Class Loading in a JVM" for more background on this concept.

- **No dependency awareness between JARs**: There is no awareness outside the internal packaging namespace used in the Java classes themselves and whatever caution is exerted by the creator of each JAR as to which classes depend on one another. At best, this can cause the tiresome burden of hunting down unmet class dependencies in an application, or at worst, the versioning clashes already mentioned.

- **No modifications to a running JVM**: Unless a JVM instance is completely stopped and restarted again, no upgrade can be performed on either classes or JARs.

CLASS LOADERS: CUSTOM CLASS LOADING IN A JVM

A JVM can support multiple classes by the same name and different version but only using custom class loaders.

By default a JVM has two class loaders, a bootstrap class loader for JVM classes and a system class loader for classes declared in the `CLASSPATH` variable. Additional class loaders can provide isolation for multiple classes by the same name and different version. The following diagram illustrates this class loader hierarchy.

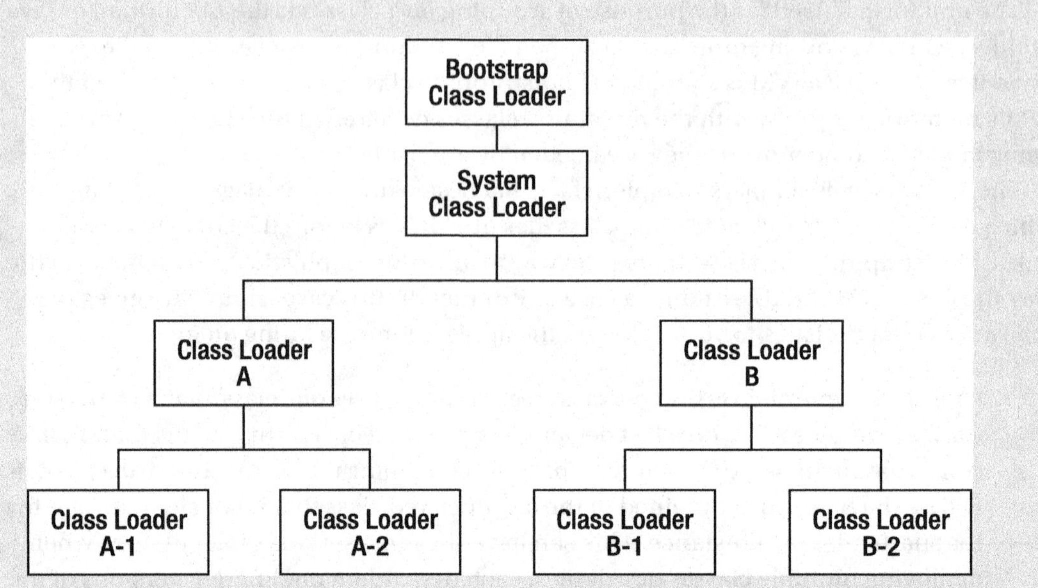

However, adding more class loaders requires using Java APIs, making class loaders an integral part of an application's design that have to be contemplated from the outset. For this reason, most applications rely on the single-system class loader provided by the JVM, complicating the use of multiple classes by the same name and different version.

Java EE application servers are the perfect example of class loader use, providing an environment running on a JVM in which multiple Java applications are deployed. In such cases, class loaders are fundamental to avoid conflicts between applications running on a server. The subject of class loaders and Java EE application servers is expanded in Chapter 3.

At first sight, these characteristics may seem minor or even be seen as unreasonable criticism by someone who is just looking for drawbacks in Java's `CLASSPATH` variable and class file loading. But if thoroughly analyzed, you can conclude they contribute heavily to some errors and undesired behaviors that are all too common in Java applications.

One such error is that of class-loading conflicts, on occasion referred to as "JAR Hell" or simply observed as `java.lang.IncompatibleClassChangeError`. This type of error is increasingly common in JVMs used for deploying enterprise applications, given the size of these applications and their often intertwined relationships.

If a sufficiently large application of this kind is deployed on a JVM, it can be extremely difficult to debug and correct. That can happen, for example, if an application relies on both library A and library B, and each of these libraries in turn relies on different versions of the same XML parser or application logger.

Similarly, another error that can be attributed to the characteristics of the `CLASSPATH` variable is `java.lang.OutOfMemoryException`, which is thrown when a JVM cannot allocate more memory to fulfill its operations. This error is often associated with memory leaks, due to circular references or unallocated objects in the life cycle of an application.

Last but not least, let's not forget `java.lang.ClassNotFound`, which indicates an application is missing one particular class in the classpath in order to fulfill its intended purpose. Since each JAR file does not explicitly indicate what classes it needs or what it can offer the outside world, solving a `java.lang.ClassNotFoundException` error can become a pretty expensive trial-and-error process of adding and removing classes to the `CLASSPATH` variable, with the potential of introducing versioning conflicts.

The characteristics of the JVM and `CLASSPATH` also make it awkward, and perhaps risky, to make changes to a running Java application. When an application is running on a stand-alone workstation or PC, it may seem trivial to stop and restart it. But as uptime requirements get more demanding, and availability more essential, it becomes steadily less acceptable to stop a JVM for class upgrades.

As you've probably realized, most of the JVM and `CLASSPATH` issues presented in the preceding text exist because they are overlooked by the current JVM technology curve. So let's now shift our attention to OSGi's feature set, which solves many of these issues, and get moving toward an OSGi-based architecture.

The OSGi Bundle

If there is a central theme to OSGi, it is that of a bundle. A *bundle* is a group of Java classes and additional resources equipped with a detailed manifest on all its contents, as well as additional services needed to give the included group of Java classes more sophisticated behaviors, to the extent of deeming the entire aggregate a *component*.[3]

The first thing you need to realize is that an *OSGi bundle is a JAR file*. This statement has one very important consequence: OSGi's primary building block is not a radical departure from the packaging model used throughout the Java world; it's simply a richer type of JAR file.

Still, you may question why the need to reinvent a proven format like a JAR. As it turns out, a JAR file's contents are isolated from every other surrounding Java class and action that occurs inside the JVM, so how do you make a JAR file aware of its surroundings?

This is actually quite easy. State what a JAR file needs to be informed about, what it requires from the outside world, and what it can offer outsiders. How? By adding OSGi headers to the `MANIFEST.MF` file already included in a JAR.[4]

A `MANIFEST.MF` file is a simple text file attached to an underlying JAR structure—inside the `META-INF` directory—that contains information about its contents. In the case of OSGi headers, these values express numerous behaviors that allow its contents to reap the benefits of dynamic loading and all the virtues this entails. Listing 1-1 illustrates a basic `MANIFEST.MF` file with OSGi headers.

---

3. OSGi Alliance, "OSGi Technology—Conclusion," `http://www.osgi.org/About/Technology#Conclusion`
4. Sun Microsystems, "Java Archive (JAR) files," `http://java.sun.com/j2se/1.5.0/docs/guide/jar/index.html`

Listing 1-1. *MANIFEST.MF File with OSGi Headers*

```
Bundle-Name: Hello World
Bundle-Description: A Hello World bundle for Pro-Spring OSGi
Bundle-Version: 1.0.0
Bundle-Activator: com.apress.springosgi.ch1.Activator
Export-Package: com.apress.springosgi.ch1;version="1.0.0"
Import-Package: org.osgi.framework;version="1.3.0"
```

The meaning of the contents in Listing 1-1 is as follows:

- `Bundle-Name`: Simply assigns a short name to the bundle
- `Bundle-Description`: Expresses a lengthier description for what the bundle will do
- `Bundle-Version`: Designates a version number to the bundle
- `Bundle-Activator`: Indicates the class name to be invoked once a bundle is activated
- `Export-Package`: Expresses what Java packages contained in a bundle will be made available to the outside world
- `Import-Package`: Indicates what Java packages will be required from the outside world, in order to fulfill the dependencies needed in a bundle

OSGI MANIFEST HEADERS

For those of you wishing to explore the full set of available OSGi manifest headers, you can browse through the Appendix, which contains a complete list of values. The Appendix is available online at the Apress web site in the Book Extras section at `http://www.apress.com/book/view/9781430216124`.

OSGi's dynamic behavior can best be understood by first looking at the use of `Export-Package` and `Import-Package`, given that these values set the stage for a leaner and smarter packaging format than that offered by JAR files.

By explicitly declaring these values, a JAR file transformed into an OSGi bundle can effectively avoid including all but its utmost essential packages and also expose its core packages to the benefit of other bundles running in the same system. Notice how Listing 1-1 assigns Java package values to the manifest headers `Import-Package` and `Export-Package`. This allows OSGi to dynamically import packages from other bundles, as well as export packages so they can be dynamically discovered by other bundles. This makes an application's JARs smaller and smarter in terms of the classes it uses.

Also notice how the imported and exported packages in Listing 1-1 are appended with version values. This further classifies the package version needed by a bundle, as well as the hosted package version available to other bundles. Note that if version values are omitted, packages are assumed to be unique.

CLASS LOADERS REVISITED: THE OSGI WAY

A benefit to using OSGi's bundle format is that an OSGi environment assigns a class loader to each bundle. This design is the basis on which the OSGi headers `Export-Package` and `Import-Package` function, with each class loader working as a gateway exposing and accessing only those packages explicitly declared in a manifest.

However, these class loaders are not the same as those created via Java APIs and added to a JVM's system class loader; these are OSGi-administered class loaders. The difference could not be more critical, because instead of designing a class loader hierarchy yourself, OSGi automatically creates one for you based on bundles. The following diagram illustrates this class loader hierarchy:

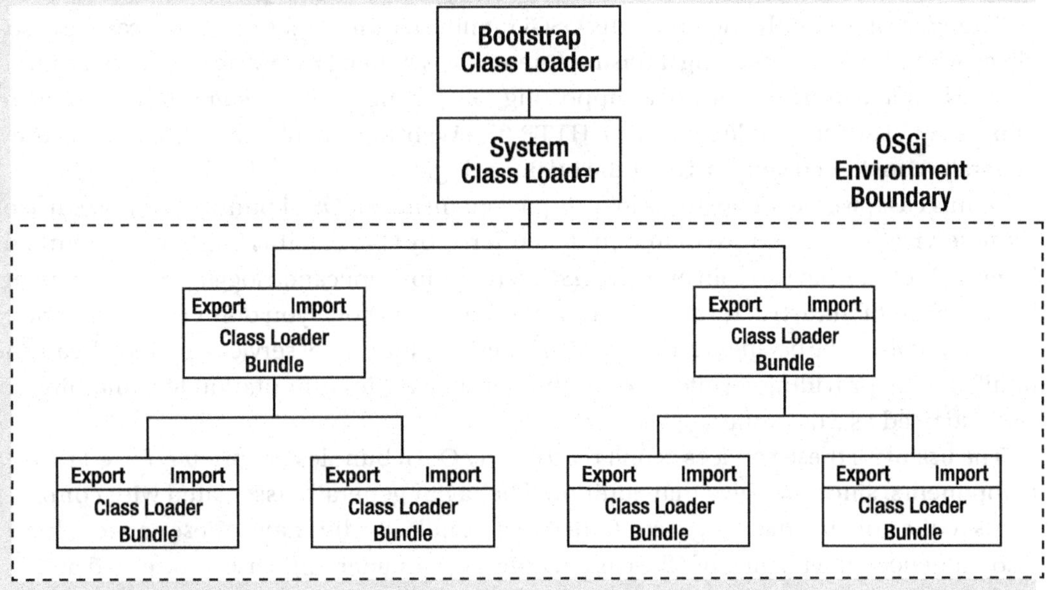

So where does this leave the `CLASSPATH` variable and a JVM's default class loaders? In the same place, everything keeps running under the system class loader. It only means an OSGi environment manages a separate class loader hierarchy, which is in contact with the parent system class loader.

Still, another important piece that has dynamic implications in this OSGi manifest is the value pertaining to `Bundle-Activator`. Whereas `Export-Package` and `Import-Package` simply contain values to packages that would otherwise form part of a standard JAR file, the value for `Bundle-Activator`—which is a Java class in itself—contains logic that implements *OSGi services*.

OSGi services are a critical step to understanding OSGi's "big picture," so with a keen eye read and reread the following paragraphs if necessary until you firmly grasp the concept. Loosely speaking, an OSGi bundle can have three types of services:

- **Management services** that are *completely agnostic to the business logic* contained in the Java packages that make up the bundle
- **Infrastructure services** that *support the business logic* contained in the packages that make up the bundle
- **Business services** that *expose actual business logic* contained in the Java packages that make up bundle

Referring back to the OSGi manifest you just saw, the class assigned to `Bundle-Activator` contains services related to the life cycle of a bundle—what actions to take once a bundle is loaded into memory—and hence can be considered a management service.

Though not explicitly shown in this OSGi manifest, other types of classes can be associated with a bundle containing infrastructure services. When I use the term "infrastructure services," it's to exert the idea of a supporting role for the business logic contained in an application: services like logging, I/O, HTTP (the Web's protocol), and XML parsing are generally considered supportive of the business logic.

In this case, whatever business logic is packed inside an OSGi bundle can make use of these services in the same dynamic context offered by OSGi. At this juncture, it might not be entirely clear what you gain by using OSGi services for application logging or XML parsing, but every bit of infrastructure service reuse is that much code you don't have to rewrite.

Finally comes the business service, which is perhaps the type of service you may already be familiar with, providing results on everything from a basic computation to something as sophisticated as a data query.

The use of all these services is one reason why OSGi bundles are often referred to as components, since they give that additional behavior generally associated with components to the core business logic contained in a bundle. Additionally, these services have also influenced the tagging of OSGi as a technology for enabling service-oriented architecture (SOA).

The OSGi specification sets forth a series of predefined services, so up next the discussion will focus on this subset of OSGi services as you familiarize yourself with the actual OSGi framework.

Note The OSGi specification makes no distinction between services as it's expressed in this last section. In order to help explain the concept of a bundle, this division of management, infrastructure, and business services was made to let you know some of OSGi's services are there to serve the bundle itself, others to support the business logic contained in a bundle, and others to expose business logic. In the remainder of the book, you will see the term "service" used universally no matter what purpose it serves for a bundle.

The OSGi Framework

You're now aware of a few benefits that OSGi's bundle architecture can bring to your applications, such as the `Import` and `Export` package mechanisms that lay the foundations for sharing classes, but what about those OSGi services than can also be integrated into bundles? What are they all about? Figure 1-1 illustrates the various layers that make up the OSGi framework, many of which map to the different types of services.

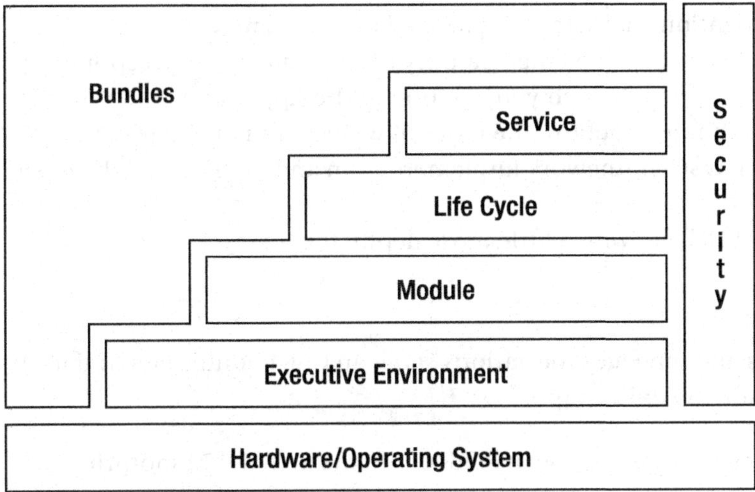

Figure 1-1. *OSGi framework layers*

Most of these OSGi layers possess a comprehensive API—like you would expect in any other Java framework—with which it's possible to dictate the required service behaviors for each bundle through Java classes, which are associated to the bundle through its corresponding manifest.

For now, I won't bog down this introductory discussion on the OSGi framework with the dense subject of API classes and methods, but rather state what each of these layers brings to the table and the capabilities it offers OSGi bundles.

The Security Layer

This subset of the OSGi framework refers to everything related to the security rights of a bundle. Based on the Java 2 security architecture, it defines how a bundle can be digitally signed and how security checks can be enforced in the context of the framework.

As OSGi security is based on the Java 2 security model, there is no OSGi security service API. Instead the framework relies on the presence of this former API to provide security functionality to a bundle.

As far as the actual security checks are concerned, these are integrated with the OSGi service APIs pertaining to the life-cycle layer, which is described in the upcoming paragraphs.

The Module Layer

Much like the security layer, the module layer doesn't have any specific service API, but rather defines the modularization characteristics needed by the framework itself.

In this sense, the module layer defines the anatomy of a bundle, the corresponding manifest values it needs to support (which you can find in the Appendix), and how the class-loading architecture should function, the latter of which would primarily be of interest to those creating an OSGi framework implementation and not necessarily those using it.

So let's move on to an OSGi layer with a little more depth: the life-cycle layer.

The Life-Cycle Layer

The life-cycle layer defines and manages the various *states* an OSGi bundle can find itself in at any time, which include the following:

- **Active state**: Indicates a bundle has been loaded into the actual JVM footprint
- **Uninstalled state**: Indicates a bundle is effectively uninstalled, meaning no verification process has taken place
- **Installed state**: Indicates a bundle has been validated and is prepared to be activated
- **Resolved state**: Indicates all dependencies declared for a bundle have been resolved
- **Starting state**: Indicates a bundle is in the process of transitioning to an active state
- **Stopping state**: Indicates a bundle is in the process of being stopped

The transition of a bundle from each of these states is caused by either an administrative console in which a user inputs some of these changes or the framework performing dynamically based on what other actions are taking place in dependent bundles. Figure 1-2 illustrates the life cycle of an OSGi bundle.

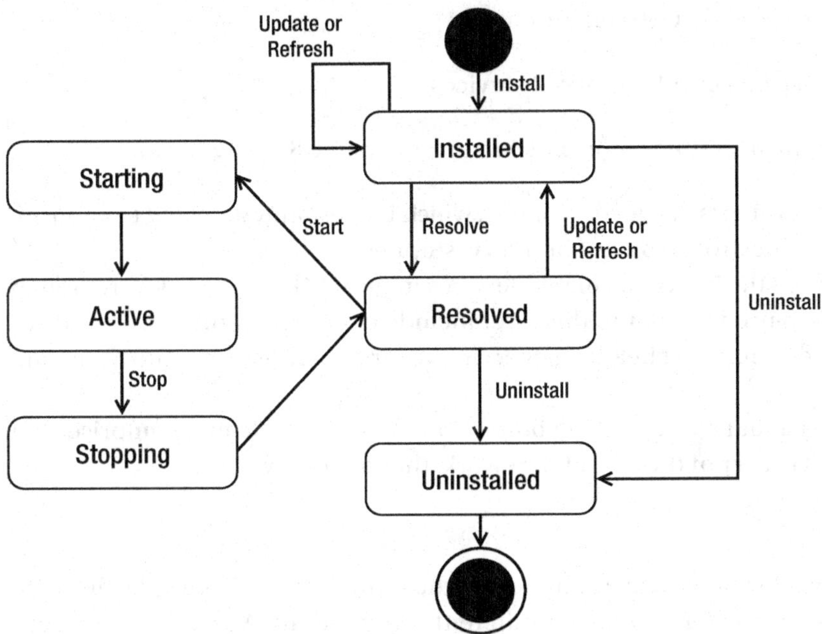

Figure 1-2. *OSGi bundle life cycle*

Events are another subject inevitably related to life cycles and state changes. In OSGi's case, each state transition in the life cycle of a bundle is associated to an event—such as on install, on update, or on start—which in turn corresponds to an API *listener* method that can be used to invoke other services at the time each event presents itself.

If you look back at the OSGi manifest in Listing 1-1, you'll realize you're already familiar with the concept. The Java class assigned to `Bundle-Activator` is precisely a class containing OSGi API methods like `start()` and `stop()` that are listening for a bundle to enter and exit its active state, respectively. As for the logic executed inside these methods, it can be pretty much open-ended like any other Java class, though it's more likely to contain logic related to other OSGi services.

Another aspect related to the life cycle of a bundle is its *context*. If you are familiar with developing server-side Java with servlets, a context in OSGi works in the same way. It simply serves as a proxy for the underlying component in the process of executing operations, such as the following:

- Installing new bundles into an OSGi environment
- Interrogating other bundles installed in an OSGi environment
- Obtaining a persistent storage area
- Registering services in an OSGi environment
- Retrieving service objects of registered services
- Subscribing or unsubscribing to events broadcast by an OSGi environment

Each bundle upon starting is assigned a context, which is constantly accessed to perform these operations and is destroyed once a bundle is stopped.

With this I've covered the bulk of available services in the OSGi life-cycle layer, though other operations you may encounter in this layer include update methods for a bundle, the capability to retrieve manifest headers, querying security permissions, and accessing resources.

Next, you will learn about a closely knit companion to the life cycle that comprises the last and most extensive layer of the OSGi framework: the service layer.

The Service Layer

Let's start by clearing up what exactly is implied by the term "service" in this layer, since in today's software world the term often has different connotations. A service in OSGi is a Java object inside a bundle, which is listed in an OSGi service registry for the benefit of other bundles running in the same JVM.

Based on this, a bundle only has a few courses of action with a service. It can register a service, it can search for a service, or it can opt to receive notifications when a service changes.

The actual composition of a Java object functioning as a service is a little more comprehensive, since as mentioned earlier it can fulfill many duties. The recommended practice for OSGi services, though, is that they be composed of a Java interface accompanied by an implementing Java class. This decoupling favors changes to a Java object, without disturbing the interface on which services are published.

Next, let's investigate the service interfaces that OSGi provides out of the box—those that form part of every OSGi distribution. Table 1-1 shows a description of all the OSGi service interfaces as of OSGi v.4.1

Table 1-1. *OSGi Service Interfaces*

OSGi Service	Function/Purpose
Logging	Provides the facilities to log information and retrieve current or older logger data
Http Service	Allows formation to be sent and received from OSGi using HTTP, the Web's protocol
Device Access	Facilitates the coordination of automatic detection and attachment of existing devices
Configuration Admin	Allows an operator to set the configuration information of deployed bundles
Metatype	Allows services to specify the type information of data (metadata) to use as arguments
Preferences	Offers an alternative, more OSGi-friendly mechanism to using Java's default `java.util.Properties` for storing preference
User Admin	Provides authorization based on who runs the code, instead of using the Java code-based permission model
Wire Admin	Comprises an administrative service used to control the wiring topology (Note that this is intended to be used by user interface or management programs that control the wiring of services.)
IO Connector	Offers an extendable communication API capable of handling different communication protocols, on different networks, firewalls, and intermittent connectivity
Initial Provisioning	Defines how a management agent can make its way to the service platform
UPnP Device Service	Specifies how OSGi bundles can be developed to interoperate with Universal Plug and Play (UPnP) devices
Declarative	Addresses some of the complications that arise when the OSGi service model is used for larger systems and wider deployments
Event Admin	Provides an interbundle communication mechanism based on a publish-and-subscribe model
Deployment Admin	Standardizes access to some of the responsibilities of the management agent
Auto Configuration	Defines the format and processing rules that allow the autoconfiguration of bundles
Application Admin	Simplifies the management of an environment with many different types of applications that are simultaneously available

Table 1-1. *OSGi Service Interfaces (Continued)*

OSGi Service	Function/Purpose
DMT Admin	Defines an API for managing a device using concepts from the Open Mobile Alliance (OMA) device management specifications
Monitor Admin	Outlines how a bundle can publish status variables and how administrative bundles can discover the same variables
Foreign Application Access	Enables foreign applications—such as Mobile Information Device Profile (MIDP), applets, and other Java application models—to participate in the OSGi SOA
Service Tracker	Allows for the tracking of services as they are registered and unregistered
XML Parser	Addresses how the classes defined in JAXP can be used in an OSGi service platform
Position	Provides a consistent way of handling geographic positions in OSGi applications
Measurement and State	Allows and simplifies the correct handling of measurements in an OSGi service platform

Depending on the nature of your OSGi-based design, these service interfaces can either form the backbone of your entire application or simply be reserved for a later phase when your requirements indicate a need for such services.

Now let's move forward and explore another type of service you may encounter in an OSGi bundle: *a business service.* Listing 1-2 presents a Java interface and implementing Java class that show how a custom service would look like as an OSGi service.

Listing 1-2. *Java Interface and Java Class Used As an OSGi Service*

```
public interface Calculator {

 public double sum(double a, double b);

 public double substract(double a, double b);

}

public class CalculatorImpl implements Calculator {

 public double sum(double a, double b) {
  return a+b;
 }
 public double substract(double a, double b) {
  return a-b;
 }
}
```

You don't need to be very familiar with OSGi to understand this last code snippet. It is simply a run-of-the-mill Java interface with an accompanying Java class implementing some business logic. So what gives? What's so special about it that it can be called an OSGi calculator service? Well, the code in itself is nothing special, but the way it can interact with other services and the way it's deployed *is* what makes it special.

But let's explore in a little more detail how this microcosm of services actually works. Each OSGi service (whether derived from the framework itself or a business service like the one just illustrated) needs to be registered to be discovered by other classes in the JVM.

The service registration process is reliant on the state of a bundle. When a bundle enters its active state, it becomes an ideal state in which to perform the registration of services a bundle has to offer. Similarly, a bundle's transition into an active state also becomes a perfect time to search for services a bundle depends on, services that were registered by other bundles.

Since there is a correlation between a bundle's state and services, every other state change in a bundle has influence over the services it provides or accesses. Depending on an application's overall design, business services can rely on the framework's listener methods—those listening for bundle transitions—in order to activate, search, or update services explicitly.

In essence, what you will have is an array of services dynamically coordinated among each other, contained in bundles and managed by the OSGi service registry.

OSGI SERVICE REGISTRY

It's equally important that you realize OSGi possesses a registry to manage the services included in each OSGi bundle, and apply whatever changes or requests are made to these services. Depending on the OSGi implementation you choose, an OSGi service registry can have everything from a sophisticated administrative interface in which it's possible to consult the state of each deployed bundle providing a snapshot of the systems services, to pretty much a "black box" in which the OSGi service registry operates in the background within your JVM.

Conceptually speaking, you now know exactly what is needed to navigate OSGi waters, so it's time for you to write your first OSGi application.

OSGi Hello World Application

The Hello World application you are about to write will take you through OSGi's most basic steps, such as setting up the framework with a JVM and creating your first bundle, to more advanced topics like leveraging third-party bundles and making OSGi services accessible through the Web. Figure 1-3 illustrates the bundles that will make up the application and the relationship between each one.

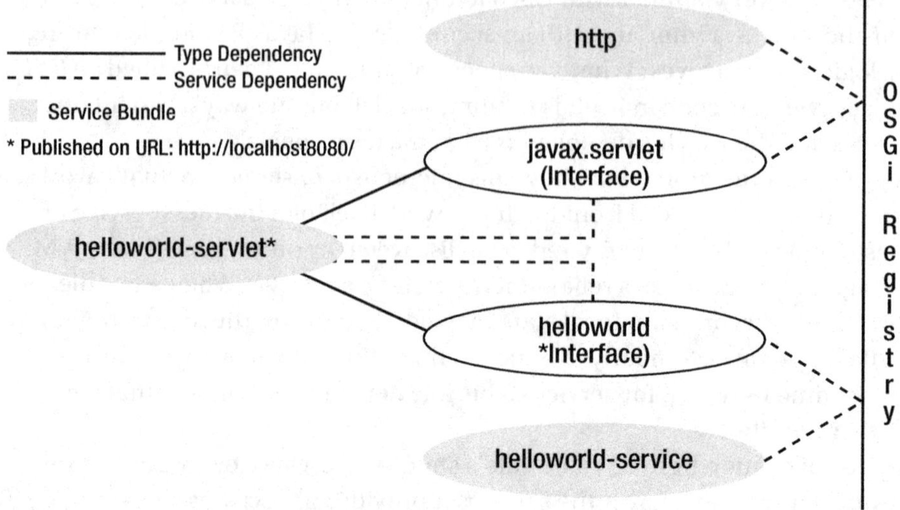

Figure 1-3. *OSGi Hello World application bundles and relationships*

Prerequisites and Downloads

Table 1-2 lists the software you will need to download and install before embarking on your first OSGi project.

Table 1-2. *OSGi Hello World Prerequisites and Downloads*

Software	Function	Download site
Java Standard Edition (SE) 5 or higher	Java's runtime environment	`http://java.sun.com/javase/downloads/index.jsp`
Apache Ant 1.6 or higher	Popular Java build project, used for easing the compilation and creation of OSGi bundles	`http://www.apache.org/dist/ant/binaries/apache-ant-1.7.1-bin.zip`
Apache Felix 1.2.0	OSGi 4.0 reference implementation developed by the Apache Software Foundation	`http://www.apache.org/dist/felix/felix-1.2.0.zip`
OSGi 1.0.1 compendium API bundle	The necessary interfaces for OSGi services	`http://www.apache.org/dist/felix/org.osgi.compendium-1.2.0.jar`
Java Servlet 1.0 OSGi bundle	Classes for deploying servlets with OSGi's Http Service	`http://www.apache.org/dist/felix/javax.servlet-1.0.0.jar`
OBR 1.1.2 HttpService bundle	An implementation for OSGi's Http Service based on Jetty	`http://oscar-osgi.sf.net/repo/http/http.jar`

It's very likely you may have some of this software already installed on your workstation. If so, just ensure that you have the suggested versions, as minor version variations may hold you back in getting through the outlined steps.

Installing Java SE

Installing Java SE should be straightforward: simply executing the downloaded file and following its short instructions should set it up.

Perform the following test to ensure Java SE's correct operation: place yourself on any system directory and execute `java -version`; this will display Java SE's version and ensure Java is accessible from any working directory in the system. In case this test fails, do the following:

- **Verify the `JAVA_HOME` variable**: Check that the variable `JAVA_HOME` is defined on your system and is pointing to Java SE's root directory.
- **Verify the `PATH` variable**: Check that your system's `PATH` variable contains a value pointing to Java SE's `bin` directory.

Installing Apache Ant

The process for installing Apache Ant consists of the following steps:

1. Unzip the downloaded Apache Ant file into a directory of your choice.
2. Define the system variable `ANT_HOME` with a value equivalent to the unzipped directory generated in the previous step.
3. Modify your system's `PATH` variable to include the `bin` subdirectory directly under the `ANT_HOME` value.

Perform the following test to ensure Apache Ant is operating correctly: place yourself on any system directory and execute `ant -version`; this will display Apache Ant's version and ensure Apache Ant is accessible from any working directory in the system. In case this test fails, do the following:

- **Verify the `ANT_HOME` variable**: Check that the variable `ANT_HOME` is defined on your system, and its value is pointing toward Apache Ant's root directory.
- **Verify the `PATH` variable**: Check that your system's `PATH` variable contains a value pointing to Apache Ant's `bin` directory.

Installing Apache Felix

The process for installing Apache Felix consists of just one step: unzipping the downloaded file into a directory of your choice. Perform the following test to ensure Apache Felix's correct operation:

1. Place yourself in Apache Felix's root directory and execute `java -jar bin/felix.jar` to start an OSGi session.

2. You will then be prompted to enter a profile name. Introduce `HelloWorld`.

   A profile name is used to keep track of OSGi deployments—think of it as a project name. Apache Felix will automatically create a subdirectory by this name under a user's home directory (`~/.felix/HelloWorld` on Unix), and inside, it will keep track of things like bundle versions, locations, IDs, and states, among other things.

■ **Note** You should not attempt to modify this structure directly.

---

3. At this point, you will be placed inside an OSGi shell. You can type **help** to see the available options.

4. Don't worry if the options don't make much sense now; we will get to them in a little while. Press Ctrl+C to quit the shell.

Installing Remaining Downloads

The remaining downloads are simply OSGi bundles that will aid you in the creation of the Hello World application. Just take note of their location; we will move them around when the need arises.

Setting Up the Hello World "Playground" Directory Structure

Now that you've got the tools working, it's time to create the proper workspace in which to maneuver. It's nothing too elaborate, though, just a directory structure like the one illustrated in Figure 1-4.

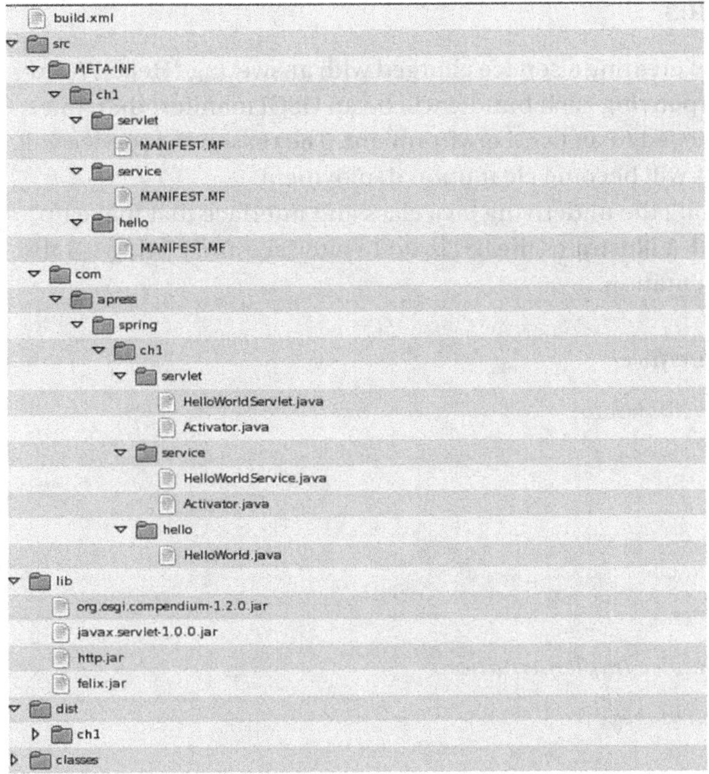

Figure 1-4. *Directory structure for the Hello World "playground"*

The directory structure functions as follows:

- `build.xml`: This is the main Apache Ant configuration file containing the necessary tasks to build the application.
- `classes`: All compiled Java classes are placed in this directory.
- `dist`: All built bundles are placed in this directory.
- `lib`: All JARs and OSGi bundles needed to compile Java sources are placed in this directory.
- `src`: All Java sources files composing the application are placed accordingly in subdirectories inside this directory, including bundle manifests inside `META-INF`.

Your First OSGi Bundles

Your first bundles will consist of creating a service charged with answering “Hello World” to all incoming queries. Accompanying each bundle will be an OSGi manifest that, once packaged as a unit, can be deployed to an OSGi environment. The reason the service will consist of two separate bundles will become clear upon deployment.

Let’s kick things off by defining the underlying Java class and interface that make up the `HelloWorld` service. Listing 1-3 illustrates the `HelloWorld` interface and Listing 1-4 the corresponding service implementation.

Listing 1-3. *`HelloWorld` Service Interface*

```
package com.apress.springosgi.ch1.hello;

public interface HelloWorld
{
 public String hello();
}
```

Listing 1-4. *`HelloWorldService` Service Implementation*

```
package com.apress.springosgi.ch1.service;

import com.apress.springosgi.ch1.hello.HelloWorld;

public class HelloWorldService implements HelloWorld
{
 public String hello() {
  return "Hello World 1.0";
      }
}
```

That’s all the business logic for our simple service; now let’s take a look at what is needed to register this `HelloWorld` service as an OSGi service. Listing 1-5 illustrates the `Activator` class used for this purpose.

Listing 1-5. *`Activator` Class for the `HelloWorld` Service*

```
package com.apress.springosgi.ch1.service;

import com.apress.springosgi.ch1.hello.HelloWorld;

import java.util.Properties;
```

```
import org.osgi.framework.BundleActivator;
import org.osgi.framework.BundleContext;

public class Activator implements BundleActivator
{
 public void start(BundleContext context)
 {
  Properties props = new Properties();
  context.registerService(
   HelloWorld.class.getName(), new HelloWorldService(),props);
 }

 public void stop(BundleContext context)
 {
  //Note: The service is automatically unregistered
 }
}
```

The Activator class implements BundleActivator—which forms part of the OSGi framework—providing the necessary wiring to execute logic at the time a bundle is started and stopped, which is done inside the start() and stop() methods, respectively.

The start() method consists of two declarations, a Properties object used to associate values with a service and the actual registration performed via the registerService() method of a bundle's context. In this case, the Properties object is left empty, but it can contain values to further characterize a service. On the other hand, the registerService() method receives three input parameters: the service type, HelloWorld.class.getName(); an object instance of the service itself, new HelloWorldService(); and a Properties object associated to the service.

The stop() method for our BundleActivator contains no code, because the service is automatically unregistered once a bundle is deactivated. The only circumstances under which the stop() method would contain logic would be to deallocate nonservice resources assigned during the start of a bundle, which is not the case for this scenario.

It should be noted that this is all it takes for a service to be accessible from other OSGi bundles in a JVM, and consequently the service registration is identical for any OSGi-bound service, whether it's performed once a bundle is activated, stopped, or executed on account of another system event.

This concludes creating the classes needed to make up your first OSGi bundles. Now let's put together the bundles—one for the service and another for its accompanying interface

To start building the bundles, move over to the Hello World "playground" directory structure you created earlier, and follow these steps:

1. Place the bundles' source files—those created in the earlier section—into the subdirectory `src/com/apress/springosgi/ch1/hello/` and `src/com/apress/springosgi/ch1/service/`. based on the listing's package value.

2. Copy the `felix.jar` bundle—included in the `bin` directory of the Apache Felix distribution—to the `lib` directory of the "playground."

3. Copy the `javax.servlet-1.0.0.jar` bundle to the `lib` directory of the "playground."

4. Copy the `org.osgi.compendium-1.2.0.jar` bundle to the `lib` directory of the "playground."

The previous steps set up the bundles' source files for compilation, with the movement of prebuilt bundles (JARs) serving to fulfill dependencies at compile time. The actual compilation process you will now embark on will be carried out using Apache Ant.

Apache Ant relies on an XML-based file to define its tasks. Listing 1-6 shows the first iteration of this file used to build your first OSGi bundles.

Listing 1-6. *Apache Ant `build.xml` File for Compiling Classes*

```
<?xml version="1.0"?>

<project default="init" basedir=".">

  <target name="init" description="Apress - Pro Spring-OSGi">
  <tstamp/>
  <property name="projectname" value="Pro Spring-OSGi"/>

  <echo message="-------${projectname}------"/>

  <property name="debug"          value="on"/>
  <property name="optimize"       value="off"/>
  <property name="deprecation"    value="off"/>
  <property name="build.compiler" value="modern"/>
  <property name="target.vm"      value="1.5"/>
  <property name="build.dir"      value="classes"/>
  <property name="dist.dir"       value="dist"/>
  <property name="src.dir"        value="src"/>
  <property name="lib.dir"        value="lib"/>
```

```
  <!-- Load JARs onto the classpath, taken from lib sub-dir -->
  <path id="classpath">
   <fileset dir="${lib.dir}">
    <include name="*.jar"/>
   </fileset>
   <pathelement location="${build.dir}"/>
  </path>

 </target>

 <target name="compile" depends="init" description="Compile code">

  <echo message="-------Compiling code for Pro-Spring OSGi------"/>

  <mkdir dir="${build.dir}"/>
  <mkdir dir="${dist.dir}"/>

  <javac srcdir="${src.dir}"
         destdir="${build.dir}"
         debug="${debug}"
         optimize="${optimize}"
         deprecation="${deprecation}"
         target="${target.vm}">
     <classpath refid="classpath"/>
  </javac>

  <copy todir="${build.dir}">
           <fileset dir="${src.dir}">
<!-- Some of the following statements are relevant to Ch2 -->
<!-- They are present here because the same compile task is used -->
               <include name="**/*.properties"/>
               <include name="**/*.xml"/>
               <exclude name="**/*.java"/>
               <exclude name="META-INF/**"/>
               <exclude name="WEB-INF/**"/>
               <exclude name="GUI/**"/>
             </fileset>
  </copy>
  </target>
</project>
```

In summary, this `build.xml` file defines the numerous flags used in the Java compilation process, indicates where the bundles' source files are located, defines where the compiled classes are to be placed, copies property files from the source directory to the compiled class directory, and modifies the default `CLASSPATH` value to include additional JAR files and the compiled class directory.

With this `build.xml` file in hand and placed under the root directory of your Hello World "playground," execute the command `ant compile`; this step will compile the bundles' classes and place them under the `classes` subdirectory.

OK, you now have the bundles' classes compiled, but what's missing before packaging? The OSGi manifests. Listing 1-7 and Listing 1-8 contain the OSGi manifests that need to accompany the compiled classes, which you need to copy into the `/src/META-INF/ch1/hello/` and `/src/META-INF/ch1/service/` directories, respectively, of your Hello World "playground."

Listing 1-7. *OSGi Manifest for* `HelloWorld` *Interface Bundle*

```
Bundle-Name: Hello World
Bundle-Description: H.W Pro-Spring OSGi
Bundle-Version: 1.0.0
Export-Package: com.apress.springosgi.ch1.hello
```

Listing 1-8. *OSGi Manifest for* `HelloWorld` *Service Bundle*

```
Bundle-Name: Hello World Service
Bundle-Description: H.W Service Pro-Spring OSGi
Bundle-Version: 1.0.0
Bundle-Activator: com.apress.springosgi.ch1.service.Activator

Import-Package: org.osgi.framework,
 com.apress.springosgi.ch1.hello
```

Earlier in Listing 1-1 you got a glimpse of an OSGi manifest, but to recap, `Bundle-Name` and `Bundle-Description` are there to provide friendly naming values to the bundle, whereas the `Bundle-Version` value is used to keep track of bundle releases. The remaining values in both manifests differ, so let's tackle each one separately.

Listing 1-7 makes use of `Export-Package`, indicating that the respective package value, which contains the service interface in Listing 1-3, will be made available to the other bundles' class loaders running in the system.

Listing 1-8 starts off with the Bundle-Activator statement, indicating what class to execute once a bundle is activated. Import-Package is used to indicate what Java packages a bundle requires from the outside and need to be loaded onto a bundle's class loader.

Copy the MANIFEST.MF file in Listing 1-7 to the /src/META-INF/ch1/hello/ directory of the Hello World "playground" and the MANIFEST.MF file in Listing 1-8 to the directory /src/META-INF/ch1/service/ of the same "playground."

Knowing what the manifests need to contain, let's switch back over to Apache Ant and define a task for creating the bundles in a more automated fashion. Listing 1-9 contains the Apache Ant task needed to create the OSGi HelloWorld service and interface bundles.

Listing 1-9. *Apache Ant Target for Building OSGi HelloWorld Service and Interface Bundles*

```
<target name="ch1" depends="compile" description="Build Chapter 1 Bundles">
  <echo message="-Building Chapter 1 bundles for Pro-Spring OSGi-"/>

  <property name="ch1.dir"          value="${dist.dir}/ch1/"/>
  <mkdir dir="${ch1.dir}"/>

  <jar destfile="${ch1.dir}/helloworld.jar" manifest="${src.dir}/META-INF/ch1/➥
hello/MANIFEST.MF">
    <fileset dir="${build.dir}" includes="com/apress/springosgi/ch1/hello/**"/>

  </jar>
  <jar destfile="${ch1.dir}/helloworld-service.jar" manifest="${src.dir}/➥
META-INF/ch1/service/MANIFEST.MF">

    <fileset dir="${build.dir}" includes="com/apress/springosgi/ch1/service/**"/>

  </jar>

 </target>
```

If you edit your build.xml file to include this last Ant definition and under the root directory of your Hello World "playground" execute ant ch1, bundles helloworld.jar and helloworld-service.jar will be generated inside the dist/ch1 subdirectory.

That's it! You now have your first OSGi bundles packaged and ready for the final step: deployment.

The first thing you will need to do in order to deploy an OSGi bundle is start an OSGi session, so go straight to the directory where you unzipped Apache Felix and execute `java -jar bin/felix.jar` to do so.

You will then be prompted for a profile name; enter **HelloWorld**. At this juncture, your OSGi session is active and awaiting further instructions. Enter the command **ps** to search for the current bundles in the session. You should see the system bundle and three more bundles pertaining to Felix itself. Listing 1-10 contains the screen output for the series of steps just outlined.

Listing 1-10. *Apache Felix Session Start*

```
$ java -jar bin/felix.jar

Welcome to Felix.
=================

Enter profile name: HelloWorld

DEBUG: WIRE: 1.0 -> org.osgi.service.packageadmin -> 0
DEBUG: WIRE: 1.0 -> org.osgi.service.startlevel -> 0
DEBUG: WIRE: 1.0 -> org.ungoverned.osgi.service.shell -> 1.0
DEBUG: WIRE: 1.0 -> org.osgi.framework -> 0
DEBUG: WIRE: 1.0 -> org.apache.felix.shell -> 1.0
DEBUG: WIRE: 2.0 -> org.osgi.framework -> 0
DEBUG: WIRE: 2.0 -> org.apache.felix.shell -> 1.0
DEBUG: WIRE: 3.0 -> org.osgi.service.obr -> 3.0
DEBUG: WIRE: 3.0 -> org.osgi.framework -> 0
DEBUG: WIRE: 3.0 -> org.apache.felix.shell -> 1.0
-> ps
START LEVEL 1
   ID   State         Level  Name
[   0] [Active     ] [    0] System Bundle (1.2.0)
[   1] [Active     ] [    1] Apache Felix Shell Service (1.0.2)
[   2] [Active     ] [    1] Apache Felix Shell TUI (1.0.2)
[   3] [Active     ] [    1] Apache Felix Bundle Repository (1.2.0)
->
```

Next, you will need to install the `helloworld.jar` and `helloworld-service.jar` bundles, executing the following instruction from this same OSGi session shell: `install file:/<playground_root_directory>/dist/ch1/helloworld.jar` and `file:/<playground_root_directory>/dist/ch1/helloworld-service.jar`. This last step will incorporate the `HelloWorld` OSGi bundle into the OSGi session. Enter the **ps** command once again, and you will see the bundle listed as shown in Listing 1-11.

Listing 1-11. *Apache Felix* `HelloWorld` *Bundle Installed*

```
-> install file:/<playground_root_directory>/dist/ch1/helloworld.jar
Bundle ID: 4
-> install file:/<playground_root_directory>/dist/ch1/helloworld-service.jar
Bundle ID: 5
-> ps
START LEVEL 1
   ID   State         Level  Name
[   0] [Active     ] [    0] System Bundle (1.2.0)
[   1] [Active     ] [    1] Apache Felix Shell Service (1.0.21)
[   2] [Active     ] [    1] Apache Felix Shell TUI (1.0.21)
[   3] [Active     ] [    1] Apache Felix Bundle Repository (1.2.0)
[   4] [Installed  ] [    1] Hello World (1.0.0)
[   5] [Installed  ] [    1] Hello World Service (1.0.0)
```

If you look closely at the bundle state listings at this point, you will notice that both bundles have an `Installed` state. Let's change the state of the bundle using the `start` command. Execute `start 5`, where 5 indicates the ID assigned to the `HelloWorld` service bundle.

If you enter **ps** again to observe the session bundles, you will note the `HelloWorld` service bundle now has an `Active` state and the `HelloWorld` interface bundle has a `Resolved` state. Even though you took no action on the `HelloWorld` interface bundle (ID 4), its state changed to `Resolved` because the service bundle (ID 5) that you did activate requires importing a package from this bundle (ID 4) per the manifest values presented in Listing 1-8. The `Active` state on the service bundle further implies the bundle's services have been registered into the environment on account of the bundle's `Activator` class. Additionally, if you enter the command **services**, you will see the `HelloWorld` service bundle provides a service by the same name. Listing 1-12 illustrates these last steps.

Listing 1-12. *Apache Felix* `HelloWorld` *Bundle Activated*

```
-> start 5
DEBUG: WIRE: 54.0 -> com.apress.springosgi.ch1.hello -> 4.0
DEBUG: WIRE: 54.0 -> org.osgi.framework -> 0
DEBUG: WIRE: 4.0 -> com.apress.springosgi.ch1.hello -> 4.0

-> ps
START LEVEL 1
   ID   State         Level  Name
[   0] [Active     ] [    0] System Bundle (1.2.0.4)
[   1] [Active     ] [    1] Apache Felix Shell Service (1.0.2)
[   2] [Active     ] [    1] Apache Felix Shell TUI (1.0.2)
[   3] [Active     ] [    1] Apache Felix Bundle Repository (1.2.0)
```

```
[   4] [Resolved    ] [    1] Hello World (1.0.0)
[  5] [Active     ] [    1] Hello World Service (1.0.0)
-> services

System Bundle (0) provides:
---------------------------
org.osgi.service.startlevel.StartLevel
org.osgi.service.packageadmin.PackageAdmin

Apache Felix Shell Service (1) provides:
----------------------------------------
org.apache.felix.shell.ShellService, org.ungoverned.osgi.service.shell.ShellService

Apache Felix Bundle Repository (3) provides:
--------------------------------------------
org.osgi.service.obr.RepositoryAdmin

Hello World (5) provides:
-------------------------
com.apress.springosgi.ch1.hello.HelloWorld
->
```

Your HelloWorld service and interface bundles including the accompanying application service are now deployed, but before we move on to doing more things with your first OSGi bundle, close the OSGi session by pressing Ctrl+C.

This last step exits the OSGi shell and kills the Java process containing the installation sequence and bundle state modification you just did. What would you expect to see if you started another OSGi session? Well, if you invoke `java -jar bin/felix.jar` once again and introduce the profile name HelloWorld, you might be surprised to see that the list of bundles—including their state—is just as it was before you closed the first session.

The reason for this is that Apache Felix keeps track of all changes made to bundles, copying each installed bundle to a separate location and maintaining whatever changes are propagated to the bundle. This tracking and location mechanism is based on the profile name you enter upon starting a session. In this case, Apache Felix creates a directory by the name <User_Home>/.felix/HelloWorld/—where <User_Home> is the process owner for Apache Felix—in which all bundles and their state are persisted for future sessions initiated under the same profile name.

DEPLOYMENT AND DEVELOPMENT OF OSGI BUNDLES

The process for deploying OSGi bundles is highly specific to the OSGi implementation you choose. In this case, Apache Felix, in its out-of-the-box state, requires that you enter its shell to perform the tasks of installing bundles, but this may not be so for other OSGi implementations.

Some OSGi implementations provide fancier GUIs for deployment operations or "hot" directories in which a bundle is simply placed and installed immediately. Similarly, OSGi-based Java products like application servers or integrated development environments (IDEs) might not even hint at the use of an OSGi implementation in their startup sequence, but simply operate OSGi in the underlying JVM and handle whatever OSGi'fied packages compose their architecture.

On the development front, I opted to use Apache Ant because of its simple setup and greater familiarity in the Java community, though it should be mentioned that there are already a few IDEs, such as Eclipse, that aid in the creation of OSGi bundles, something that reduces or even eliminates the need to create and update OSGi manifest values by hand. (Note that as well as aiding in the development of OSGi applications, Eclipse itself is an OSGi application.)

The Http Service OSGi Bundle

Congratulations! You have now implemented and deployed your `HelloWorld` OSGi service, so this would be a perfect time to deepen your knowledge of other OSGi services, especially those mentioned earlier that form part of the OSGi framework.

Unlike the `HelloWorld` service that you just created from scratch, the OSGi framework sets forth a series of contracts that certain services need to adhere to, contracts that were mentioned in Table 1-1.

By far the most notable of this group of OSGi services—or at least more widely known by its backing function—is the Http Service, a service that supports the same backing protocol for operations on the Web. Listing 1-13 illustrates the interface defined by OSGi for the Http Service.

Listing 1-13. *OSGi Http Service Interface*

```
public interface HttpService
{

      public HttpContext createDefaultHttpContext();

      public void registerServlet(
        String alias, Servlet servlet, Dictionary params, HttpContext context)
        throws ServletException, NamespaceException;
```

```
    public void registerResources(
      String alias, String name, HttpContext context)
      throws NamespaceException;

    public void unregister(String alias);
}
```

The interface for the Http Service defines methods for tasks typically associated with Java web applications, such as registering servlets, which form the building blocks for most Java web applications; registering resources, which are ancillary pieces to a web application like images, CSS files, or JavaScript files; and creating an `HttpContext`, which serves to manipulate servlets and resources.

Fortunately, there are already freely available Http Service implementations, avoiding the need to reinvent the wheel.

You've already downloaded an OSGi bundle containing such a service, one based on the Jetty Java web server, so let's get on with the task of deploying this bundle and its accompanying service.

In order to deploy the Http Service OSGi bundle, start an Apache Felix session executing `java -jar bin/felix.jar` and enter the profile name **HelloWorld**. Once inside Felix's shell, perform the following steps:

1. Install `javax.servlet-1.0.0.jar`, which is a required bundle dependency for the Http Service bundle.
2. Install `http.jar`, which is the actual Http Service OSGi bundle.
3. Start `http.jar`. This will activate the Http Service, along with its underlying web server.

Listing 1-14 contains the screen output for these steps.

Listing 1-14. *Apache Felix Http Service Activation*

```
START LEVEL 1
   ID   State         Level  Name
[   0] [Active     ] [    0] System Bundle (1.2.0)
[   1] [Active     ] [    1] Apache Felix Shell Service (1.0.2)
[   2] [Active     ] [    1] Apache Felix Shell TUI (1.0.2)
[   3] [Active     ] [    1] Apache Felix Bundle Repository (1.2.0)
[   4] [Active     ] [    1] Hello World (1.0.0)
[   5] [Active     ] [    1] Hello World Service (1.0.0)
```

```
-> install file:bundle/javax.servlet-1.0.0.jar
Bundle ID: 6
-> install file:bundle/http.jar
Bundle ID: 7
-> start 7
DEBUG: WIRE: 7.0 -> javax.servlet.http -> 6.0
DEBUG: WIRE: 7.0 -> javax.servlet -> 6.0
DEBUG: WIRE: 7.0 -> org.osgi.service.http -> 7.0
DEBUG: WIRE: 7.0 -> org.osgi.framework -> 0
11:21:06.171 EVENT  Starting Jetty/4.2.x
11:21:06.397 EVENT  Started SocketListener on 0.0.0.0:8080
11:21:06.419 EVENT  Started org.mortbay.http.HttpServer@110b053
```

If you look at the output for this last sequence, you will notice that near the end there is a line that reads `Starter SocketListener on 0.0.0.0:8080`, which indicates a web server has started on the localhost under port 8080.

So go ahead and open a browser pointing to the address `http://localhost:8080/`. You should get a 404 Not Found page. The reason for this is that even though you've deployed two bundles with accompanying services, neither of these bundles is designed to expose data on the Web.

OSGi Bundle for the Web

If you've done web development in Java, you should be familiar with the default component used for exposing business logic on the Web: the servlet. A servlet provides the underlying structure to manage the stateless nature of the Web and is an important building block to many of the Java frameworks and applications built around Java EE.

Given this background, using a servlet would also be a natural choice for creating a web interface for the OSGi Hello World application, so next you will learn how to integrate a servlet into an OSGi bundle.

Since servlets are broadly used, they come in many shapes and forms; some work as facades for other components, some access the data tier directly, while some may be stacked against each other to achieve a goal set by a particular web framework. The servlet you are about to create, however, has one particularity you've probably never seen: it will be built and supported by OSGi services.

Listing 1-15 illustrates the `HelloWorldServlet` class that makes use of the `HelloWorld` service created earlier.

Listing 1-15. *HelloWorldServlet Class*

```
package com.apress.springosgi.ch1.servlet;

import com.apress.springosgi.ch1.hello.HelloWorld;

import java.io.IOException;

import javax.servlet.ServletException;

import javax.servlet.ServletOutputStream;

import javax.servlet.http.HttpServlet;

import javax.servlet.http.HttpServletResponse;

import org.osgi.util.tracker.ServiceTracker;

public class HelloWorldServlet extends HttpServlet {

    private static final long serialVersionUID = 42L;

        private ServiceTracker serviceTracker;

        public HelloWorldServlet(ServiceTracker serviceTracker) {

                this.serviceTracker = serviceTracker;
        }
        protected void doGet(HttpServletRequest httpServletRequest,

                        HttpServletResponse httpServletResponse) throws ➥
ServletException,

                        IOException {

                httpServletResponse.setContentType("text/html");

                ServletOutputStream out = httpServletResponse.getOutputStream();

                out.println("<html><body>");
```

```
            HelloWorld service = (HelloWorld) serviceTracker

                            .getService();

            if (service != null) {

                    out.println(service.hello());

            }

            out.println("</body></html>");

            out.close();

    }

}
```

The servlet creates an HTML response with the value returned by the `hello()` method belonging to a `HelloWorld` interface—which is backing the service object itself—looked up via OSGi's `ServiceTracker`; other than this, the servlet's structure is pretty much standard, with its `doGet()` method and piping out a `ServletOutputStream` value to the browser. So the question now is how does this servlet get ahold of the OSGi `HelloWorld` service? And more importantly, how does it get published to the web server you started a while ago?

Well, let's address the publishing issue of the servlet first. As it turns out, the OSGi Http Service possesses a method named `registerServlet()` that does exactly this; it takes a servlet object and wires it up for external access. This means that the servlet in one way or another needs to enter in contact with both OSGi services, with the question now turning from how to where. What better place to do so than in the bundle's `Activator` class, which is an integral part of a bundle and where instructions are always executed at the outset. Listing 1-16 shows the `Activator` class that would accompany the bundle containing the `HelloWorldServlet`.

Listing 1-16. *`Activator` Class for `HelloWorldServlet`*

```
package com.apress.springosgi.ch1.servlet;

import com.apress.springosgi.ch1.hello.HelloWorld;

import org.osgi.framework.BundleActivator;

import org.osgi.framework.BundleContext;
```

```
import org.osgi.framework.ServiceReference;

import org.osgi.service.http.HttpService;

import org.osgi.util.tracker.ServiceTracker;

public class Activator implements BundleActivator
{

     private ServiceTracker httpServiceTracker;

        private ServiceTracker helloWorldServiceTracker;

        public void start(BundleContext context) throws Exception {

                // create new ServiceTracker for HelloWorldService via ➥
HelloWorld interface

                helloWorldServiceTracker = new ServiceTracker(context,

                                HelloWorld.class.getName(), null);

                // create new ServiceTracker for HttpService

                httpServiceTracker = new ServiceTracker(context, HttpService.class

                                .getName(), null) {

                        public Object addingService(ServiceReference reference) {

                                HttpService httpService = (HttpService) super

                                                .addingService(reference);

                                try {

                                        httpService.registerServlet("/", ➥
new HelloWorldServlet(helloWorldServiceTracker),

                                                        null, null);
```

```
                } catch (Exception e) {
                    e.printStackTrace();
                }
                return httpService;
            }
            public void removedService(ServiceReference reference,
                    Object service) {
                ((HttpService) service).unregister("/");
                super.removedService(reference, service);
            }
        };
        // open service tracker to start tracking
        helloWorldServiceTracker.open();
        httpServiceTracker.open();
    }
    public void stop(BundleContext context) throws Exception {
        // open service tracker to stop tracking
        httpServiceTracker.close();
        helloWorldServiceTracker.close();
    }
}
```

The first thing to note about this Activator class is its ample use of OSGi's Service Tracker. As its name implies, the ServiceTracker class allows a bundle to keep track of an OSGi environment's registered services in case these are upgraded or uninstalled. In Listing 1-16, the first actions performed in the start() method of the Activator class are to keep track of the services you've already deployed, the HelloWorld service, as well as the Http Service (for the web server).

Once these preexisting services are associated with OSGi's Service Tracker, the services are then bound using the addingService method. Inside this last method, you will find the statement httpService.registerServlet("/", new HelloWorldServlet(helloWorldServiceTracker), null, null). This statement executes the registerServlet() method—part of the Http Service—taking as input an instance of the HelloWorldServlet, which in itself receives a reference to the Service Tracker HelloWorld service, as well as the / value, indicating the servlet is to be deployed in the root directory of the underlying Http Service.

Then you can find the removedService method, which performs exactly the opposite instructions as its counterpart addingService method, in this case using the unregister method to eliminate the servlet from the root directory / of the underlying Http Service. Capping off the Activator start() method, you will find both Service Tracker references declared in the class invoking the open() method in order to initiate the tracking services. Though of lesser importance, finally there is the stop()) method for the Activator class, called when a bundle is stopped and which in this case simply invokes the close() method on the Service Tracker references to halt the tracking of services.

So there you have it, a servlet ready to make use of OSGi services. Let's take the next step, linking it to its Activator class by building a bundle.

You're already familiar with the process of building a bundle with Apache Ant, so let's cut to the chase. Listing 1-17 shows this bundle's manifest file, while Listing 1-18 contains the additional instructions you will need to add to your build.xml—into the existing ch1 target—in order to build the helloworld-servlet.jar bundle.

Listing 1-17. *OSGi HelloWorldServlet Bundle Manifest*

```
Bundle-Name: Servlet for Hello World
Bundle-Description: Servlet for Hello World Pro Spring-OSGi
Bundle-Version: 1.0.0
Bundle-Activator: com.apress.springosgi.ch1.servlet.Activator
Import-Package:  org.osgi.framework,
 org.osgi.util.tracker,
 javax.servlet,
 javax.servlet.http,
 org.osgi.service.http,
 com.apress.springosgi.ch1.hello
```

Listing 1-18. *Apache Ant Target for Building OSGi* `HelloWorldServlet` *Bundle*

```
<target name="ch1" depends="compile" description="Build Chapter 1 Bundles">
  <echo message="-Building Chapter 1 bundles for Pro Spring-OSGi"/>

  <property name="ch1.dir"          value="${dist.dir}/ch1/"/>
  <mkdir dir="${ch1.dir}"/>

   <jar destfile="${ch1.dir}/helloworld.jar" manifest="${src.dir}/META-INF/ch1/ ➥
hello/MANIFEST.MF">
   <fileset dir="${build.dir}" includes="com/apress/springosgi/ch1/hello/**"/>

  </jar>
<jar destfile="${ch1.dir}/helloworld-service.jar" manifest="${src.dir}/META-INF/➥
ch1/service/MANIFEST.MF">

   <fileset dir="${build.dir}" includes="com/apress/springosgi/ch1/service/**"/>

  </jar>

 <jar destfile="${ch1.dir}/helloworld-servlet.jar" manifest="${src.dir}/➥
META-INF/ch1/servlet/MANIFEST.MF">
         <fileset  dir="${build.dir}" includes="com/apress/springosgi/ch1/➥
servlet/**"/>

     </jar>
 </target>
```

Things to note about this particular bundle's build process include the following: its specific manifest headers, which now include the `javax.servlet` and `javax.servlets.http` packages, and of course that its class files include only those in the `com.apress.springosgi.ch1.servlet` package, which are the `HelloWorldJava.class` and its corresponding `Activator.class`.

Now on to the final step for your servlet bundle: deployment.

Once again, start an Apache Felix session executing `java -jar bin/felix.jar` and enter the profile name **HelloWorld**. From there you will need to install and later start the `helloworld-servlet.jar` bundle. Listing 1-19 shows the sequence of events.

Listing 1-19. *Apache Felix* `HelloWorldServlet` *Activation*

```
START LEVEL 1
   ID   State         Level  Name
[   0] [Active     ] [    0] System Bundle (1.0.3)
[   1] [Active     ] [    1] Apache Felix Shell Service (1.0.0)
```

```
[   2] [Active     ] [    1] Apache Felix Shell TUI (1.0.0)
[   3] [Active     ] [    1] Apache Felix Bundle Repository (1.0.2)
[   4] [Resolved   ] [    1] Hello World (1.0.0)
[   5] [Active     ] [    1] Hello World Service (1.0.0)
[   6] [Resolved   ] [    1] Servlet 2.1 API (1.0.0)
[   7] [Active     ] [    1] HTTP Service (1.1.2)
-> install file:bundle/helloworld-servlet.jar
Bundle ID: 8
-> start 8
DEBUG: WIRE: 8.0 -> javax.servlet.http -> 6.0
DEBUG: WIRE: 8.0 -> javax.servlet -> 6.0
DEBUG: WIRE: 8.0 -> com.apress.springosgi.ch1.hello -> 4.0
DEBUG: WIRE: 8.0 -> org.osgi.service.http -> 7.0
DEBUG: WIRE: 8.0 -> org.osgi.framework -> 0

11:25:53.232 EVENT  Started ServletHttpContext[/]
```

Once you start the helloworldservlet.jar bundle, open up a browser and point it to the address http://localhost:8080/. You will then be able to see the "Hello World 1.0" message on your screen, and with it successfully conclude the deployment of a web-based application based on an OSGi architecture.

But before you close everything up, there is one more aspect worth exploring in your first OSGi application: the update mechanism available in OSGi.

Updating OSGi Bundles

Requirement changes are practically ingrained in the life cycle of a software application, so let's see how our OSGi-based application can cope with a few updates.

Go to the Hello World "playground" and modify the source file HelloWorldService.java (Listing 1-4) to return a new string that reads "Hello World 2.0." Once you do this, rebuild the helloworld-service.jar bundle, executing Apache Ant's task, ant ch1; a new bundle reflecting this change will be created under the dist/ch1 subdirectory.

Since you should already have an installed helloworld-service.jar bundle under your HelloWorld profile, what you need to do next is perform an update process from inside an Apache Felix session. To perform this update, execute the instruction update 5, where 5 is the ID assigned to the initial helloworld-service.jar bundle.

Now open up a browser and point it to http://localhost:8080/. You should see "Hello World 2.0." The interesting part about this whole update sequence is that the underlying Java process was never stopped; the changes were simply propagated and automatically incorporated into the bundles that relied on the updated service.

Having performed this update, the bundle-partitioning scheme for the application illustrated in Figure 1-3 can be explained more easily. The helloworld-servlet has two type and two service dependencies, with the type dependency bundles providing the necessary interfaces to access the backing service bundles. So why are there four bundles? Couldn't an interface and its service be packaged in the same bundle, reducing the number to two instead of four?

The problem with type dependencies is that they are tightly coupled to the bundles using them. This means that updating bundles with type dependencies requires OSGi to refresh—uninstall and reinstall—all bundles in the dependency hierarchy.

In this case, if the `helloworld` service were to have been packaged in the same bundle as the `helloworld` interface, an update to the `helloworld` service would have required OSGi to refresh—uninstall and reinstall—all bundles tied to the type dependency hierarchy. A service might be the only thing being updated, but if other bundles have type dependencies on this same updated bundle, OSGi ensures changes are propagated to all dependent bundles by uninstalling and reinstalling each one.

This is not the case with services, since services are always consulted via OSGi's registry. If a bundle only contains services and is updated, there is no need to propagate updates to bundles using this service; the OSGi registry will ensure all consuming bundles obtain a reference to the updated service the next time it is accessed.

In this case, by having the `helloworld` service decoupled from its interface, the service bundle can be updated without incurring the overhead of refreshing additional bundles. Therefore, it's often advised to package OSGi services and their corresponding interfaces in different bundles.

OSGi Hello World Application Conclusions

Hello World applications are meant to be bare-bones examples illustrating the capabilities behind a technology, but often in this simplicity, important lessons are overlooked. So here are a few takeaway points on the OSGi Hello World application you just made:

- **Everything is a service**: OSGi bundles rely on a wide gamut of services. In this application you worked with two services, but the basis for every OSGi application no matter its size is always the same: publishing and reusing services.

- **No WAR files**: Even though you deployed a Java web application, notice there is no trace of Web Archive (WAR) files, which are the norm for deploying this kind of application.

- **Bundles are a generic packaging format**: With services forming the cornerstone to OSGi, a bundle's structure can package or use services destined for many purposes. This application demonstrated how a bundle can be used to package a servlet and make it accessible to a browser.

- **Hot-pluggability**: When a bundle is updated, changes are propagated immediately to dependent bundles with no interruptions in the system. This application showed that upon updating the Hello World service's logic, changes are reflected instantly up to the browser interface without interrupting the Http Service.

Though you may still have some looming questions on this web-enabled OSGi Hello World application, such as the access to a Relational Database Management System (RDBMS) or a more sophisticated interface design, OSGi services by themselves are not well suited for so many tasks, so the next chapter will introduce a framework that has gained tremendous traction as an end-to-end solution for building web-enabled applications in the enterprise: the Spring Framework.

WHY DOESN'T JAVA SE SUPPORT OSGI?

At this juncture you may be impressed at the capabilities OSGi brings to the JVM, but you may still be wondering, "If OSGi is such a boon, why hasn't it been incorporated into Java's Standard Edition like so many other APIs throughout the years?" The short answer is, it's already in the pipeline as JSR-291 (`http://www.jcp.org/en/jsr/detail?id=291`), targeting Java 1.2, 1.3, and 1.4 and Java SE 5.0 and 6.0.

The longer answer, as in when OSGi will be an integral part of mainstream Java SE, is a lot more difficult to predict, given Java SE's more conservative evolutionary path. Since Java SE forms the backbone to many products across several industries—and OSGi in many ways influences and modifies the underlying operation of the JVM—incorporating OSGi into Java SE is not as simple as incorporating a niche JSR.

Like most processes involving technology standards, a standard making its way into a product will depend heavily not just on being a best-of-breed technology, but also on a mix of business interests, corporate politics, and when the user community acknowledges its pressing need. Though for now OSGi is separate from Java SE, rest assured the technology has been given a vote of confidence by the same group that oversees the Java platform.

Summary

In this chapter you learned how OSGi brings a wealth of versatility to the already robust and popular Java platform, enhancing the way Java class loading operates and augmenting its capabilities to support dynamic behaviors in this same context, supporting features like hot-pluggability and autodiscovery of classes.

To support these features, you also learned how OSGi relies on its own packaging model of a bundle, which is identical to a JAR except in having an OSGi manifest.

Additionally, you explored the inner workings of OSGi bundles and how these rely on the use of services, either registering services for the use of other bundles in a system or consuming services from other bundles in the same system, as well as relying on services offered by the framework itself or creating custom services for fulfilling business logic, and last but not least, how this service management is achieved through an OSGi registry.

You also saw how to create numerous bundles in different capacities: one bundle used to register a `HelloWorld` service, a second using an Http Service to offer web access to other OSGi bundles, and a third leveraging both the `HelloWorld` and Http Service to publish a Java servlet and access it through the Web.

Finally, you learned how an OSGi bundle is a universal packaging format, perfectly capable of supplanting other packaging formats like WARs, which are typically used for deploying Java web application, and how the Java SE is already in the process of incorporating OSGi's features into its building blocks through JSR-291.

CHAPTER 2

Introducing Spring

Spring is a Java framework that emerged to address many of the shortcomings present in the initial versions of the de facto Java platform targeting the enterprise market or server-side space: J2EE (Java 2 Enterprise Edition), today just Java EE. In this sense, Spring is a true grassroots movement that came about from two best practices books on this platform entitled *J2EE Design and Development*[1] and *J2EE Development without EJB*.[2]

To one of the authors of these books—Rod Johnson, who was Spring's lead architect—there were many complexities that needed to be addressed in order to embark on a server-side Java project using J2EE. Chief among these complexities was EJB (as implied by one of these titles), and the principles that emerged for designing applications without EJBs became the foundation of the Spring Framework.

While the landscape in server-side Java development has changed remarkably since the ideas underpinning Spring emerged, with the flagship enterprise Java platform undergoing three major revisions (J2EE 1.3, J2EE 1.4, and Java EE 5) and the "black sheep" in question, EJB, also being revamped the same number of times, Spring has continued to strike a chord with many Java practitioners dedicated to server-side development.

Today, Spring is considered a one-stop shop, or full stack, for all the needs encountered in the development life cycle of an enterprise Java project, providing everything from its own Model-View-Controller (MVC) module, which is a common paradigm used in server-side developments, to tight support of object-relational mapping tools, which are pretty much the norm for bridging Java objects to the relational database world that dominates enterprise IT data centers. Equipped with this brief background and awareness of the place Spring holds in the Java ecosystem, let's explore the technical foundations of Spring.

Spring Concepts and Architecture

Software applications are generally chock-full of dependencies, whether to another application, an external resource, or some other type of mechanism. Each of these dependencies helps to make an application "tick" the way you intended it to. If you drill down deep

1. Rod Johnson, *J2EE Design and Development* (Indianapolis, Indiana: Wrox, 2002)
2. Rod Johnson, Juergen Hoeller, *J2EE Development without EJB* (Indianapolis, Indiana: Wrox, 2004)

enough at the code level—in the Java classes themselves—you will find that this same behavior continues to hold true.

You may find a few Java classes depend on the use of some third-party API, others on an external resource like a database connection, and yet others on an inheritance hierarchy imposed by some other classes. So you could effectively say dependencies are everywhere, but while these dependencies in themselves are necessary to achieve the ultimate goal of a functioning application, the way you go about defining them can have broad implications in the overall design of an application.

Take for instance the classes presented in Listing 2-1 and Listing 2-2, both of which illustrate how to reference an external resource, or define a dependency. They differ, however, in the way this is done.

Listing 2-1. *Defining Resource Dependencies in Java*

```
public class Sales {

    public double getMonthlySales(String month) {
        InitialContext ctx = new InitialContext();
        DataSource ds = (DataSource) ctx.lookup("java:comp/enb/jdbc/mysql");
        Connection conn = ds.getConnection();

        try {
            Statement stm = conn.createStatement();
            // Extract actual monthly sales
            return monthlySales;
        } catch (SQLException e) {
            // Handle error


        } finally {
            conn.close();
        }
    }
}
```

Listing 2-2. *Defining Resource Dependencies in Java via Dependency Injection*

```
public class Sales {
    private DataSource ds;

    public void setDataSource(DataSource ds) {
        this.ds = ds;
    }
```

```
    public double getMonthlySales(String month) {
        Connection conn = this.ds.getConnection();

        try {
            Statement stm = conn.createStatement();
            // Extract actual monthly sales
            return monthlySales;
        } catch (SQLException e) {
            // Handle error


        } finally {
            conn.close();
        }
    }
}
```

Notice how the class in Listing 2-1 relies on an explicit lookup sequence that requires the use of an API—the JNDI API—while the one in Listing 2-2 is apparently devoid of any such mechanism, relying solely on the use of a method to gain access to the same `DataSource`. In reality, the Java class in Listing 2-2 is gaining access to the same resource as the one in Listing 2-1, except it's obtaining the resource characteristics from another location. How can this be so? Through Inversion of Control.

Inversion of Control and Dependency Injection

Inversion of Control (IoC) is a software design pattern in which the flow of a system is inverted with respect to a traditional sequence of procedural calls; the flow is instead delegated over to an external entity, which then performs the sequence of calls based on a predefined set of instructions.[3]

In Spring's case, it is said to be an *IoC container* since it's precisely Spring that fulfills the part of an external entity in the IoC definition sense. Spring implements a particular type of IoC, Dependency Injection (DI), which is the pattern illustrated in Listing 2-2. In light of this IoC definition, the differences between Listing 2-1 and Listing 2-2 should become more evident. It's not that Listing 2-2 is devoid of dependencies, but rather that its dependencies are *injected* from an external entity—the Spring IoC container—that has been configured with a set of predefined values.

---

3. Martin Fowler, InversionOfControl definition, `http://martinfowler.com/bliki/InversionOfControl.html`

The actual *injection* of values takes place when an object of the corresponding class is instantiated, either via its constructor method or setter methods—as is the case in Listing 2-2 using a setter method.

This is in contrast to Listing 2-1, in which the class itself takes responsibility for accessing the resource, therefore requiring a traditional sequence of procedural calls. DI can be used to tackle many types of dependencies in Java classes, not just resources as illustrated in Listing 2-2. For example, another case of DI could consist of a business service being injected into another business service, avoiding code dependencies between each service to be intertwined in the same location.

DI effectively allows you to simplify the thought process for designing programs, since you don't have to think of multiple sequences that need to be fulfilled at once, but rather individual sequences that can later be injected into certain locations of a program.

If you are new to developing enterprise applications, you may not see an immediate benefit to using DI until you immerse yourself in a typical enterprise-level project.

For the most part, enterprise applications are full of dependencies in the form of services and resources that are closely intertwined with the business logic they attempt to fulfill; things like data sources, transactions, security, and logging data are all carefully coordinated *aspects* that are taken into account in projects of this nature.

Were it not for the sheer size and life span of enterprise applications, using something like DI might be seen as a purely academic practice, but it is exactly the size and constant flux of enterprise projects that has given Spring and its DI approach an important market share in the area of enterprise Java projects.

By effectively separating business logic from all its underlying services and resources, a project's code base is kept increasingly clean, favoring what are four important characteristics in enterprise software: simplicity, maintenance, testing, and reusability.

Which takes us to another construct central to Spring that fosters these last characteristics: Plain Old Java Objects (POJOs).[4]

WHY IS SPRING OFTEN CALLED A LIGHTWEIGHT CONTAINER?

In relation to Spring, the allusion to the word "container" is due to how Java applications are deployed in the Java EE platform. Java EE relies on application servers composed of containers—a web container and often an EJB container—that enable access to the resources and services needed by an application. However, the majority of classes that make up an application also need to be designed against the APIs provided in these containers, further allowing classes to access the resources and services they supply—such as transactions, data sources, and security.

4. Martin Fowler, POJO definition, `http://martinfowler.com/bliki/POJO.html`

With the emergence of Spring and its IoC design, application classes no longer need to be pegged against any container APIs. Spring allows Java application classes to cooperate without requiring the use of any particular API, further allowing such classes to access the resources and services provided by a container via DI, making for a more lightweight process than that associated with using container APIs. So because Spring does not impose the use of any particular API for creating applications and still provides access to the same services and resources available in Java EE containers but in a more simplified way, the term "lightweight container" emerged.

Plain Old Java Objects

A POJO is an object instantiated from a Java class that possesses a few of the following technical characteristics:

- It has numerous properties/fields.
- Its properties/fields are accessed and assigned via getter and setter methods, respectively.
- It may have other methods containing business logic, for manipulating either its properties/fields or other resources.

At first glance, these behaviors might seem strikingly similar to those of a Java Bean—as defined by the Java platform—and in fact, they have the same characteristics. So why not just say Java Bean and be done with it? Why POJO?

The term "POJO" started being thrown around when the original Java EE platform showcased its first versions of Enterprise Java Beans (EJBs). In order to differentiate from this last Java Bean incarnation, which is a completely different beast from a run-of-the-mill Java Bean, many started prefixing the "Plain Old" phrase when referring to non-EJB objects.

Further defining the term POJO was the fact that EJBs required the use of a nonstandard JVM life-cycle contract. A nonstandard life cycle implies that a Java object is required to go through certain steps not defined by a JVM—such as create, remove, activate, and passivate—that were a requirement in EJB objects. And by contract, it is to be understood that an EJB class needed to implement an interface defined by the EJB standard—the framework—in order to enforce this special life cycle.

Ever since then, the definition has taken on a life of its own, making POJOs a household name in the area of enterprise Java applications. So far you've seen a POJO's technical characteristics enumerated; next you will learn more about its behavioral characteristics.

Simplicity

It should be somewhat obvious that "Plain Old" goes hand in hand with simplicity. In a POJO's case, its most clear traces of simplicity come through with its often scant use of third-party APIs and light reliance on class inheritance hierarchies.

This is not to say a POJO can't or doesn't use third-party APIs, but more often than not, a POJO's `import` statements are reduced to either a few classes in the core Java SE platform or limited to a few constructs from some third-party library.

Similarly, most POJOs don't have deep inheritance hierarchies as is often the case with some object-oriented (OO) designs. With respect to interfaces, POJOs never rely on any framework interfaces that might tie them to a nonstandard life cycle, as outlined earlier. If employed at all, interfaces in POJOs are used to enforce business method contracts.

While it may indeed be a slippery slope to characterize a POJO by its number of import statements or its inheritance hierarchy, as a colleague once put it, "If at first glance a class doesn't look simple, needless to say it isn't a POJO," and there is nothing like the use of too many APIs or deep inheritance hierarchies to make a class look complicated even to the trained eye.

Maintenance

For the massive undertaking that is developing enterprise-grade applications, most projects of this nature portray a considerable investment to any organization and are seen as a critical business asset once placed in production, hence maintenance proves to be an important factor with the natural changing of business requirements.

When it comes to enterprise applications, it's not strange for numerous groups of people—internal employees or contractors—to work on the same application. Add to this the effective life span of most applications is in terms of years, and maintenance can prove to be a nightmare if different people are brought in to modify an overly complex code base.

The point here is that the kiss of death to maintenance is complexity, and in software development, we can draw from the well-known acronym KISS—keep it short and simple.

It doesn't matter if a code wizard's über-class concoction can shave days off a project's schedule. When maintenance or upgrade time comes around, having a code base composed of POJOs—even if this requires lengthier times—will pay off handsomely, not only because POJOs will allow different people to navigate a code base more easily, but also because it favors another important aspect to software development: testing.

Testing

In any software application, errors are something that users and development teams have come to live with; in thousands of lines of code, there is a high probability that buried amidst all the logic is some unforeseen sequence of calls that will break the intended purpose of an application. To solve this nuisance, testing has proven to be the most effective solution.

However, the issue with testing is that it's often a continuous process. More testing will tend to uncover more unforeseen behaviors, though it's a known fact that the sooner these unforeseen behaviors—errors—are uncovered, the less disruptive and expensive they become.

Until recently, most software testing took place once the first end users got their hands on a piece of software; however, a new approach named *test-driven development*[5] started to make its way into the development world. This approach consisted of testing code at the same time classes were being written, effectively shifting testing to one of the earliest possible phases in the life span of an application.

Test-driven development proves easiest to implement when applied to POJOs, due to their minimalistic approach and limited number of dependencies—especially dependencies on infrastructure resources.

In order to perform testing, it's critical to replicate everything a class would use in a production system. As a consequence, if a class depends on infrastructure resources, like a data source, or it depends on a nonstandard JVM life cycle, like an EJB that requires its own environment, testing can become difficult. Hence, it's much easier to write a test for a potential outcome when a class's logic is less convoluted with dependencies, like it is in POJOs.

Similarly, such tests at a class level also serve the purpose of "safety nets" once a project's code base starts being modified. By having such tests, each time an application is modified it can be checked against these benchmarks, guaranteeing that earlier logic contained in a class has not been compromised due to some unintended modification in the code base.

Testing is an extremely ample subject, and I won't even attempt to summarize all its benefits here. The objective was simply to emphasize that POJOs lend themselves extremely well to the whole testing paradigm, something that will become more evident once you create your first Spring application in the upcoming section.

Reusability

Reusability is one of the many goals pursued in OO projects, but it can be hard to achieve. The reason reusability proves difficult is because classes often fulfill too many duties in an OO project. This not only causes reusable logic to be obscured in large classes, but also breeds the mentality of "It's easier to rewrite it than to learn how to use it" given the complexity of some classes.

While reusability is undeniably linked to getting a project's "big picture" from the outset, there are many factors that foster it, and one of them is POJOs. Since POJOs themselves foster simplicity, this has the side effect of smaller and more understandable classes, which in turn favor reusability.

POJOs force a developer to think in terms of more manageable units and not get carried away with what a single class attempts to fulfill. This benefits not only an individual developer's efforts to reuse classes, but also the efforts of an entire team that can clearly understand

---

5. Wikipedia, "Test-driven Development," `http://en.wikipedia.org/wiki/Test-driven_development`

a class's logic and therefore reuse it more easily. Having described a POJO's primary characteristics, let's finish the discussion on Spring's concepts and architecture with a look at the numerous parts that make up Spring.

Spring Portfolio

Spring's popularity has seen it blossom from a grassroots project in the Java community to a federated portfolio of projects spanning beyond the Java platform. Table 2-1 presents a summary of the various projects that comprise the Spring portfolio.

Table 2-1. *Spring Portfolio Projects*[a]

Project	Function	Home Page
Spring Framework (Core)	The core framework, Spring's main offering	`http://www.springsource.com/products/springframework`
Spring Security	Project that provides authentication and authorization services for enterprise applications based on Spring tenets	`http://www.springsource.com/products/springsecurity`
Spring Web Flow	A web application front-end framework based on Spring principles	`http://www.springframework.org/webflow`
Spring Web Services	A framework designed to make the management of SOAP and Plain Old XML (POX) web services easier	`http://www.springsource.com/products/springwebservices`
Spring Dynamic Modules for OSGi	Project designed to make use of OSGi features in Spring	`http://www.springsource.com/products/springdynamicmodules`
Spring Batch	A batch-processing framework based on Spring principles	`http://www.springsource.com/products/springbatch`
Spring IDE	A set of GUIs for Spring configuration files, built as Eclipse plug-ins	`http://www.springsource.com/products/springide`
Spring Modules	A collection of tools, add-ons, and modules to extend the Spring Framework	`https://springmodules.dev.java.net/`
Spring Java Configuration	Project that provides a type-safe, pure-Java option for configuring the Spring IoC container	`http://www.springframework.org/javaconfig`
SpringBeanDoc	Project that facilitates documentation and graphing of Spring bean factories and application context files	`http://spring-beandoc.sourceforge.net/`

Table 2-1. *Spring Portfolio Projects*[a]

Project	Function	Home Page
Spring .NET	Project for the .NET Framework, based on the same principles as its Java counterpart	`http://www.springsource.com/products/springdotnet`
Spring LDAP	An LDAP library based on Spring principles	`http://www.springframework.org/ldap`
Spring Rich Client	Project designed to leverage Spring's approach to the development of rich clients	`http://www.springframework.org/spring-rcp`
Spring Integration	Project designed to address Enterprise Integration Patterns in the context of Spring applications	`http://www.springsource.com/products/springintegration`
SpringSource dm Server	A module-based Java application server designed to leverage Spring, Apache Tomcat, and OSGi	`http://www.springsource.com/products/suite/applicationplatform`

a. `http://www.springframework.org/projects`

This book will cover every aspect related to the Spring Dynamic Modules for OSGi project and also introduce the SpringSource dm Server, the latter of which facilitates the use of OSGi and Spring technology in the enterprise.

However, before we get to those subjects, it's important for you to get a feel for what the Spring platform can accomplish without the use of OSGi and have a firsthand account on the use of POJOs; IoC, DI, and testing, among other core subjects related to Spring. Up next you will embark on the task of creating a Hello World application using Spring.

Spring Hello World Application

The Hello World application you are about to start will take you through the most basic steps in using Spring, such as defining your domain model and POJOs, to more advanced topics, such as connecting to a relational database using Object-Relational Mapping (ORM) principles and making use of the MVC pattern to enable applications on the Web.

Be advised that this is a "show it all" Hello World example on the Spring Framework, and not your typical one-line Hello World program. This is done with good reason, since the integration between OSGi and Spring requires an understanding on all the subjects presented in this example.

Though the following Hello World application might take you a little longer to re-create than most Hello World examples, it will save valuable time and effort if you are not familiar with Spring, since the application is the essence of entire books covering the Spring Framework.

Figure 2-1 illustrates the different layers and components that will make up this application using the Spring Framework.

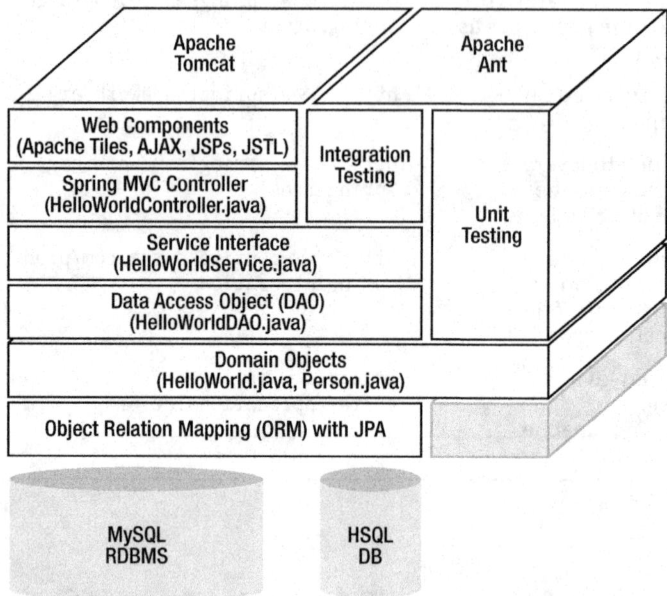

Figure 2-1. *Spring Hello World application layers and components*

Prerequisites and Downloads

Table 2-2 lists the software you will need to download and install prior to embarking on your first Spring application.

Table 2-2. *Spring Hello World Prerequisites and Downloads*

Software	Function	Download Site
Java SE 5 or higher	Java's runtime environment	`http://java.sun.com/javase/downloads/index.jsp`
Java Ant 1.6 or higher	Popular Java build project, used for easing the compilation and creation of Spring applications	`http://www.apache.org/dist/ant/binaries/apache-ant-1.7.1-bin.zip`
Spring Framework 2.5.4 (with dependencies)	Spring Framework's core libraries	`http://www.springframework.org/download`

Table 2-2. *Spring Hello World Prerequisites and Downloads*

Software	Function	Download Site
Spring Web Flow 2.0.2	Project that aids in the creation of Java web applications using Spring's MVC paradigm	`http://www.springframework.org/download#webflow`
Apache Tiles 2.0.6	Web templating system used to incorporate Asynchronous JavaScript and XML (AJAX) functionality into Spring MVC designs	`http://tiles.apache.org/download.html`
Apache Tomcat Core 5.5.26	Java container for deploying applications on the Web	`http://www.apache.org/dist/tomcat/tomcat-5/v5.5.26/bin/apache-tomcat-5.5.26.zip`
Java Persistence API (JPA) reference implementation 1.0	Java's de facto ORM API for persisting Java objects to a Relational Database Management System (RDBMS)	Included in the Spring Framework with dependencies download
MySQL Community Server 5.0	An open source RDBMS	`http://dev.mysql.com/downloads/mysql/5.0.html`
MySQL Connector/J Driver 5.1	MySQL-Java driver	`http://dev.mysql.com/downloads/connector/j/5.1.html`
HSQLDB 1.8	A lightweight in-memory RDBMS used for testing	Included in the Spring Framework with dependencies download
JUnit 4.4	Java framework used for unit testing	Included in the Spring Framework with dependencies download

It's very likely you may have some of this software already installed on your workstation; if so, just ensure that you have the suggested versions, as minor version variations may hold you back in getting through the outlined steps.

Additionally, since some of this software was already used in the OSGi Hello World application presented in Chapter 1, installation instructions for those packages will not be presented here, so please refer to Chapter 1 for detailed installation instructions.

Installing Spring Framework

The process for installing the Spring Framework consists of just one step: unzipping the downloaded file into a directory of your choice. As mentioned earlier, Spring consists of numerous parts, many of which I can't talk about in this introductory application, so while you are free to browse and explore on your own, it's only the following directories and files that will be of interest to you:

- `dist`: Contains the main distribution file `spring.jar` used by every Spring application.
- `modules` (inside `dist`): Includes the numerous modules that form part of the Spring distribution. Among the ones used in this application will be `spring-webmvc.jar` and `spring-orm.jar`.
- `lib`: Contains the various dependencies used by Spring, many of which are amply used in enterprise applications and will also serve your Hello World application, among them JUnit, JPA, and HSQLDB.

Installing Apache Tomcat

The process for installing Apache Tomcat also consists of one step: unzipping the downloaded file into a directory of your choice. Once you do this, descend into the unzipped directory and perform the following test.

While in Apache Tomcat's `bin` directory, execute `java -jar bootstrap.jar`; this will start Apache Tomcat under port 8080. Next, open a browser and attempt to access the address `http://localhost:8080/`; you should see an Apache Tomcat Welcome page. In case this test fails, verify that port 8080 is not busy: check that no other application is running on the same default port (8080) as Apache Tomcat.

Installing MySQL

Depending on your operating system, follow the instructions included in your download, which can vary from those given in a simple Installation Wizard on Windows, to executing a few scripts on Unix-type systems. Once you have installed MySQL's base system, you will need to create a database in order to place your application data. Follow these steps:

1. Create a database: execute the command `mysqladmin create springosgi`, which will create a database instance by the name `springosgi`.

Note You may be required to introduce MySQL's root password to create a new database. Use the following command if this is the case: `mysqladmin -u root -p<rootpassword> create springosgi`.

---

2. Create/Grant privileges to an application user: log in to the main database—mysql—with the command `mysql -u root -p<rootpassword> -D mysql`, and then execute the instructions `GRANT ALL PRIVILEGES ON springosgi.* to hello@localhost IDENTIFIED BY 'world'`. This process will grant connection rights to the user `hello` with the password `world` on the `springosgi` database, credentials that will be used to connect from Java to MySQL.

3. To ensure that the proper connection rights have been established, execute the following command from a command prompt: `mysql -u hello -pworld -D springosgi`. Upon performing this instruction, you should be placed inside a MySQL shell.

4. In case this test fails, verify `springosgi` database credentials: ensure that the user/password credentials for the database were granted as outlined in the previous steps.

CAN I USE ANOTHER RDBMS?

The reason MySQL was chosen for the examples is simply because of its open source licensing scheme, which is popular in development circles, and its somewhat easy installation process. However, you can easily use another RDBMS, such as the ones produced by Oracle or IBM.

You will only be using an RDBMS for the purpose of persisting Java objects within Spring via the JPA, and as you will observe in that particular part of the exercise, changing the RDBMS in a Spring/JPA-enabled application is only a matter of modifying a few configuration lines.

Installing Remaining Downloads

The remaining downloads simply contain JAR files that will aid you in the creation of the Hello World application. Just take note of their location—you will move them around when the need arises.

Setting Up the Hello World "Playground" Directory Structure

Now that you've got the tools working, it's time to create the proper workspace in which to maneuver, a directory structured like the one illustrated in Figure 2-2.

The directory structure functions as follows:

- `build.xml`: This is the main Java Ant configuration file containing the necessary tasks to build the application.

- `classes`: All compiled Java classes are placed in this directory.

- `dist`: All built applications are placed in this directory.

- `lib`: All JARs needed to compile Java sources are placed in this directory.

- `src`: All Java sources files composing the application are placed accordingly in subdirectories inside this directory, including application web descriptors in `WEB-INF`, metadata files in `META-INF`, and application user interfaces (like JSPs) in `GUI`.

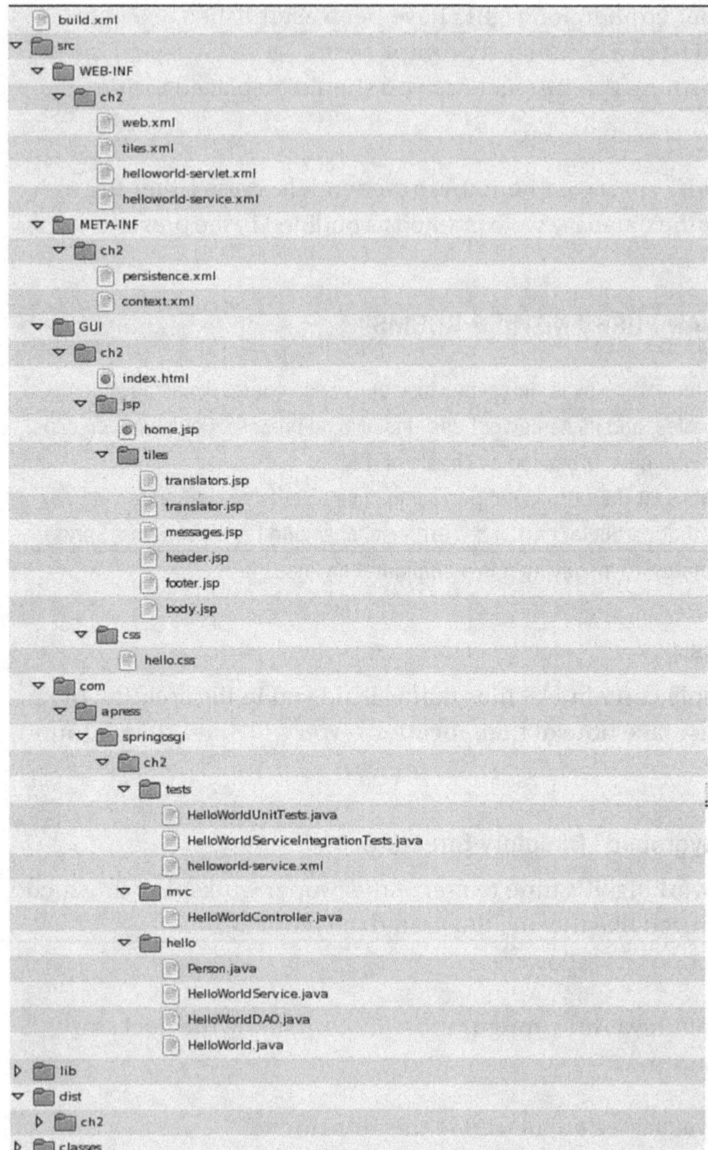

Figure 2-2. *Directory structure for the Hello World "playground"*

The Domain Model

A *domain model* is used to describe a system's core competencies in terms of classes. Given the requirements of most Hello World examples, our domain model will be extraordinarily simple, consisting of just two classes: one used to associate "Hello World" messages in different languages, and another to associate a person performing the translation of each "Hello World" message.

In OO modeling terms, the domain model will consist of a single one-to-one relationship: each "Hello World" message will have one person, and consequently, each person will also have one "Hello World" message. Listing 2-3 illustrates the `HelloWorld` class, while Listing 2-4 contains the `Person` class.

Listing 2-3. *`HelloWorld.java` POJO*

```
package com.apress.springosgi.ch2.hello;

import java.util.Date;

public class HelloWorld {

    private long id;
    private String language;
    private String message;
    private Date transdate;
    private Person translator;

    public HelloWorld(String language, String message, Date transdate,➥
Person translator) {
        this.language = language;
        this.message = message;
        this.transdate = transdate;
        this.translator = translator;
    }

    public HelloWorld() {
    }

    public void setId(long id) {
        this.id = id;
    }

    public long getId() {
        return id;
    }

    public void setLanguage(String language) {
        this.language = language;
    }
```

```
    public String getLanguage() {
        return language;
    }

    public void setMessage(String message) {
        this.message = message;
    }

    public String getMessage() {
        return message;
    }

    public void setTransdate(Date transdate) {
        this.transdate = transdate;
    }

    public Date getTransdate() {
        return transdate;
    }

    public Person getTranslator() {
        return translator;
    }

    public void setTranslator(Person translator) {
        this.translator = translator;
    }

}
```

Listing 2-4. *Person.java POJO*

```
package com.apress.springosgi.ch2.hello;

public class Person {

    private long id;
    private String firstName;
    private String lastName;
    private double hourlyRate;
```

```
    public Person(String firstName, String lastName, double hourlyRate){
        this.firstName = firstName;
        this.lastName = lastName;
        this.hourlyRate = hourlyRate;
    }

    public Person() {
    }

    public double getHourlyRate() {
        return hourlyRate;
    }

    public void setHourlyRate(double hourlyRate) {
        this.hourlyRate = hourlyRate;
    }

    public String getLastName() {
        return lastName;
    }

    public void setLastName(String lastName) {
        this.lastName = lastName;
    }

    public String getFirstName() {
        return firstName;
    }

    public void setFirstName(String firstName) {
        this.firstName = firstName;
    }

    public void setId(long id) {
        this.id = id;
    }

    public long getId() {
        return id;
    }
}
```

Both class listings are in line with the POJO characteristics outlined earlier: each class has numerous fields, possesses various getter and setter methods to access and assign values to each field, and contains no framework-specific interfaces.

Also notice that at this juncture, there is no indication as to what objects of either the `HelloWorld` or `Person` class will do. Will they be presented on a web page? Will they be persisted to a database? Will they be presented on a desktop GUI? This is the whole point of using POJOs and Spring's IoC—having API-agnostic code with all the benefits mentioned in the last section.

Now, these two classes by themselves only represent the application's objects and their corresponding properties, but what about the application's actions? For that, you will need to define a service interface containing all the possible actions on this pair of objects. Listing 2-5 illustrates such an interface.

Listing 2-5. *`HelloWorldService.java` Interface*

```
package com.apress.springosgi.ch2.hello;

import java.util.List;

public interface HelloWorldService {

    public HelloWorld findById(long id);

    public List<HelloWorld> findAll();

    public HelloWorld update(HelloWorld hw);

    public void save(HelloWorld hw);

    public void delete(HelloWorld hw);

    public void deleteMessage(long id);

    public List<HelloWorld> findByTranslatorFirstName(String firstName);

    public List<HelloWorld> findByTranslatorLastName(String lastName);

    public List<HelloWorld> findByTranslatorHourlyRateOver(double hourlyRate);

    public List<HelloWorld> findByLanguage(String language);
```

```
    public List<HelloWorld> findByMessage(String message);

}
```

This last interface illustrates a typical contract for actions performed on class objects linked to a data store; things like the findByX search methods, as well as the update, save, and delete methods, are all indicative of some type of persistence operation being involved.

But still, aside from using the HelloWorld class as an input parameter and returning Java lists of HelloWorld objects in various methods, there is still no trace of how persistence or an RDBMS will be involved in the Hello World application.

So up next, we will explore how you would go about persisting the application's domain model using the JPA and how to create a Data Access Object (DAO) out of this last interface with the aid of the same JPA and Spring.

Persisting the Domain Model with JPA

A little background on the whole issue of persistence in Java may be in order to explain why JPA[6] was chosen for this application. If there is more than one way to skin a cat, the Java world has seen its fair share of cat skinning throughout the years for persisting data. Among these approaches you will find things like JDBC, JDO, Entity EJBs, Object-Relational Mappers (ORMs), and perhaps some other standards or home-brewed processes to achieve the same results.

Java aside, many in the object-oriented community have always favored the approach and results offered by ORMs for persisting objects to RDBMSs; however, until recently the issue with Java ORMs was that they were extremely fragmented, resulting in many contrasting ways of doing Object-Relational Mapping in the Java platform, that is, until JPA came to fruition.

JPA is now the standard API for performing Object-Relational Mapping in Java, and since its emergence, many Java ORM vendors have pegged their products against this API, with the biggest beneficiaries of this whole process being application developers, since a single and unified API can now be used across the board for object-relational purposes. This is why the Hello World application will use JPA.

Though the Hello World application will use a very basic set of JPA instructions, and Spring does an excellent job of abstracting away many direct uses of the API through its IoC/DI approach, be aware that JPA is an extensive technology in itself, with entire books written on the subject. That said, let's get started decorating the Hello World application POJOs with JPA annotations.

Listing 2-6 contains a modified version of the HelloWorld class decorated with JPA annotations.

---

6. http://java.sun.com/javaee/overview/faq/persistence.jsp

Listing 2-6. *`HelloWorld.java` POJO with JPA Annotations*

```
package com.apress.springosgi.ch2.hello;

import java.util.Date;

import javax.persistence.CascadeType;
import javax.persistence.Column;
import javax.persistence.Entity;
import javax.persistence.GeneratedValue;
import javax.persistence.Id;
import javax.persistence.OneToOne;
import javax.persistence.Temporal;
import javax.persistence.TemporalType;

@Entity
public class HelloWorld {

    @Id
    @GeneratedValue
    private long id;
    @Column
    private String language;
    @Column
    private String message;
    @Temporal(TemporalType.DATE)
    private Date transdate;
    @OneToOne(cascade = CascadeType.ALL)
    private Person translator;

    // Followed by methods identical to Listing 2-3
}
```

The first thing to note about this listing is its various `import` statements, which represent JPA annotations and behaviors. Starting things off is the `@Entity` annotation used to decorate the class itself, indicating to the Java persistence runtime that the class represents an object that will be persisted using the JPA.

Immediately after, you find the remaining JPA annotations decorating the numerous fields belonging to the class. The `@Id` annotation indicates a class's field will be used as the primary key in a relational table, with the `@GeneratedValue` further specifying the strategy for the primary key, in this case a default strategy.

Next are two `@Column` annotations indicating the fields in question will be represented as columns in a relational table, with the `@Temporal(TemporalType.DATE)` serving the same purpose as the @Column annotation, except the former is specifically used for fields related to dates.

Finally, you find the @OneToOne annotation, which is used to represent a field's association to another class. In this case, the annotation indicates that the translator field is another entity class in the application, and hence has its own relational table. Of particular importance in this last annotation are its attributes, cascade = CascadeType.ALL, used to specify that any persistence operation occurring in the field be propagated out to its respective entity.

Listing 2-7 illustrates the other POJO used in the Hello World application decorated with JPA annotations.

Listing 2-7. *Person.java POJO with JPA Annotations*

```
package com.apress.springosgi.ch2.hello;

import javax.persistence.Column;
import javax.persistence.Entity;
import javax.persistence.GeneratedValue;
import javax.persistence.Id;

@Entity
public class Person {

    @Id
    @GeneratedValue
    private long id;
    @Column(name = "FNAME")
    private String firstName;
    @Column(name = "LNAME")
    private String lastName;
    @Column(precision=4, scale=2)
    private double hourlyRate;

    // Followed by methods identical to Listing 2-4
}
```

The JPA annotations used in the Person class are pretty much the same as the ones used in the HelloWorld class, with the exception of the attributes included in the @Column annotation. In this particular case, the attributes used in the @Column annotation override the default properties assigned to columns in a relational table, where name is used to indicate a specific column name, and precision along with scale are used to indicate a number column's characteristics.

An extremely important aspect to emphasize before moving on is that both these classes still remain POJOs. The JPA annotations allow each class's logic to remain free of any clutter needed to persist objects, relying instead on the runtime interpretation of such annotations to perform the actual persistence work, while maintaining a class structure that favors simplicity, maintenance, and testing. See the sidebar "POJOS and Annotations: Hot Button" for the controversy surrounding this definition of a POJO.

POJOS AND ANNOTATIONS: HOT BUTTON

Mixing the term "POJOs" with "annotations" is often cause for controversy in many Java circles, since annotations implicitly represent a dependency on a framework or API, going against the strictest definition of a POJO. In the case of Listings 2-6 and 2-7, both classes are being tied to the JPA.

Since the JPA can be implemented using either annotations (as illustrated in Listings 2-6 and 2-7) or implemented using interfaces like `PersistenceEntity`, it raises the following controversy: does using one approach over the other make a class any more or any less of a POJO?

What makes annotations different is that dependencies are *injected*, not enforced through interfaces. To some, the shedding of interfaces is sufficient to qualify a class as a POJO, since there is no explicit use of framework APIs or nonstandard JVM life cycle. To others, the use of annotations is simply turning a "blind eye" to a dependency that still ties a class to a particular framework API or nonstandard JVM life cycle, in another part of an application.

The topic is controversial depending on how rigid your definition of a POJO is, so I'll leave you to measure the semantics of a POJO with annotations against your own criteria.

Though having these two JPA-decorated classes is an important part to persisting `HelloWorld` and `Person` objects, you're still in need of another important part of the puzzle in order to make use of such objects: a DAO.

Since both aforementioned classes persist objects to an RDBMS, a mechanism in which to retrieve such objects still needs to be established, and though you might not have realized it, you already set the groundwork for creating a DAO back in Listing 2-5, which defined the numerous actions the Hello World application would be able to perform.

Under normal circumstances, creating a class to serve as a DAO would entail not only implementing all the methods contained in an interface like the one in Listing 2-5, but also extensive use of the JPA in order to perform the necessary logic against an RDBMS to obtain the desired results.

Fortunately, this is one area where Spring makes its presence felt with a very simple and straightforward manner of implementing a DAO. Listing 2-8 illustrates the `HelloWorldDAO` class using JPA and implementing the `HelloWorldService` interface defined in Listing 2-5.

Listing 2-8. *HelloWorldDAO.java DAO Class*

```
package com.apress.springosgi.ch2.hello;

import org.springframework.transaction.annotation.Propagation;
import org.springframework.transaction.annotation.Transactional;

import java.util.List;

import org.springframework.orm.jpa.support.JpaDaoSupport;

public class HelloWorldDAO extends JpaDaoSupport implements HelloWorldService {

    public HelloWorld findById(long id) {
        return getJpaTemplate().find(HelloWorld.class, id);
    }

    public List<HelloWorld> findAll() {
        return getJpaTemplate().find("select e from HelloWorld e");
    }

    public HelloWorld update(HelloWorld emp) {
        return getJpaTemplate().merge(emp);
    }

    public void save(HelloWorld emp) {
        getJpaTemplate().persist(emp);

    }

    public void delete(HelloWorld emp) {
        getJpaTemplate().remove(emp);
    }


    public List<HelloWorld> findByTranslatorFirstName(String firstName) {
        return getJpaTemplate().find("select e from HelloWorld e➥
where e.translator.firstName = ?1", firstName);
    }
```

```
    public List<HelloWorld> findByTranslatorLastName(String lastName) {
        return getJpaTemplate().find("select e from HelloWorld e where➥
e.translator.lastName = ?1", lastName);
    }

    public List<HelloWorld> findByTranslatorHourlyRateOver(double hourlyRate) {
        return getJpaTemplate().find("select e from HelloWorld e where➥
e.translator.hourlyRate > ?1", hourlyRate);
    }

    public List<HelloWorld> findByLanguage(String language) {
        return getJpaTemplate().find("select e from HelloWorld e where➥
e.language = ?1", language);
    }

    public List<HelloWorld> findByMessage(String message) {
        return getJpaTemplate().find("select e from HelloWorld e where➥
e.message = ?1", message);
    }

    @Transactional(propagation = Propagation.REQUIRED)
    public void deleteMessage(long id) {
        HelloWorld hw = getJpaTemplate().find(HelloWorld.class, id);
        getJpaTemplate().remove(hw);

    }

}
```

The bulk of the work behind this DAO class is performed by the `org.springframework.orm.jpa.support.JpaDaoSupport` class and its `getJpaTemplate()`. Notice that each of the class's methods contain calls to `getJpaTemplate()`, along with other nested calls to methods like `persist()`,`merge()`,`delete()`, and `find()`, which is accompanied by Java Persistence Query Language (JPQL), an SQL-esque syntax for Java.

In this scenario, the `JpaDaoSupport` class takes care of the intricacies of using the JPA, such as explicitly managing a persistence context and its corresponding JPA Entity Manager, as well as the handling of transactions. Hence, each call to `getJpaTemplate()` performs an atomic operation to whatever underlying data source is bound to the JPA Entity Manager.

The last method in the DAO class is different in the sense that it uses the transactional Spring annotation `@Transactional(propagation = Propagation.REQUIRED)`, indicating that the operations included in the method will be performed under a single transaction. In this case, since the method is performing two operations against a data source—find and remove—this annotation overrides the default behavior of initiating a new transaction on each of the two calls made to `getJpaTemplate()`.

This is all it takes to perform object-relational actions using Spring and JPA. Now you may be questioning where exactly this `HelloWorldDAO` class is getting its information, such as on what database to perform its queries. A very valid question, of course, but also one with a very simple answer: descriptors.

Descriptors for Spring and JPA

All the JPA annotations and queries presented in this section are of no use if an application is not aware of where to persist and find such objects; as a consequence, you need to rely on the use of XML descriptors to provide such information.

The JPA standard dictates that a descriptor by the name `persistence.xml` be used to contemplate all the JPA code contained in a set of classes, indicate an Entity Manager, RDBMS connection parameters, and classes to be persisted, among other things.

As you've already been forewarned, JPA is a very deep subject, and its corresponding `persistence.xml` file can also become elaborate; fortunately, since you're already relying on Spring to aid you in the implementation of a DAO using JPA, you can delegate much of the work in this file over to Spring.

Nevertheless, given that the JPA requires the use of a `persistence.xml` descriptor, you can't forgo this requirement, so you need to include a minimum set of instructions in such a file. Listing 2-9 contains the typical `persistence.xml` descriptor used in Spring applications employing JPA, which will also be used for the Hello World example.

Listing 2-9. *`persistence.xml` Used in JPA-Spring Applications*

```
<persistence xmlns="http://java.sun.com/xml/ns/persistence" version="1.0">

    <persistence-unit name="proSpringOSGiJpa" transaction-type="RESOURCE_LOCAL"/>

</persistence>
```

The remaining configuration parameters for using JPA in a Spring application are left in the hands of a service descriptor containing numerous Spring constructs. Listing 2-10 illustrates the `helloworld-service.xml` descriptor used in this Hello World application, with some of its values further explained in Table 2-3 and Table 2-4 a little later in this section for cases in which different RDBMSs are used.

Listing 2-10. *`helloworld-service.xml` Used in the JPA-Spring Hello World Application*

```
<?xml version="1.0" encoding="UTF-8"?>
<beans xmlns="http://www.springframework.org/schema/beans"
       xmlns:tx="http://www.springframework.org/schema/tx"
       xmlns:xsi="http://www.w3.org/2001/XMLSchema-instance"
```

```
        xsi:schemaLocation="http://www.springframework.org/schema/beans
                            http://www.springframework.org/schema/beans/➥
spring-beans.xsd
                            http://www.springframework.org/schema/tx
                            http://www.springframework.org/schema/tx/➥
spring-tx-2.5.xsd">

   <tx:annotation-driven/>

   <bean id="helloWorldService"
         class="com.apress.springosgi.ch2.hello.HelloWorldDAO">
     <property name="entityManagerFactory" ref="entityManagerFactory"/>
   </bean>

   <bean id="entityManagerFactory"
         class="org.springframework.orm.jpa.LocalContainerEntityManagerFactoryBean">
     <property name="dataSource" ref="dataSource"/>
     <property name="jpaVendorAdapter">
      <bean
         class="org.springframework.orm.jpa.vendor.OpenJpaVendorAdapter">
           <!-- See Table 2-3 for valid property values in this bean -->
      </bean>
     </property>
     <property name="loadTimeWeaver">
      <bean
         class="org.springframework.instrument.classloading.SimpleLoadTimeWeaver"/>
     </property>
   </bean>

   <bean id="dataSource" class="<!-- See Table 2-4 for valid class values -->">
     <!-- See Table 2-4 for valid property values in this bean -->
   </bean>

   <bean id="transactionManager" class="org.springframework.orm.jpa.Jpa➥
TransactionManager">
      <property name="entityManagerFactory" ref="entityManagerFactory"/>
      <property name="dataSource" ref="dataSource"/>
   </bean>

</beans>
```

The first thing to note about Listing 2-9 is its ample use of `<bean>` declarations, each having its own ID, as well as numerous properties to assign more specific behaviors to the bean in question. This is what most Spring configuration files look like; after all, Spring is mostly about enabling Java Beans—POJOs—with IoC/DI.

The initial bean declaration `<bean id="helloWorldService">` is related to the DAO class you created earlier, associated through the class attribute with a value of `com.apress.springosgi.ch2.hello.HelloWorldDAO`. Inside the bean, however, you will find a property name and reference to `entityManagerFactory`, which indicates a dependence on another bean by this name that is charged with the management of entities.

Searching for a bean with an `id` value of `entityManagerFactory`, you will come to the second bean declaration in the file, the `entityManagerFactory` bean, which is associated to the class `org.springframework.orm.jpa.LocalContainerEntityManagerFactoryBean`, a Spring Framework factory class for JPA operations.

In terms of properties, this last bean is a little a more interesting than the first one, not only because it has three properties, but also because these properties are beans themselves. The meaning behind each of the properties in Spring's JPA Entity Manager factory are as follows:

- `dataSource`: Defines the actual data source that is going to be managed by the factory, with its value pointing to yet another `<bean>` ID containing the data source's properties.
- `jpaVendorAdapter`: Indicates the JPA vendor adapter used by the Entity Manager, which provides JPA behaviors like vendor-specific RBDMS mapping and SQL creation strategies. Its value is another `<bean>`—in this case nested—pointing to the Spring-provided adapter class `OpenJpaVendorAdapter` (with other available Spring adapters classes being `HibernateJpaVendorAdapter` and `EclipseLinkJpaVendorAdapter`). The internal properties for the `jpaVendorAdapter` bean used in this application can be found in Table 2-3.
- `loadTimeWeaver`: Provides the necessary weaving behaviors for using JPA with Spring, assigning the Spring-provided class `org.springframework.instrument.classloading.SimpleLoadTimeWeaver`.

Note I will elaborate on the use and need of weaving toward the end of this chapter in the sidebar "What Is Weaving? And Why Is It Important?"

Amid the properties defined for the `entityManagerFactory` bean, recall there was a property named `dataSource` pointing to a bean by the same name, which is precisely declared as the third top-level bean in the `hellworld-service.xml` descriptor.

Table 2-3. *Spring Open JPA Vendor Adapter Bean Properties*

Property	Values	Sample	Description
showSql	true/false	<property name= "showSql" value="true"/>	Outputs SQL in the log or console
generateDdl	true/false	<property name= "generateDdl" value="true"/>	Specifies whether to execute Data Definition Language (DDL) each time the Entity Manager is initialized, that is, whether to create and update the respective relational tables associated with each managed entity
databasePlatform	FirebirdDictionary, H2Dictionary, JDataStoreDictionary, AccessDictionary, OracleDictionary, EmpressDictionary, DBDictionary, MyQSLDictionary, HSQLDictionary, InformixDictionary, SQLServerDictionary, InterbaseDictionary, DB2Dictionary, PointbaseDictionary, SybaseDictionary, FoxProDictionary, DerbyDictionary, PostgresDictionary (all inside package org.apache.openjpa.jdbc.sql)	<property name= "databasePlatform" value="org.apache.openjpa.jdbc.sql.HSQLPlatform"/>	Indicates what specific platform to use for JPA mapping

Not to be confused with the JPA Entity Manager factory bean, which defines *how* to persist objects to a specific RDBMS, the data source bean defines *where* to persist such objects including an RDBMS's connection parameters. In Spring, there are two primary ways you can go about the process, as described in Table 2-4.

Table 2-4. *Spring Data Source Bean Alternatives*

Type	Class	Sample	Notes
Spring administered	`org.springframework.jdbc.datasource.DriverManagerDataSource`	`<bean id="dataSource" class="org.springframework.jdbc.datasource.DriverManagerDataSource"> <property name="driverClassName" value="org.hsqldb.jdbcDriver"/> <property name="url" value="jdbc:hsqldb:mem:springosgi"/> <property name="username" value="sa"/> <property name="password" value=""/></bean>`	The data source is completely administered by Spring. In this case, the bean declares in-line properties related to the driver and username/password needed to connect to the RDBMS.
Externally administered	`org.springframework.jndi.JndiObjectFactoryBean`	`<bean id="dataSource" class="org.springframework.jndi.JndiObjectFactoryBean"> <property name="jndiName" value="java:comp/env/jdbc/springosgi" /></bean>`	The data source is administered externally; Spring simply accesses the data source via the provided JNDI name. In this case, it's a Java application server/container that administers the data source and makes it available via JNDI, where the corresponding RDBMS properties—driver, username, password—are configured in the JNDI data source itself.

WHICH JPA-SPRING DATA SOURCE TO CHOOSE?

Choosing between the two data source approaches presented in Table 2-4 will depend heavily on the usage scenario of an application. For most development and testing circumstances, using a Spring-administered data source is justifiable and easier since it doesn't require extra effort to set up.

However, the benefit to using an externally administered data source is that most JNDI data sources are administered by an application server/container and have more sophisticated mechanisms, such as connection pooling, that enhance connectivity to an RDBMS, albeit the use of an external data source also entails setting up an additional resource outside of Spring.

In the upcoming sections, you will explore both approaches: using a Spring-administered data source to perform testing and using an externally administered data source when the application is deployed on the Web via an application server/container.

Finally, we come to the last bean in the helloworld-service.xml descriptor, one related to another important part to working with RDBMSs: transactions. The transactionManager bean is associated to the Spring-provided class org.springframework.orm.jpa.JpaTransactionManager, which is then charged with managing transactions on none other than the entityManagerFactory and dataSource beans, as can be seen by the respective <property> fields.

And last but not least, let's not forget the topmost declaration in the form, <tx:annotation-driven/>, which is used to tell Spring to inspect declared beans for annotations related to transactions that in this case will enforce the transaction annotations specified in the DAO class.

With this, you now know the necessary descriptors for using JPA and Spring in the same application. For the moment, it's not important to know where these descriptor files need to be placed; in due time I will tell you where they should go.

Compiling the Domain Model

Before leaving your domain model POJOs decorated with JPA annotations and moving on to the next section, it's convenient to compile the classes not only to give this section closure, but also because the next section builds on compiled versions of these classes.

If you've been following along since Chapter 1, which presented a Hello World OSGi application and introduced the Hello World "playground," you may recall the compilation process for the book's applications rely on the use of Apache Ant.

Use the same Java Ant build.xml file presented back in Chapter 1—specifically Listing 1-6, which was used to compile classes—and place this chapter's classes according to their packages in the Hello World "playground" directory presented in Figure 2-1. Now follow these steps to enact the compilation process:

1. Copy dependent JAR files to the lib directory: as the domain model classes rely on several third-party libraries, you need to copy each of the following JARs to the HelloWorld "playground" lib directory.

   - persistence.jar: Located in the lib/j2ee directory of the Spring Framework with dependencies download

   - spring-beans.jar: Located in the dist/modules directory of the Spring Framework with dependencies download

   - spring-core.jar: Located in the dist/modules directory of the Spring Framework with dependencies download

- `spring-orm.jar`: Located in the `dist/modules` directory of the Spring Framework with dependencies download

- `spring-tx.jar`: Located in the `dist/modules` directory of the Spring Framework with dependencies download

2. Execute `ant compile`: while in the root directory of the Hello World "playground," execute the command `ant compile`. This will initiate the compilation process and place the compiled classes under the `classes` directory.

You've now finished creating and compiling your `HelloWorld` domain model. It's time to get some hands-on experience on another area touted from the outset in Spring: testing.

Testing Your Domain Model

Similar to the use of JPA in the last section, this exploration into the world of Java testing with Spring will be limited to a few basic constructs, since in much the same way, testing in itself is an extremely big subject, with numerous types and tools to support it in Java. That said, the two types of testing this Hello World application will demonstrate are unit testing and integration testing.

Unit Testing

Unit testing refers to process of guaranteeing the integrity of individual classes—hence the term "unit." It is the simplest form of software testing, because creating tests on individual classes is relatively easy.

Take for example your `HelloWorld` or `Person` class. Both contain numerous getter and setter methods, so creating a unit test for either class would consist of generating an object of each kind, invoking a series of setter and getter sequences, and later proving whether the outcome for the sequences turned out with the expected results. It's a classic process of "getting what you expect" from "what you put in": if you don't get the expected results, it means a class's logic is broken in some way.

In this Hello World application, things can't go terribly awry with the two classes in question, but in POJOs performing more elaborate logic, unit testing can avoid the presence of some pretty nasty behavioral errors that would be impossible to detect at compile time.

Listing 2-11 shows a unit test for both the `HelloWorld` and `Person` classes.

Listing 2-11. *Hello World Application Unit Test Using JUnit*

```
package com.apress.springosgi.ch2.tests;

import java.util.Date;
import junit.framework.TestCase;

import com.apress.springosgi.ch2.hello.HelloWorld;
import com.apress.springosgi.ch2.hello.Person;

public class HelloWorldUnitTests extends TestCase {

    private Person  trans1, trans2;
    private HelloWorld   hw1, hw2;
    protected void setUp() throws Exception {

        trans1 = new Person("John","Smith",45.00);

        trans2 = new Person();
        trans2.setFirstName("Carlos");
        trans2.setLastName("Perez");
        trans2.setHourlyRate(40.00);

        hw1 = new HelloWorld("English","Hello World!",new Date(),trans1);
        hw2 = new HelloWorld();
        hw2.setLanguage("Spanish");
        hw2.setMessage("Hola Mundo!");
        hw2.setTransdate(new Date());
        hw2.setTranslator(trans2);
    }
    public void testPerson() throws java.text.ParseException  {
        assertEquals("John", trans1.getFirstName());
        assertEquals("Smith", trans1.getLastName());
        assertEquals(45.00, trans1.getHourlyRate());

        assertEquals("Carlos", trans2.getFirstName());
        assertEquals("Perez", trans2.getLastName());
        assertEquals(40.00, trans2.getHourlyRate());
    }
```

```
    public void testHelloWorld() {
        assertEquals("English", hw1.getLanguage());
        assertEquals("Hello World!", hw1.getMessage());
        assertEquals(new Date(), hw1.getTransdate());
        assertEquals(trans1, hw1.getTranslator());

        assertEquals("Spanish", hw2.getLanguage());
        assertEquals("Hola Mundo!", hw2.getMessage());
        assertEquals(new Date(), hw2.getTransdate());
        assertEquals(trans2, hw2.getTranslator());
    }
}
```

The unit test in this last listing leverages the Java testing framework JUnit, which provides an excellent environment in which to perform such tests. First off, notice how the unit test class inherits its behavior from the `TestCase` class, which forms part of the JUnit framework.

The first method in the unit test is the `setUp()` method, which takes care of instantiating two `Person` objects and two `HelloWorld` objects, with each object being generated through different means—in one case through a class's overloaded constructor method, and in another using the class's default constructor and later using its corresponding setter methods.

An important aspect of the JUnit framework is that each of the objects generated in the `setUp()` method will be created at the outset of a test, further making these objects available to other methods in the unit test for future usage.

Continuing with the sequence of methods, you will find the `testPerson()` method, which is charged with testing the `Person` class. Inside this last method are various statements starting with `assertEquals()`—which is a JUnit method—used to invoke various getter methods on the `Person` objects created in `setUp()`, and comparing them to the expected values as inputted in this latter method. If for some reason the assertion fails, the unit test is said to have failed.

The `testHelloWorld()` method does pretty much the same as its `testPerson()` counterpart, except it does so for the `HelloWorld` class, identically using JUnit's `assert()` method to prove an object's getter methods return the expected values as inputted in the `setUp()` method.

This is basically the same process for performing any unit test using the JUnit framework, so you could easily add another `testXXX()` method to include more `assert` statements—or some other JUnit variation—to unit test any other class.

As far as the actual bootstrapping and execution of unit tests is concerned, JUnit offers various approaches, ranging from its own stand-alone GUI, to external support in IDEs like Eclipse, to the Java build utility you've already used and will be the tool of choice: Apache Ant. But before you get to executing unit tests, let's take a look at how you can perform integration testing on your Hello World application.

Integration Testing

Integration testing can be a little more elaborate than unit testing, since it consists of taking numerous parts—units—and testing how they interact with one another, with the addition of acquiring other resources and services to perform the necessary tests on the underlying logic.

In your Hello World application, you have a perfect candidate to perform integration testing on, the DAO class presented back in Listing 2-10. In this case, the integration test would consist of guaranteeing that each of the DAO's actions returned the appropriate results from an RDBMS.

This process is by far lengthier than the earlier unit test, since it entails prepopulating an RDBMS with values, performing a class's operations against an RDBMS, and verifying the output from the RDBMS is returned as expected. Fortunately, and as you will now see, Spring has excellent built-in support for bootstrapping resources like RDBMS for the purpose of testing. Listing 2-12 contains the integration test used for the `HelloWorldService` DAO class.

Listing 2-12. *Hello World Application Integration Test Using Spring*

```
package com.apress.springosgi.ch2.tests;

import java.util.Date;
import java.util.List;

import com.apress.springosgi.ch2.hello.HelloWorld;
import com.apress.springosgi.ch2.hello.Person;
import com.apress.springosgi.ch2.hello.HelloWorldService;

import org.springframework.test.jpa.AbstractJpaTests;

public class HelloWorldServiceIntegrationTests extends AbstractJpaTests {

    private HelloWorldService helloWorldService;

    private long EnglishId;
    private long SpanishId;
    private long FrenchId;

    public void setHelloWorldService(HelloWorldService helloWorldService) {
        this.helloWorldService = helloWorldService;
    }
```

```
    protected String[] getConfigLocations() {
        return new String[] { "classpath:/com/apress/springosgi/ch2/tests/➥
helloworld-service.xml" };
    }

    protected void onSetUpInTransaction() throws Exception {
        HelloWorld hw1 = new HelloWorld("English",
                                       "Hello World!", new Date(),
                                       new Person("John","Smith",45.00));
    HelloWorld hw2 = new HelloWorld("Spanish",
                                       "Hola Mundo!", new Date(),
                                       new Person("Carlos","Perez",40.00));
    HelloWorld hw3 = new HelloWorld("French",
                                       "Bonjour Monde!", new Date(),
                                       new Person("Pierre","LeClair",40.00));

        helloWorldService.save(hw1);
        helloWorldService.save(hw2);
        helloWorldService.save(hw3);

        EnglishId = helloWorldService.findByLanguage("English").get(0).getId();
        SpanishId = helloWorldService.findByLanguage("Spanish").get(0).getId();
        FrenchId = helloWorldService.findByLanguage("French").get(0).getId();
    }

    public void testFindById() {
        HelloWorld hw = helloWorldService.findById(EnglishId);
        assertNotNull(hw);
        assertEquals("English", hw.getLanguage());
    }

    public void testFindByDoesNotExistId() {
        HelloWorld hw = helloWorldService.findById(10000);
        assertNull(hw);
    }

    public void testFindByLanguage() {
        List<HelloWorld> hws = helloWorldService.findByLanguage("Spanish");
        assertEquals(1, hws.size());
        HelloWorld hw = hws.get(0);
        assertEquals("Hola Mundo!", hw.getMessage());
    }
```

```
  public void testFindByBadLanguage() {
        List<HelloWorld> hws = helloWorldService.findByLanguage("Catalan");
        assertEquals(0, hws.size());
    }

    public void testFindByTranslatorFirstName() {
        List<HelloWorld> hws = helloWorldService.findByTranslatorFirstName("John");
        assertEquals(1, hws.size());
        HelloWorld hw = hws.get(0);
        assertEquals(EnglishId, hw.getId());
    }

    public void testFindByTranslatorLastName() {
        List<HelloWorld> hws = helloWorldService.findByTranslatorLastName➥
("LeClair");
        assertEquals(1, hws.size());
        HelloWorld hw = hws.get(0);
        assertEquals(FrenchId, hw.getId());
    }
   public void testFindByTranslatorFirstNameDoesNotExist() {
        List<HelloWorld> hws = helloWorldService.findByTranslatorFirstName("Bill");
        assertEquals(0, hws.size());
    }

    public void testFindByTranslatorLastNameDoesNotExist() {
        List<HelloWorld> hws = helloWorldService.findByTranslatorLastName➥
("Matsusaka");
        assertEquals(0, hws.size());
    }

    public void testFindByTranslatorHourlyRateOver() {
        List<HelloWorld> hws = helloWorldService.findByTranslatorHourly➥
RateOver(42.00);
        assertEquals(1, hws.size());

    }
 public void testModifyHelloWorldMessage() {
        String oldHelloMessage = "Bonjour Monde!";
        String newHelloMessage = "Bonjour Le Monde!";
        HelloWorld hw = helloWorldService.findByLanguage("French").get(0);
        hw.setMessage(newHelloMessage);
```

```
        HelloWorld hw2 = helloWorldService.update(hw);
        assertEquals(newHelloMessage, hw2.getMessage());

        List<HelloWorld> hw3 = helloWorldService.findByMessage(oldHelloMessage);
        assertEquals(0, hw3.size());

        hw3 = helloWorldService.findByMessage(newHelloMessage);
        assertEquals(1, hw3.size());
        HelloWorld newhw3 = hw3.get(0);
        assertEquals(newHelloMessage, newhw3.getMessage());
    }
 public void testDeleteHelloWorldCascade() {
        String transFirstName = "Carlos";
        HelloWorld hw = helloWorldService.findByTranslatorFirstName➥
(transFirstName).get(0);
        int transCountBefore = countRowsInTable("person");
        int helloCountBefore = countRowsInTable("helloworld");
        helloWorldService.delete(hw);
        List<HelloWorld>  hws = helloWorldService.findByTranslator➥
FirstName(transFirstName);
        assertEquals(0, hws.size());
        int transCountAfter = countRowsInTable("person");
        int helloCountAfter = countRowsInTable("helloworld");
        assertEquals(transCountBefore -1, transCountAfter);
        assertEquals(helloCountBefore -1, helloCountAfter);
    }

    public void testFindAll() {
        List<HelloWorld> hws = helloWorldService.findAll();
        assertEquals(3, hws.size());
    }
}
```

Much like the DAO class itself, which relies on one of Spring's core classes to facilitate the use of JPA, this integration test class inherits it behavior from another Spring class named `org.springframework.test.jpa.AbstractJpaTests`.

As you will likely notice in the last listing, the layout in terms of methods and their names is strikingly similar to the earlier unit test. The first difference, though is the use of the `setHelloWorldService()` method, which injects an instance of `HelloWorldService` into the test. Next, you will find two methods that are executed at the outset of a test: `getConfigLocations()` and `onSetUpInTransaction()`.

The getConfigLocations() method is used to locate the RDBMS's parameters against which the integration tests will be performed, with the assigned value being a Spring-JPA descriptor file like the one described in Listing 2-13 in the next section. On the other hand, the onSetUpInTransaction() is charged with creating and saving three HelloWorld objects—and their corresponding Person objects—to the RDBMS for further use by the class's testing methods.

The testing methods that start with the prefix testXXX() perform various operations against the RDBMS using the DAO methods, later leveraging methods like assertEquals() and countRowsInTable() to verify that the returned results are in line with the input objects created in the onSetUpInTransation() method.

Now let's take a brief sidestep and see what the RDBMS's parameters bootstrapped in the getConfigLocations() method look like.

JPA Descriptor Files for Integration Testing

Since integration testing is mostly performed on development workstations and tends to be limited to a one-time affair, you will be taking the simplest and shortest route possible to set-up an RDBMS: a data source managed by Spring and an in-memory RDBMS to avoid any extra configuration steps.

Listing 2-13 illustrates the helloworld-service.xml descriptor used for integration testing.

Listing 2-13. *helloworld-service.xml Used in JPA-Spring for Integration Testing*

```
<?xml version="1.0" encoding="UTF-8"?>
<beans xmlns="http://www.springframework.org/schema/beans"
       xmlns:xsi="http://www.w3.org/2001/XMLSchema-instance"
       xsi:schemaLocation="http://www.springframework.org/schema/beans
                           http://www.springframework.org/schema/beans/➥
spring-beans.xsd">

   <bean id="helloWorldService"
         class="com.apress.springosgi.ch2.hello.HelloWorldDAO">
     <property name="entityManagerFactory" ref="entityManagerFactory"/>
   </bean>

   <bean id="entityManagerFactory"
         class="org.springframework.orm.jpa.LocalContainerEntityManagerFactoryBean">
     <property name="dataSource" ref="dataSource"/>
     <property name="jpaVendorAdapter">
      <bean
```

```
        class="org.springframework.orm.jpa.vendor.OpenJpaVendorAdapter">
            <property name="showSql" value="true"/>
            <property name="generateDdl" value="true"/>
          <property name="databasePlatform" value="org.apache.openjpa.jdbc.sql.➥
HSQLDictionary"/>
      </bean>
    </property>
    <property name="loadTimeWeaver">
      <bean
        class="org.springframework.instrument.classloading.SimpleLoadTimeWeaver"/>
    </property>
  </bean>

  <bean id="dataSource" class="org.springframework.jdbc.datasource.Driver➥
ManagerDataSource">
      <property name="driverClassName" value="org.hsqldb.jdbcDriver"/>
      <property name="url" value="jdbc:hsqldb:mem:springosgi"/>
      <property name="username" value="sa" />
      <property name="password" value="" />
  </bean>

  <bean id="transactionManager" class="org.springframework.orm.jpa.JpaTransaction➥
Manager">
      <property name="entityManagerFactory" ref="entityManagerFactory"/>
      <property name="dataSource" ref="dataSource"/>
  </bean>

</beans>
```

The RDBMS parameters specified in this last descriptor belong to the HSQL database—`databasePlatform = HSQLPlatform`—a popular in-memory RDBMS with the same general behaviors as more heavyweight RDBMSs, while specifying that JPA generate logging information—`showSQL=true`—and that it attempt to generate and update relational tables each time the Entity Manager is initialized—`generateDdl=true`. Additional parameters also include those for the data source, which are the HSQLDB driver, connection URL, and the default username and password for HSQLDB.

It should also be noted that since HSQLDB is configured an in-memory solution, data never survives beyond the parent process that initiates it, though for the purpose of testing and since JPA uses `generateDdl=true`, this is a perfectly reasonable trade-off.

Besides the `helloworld-service.xml` descriptor shown here, the JPA also requires a default `persistence.xml` descriptor. Whether used in the context of testing or deploying production-type Spring JPA applications, this file never changes, and hence can be taken from the code presented in Listing 2-9 earlier.

With this you finish up all aspects related to integration testing on your Hello World Spring application; now it's time to execute this test along with the corresponding unit test created earlier.

Running Tests

For executing the Hello World application tests, you will once again rely on the Apache Ant build tool. Prior to defining this Ant task, though, make sure you have incorporated all the following steps into your Hello World "playground":

1. Copy the test classes to the appropriate directory: ensure the sources for both the unit and integration tests are placed according to their package in the subdirectory `src/com/apress/springosgi/ch2/tests/`.

2. Copy the Spring-JPA descriptor to the appropriate directory: make sure the `helloworld-service.xml` descriptor in Listing 2-13 is also located under the subdirectory `src/com/apress/springosgi/ch2/tests/`.

3. Copy the JPA default descriptor to the appropriate directory: a copy of the `persistence.xml` file from Listing 2-9 should be placed under the subdirectory `src/META-INF/ch2/`.

4. Copy dependent JAR files to the `lib` directory: the test classes incorporate new dependencies into the application. Copy each of the following JARs to the Hello World "playground" `lib` directory:

    - `commons-logging.jar`: Located in the `lib/jakarta-commons` directory of the Spring Framework with dependencies download

    - `commons-lang.jar`: Located in the `lib/jakarta-commons` directory of the Spring Framework with dependencies download

    - `commons-collections.jar`: Located in the `lib/jakarta-commons` directory of the Spring Framework with dependencies download

    - `hsqldb.jar`: Located in the `lib/hsqldb` directory of the Spring Framework with dependencies download

    - `junit.jar`: Located in the `lib/junit` directory of the Spring Framework with dependencies download

    - `jta.jar`: Located in the `lib/j2ee` directory of the Spring Framework with dependencies download

- `serp.jar`: Located in the `lib/serp` directory of the Spring Framework with dependencies download
- `spring.jar`: Located in the `dist` directory of the Spring Framework with dependencies download
- `spring-test.jar`: Located in the `dist/modules` directory of the Spring Framework with dependencies download
- `openjpa.jar`: Located in the `lib/openjpa` directory of the Spring Framework with dependencies download

5. Copy `junit.jar` to Apache Ant's `lib` directory: ensure the `junit.jar` file—located in the `lib/junit` directory of the Spring Framework with dependencies download—is copied over to Apache Ant's `lib` directory.

With all dependencies, classes, and descriptor files in place, define an Ant task for the purpose of performing the application's unit and integration tests. Listing 2-14 shows such a task.

Listing 2-14. *Ant Task for Performing Unit and Integration Tests*

```
<target name="ch2" depends="compile" description="Build Chapter 2 ➥
Spring Application">

    <echo message="-------------- Building Chapter 2 Spring Application for ➥
Pro Spring-OSGi --------------"/>

     <property name="ch2.dir"          value="${dist.dir}/ch2/"/>
     <mkdir dir="${ch2.dir}"/>

     <property name="test.dir"        value="${ch2.dir}/tests"/>
     <mkdir dir="${test.dir}"/>

     <mkdir dir="${ch2.dir}/lib/"/>
     <mkdir dir="${build.dir}/META-INF"/>

     <copy file="${src.dir}/META-INF/ch2/persistence.xml" tofile=➥
"${build.dir}/META-INF/persistence.xml"/>

  <junit printsummary="yes">
      <classpath refid="classpath"/>
      <formatter type="brief"/>
```

```
        <batchtest todir="${test.dir}">
          <fileset dir="${build.dir}">
            <include name="com/apress/springosgi/ch2/tests/*"/>
          </fileset>
        </batchtest>
    </junit>

</target>
```

This Ant task starts off by declaring a dependency on the `compile` target, ensuring that prior to attempting any tests, all classes are properly compiled. It then sets off on a few housekeeping tasks, creating a `ch2` and `test` build directory to output results, and copying the `persistence.xml` descriptor over to the project's build directory, so it can be picked up by Java's classpath as required by the integration test.

Then you can observe the `<junit>` task, which in itself contains the `printsummary="yes"` attribute used for outputting one-line statistics on each test. Nested inside `<junit>`, you will also find numerous declarations used for the following:

- `<classpath>`: Indicates the Ant variable to use as the Java `CLASSPATH` for executing tests, in this case containing a value pointing to the `lib` and `compiled` class directories.
- `<formatter>`: Specifies the type of formatting to use for the results obtained on each test.
- `<batchtest>`: Defines the location in which to place testing reports, as well as where to locate the classes containing the tests via a `<fileset>` directive. In this case, notice that the `<fileset>` directive points toward the `com/apress/springosgi/ch2/tests/` subdirectory, which is where the compiled tests classes are placed.

Now, while inside the root directory of the Hello World "playground," invoke `ant ch2`. This last instruction will trigger the tests, presenting a one-line summary of the results on the console, and if you go to the `dist/ch2/test` subdirectory, you will be able to consult a detailed report on every test, including error stacks for failed tests and SQL logging information for integration tests, among other things.

You now have a tested domain model connecting to an RDBMS via JPA, but still no graphical interface for showing off such logic. It's time to switch gears over to another application tier in which Spring can also aid you with its POJO approach: the web tier.

Using Spring's MVC

Java web development often goes hand in hand with the MVC pattern, an approach that supports the multitier and stateless nature of web-enabled applications. Nowadays, nearly all

Java web frameworks make use of the MVC pattern to a greater or lesser extent, and in Spring's case, it offers its own brew designed to accommodate the same IoC nature you saw in the domain model.

To integrate the MVC pattern in the Hello World Spring application, you already have your work cut out for you, since what you did in the last section as your domain model is the equivalent to the "Model" in MVC. The next thing you have to do is create a controller that will be charged with hooking up the model with the different views in the system.

Creating a Spring Controller

A Spring controller in the context of the MVC pattern takes care of brokering all incoming requests made to a web application, performing any corresponding action requested by the originating party—creating, reading, updating, or deleting data—and later delegating each request to an appropriate view indicating the outcome.

Listing 2-15 contains the controller used for the Hello World application.

Listing 2-15. *HelloWorldController.java*

```
package com.apress.springosgi.ch2.mvc;

import java.util.List;
import java.util.Date;

import org.springframework.beans.factory.annotation.Autowired;
import org.springframework.stereotype.Controller;
import org.springframework.web.bind.annotation.RequestMapping;
import org.springframework.web.bind.annotation.RequestMethod;
import org.springframework.web.bind.annotation.RequestParam;
import org.springframework.web.bind.annotation.ModelAttribute;
import org.springframework.ui.ModelMap;

import com.apress.springosgi.ch2.hello.HelloWorld;
import com.apress.springosgi.ch2.hello.Person;
import com.apress.springosgi.ch2.hello.HelloWorldService;

@Controller
public class HelloWorldController {

    private HelloWorldService helloWorldService;
```

```
    @Autowired
    public HelloWorldController(HelloWorldService helloWorldService) {
        this.helloWorldService = helloWorldService;
    }

    @RequestMapping(method = RequestMethod.GET)
    @ModelAttribute("helloworlds")
    public List<HelloWorld> home() {
        return this.helloWorldService.findAll();
    }

    @RequestMapping(method = RequestMethod.GET)
    public String translator(@RequestParam("id") Long id, ModelMap model) {
     Person translator = helloWorldService.findById(id).getTranslator();
     List<HelloWorld> hws = helloWorldService.findAll();
     model.addAttribute("helloworlds",hws);
     model.addAttribute("translator",translator);
     return "home";
    }

    @RequestMapping(method = RequestMethod.GET)
    public String deleteMessage(@RequestParam("id")
    Long id) {
        helloWorldService.deleteMessage(id);
        return "redirect:home";
    }
}
```

The first thing that will likely strike you about this listing is its ample use of annotations, which are Spring controller annotations. Let's break down what each of them means.

At the top of the listing you will see that the class is designated with a `@Controller` annotation, which is simply indicating the class will be used for this purpose. Moving along, you will encounter the `@Autowired` annotation on the class's constructor method, which indicates it will be auto-wired with Spring's dependency injection facilities. What this means is that the controller will gain access to whatever beans are declared inside its constructor, in this case a `HelloWorldService` bean and all its corresponding methods that have access to an RDBMS.

Next, you will find three methods decorated with the `@RequestMapping` annotation. The `@RequestMapping` annotation dictates on what incoming request a method's actions will be executed; in this case, the value `(method = RequestMethod.GET)` is an open-ended way to inspect all incoming requests and match them against a method's name.

For example, if this controller handled a request in the form http://localhost/home, this would trigger the actions of the home() method; similarly, a request for http://localhost/translator?id=2 would execute the logic in the translator() method, and so on.

In a similar manner, if a request came into this controller and no corresponding method by that name was found—for example, http://localhost/foobar—no action would taken. Alternatively, @RequestMapping can also take a hard-coded value in case an incoming request requires it to match long or different method names (e.g., the annotation @RequestMapping("/zipcode") decorating the method searchInAVeryLongNameMethodForZipcodes() would result in the method being executed on a request to the URL http://localhost/zipcode).

While the @RequestMapping annotation manages incoming requests, the @ModelAttribute annotation defines how the data for each method is transferred over to a corresponding view. For example, in the topmost controller method, home(), the value @ModelAttribute("helloworlds") indicates that whatever values are returned by the method in question will be placed inside a variable by the name helloworlds to later be manipulated inside a view template.

The remaining two methods make use of the find @RequestParam annotation, which extracts a parameter from the incoming request URL and passes it as an input value to a controller method. Of noted importance is that these same two methods don't make use of the @ModelAttribute annotation. So does this mean they don't return data to a view template? No, they still do, they just do it differently.

The second method makes use of a ModelMap object, which assigns two objects obtained from DAO service calls, information that will later be made available to a view template through the helloworld and translator values. In this scenario, the return value for the method indicates the name of the view to which control will be rescinded.

Before we move to the last method in the controller, you may be wondering what view name the first method returns control to, being it returns data. That would be to a method's default view, the one with the same name as the method, so the home() method would relinquish control over to a view named home, the same view explicitly returned in the second method.

Finally, we come to the third method in the controller, which eliminates a record from the RDBMS. This method rescinds control using the string redirect:home, signifying that the request be redirected to the home() method for further processing, further executing this last method's logic—obtaining all the messages in the RDBMS—and making them available to the home view. The logic behind this last controller method will become more obvious once you see its use in fulfilling AJAX type requests.

All the views—or the home view in this application—designated by Spring controllers are said to be *logical views*; in other words, they are not a physical view template (a file by that name) but are rather further mapped to one of the many view technologies supported by

Spring's MVC, which include JavaServer Pages (JSP), JSP Standard Tag Library (JSTL), JavaServer Faces (JSF), and Apache Tiles, among others.

So let's see how a logical view in a Spring controller gets mapped to a view technology.

Creating Views with Tiles

In the context of Spring's MVC, a view can consist of everything from a vanilla HTML page, to an XML document, run-of-the mill JSP, or JSF, to a more sophisticated view system like Apache Tiles.

For your Hello World application, you will be using Apache Tiles, a comprehensive templating system that allows a web page to be divided into different units, permitting each unit to have its own structure made of either JSTL tags, JSP code, or simple text.

Its design is tailor-made to providing solutions for many of the layout issues faced in web applications, like avoiding monolithic pages and instead dividing a layout in terms of header, footer, sidebars, and body templates. Additionally, Apache Tiles integrates nicely with Spring's Web Flow project, a front-end companion to Spring's MVCs that supports complex page navigations and also includes the necessary libraries to use AJAX in Spring, and which will also be touched upon in this application.

Now that you know why I opted to have you use Apache Tiles as the view technology, take a look at Listing 2-16, which contains the main definition file for the tiles used in the Hello World application.

Listing 2-16. *Apache Tiles Definition File—*`tiles.xml`

```
<?xml version="1.0" encoding="ISO-8859-1"?>
 <!DOCTYPE tiles-definitions PUBLIC
       "-//Apache Software Foundation//DTD Tiles Configuration 2-0//EN"
       "http://tiles.apache.org/dtds/tiles-config_2_0.dtd">
<tiles-definitions>

  <definition name="home" template="/jsp/home.jsp">
      <put-attribute name="title" value="Hello World - Pro Spring-OSGi"/>
      <put-attribute name="header" value="/jsp/tiles/header.jsp"/>
      <put-attribute name="content" value="index.body"/>
      <put-attribute name="footer" value="/jsp/tiles/footer.jsp" />
  </definition>

  <definition name="index.body" template="/jsp/tiles/body.jsp">
      <put-attribute name="helloMessages" value="/jsp/tiles/messages.jsp" />
      <put-attribute name="helloTranslators" value="/jsp/tiles/translators.jsp" />
      <put-attribute name="translator" value="/jsp/tiles/translator.jsp" />
  </definition>

</tiles-definitions>
```

The main page layout is contained in the <definition> named home, which points to a template named /jsp/home.jsp. Notice though that nested inside the home <definition> element are numerous <put-attribute> values, each of which represents a tile for the template.

One of these <put-attribute> elements declares a String value, while two others point to different JSP code, and yet another points to index.body, which is a <definition> statement also defined in the file. Listing 2-17 shows what the main Apache Tiles template, /jsp/home.jsp (which is assigned to the home <definition>), looks like.

Listing 2-17. *Home Page (home.jsp) Using Apache Tiles*

```
<!DOCTYPE HTML PUBLIC "-//W3C//DTD HTML 4.01//EN"
        "http://www.w3.org/TR/html4/strict.dtd">
<%@ taglib uri="http://tiles.apache.org/tags-tiles" prefix="tiles" %>
<%@ taglib prefix="c" uri="http://java.sun.com/jsp/jstl/core" %>
<html>
<head>
        <title><tiles:getAsString name="title"/></title>
        <link href="/springhelloworld/css/hello.css" rel="stylesheet" ➥
type="text/css">
        <script type="text/javascript" src="<c:url value="/resources/dojo/➥
dojo.js" />"> </script>
        <script type="text/javascript" src="<c:url value="/resources/spring/➥
Spring.js" />"> </script>
        <script type="text/javascript" src="<c:url value="/resources/spring/➥
Spring-Dojo.js" />"> </script>
</head>
<body>

<div id="wrap">
         <div id="header">
          <h1><tiles:insertAttribute name="header"/></h1>
         </div>

         <div id="content">
          <tiles:insertAttribute name="content"/>
         </div>

         <div id="footer">
          <h3><tiles:insertAttribute name="footer"/></h3>
         </div>
</div>
</body>
</html>
```

Notice how this template has numerous `<tiles:insertAttribute>` elements scattered with plain HTML, and that each of these values corresponds to a `<put-attribute>` `name` as declared in the Apache Tiles definition file.

What Apache Tiles will do upon rendering this particular template is replace each of these values with those declared in the definition file, so `<tiles:getAsString name="title"/>` will be replaced by the string `'Hello World - Pro Spring-OSGi'`, `<tiles:insertAttribute name="header"/>` with the contents of the file `/jsp/tiles/header.jsp`, and so on.

It's a powerful layout approach, and one that can be nested to numerous degrees as can be observed in the `content` tile value, which points to another template that itself is composed of even more tiles.

Shifting the focus back to the controller designed earlier, recall that it was precisely the controller that is required to send control back to a logical view named `home`. As it turns out, each of the `<definition> names` in an Apache Tiles definition file maps to a logical view; this means that when a request comes into `http://localhost/home`, the logic inside the controller method `home()` will executed, returning a rendered Apache Tiles `home` view with all its nested tiles back to an end user.

Also remember the controller `home()` method returns a set of data extracted from the RDBMS that would be made available under the `helloworlds` name, so where is this information? This data is being manipulated in a tile within a tile, the `helloMessages` tile pointing to the `jsp/tiles/messages.jsp` file, which of course still forms part of the logical `home` view, nested as it may be. Listing 2-18 shows what the `helloMessages` tile's underlying JSP looks like and how it processes data sent by the controller.

Listing 2-18. *`HelloMessage` Tile (`messages.jsp`) Processing Controller Data with AJAX Calls*

```
<%@ taglib prefix="c" uri="http://java.sun.com/jsp/jstl/core" %>
<%@ taglib prefix="fmt" uri="http://java.sun.com/jsp/jstl/fmt" %>
 <div id="helloMessages">
 <c:forEach var="hello" items="${helloworlds}">
   <div style="border:red 2px dashed;margin:10px;padding:5px">
       <b><c:out value="${hello.language}"/></b>
       <c:out value="${hello.message}"/> - Translated on:  <fmt:formatDate ➥
value="${hello.transdate}" dateStyle="long" /> <br/>
       <a id="deleteMessage_${hello.id}" href="deleteMessage?id=${hello.id}">➥
Delete Message </a>
       <script type="text/javascript">
               Spring.addDecoration(new Spring.AjaxEventDecoration({
               elementId:"deleteMessage_${hello.id}",
               event:"onclick",
               params: {fragments:"helloMessages,helloTranslators"}
        }));
```

```
        </script>
        <br/>

      </div>
  </c:forEach>
</div>
```

The JSP for this last tile makes use of the JSTL core library for iterating over the `helloworlds` data set sent by the controller and lays out each message inside an HTML `<div>` element. This tile has another important aspect of the Hello World application: an AJAX call.

In case you are unfamiliar with the term "AJAX," what this technique allows a web application to do is perform an *out-of-band* call from a browser back to a server-side controller, without the user experiencing a complete page refresh; in essence, only a piece of a page is updated.

The AJAX call in this tile is brought to you by the HTML link `<a id="deleteMessage_${hello.id}" href="deleteMessage?id=${hello.id}">Delete Message </a>`, which effectively calls `deleteMessage?id=${hello.id}`, invoking the `deleteMessage()` controller method, which in turn eliminates the message from the RDBMS.

This last HTML link doesn't act like a standard HTML link on account of the JavaScript declaration right next to it, the one starting with a JavaScript method `Spring.addDecoration()` that has the nested `Spring.AjaxEventDecoration()` method, which includes the following definitions:

- `elementId`: This parameter associates a given HTML ID to an AJAX event. In this case, the value `deleteMessage_${hello.id}` signifies that each of the corresponding links (`<a>`) to delete a message will be associated with an AJAX call, hence overriding the default behavior of links to navigate to a new page.

- `event`: This parameter indicates on what action the AJAX event will be triggered. In this case, an `onclick` event on the given `elementId` will trigger the AJAX call.

- `params`: This parameter indicates what tile and HTML ID to re-render once the AJAX call has completed. In this case, since you are eliminating messages, `params` is indicating that both the `helloMessages` and `helloTranslators` tiles and HTML IDs—which contain messages—will be re-rendered, with the remaining tiles in the page remaining without update.

All this AJAX functionality comes from Spring's JavaScript module, which forms part of the grander Spring Web Flow project, the latter of which is a companion to projects made around Spring's MVC module. Here, the actual JavaScript libraries are made available through declarations at the top of the main template in Listing 2-17.

The remaining tiles composing the home page view contain another similar AJAX call and a few more basic constructs made up of text, HTML, and JSTL. Listings 2-19 through 2-25 show the application's remaining tiles, main index, and CSS file.

Listing 2-19. *Header Tile (`header.jsp`) for Hello World*

```
Spring Application - Pro Spring-OSGi
```

Listing 2-20. *Footer Tile (`footer.jsp`) for Hello World*

```
Pro Spring OSGi by Daniel Rubio - Published by Apress
```

Listing 2-21. *Body Tile (`body.jsp`) for Hello World*

```
<%@ taglib uri="http://tiles.apache.org/tags-tiles" prefix="tiles" %>
     <div id="index.body">
       <div id="main">
               <h2>Hello World Messages </h2>
               <tiles:insertAttribute name="helloMessages"/>
       </div>
       <div id="sidebar">
            <h2>Translators </h2>
              <tiles:insertAttribute name="helloTranslators"/>

              <tiles:insertAttribute name="translator"/>
       </div>
    </div>
```

Listing 2-22. *HelloTranslators Tile (`translators.jsp`) for Hello World*

```
<%@ taglib prefix="c" uri="http://java.sun.com/jsp/jstl/core" %>
<div id="helloTranslators">
 <ul>
  <c:forEach var="hello" items="${helloworlds}">
       <li><c:out value="${hello.language}"/>
       <a id="showTranslator_${hello.id}" href="translator?id=${hello.id}">➥
Translator Details </a>
       <script type="text/javascript">
               Spring.addDecoration(new Spring.AjaxEventDecoration({
               elementId:"showTranslator_${hello.id}",
               event:"onclick",
               params: {fragments:"translator"}
        }));
       </script></li>
```

```
  </c:forEach>
 </ul>
</div>
```

Listing 2-23. *Translator Tile (`translator.jsp`) for Hello World*

```
<%@ taglib prefix="c" uri="http://java.sun.com/jsp/jstl/core" %>
 <div id="person">
  <div style="border:red 2px dashed;margin:10px;padding:5px;">
   <b>Name</b> :<c:out value="${translator.firstName}"/> ➥
<c:out value="${translator.lastName}"/><br/>
   <b>Hourly Rate</b> : $<c:out value="${translator.hourlyRate}"/><br/>
  </div>
</div>
```

Listing 2-24. *Main Index (`index.html`) for Hello World*

```
<html>
<head>
  <meta http-equiv="Refresh" content="0; URL=spring/home">
</head>
</html>
```

Listing 2-25. *Cascading Style Sheet (`hello.css`) for Hello World*

```
body,
html {
        margin:0;
        padding:0;
        background:#a7a09a;
        color:#000;
}

body {
        min-width:750px;
}

#wrap {
        background:#ffffff;
        margin:0 auto;
        width:750px;
}
```

```
#header {
        background:#cfcfcf;
}

#header h1 {
        padding:5px;
        margin:0;
        text-align:center;
}
#main {
        background:#dfdfdf;
        float:left;
        width:500px;
}

#main h2, #main h3, #main p {
        padding:0 10px;
}

#sidebar {
        background:#ffffff;
        float:right;
        width:240px;
}

#sidebar ul {
        margin-bottom:0;
}

#sidebar h3, #sidebar p {
        padding:0 10px 0 0;
}
#footer {
        background:#bfbfbf;
        clear:both;
        text-align:center;
}

#footer p {
        padding:5px;
        margin:0;
}.
```

Copy the following files to the specified directories in the Hello World "playground": the main `index.html` file in Listing 2-24 to the `src/GUI/ch2/` directory, the `hello.css` file in Listing 2-25 to the `src/GUI/ch2/css/` directory, and the `home.jsp` file in Listing 2-17 to the `src/GUI/ch2/jsp/` directory. You will also need to copy all tiles in Listings 2-18 through 2-23 to the directory `src/GUI/ch2/jsp/tiles/`.

Up next, you will create the corresponding descriptors needed to accompany the controller class, Apache Tiles definition file, and Apache Tiles templates you just created.

Spring MVC Descriptors

A Spring MVC project is always accompanied by the de facto descriptor used in Java web applications and a few other descriptors containing Spring's MVC behaviors. Listing 2-26 contains the `web.xml` file that is always used in Java web applications, applied to the Hello World application.

Listing 2-26. *`web.xml` for the Hello World Spring Application*

```
<?xml version="1.0" encoding="UTF-8"?>
<web-app id="WebApp_ID" version="2.4" xmlns="http://java.sun.com/xml/ns/j2ee" ➥
xmlns:xsi="http://www.w3.org/2001/XMLSchema-instance" xsi:schema➥
Location="http://java.sun.com/xml/ns/j2ee http://java.sun.com/xml/ns/➥
j2ee/web-app_2_4.xsd">
        <display-name>Pro Sprng-OSGi</display-name>
        <context-param>
            <param-name>contextConfigLocation</param-name>
            <param-value>/WEB-INF/helloworld-service.xml</param-value>
        </context-param>
        <listener>
        <listener-class>
          org.springframework.web.context.ContextLoaderListener
        </listener-class>
        </listener>

        <servlet>
           <description>
             Pro Spring-OSGi MVC Dispatch Servlet
           </description>
           <display-name>DispatcherServlet</display-name>
           <servlet-name>helloworld</servlet-name>
           <servlet-class>
              org.springframework.web.servlet.DispatcherServlet
           </servlet-class>
            <load-on-startup>1</load-on-startup>
        </servlet>
```

```
        <servlet>
           <servlet-name>ResourcesServlet</servlet-name>
           <servlet-class>org.springframework.js.resource.ResourceServlet➥
</servlet-class>
        </servlet>
  <servlet-mapping>
                <servlet-name>helloworld</servlet-name>
                <url-pattern>/spring/*</url-pattern>
        </servlet-mapping>

        <servlet-mapping>
           <servlet-name>ResourcesServlet</servlet-name>
           <url-pattern>/resources/*</url-pattern>
         </servlet-mapping>

        <welcome-file-list>
                <welcome-file>index.html</welcome-file>
        </welcome-file-list>


 <resource-ref>
      <description>Database Connection</description>
      <res-ref-name>jdbc/springosgi</res-ref-name>
      <res-type>javax.sql.DataSource</res-type>
      <res-auth>Container</res-auth>
  </resource-ref>
</web-app>
```

The `web.xml` descriptor starts off by associating the `helloworld-service.xml` descriptor—which contains the DAO, JPA, and RDBMS properties—with the application's context through Spring's `ContextLoaderListener` class. Back when you tested your domain model, you also made use of a `helloworld-service.xml` file to associate the DAO class with a JPA Entity Manager and its corresponding data source. This time around though, the file will be different.

Since the application will now be deployed on the Web, it requires a more robust approach. Listing 2-27 contains the `helloworld-service.xml` descriptor needed to use MySQL as the underlying RDBMS and leverage an externally administered data source through JNDI.

Continuing with the `web.xml` file, you will find the declaration for two servlets, one of the type `DispatcherServlet` and another of the type `ResourceServlet`. The former is part of Spring's MVC module and the latter part of Spring's Web Flow/JavaScript module, with Spring's dispatcher servlet providing the "plumbing" for most web controller actions and Spring's resource servlet providing prepackaged resources—JavaScript libraries—for actions related to AJAX.

Next are the corresponding servlet mapping declarations, indicating under what URLs the servlets in question will be executed. Spring's dispatcher servlet will be invoked on every request under the `spring` directory, and Spring's resource servlet will also make use of the same wildcard notation except under the `resources` directory.

Finally, observe the `<welcome-file-list>` and `<welcome-file>` parameters used to configure a default home page for an application, as well as a `<resource-ref>` declaration loading a JNDI data source named `jdbc/springosgi` provided by an application server/container.

As this last data source is inside `web.xml`, it has some further configuration issues you need to address: how to go about its configuration in an application server/container—which you will explore in the upcoming section—and how to associate the data source to its corresponding JPA Entity Manager and the DAO classes it will manage. Listing 2-27 contains the `helloworld-service.xml` used for this purpose, which is similar in nature to the one employed in the testing phase of the domain model.

Listing 2-27. *`helloworld-service.xml` Used in JPA-Spring for Production Deployment*

```
<?xml version="1.0" encoding="UTF-8"?>
<beans xmlns="http://www.springframework.org/schema/beans"
       xmlns:tx="http://www.springframework.org/schema/tx"
       xmlns:xsi="http://www.w3.org/2001/XMLSchema-instance"
       xsi:schemaLocation="http://www.springframework.org/schema/beans
                           http://www.springframework.org/schema/beans/➥
spring-beans.xsd
                           http://www.springframework.org/schema/tx
                           http://www.springframework.org/schema/tx/➥
spring-tx-2.5.xsd">

  <tx:annotation-driven/>

   <bean id="helloWorldService"
         class="com.apress.springosgi.ch2.hello.HelloWorldDAO">
     <property name="entityManagerFactory" ref="entityManagerFactory"/>
   </bean>

   <bean id="entityManagerFactory"
         class="org.springframework.orm.jpa.LocalContainerEntityManagerFactoryBean">
     <property name="dataSource" ref="dataSource"/>
     <property name="jpaVendorAdapter">
      <bean
```

```
        class="org.springframework.orm.jpa.vendor.OpenJpaVendorAdapter">
          <property name="showSql" value="true"/>
          <property name="generateDdl" value="false"/>
          <property name="databasePlatform" value="org.apache.openjpa.jdbc.➥
sql.MySQLDictionary"/>
      </bean>
    </property>
    <property name="loadTimeWeaver">
      <bean
        class="org.springframework.instrument.classloading.SimpleLoadTimeWeaver"/>
    </property>
  </bean>

  <bean id="dataSource" class="org.springframework.jndi.JndiObjectFactoryBean">
     <property name="jndiName" value="java:comp/env/jdbc/springosgi"/>
  </bean>

  <bean id="transactionManager" class="org.springframework.orm.jpa.Jpa➥
TransactionManager">
      <property name="entityManagerFactory" ref="entityManagerFactory"/>
      <property name="dataSource" ref="dataSource"/>
  </bean>
</beans>
```

In this Spring configuration used to wire up the DAO class with a data source and JPA Entity Manager, three things have changed from the configuration file you created for testing purposes.

One is the value `generateDdl` is set to `false`; this is done because it's not good practice for a JPA Entity Manager used in a production database to constantly refresh an RDBMS table's structure—DDL—each time it's started and stopped, which would equal each time the application itself is started and stopped.

And the other two changes correspond to the JPA data source, since the value `databasePlatform` is now pointing toward a mapping for a MySQL RDBMS, and the `datasource` bean is pointing toward an externally managed JNDI data source by an application server/container.

Next, you need to create just one more configuration file pertaining to the Spring Dispatcher servlet declared in `web.xml`. By convention, Spring looks for a Dispatcher servlet configuration file prefixed with its name. So in this case, since the Dispatcher servlet in `web.xml` is named `helloworld`, Spring will look for a configuration file named `helloworld-servlet.xml`. Listing 2-28 illustrates the `helloworld-servlet.xml` configuration file.

Listing 2-28. *helloworld-servlet.xml Used for Dispatcher Servlet*

```
<?xml version="1.0" encoding="UTF-8"?>
<beans xmlns="http://www.springframework.org/schema/beans"
       xmlns:xsi="http://www.w3.org/2001/XMLSchema-instance"
       xmlns:context="http://www.springframework.org/schema/context"
       xsi:schemaLocation="http://www.springframework.org/schema/beans
                           http://www.springframework.org/schema/beans/➥
spring-beans.xsd
                           http://www.springframework.org/schema/context
                           http://www.springframework.org/schema/context/➥
spring-context-2.5.xsd">

<context:component-scan base-package="com.apress.springosgi.ch2.mvc"/>

<bean id="urlMapper" class="org.springframework.web.servlet.handler.SimpleUrl➥
HandlerMapping">
        <property name="mappings">
         <props>
          <prop key="/**">helloWorldController</prop>
         </props>
        </property>
</bean>

<bean id="tilesConfigurer"
      class="org.springframework.web.servlet.view.tiles2.TilesConfigurer">
    <property name="definitions">
      <list>
         <value>/WEB-INF/tiles.xml</value>
      </list>
    </property>
</bean>

<bean id="tilesViewResolver" class="org.springframework.js.ajax.AjaxUrlBasedView➥
Resolver">
    <property name="viewClass" value="org.springframework.webflow.mvc.view.Flow➥
AjaxTilesView"></property>
</bean>

</beans>
```

<context:component-scan>, which is the first declaration in the Dispatcher servlet file, is used to inspect class packages for annotations. In this case, the scan will be performed

on the om.apress.springosgi.ch2.mvc package, which corresponds to the same package under which the MVC controller is located. This process will incorporate all the mappings and behaviors declared through annotations in the last class, as well as generate a Spring bean by the same name.

As you probably expected from seeing other Spring file configurations, next come various beans. The first bean declaration—urlMapper—is used to further map to the URL control that will be delegated. Given that you have only one controller class, the mapping for this Dispatcher servlet uses a wildcard to indicate that every request will be sent to the helloWorldController bean. Note that helloWorldController refers to a bean name, which is automatically available on account of the annotations used in this class and the previous component-scan declaration.

In the second bean declaration you will notice the Dispatcher servlet hooks up to the Apache Tiles logical views declared in Listing 2-16, effectively allowing the previous controller bean to redirect control to the appropriate logical tile names.

The third and last bean is a special bean provided by Spring's Web Flow project, allowing Apache Tiles to support AJAX calls to individual units. Under normal circumstances, an Apache Tiles definition file is considered to have logical names corresponding to top-level <definition> names only; as a consequence, without this definition your application would only have two logical names—home and index.body.

However, if you look back at the AJAX call described in the earlier tile (Listing 2-18), you will note that it makes use of refreshing certain internal tiles. It's with the AjaxUrlBasedViewResolver bean that each of the tile's <put-attribute> names are also converted into logical names, allowing control to be relinquished to individual tiles that provide AJAX type updates.

This concludes the review of all the parts that make up an MVC design in Spring. Up next, you will start ordering all these pieces to set the stage for final deployment.

Compiling and Preparing MVC Classes and Descriptors

Here is a list of steps you need to take from within the HelloWorld "playground" in order to compile and prepare all the MVC classes and descriptors you made in the last section.

1. Copy the MVC controller to the appropriate directory: ensure the source for the controller class is placed in its package subdirectory src/com/apress/springosgi/ch2/mvc/.

2. Copy all descriptor files to the appropriate directory: all descriptor files—helloworld-service.xml, helloworld-servlet.xml, tiles.xml, and web.xml—should be placed under the subdirectory src/WEB-INF/ch2/ of your Hello World "playground."

3. Copy all view templates to the appropriate directory: all JSP, CSS, and HTML files related to Apache Tiles should be placed inside the subdirectory `src/GUI/ch2/` and its corresponding subdirectories.

4. Copy the dependent JAR file to the `lib` directory: the MVC controller class incorporates a new dependency into the application. Copy the `spring-webmvc.jar` JAR located in Spring's `dist/modules` download to the `lib` directory of the Hello World "playground."

As soon as you've followed through with these steps, you can take the next step, packaging everything in the format that is used to distribute Java web applications: WAR (Web Archive).

Creating the Web Archive

WAR is the standard packaging format used in Java web applications. Its importance is due to the fact that all Java application server/containers are designed to execute this type of file.

This makes WAR files a common distribution format for Java web applications in general—not only those designed around Spring—allowing this type of package to be equally deployed in the various Java application servers/containers available in the market. However, for your Hello World application, you will be relying on the Apache Tomcat container.

Although a WAR file needs to adhere to a certain structure in order to be deployed, at its core, it is nothing more than a unit containing Java classes, JAR libraries, deployment descriptors, and GUI templates like JSP or CSS files—which is practically all you've created since starting the Hello World application.

At this juncture you have all that's required to create a WAR file, except one piece: a descriptor needed to tell the application server/container how to set up a JNDI data source required by Spring's MVC model. Listing 2-29 illustrates the `context.xml` descriptor file used specifically for setting up a JNDI data source on the Apache Tomcat container.

Listing 2-29. *`context.xml` Used for Configuring a JNDI Data Source*

```
<Context>
<Loader loaderClass="org.springframework.instrument.classloading.tomcat.Tomcat➥
InstrumentableClassLoader" useSystemClassLoaderAsParent="false"/>
   <Resource name="jdbc/springosgi" auth="Container" type="javax.sql.DataSource"
               maxActive="100" maxIdle="30" maxWait="10000"
               username="hello" password="world" driverClassName="com.mysql.➥
jdbc.Driver"
               url="jdbc:mysql://127.0.0.1:3306/springosgi"/>

</Context>
```

The listing starts off by declaring the use of the class `TomcatInstrumentableClassLoader` in the `<Loader>` element, a class that overrides Apache Tomcat's default class loader and enables weaving, with the attribute `useSystemClassLoaderAsParent` set to `false` in order to not lose Apache Tomcat's remaining loading of staple libraries.

The `context.xml` file then defines the actual data source through the `<Resource>` element, using a JNDI name in line with the one used in Spring's descriptor—`jdbc/springosgi`—and then indicating all the necessary connection credentials to access an RDBMS, which correspond to default MySQL values or those created when you installed MySQL.

Armed with this descriptor file, you now need to place it accordingly in the Hello World "playground," along with a few more JAR files needed by the application at runtime. The steps are as follows:

1. Copy the `context.xml` descriptor: place a copy of the `context.xml` descriptor under the subdirectory `src/META-INF/ch2/`.

2. Copy dependent JAR files to the `lib` directory: the WAR file, being a deployable unit, incorporates new runtime dependencies on the application. Copy each of the following JARs to the Hello World "playground" `lib` directory:

    - `spring-web.jar`: Located in the `dist/modules` directory of the Spring Framework with dependencies download

    - `spring-context.jar`: Located in the `dist/modules` directory of the Spring Framework with dependencies download

    - `spring-jdbc.jar`: Located in the `dist/modules` directory of the Spring Framework with dependencies download

    - `jstl.jar`: Located in the `lib/j2ee` directory of the Spring Framework with dependencies download

    - `standard.jar`: Located in the `lib/jakarta-taglibs` directory of the Spring Framework with dependencies download

    - `aopalliance.jar`: Located in the `lib/aopalliance` directory of the Spring Framework with dependencies download

    - `spring-aop.jar`: Located in the `dist/modules` directory of the Spring Framework with dependencies download

    - `springframework.webflow.jar`: Located in the `dist` directory of the Spring Web Flow download

- springframework.js.jar: Located in the dist directory of the Spring Web Flow download
- tiles-*.jar: All three located in the /(Root) directory of the Apache Tiles download
- commons-*.jar: All three located in the lib directory of the Apache Tiles download

With every single file in place to create a WAR file, it's time to make use of Apache Ant in order to create it. Listing 2-30 contains the corresponding Ant syntax needed for the process.

Listing 2-30. *Ant Task for Building the JAR and WAR Files*

```
<jar destfile="${ch2.dir}/lib/helloworld.jar">
   <fileset  dir="${build.dir}">
   <include name="com/apress/springosgi/ch2/hello/*"/>
   <include name="com/apress/springosgi/ch2/mvc/*"/>
   <include name="META-INF/persistence.xml"/>
  </fileset>
</jar>

<war destfile="${ch2.dir}/springhelloworld.war" webxml="${src.dir}/WEB-INF/ch2/➥
web.xml">
          <lib dir="${ch2.dir}/lib/">
            <include name="helloworld.jar"/>
          </lib>
          <lib dir="${lib.dir}">
             <include name="spring-core.jar"/>
             <include name="spring-beans.jar"/>
             <include name="spring-context.jar"/>
             <include name="spring-jdbc.jar"/>
             <include name="spring-orm.jar"/>
             <include name="spring-tx.jar"/>
             <include name="persistence.jar"/>
             <include name="jstl.jar"/>
             <include name="spring-web.jar"/>
             <include name="spring-webmvc.jar"/>
             <include name="standard.jar"/>
             <include name="persistence.jar"/>
             <include name="openjpa-1.0.2.jar"/>
             <include name="jta.jar"/>
             <include name="commons-collections.jar"/>
             <include name="commons-lang.jar"/>
```

```
            <include name="serp-1.13.1.jar"/>
            <include name="aopalliance.jar"/>
            <include name="spring-aop.jar"/>
            <include name="org.springframework.js-2.0.2.RELEASE.jar"/>
            <include name="org.springframework.webflow-2.0.2.RELEASE.jar"/>
            <include name="tiles-api-2.0.6.jar"/>
            <include name="tiles-core-2.0.6.jar"/>
            <include name="tiles-jsp-2.0.6.jar"/>
            <include name="commons-beanutils-1.7.0.jar"/>
            <include name="commons-digester-1.8.jar"/>
            <include name="commons-logging-api-1.1.jar"/>
        </lib>
      <webinf dir="${src.dir}/WEB-INF/ch2/"/>
      <metainf dir="${src.dir}/META-INF/ch2/"/>
      <zipfileset dir="${src.dir}/GUI/ch2/" prefix=""/>
    </war>
```

The first declaration in the listing is used to create a JAR file needed by the WAR. What this JAR file will package are all the individual classes needed by the application, including the `persistence.xml` descriptor required by the JPA.

Next is the `<war>` task, which includes two attributes, a `destfile` value indicating where to place the created file and a `webxml` value indicating the location of the `web.xml` file that is to accompany the WAR, in this case the one corresponding to Listing 2-26.

Nested inside the `<war>` task are two `<lib>` declarations indicating what files will be placed within the WAR's `lib` directory, which is where all dependent JAR files are automatically picked up by an application server/container. Among the included JAR files is the `helloworld.jar` file, which includes the application's classes, as well as the various JARS for Spring, JPA, Apache Tiles, and so on needed to properly execute the application.

Capping off this Ant listing is `<webinf>`, which copies all the application's descriptors to the WAR's `WEB-INF` directory; `<metainf>`, which copies the application's `context.xml` file (the container's JNDI data source configuration) to the WAR's `META-INF` directory, and `<zipfileset>`, which copies the application's GUI files (Apache Tiles, JSP, and CSS) to the root directory of the WAR.

By appending the previous Ant listing to the existing `ch2` target you created when testing your domain model (Listing 2-14) and reinvoking the command `ant ch2`, a WAR file by the name `springhelloworld.war` will be created under the subdirectory `dist/ch2`.

That's it! Now that your WAR file is ready, it's time to see the actual application on the Web.

Deploying on the Web

In order to deploy your Spring application on the Web, you will need to make two final adjustments to the infrastructure software that will support it: the RDBMS MySQL and Apache Tomcat.

Prepopulating the RDBMS with Data

Since the Spring application displays data from an RDBMS, you will need to prepopulate it with a data set in order to show "Hello World" messages upon visiting it. Listing 2-31 contains a script used to prepopulate MySQL with the relational tables needed by the application.

Listing 2-31. *SQL Script* `helloworld.sql` *for Prepopulating the RDBMS*

```
CREATE TABLE `HelloWorld` (
  `id` bigint(20) NOT NULL,
  `language` varchar(255) default NULL,
  `message` varchar(255) default NULL,
  `transdate` date default NULL,
  `translator_id` bigint(20) default NULL,
  PRIMARY KEY  (`id`),
  KEY `I_HLLWRLD_TRANSLATOR` (`translator_id`)
) ENGINE=InnoDB DEFAULT CHARSET=latin1;

INSERT INTO `HelloWorld` VALUES (51,'Italian','Ciao Monde!','2008-05-27',2),➥
(52,'Spanish','Hola Mundo!','2008-05-27',1),(53,'English','Hello World!',➥
'2008-05-27',5),(54,'French','Bonjour Monde!','2008-05-27',3),➥
(55,'German','Hallo Welt!','2008-05-27',4);

CREATE TABLE `OPENJPA_SEQUENCE_TABLE` (
  `ID` tinyint(4) NOT NULL,
  `SEQUENCE_VALUE` bigint(20) default NULL,
  PRIMARY KEY  (`ID`)
) ENGINE=InnoDB DEFAULT CHARSET=latin1;

INSERT INTO `OPENJPA_SEQUENCE_TABLE` VALUES (0,101);

CREATE TABLE `Person` (
  `id` bigint(20) NOT NULL,
  `FNAME` varchar(255) default NULL,
  `hourlyRate` double default NULL,
  `LNAME` varchar(255) default NULL,
  PRIMARY KEY  (`id`)
) ENGINE=InnoDB DEFAULT CHARSET=latin1;

INSERT INTO `Person` VALUES (1,'Carlos',40,'Perez'),(2,'Dino',45,'Casiraghi'),➥
(3,'Pierre',40,'LeClair'),(4,'Franz',45,'Becker'),(5,'John',45,'Smith');
```

Before you actually prepopulate the RDBMS with these relation tables and values, a short note on their meaning: the `Person` and `HelloWorld` tables are of course in line with the domain model's POJO names, but you may be wondering about that table named `OPENJPA_SEQUENCE_NAME`.

This last table accommodates the default behavior of the JPA Entity Manager used in the application, Open JPA, and its mapping behavior to the MySQL RDBMS, all based on the annotations used to decorate the domain model.

Back when you annotated the `HelloWorld` and `Person` classes (Listing 2-6 and Listing 2-7), upon using the annotation `@Id @GeneratedValue`, no strategy was specified to generate the IDs for persisting objects in these classes. In Open JPA's case as it specifically relates to MySQL, the default behavior is to consult a table by the name `OPENJPA_SEQUENCE_TABLE` in order to obtain a unique ID necessary to persist entity objects.

Be advised that this behavior is highly specific to both the JPA Entity Manager and RDBMS you are using. Other JPA/RDBMS combinations may rely on different table naming conventions, the use of an RDBMS sequence, or some other variation. And of course, all this default behavior could have been avoided if the JPA `@GeneratedValue` annotation in each class provided a strategy indicating a preexisting table or sequence to use as an ID generation source.

Next, you need to process the script so the data set makes its way to the application's database instance. While in a system shell, execute the following instruction: `mysql -u hello -pworld -D springosgi < helloworld.sql`—where `helloworld.sql` is the file containing the code from Listing 2-31. This will attempt to connect to the database instance named `springosgi` with the credentials you created at the outset, and insert the contents of the script `helloworld.sql` into the respective instance.

After the successful execution of the RDBMS script, MySQL should be prepared to offer data to the Spring application. Next, you need to prepare the hosting environment: Apache Tomcat.

Configuring Apache Tomcat

Apache Tomcat requires the incorporation of two JAR files into its underlying structure to properly execute the application, one to support the MySQL database and another to support Spring's operation within the application container itself. The steps are as follows:

1. Copy `spring-tomcat-weaver.jar`: you need to copy this file located under the subdirectory `/dist/weaving/` within the Spring with dependencies download over to `$TOMCAT_HOME/server/lib/`, where `$TOMCAT_HOME` is the root directory for Apache Tomcat.

2. Copy `mysql-connector-java-bin.jar`: you need to copy this file located under the root directory within the MySQL Connector/J driver download over to `$TOMCAT_HOME/common/lib/`, where `$TOMCAT_HOME` is the root directory for Apache Tomcat.

3. Next, you need to copy the `springhelloworld.war` file containing the application over to Apache Tomcat's `webapps` subdirectory, also located in the root directory of Apache Tomcat.

Once these three files are in place, you're ready to start up Apache Tomcat and fire up a browser to see your application.

WHAT IS WEAVING? AND WHY IS IT IMPORTANT?

I mentioned weaving in this chapter a few times in the context of the JPA and Tomcat. **Weaving** is the process by which a Java class's bytecode is "woven" with other bytecode, in essence modifying the original bytecode contained in a class.

The weaving concept primarily grew out of aspect-oriented programming, in which projects are developed separately as a set of Java classes and aspects, with both said to be joined, or "woven," at either compile time, postcompile time, or load time, giving way to the concepts of compile-time weaving, postcompile-time weaving, and load-time weaving.

Spring makes ample use of load-time weaving, hence the need to use special Spring-provided classes with weaving in some parts of an application. Combining Spring with OSGi also presents its own set of issues in terms of weaving and is one of the big pluses to using the SpringSource dm Server, which eases the use of Spring and OSGi in the same Java environment. But more on this in Chapter 5, which puts weaving in a more prominent light.

Starting Apache Tomcat

Move over to the `bin` directory inside Apache Tomcat and execute `java -jar bootstrap.jar`. Once you do this, Apache Tomcat will automatically expand `springhelloworld.war`, outputting a deployment message to the screen and making the application accessible under a virtual directory by the WAR's name.

Upon completion, Apache Tomcat will be running under port 8080 of your localhost, so if you open up a browser and point it toward `http://localhost:8080/springhelloworld/`, you will be able to access the Hello World Spring application.

Summary

In this chapter you learned how Spring emerged as a grassroots movement to address many of the shortcomings present in the earlier versions of the Java 2 Enterprise Edition (J2EE)—now Java Enterprise Edition (Java EE)—offering a fresh approach to building enterprise Java applications based on the concepts of IoC/DI and POJO architectures.

You also explored the many advantages to using a POJO-based architecture in enterprise applications, favoring such things as simplicity, maintenance, testing, and reuse.

Additionally, you gained perspective on the numerous areas the Spring Framework has influenced since its inception, going even beyond the Java platform.

Later you experienced firsthand how to create a domain model based on POJO principles, which included enabling the model to use an RDBMS and leveraging Java's de facto object-relational API, JPA.

Then you performed both unit testing and integration testing on the same domain model using the Java JUnit framework and other artifacts provided by the Spring Framework. This was followed by a brief incursion into Spring's support for the MVC and AJAX type designs, both of which are staples in today's web applications.

Finally, you learned how to actually deploy a WAR that included application classes, JSPs, Apache Tiles, CSS, and configuration files created during the chapter, coming away with a live end-to-end Spring application using JPA and Spring's MVC, with Apache Tomcat serving as the Java EE container and MySQL as the RDBMS.

CHAPTER 3

Integrating Spring and OSGi

You're fresh off exploring Spring and OSGi as stand-alone technologies. Now it's time for you to experience what both have to offer in tandem. This chapter will focus on the different layers at which a Java application designed around Spring can benefit from integrating OSGi, as well as what additional steps or software you need to make use of in order to obtain the desired results.

I wouldn't expect you to take a leap of faith and combine Spring and OSGi just because "you can," so I'll start by elaborating on the high-level benefits of doing so.

OSGi's Synergy with Spring

OSGi is about the packaging, versioning, and dynamic loading of Java applications, while Spring is about pursuing a pragmatic approach to developing Java applications using POJOs and IoC. So OSGi and Spring address orthogonal[1] concerns, as a set of mutually perpendicular axes meeting at right angles. OSGi's strengths (outlined in Chapter 1) can be greatly enhanced by leveraging the Spring Framework, gaining from the following techniques:

- OSGi's core services can make use of Spring's dependency injection approach, making the development of OSGi-bound classes simpler and more amenable to testing, traits that are highly desirable in enterprise applications.
- OSGi can leverage Spring's ample foundation for delivering enterprise-grade applications, granting it faster ramp-up times for creating RDBMS and web-bound applications.

---

1. Princeton University WordNet Search, Orthogonal definition, `http://wordnet.princeton.edu/perl/webwn?s=orthogonal`

Similarly, Spring's already popular approach has much to gain from adopting some of OSGi's features, yielding the following benefits:

- Spring's overall dependency injection technique can be performed more intelligently with the help of OSGi's dynamic-loading capabilities.
- Class libraries used in Spring applications can be shared more easily, with a lesser threat of class conflicts and an overall reduced memory footprint due to OSGi's awareness of other bundles (JARs) running in the system.
- Spring applications can be designed to support class versioning, thanks to OSGi's capabilities in this area.
- Spring beans can be registered as OSGi services, making them readily available to other bundles (JARs) running in the system.

As you can see from some of these benefits, the integration process of Spring and OSGi entails modifying the way you design Java classes themselves, the way you package Java applications, and, of course, the way in which you actually deploy this latter type of project.

The next section explores the different layers at which you will need to incorporate new approaches in order to make Spring and OSGi click together.

Layers of Integration

Due to how Spring and OSGi use techniques that are orthogonal to one another, you need to make a coordinated effort in various areas that is best understood by using layers. The following sections address such layers, including the necessary tools and resources needed to integrate Spring and OSGi.

Application Design: Services and Beans

The *application design layer* of integration refers to the classes that make up an application, which go on to form the building blocks for each platform: services for OSGi and beans for Spring.

As you learned in Chapter 1, OSGi's architecture is based primarily on the use of services, which can be accessed, searched, or registered against a central OSGi repository in order to achieve the many dynamic behaviors offered by the platform.

The way in which these services are made use of—accessed, searched, and registered—is done using a sequence of procedural calls, requiring explicit and extensive use of OSGi APIs to achieve such steps; if you don't recall the process, refer back to Listing 1-16, which contains an OSGi service registration sequence.

Similarly, the composition of services, which can range from a custom-made HelloWorld service to an HttpService, is also based on the same kind of procedural sequence for defining such things as the dependencies a service might rely on.

So what if, instead of using sequences of procedural calls to create and perform actions against OSGi services, Spring's IoC/DI technique were used? It turns out that by going down this path, OSGi services not only become simpler to access, register, and perform queries on, but also can be easier to create and test, given they will be IoC enabled, fulfilling their dependencies and further avoiding the need to make use of specific APIs.

Turning our attention to Spring's bean-centric approach, while the use of such a design has brought the framework to the mainstream in the Enterprise Java market, there are also a few lessons that can be learned from something like OSGi.

For the most part, every bean and application library that makes up a Spring application is declared on the standard Java CLASSPATH to load Java classes, a process that can lead to unresolved class dependencies and class conflicts. Add to this that beans in different JAR files are unaware of each other's presence, and you have two clear areas in which OSGi can offer its dynamic-loading capabilities, as well as its service registry for localizing cross-JAR beans.

Additionally, other areas like versioning, which come integrated with OSGi, can also bring more functionality into Spring's already powerful IoC/DI approach, making OSGi an even more compelling partner.

Of course, in order for Spring beans to accommodate all these OSGi features, they would need to morph into a type of OSGi service, thus being capable of supporting versioning, dynamic loading, and all the other features available through OSGi's framework.

In this case, all these gaps in both platforms—OSGi services morphing into Spring beans and vice versa—are filled through the use of additional artifacts like additional descriptors and classes. These are then brought together using a special glue called the Spring Dynamic Modules for OSGi, or Spring-DM.

This last initiative, spearheaded by the people behind the Spring Framework, is core to integrating both Spring and OSGi, for it is this subproject that makes sense out of those special OSGi extensions inside the context of the Spring Framework, and similarly, makes Spring extensions click inside an OSGi environment.

For the moment, I will leave the details of Spring-DM to the Hello World example presented in this chapter and the remainder of the book to concentrate on another level of integration between Spring and OSGi: application packaging.

Application Packaging: Dependencies

As you learned in Chapter 2, Spring applications make use of two widely known Java packaging formats, Java Archives (JARs), for packaging bean classes and other supporting class files, and Web Archives (WARs), which serve to deploy full-blown application units inside Java EE application servers/containers. WARs contain JARs, XML descriptors, and GUI web templates like JSPs.

Similarly, in Chapter 1 you explored how OSGi, in order to achieve its intended purpose, requires a special packaging format. This format, though similar in nature to a JAR, requires an accompanying `MANIFEST.MF` file with special OSGi headers.

The rift in this layer occurs due to these differing approaches used in both platforms. For starters, the packaging formats used by Java application servers—which are typically used to deploy Spring applications—occur in *sandboxes*, with JAR files contained in WARs operating in a sandbox isolated from communicating with any other WARs or external JARs used elsewhere.

Of course, these sandboxes are in place by design to avoid any potential conflicts or class clashes, but in OSGi sandboxes have no place, for they only thwart the intended purpose behind the platform, which is to dynamically share resources across a system; a bundle managed through an OSGi framework effectively polices resources, instead of relying on a sandbox approach.

Similarly, OSGi's core packaging unit, the bundle, fulfills the duties of both standard JAR files and of a deployable unit like a WAR. This is due to OSGi environments operating on the premise that a packaging unit is always deployable no matter what it contains—class files, libraries, descriptors—so long as it also contains the appropriate OSGi manifest.

Given these more general-purpose packaging characteristics, bundles are the preferred packaging format when integrating Spring and OSGi. The consequence though of using bundles as the packaging format under these circumstances is the need to always include special OSGi headers in a JAR's `MANIFEST.MF` file, declaring a bundle's reliance on external packages, what it can offer other running bundles in the system, and specifying the many other OSGi behaviors described in Chapter 1.

For Spring application development, this can add some overhead, since each bundle—JAR or WAR—used in an application needs to incorporate this additional manifest, a process that applies equally to classes developed for the application and any staple libraries used by the application itself, such as an XML parser, JPA implementation, or some other variation.

While nothing much can done to avoid this burden for bundles pertaining to an application's domain model, the people behind Spring have put together a repository of bundles that are typically used as libraries in Spring applications, therefore reducing the need for end users to OSGi'fy standard staple JAR libraries.[2] You will make use of this last repository along with the Spring-DM framework in the Hello World application presented in this chapter. But first, let's take a look at the last layer of integration influencing the combination of Spring and OSGi.

Application Servers: Classpath Loaders

The application servers or containers on which Spring applications are deployed are designed around a formal set of specifications defined by numerous Java EE expert groups, many of which are currently not in complete sync with OSGi's approach.

---

2. `http://www.springsource.com/repository/`

So at this level of integration between Spring and OSGi there are various workable scenarios that depend upon the application server/container you make use of, so let's explore such possibilities.

Scenario 1: Application Server Running WARs Embedded with OSGi

This is the most straightforward manner in which you can deploy Spring and OSGi applications, because it doesn't require changing the underlying infrastructure used to deploy Java EE applications. Under these circumstances though, while you could effectively use even a J2EE application server, circa 1999, and still make use of Spring and OSGi, this scenario is also one in which the benefits are less palpable. Let's see why.

You're already aware that standard application servers/containers rely on the notion of deploying WARs, as outlined earlier. However, this packaging format operates in a type of sandbox similar to how non-OSGi JARs do. Figure 3-1 illustrates just how application servers behave upon deploying WAR files.

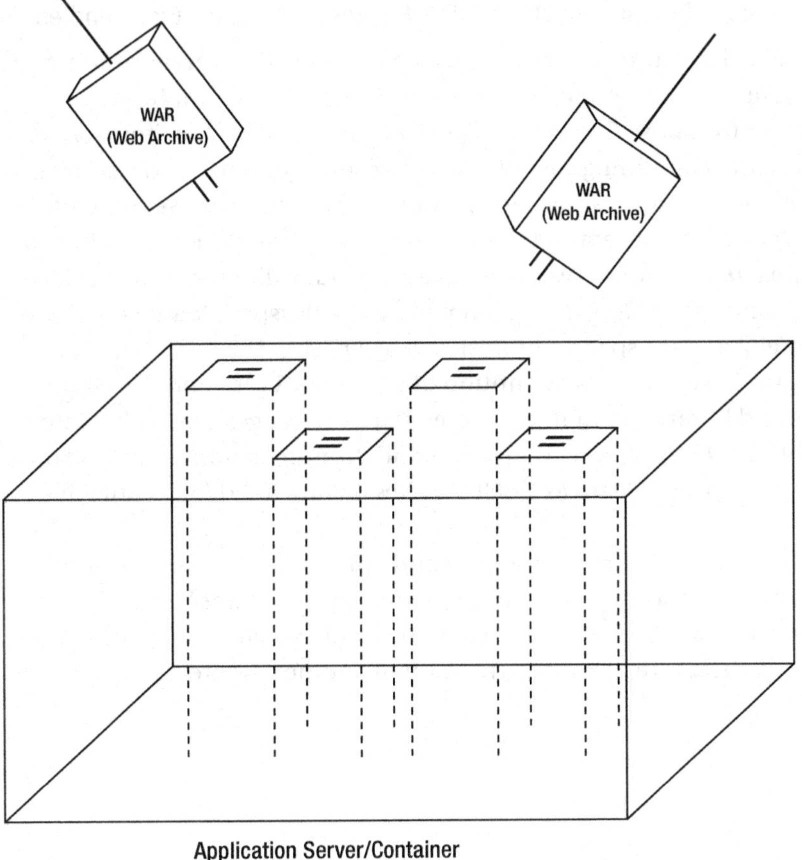

Figure 3-1. *Application server deploying WARs*

Notice how each WAR is isolated from the others. What the application server is doing is generating different class loaders for each WAR, effectively granting each WAR its own CLASSPATH sandbox on which to operate, a process that is dictated by Java EE specs.

At this level, and given OSGi's small footprint, it's viable to embed an OSGi environment inside a WAR and let it manage that one particular class loader or sandbox, in this manner granting all the potential Spring class files and Spring libraries packaged as bundles the benefits OSGi has to offer.

However, don't lose sight of the fact that while you may have one WAR file reaping the benefits of OSGi, the benefits are still confined to one sandbox, with any other application running on the same application server/container also needing to embed OSGi in its underlying WAR package.

All this again is by design, since application servers/containers *have to* support different class loaders for each deployed WAR, which begs the question, isn't there a way to have one unique classpath managed by OSGi and have all deployed WARs managed by that one instance? Well, the answer is yes, but there is a twist as to how an application server/container needs to behave with respect to class loading, which takes us to the next scenario.

Scenario 2: Application Server Running Inside an OSGi Environment with Other Bundles

You might not have realized it, but you've already used an application server running as an OSGi bundle in the example presented in Chapter 1. Back in that example, you made use of the Jetty web server to expose OSGi's HttpService. On that occasion, however, it was a stripped-down version containing solely OSGi's HttpService. What I am referring to in this scenario is a full-fledged application server/container based on these principles.

Application servers/containers operating under such principles—which from here on I will refer to as *OSGi'fied application servers*—behave in a totally different manner from those under Scenario 1, since there is absolutely no notion of classpath loaders, and we have one and only one global class space administered by OSGi.

Of course, this effectively supersedes the notion of using WAR files and the whole process of how classes and libraries contained in these latter packages are loaded into a JVM. This is on account of both the application server and the applications deployed on it relying exclusively on packages made up as OSGi bundles. Figure 3-2 depicts how this setup looks.

As you can conclude from this figure, using OSGi and Spring in such fashion entails employing an OSGi'fied application server to support and expose an application's logic; it's no doubt a step forward from Scenario 1, since there is one global class space administered by OSGi, but nevertheless represents a trade-off of another nature.

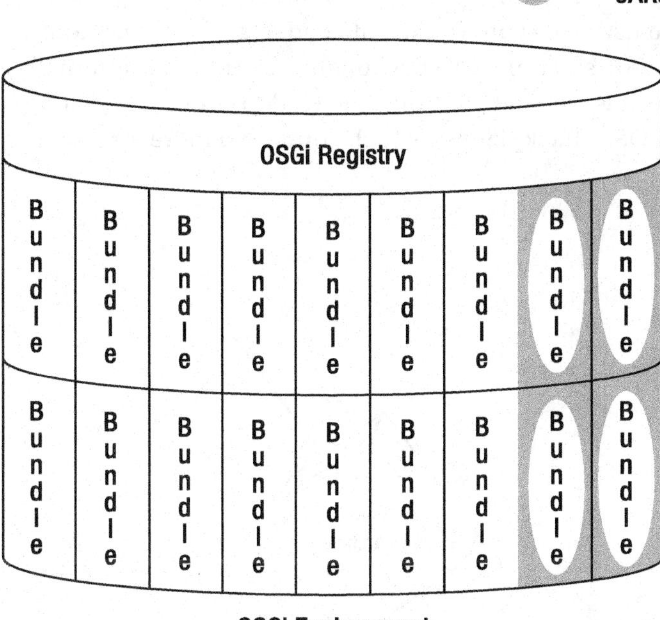

Figure 3-2. *OSGi'fied application server running alongside other OSGi bundles*

Currently, only a handful of application servers are said to be OSGi'fied, which is to say they have all their underlying JARs equipped with the corresponding OSGi manifests. But herein lies a bit of confusion, since even an OSGi'fied application server can still run without OSGi, or inclusively there are non-OSGi'fied servers running OSGi in their backplane.

Figure 3-2 depicts an application server with its main entry point being an OSGi environment, in which all requests are handled by an OSGi-administered application server; in this case, we have an OSGi'fied server communicating with other OSGi application bundles.

However, having an application server's JAR files contain an OSGi manifest doesn't necessarily mean OSGi is required. Recall that a manifest simply contains instructions, and a JAR is equally usable without OSGi. This means that all the composing application server JAR files can be bootstrapped outside OSGi, in essence having a standard Java EE application just like in Scenario 1.

The confusion in these circumstances further arises from Java EE application servers that use OSGi in their backplane, yet don't support the deployment of OSGi application bundles. In these cases, in order to use OSGi you would still need to go down Scenario 1, embedding Spring/OSGi inside a WAR, since an OSGi backplane is simply used internally. See Figure 3-3, which illustrates how this scenario plays out, and read the sidebar "OSGi'fied Application Server/Container and OSGi Backplanes," which contains a more extensive explanation on the subject.

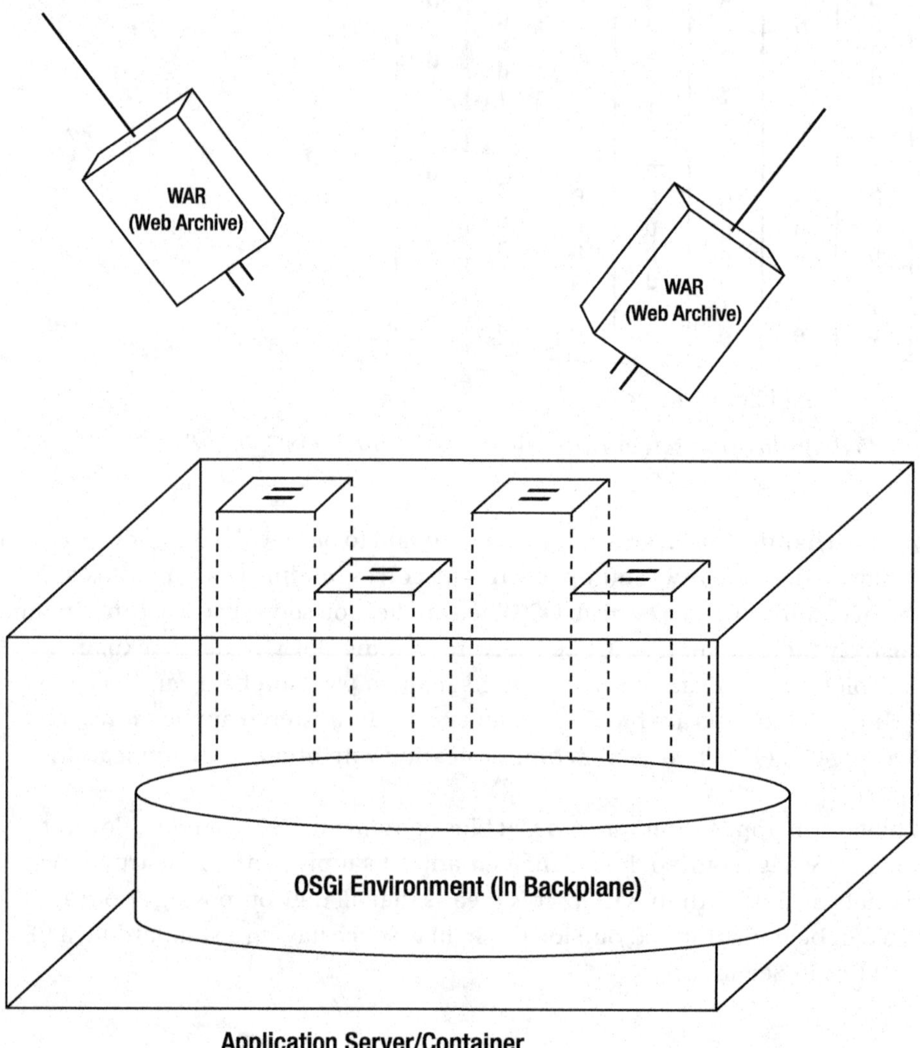

Figure 3-3. *Application server based on OSGi backplane deploying WARs*

OSGI'FIED APPLICATION SERVER/CONTAINER AND OSGI BACKPLANES

The Java EE market has seen a marked shift toward OSGi-based application servers/containers. However, there are a few notable differences you should be aware when it comes to seeing the term "OSGi" associated with an application server/container that have to do with the deployment of OSGi bundles.

Some of the pioneer Java application server vendors have long made use of OSGi in their kernel or backplane architecture to make more efficient use of resources, with many seemingly failing to announce it, because in these cases OSGi was not intended to be used in application deployment, but internally to make a better application server.

Under these circumstances, OSGi is "sealed away" and of little use to application deployment, like any other core classes used to make up a server. This is in stark contrast to having an OSGi'fied application server/container bootstrapped inside an OSGi environment (as in Figure 3-2) cohabiting with other OSGi bundles that make up an application.

The issue here becomes not that an application server/container uses OSGi, but rather to what extent the application server/container allows the deployment of OSGi bundles. Most uses of OSGi in current application servers are of the backplane kind, in which case the use of Spring/OSGi would entail placing an OSGi environment inside a WAR file, such as Scenario 1 listed earlier. The Hello World application presented in this chapter, however, will make use of Scenario 2, running an OSGi'fied application entirely within an OSGi environment, enabling the partitioning of an application into bundles.

To many the thought of using an OSGi'fied application server/container on top of an OSGi environment might seem a bit radical. After all, what are you supposed to do with all those standard WAR files you already have?

For those willing to accept a partial conversion of WAR files to OSGi bundles, Spring-DM offers support, effectively delegating a standard WAR file provisioned with an OSGi manifest—which could include servlets, JSPs, and other Java web application artifacts—to run inside an OSGi'fied application server, an architecture that you will explore first-hand in the Hello World application presented in this chapter.

But let's assume you are not the middle-ground type, and you want your WARs deployable as they currently stand but still want the capacity to potentially deploy OSGi bundles in the same environment. Isn't there an application server/container capable of supporting both? Yes, there is as a matter of fact, and Scenario 3 covers this last option for integrating Spring and OSGi in relation to application servers.

Scenario 3: Application Server Running Native OSGi Bundle and WARs

Supporting the deployment of both native OSGi bundles and WAR files is a hybrid type of application server/container, as illustrated in Figure 3-4.

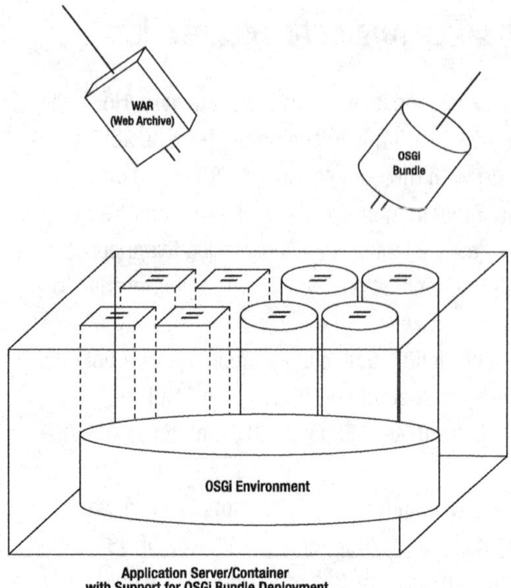

Figure 3-4. *Application server supporting OSGi bundles and WAR files*

In this image you can appreciate how the best of Scenario 1 and Scenario 2 are brought to fruition, with support for deploying standard WAR files used in Java EE applications, as well as the OSGi bundle packaging format.

As this is a relatively new paradigm for Java EE application servers, there is only one application server in the market that currently supports this scenario: the SpringSource dm Server.

The SpringSource dm Server is an application server capable of deploying standard Java EE web applications, built on the foundations of Apache Tomcat and Eclipse OSGi Equinox. (Eclipse OSGi Equinox is another OSGi implementation based on the same standard as the Apache Felix OSGi environment used in Chapter 1.) The platform also makes special provisions when it comes to dealing with class loaders and the way OSGi bundles are deployed, not to mention making use of a custom kernel to deal with cross-functional issues, like persistence to RDBMS, needed to deploy OSGi applications in enterprise settings.

While it's still early to tell with certainty whether vendors of other Java EE application servers such as IBM and Oracle/BEA will support this hybrid model of OSGi/WAR deployment in future versions of their products, the approach brings clear value to those wanting to obtain the greatest benefit from using Spring/OSGi technology, while still leaving room for standard Java EE web application deployment.

Chapter 5 will take a look at some special aspects of using the SpringSource dm Server, including its architecture and deployment style, but next it's time to get into the thick of things and create your first application using Spring and OSGi.

OSGi and Spring Hello World Application

The Hello World application you are about to start creating will take you through the most basic steps in combining Spring and OSGi technology, such as logically partitioning an application into OSGi bundles and creating the corresponding OSGi manifests, to more advanced topics like deploying an application into an OSGi'fied application server/container and making it accessible through the Web. Figure 3-5 illustrates the bundles that will make up the application and the relationship between each one.

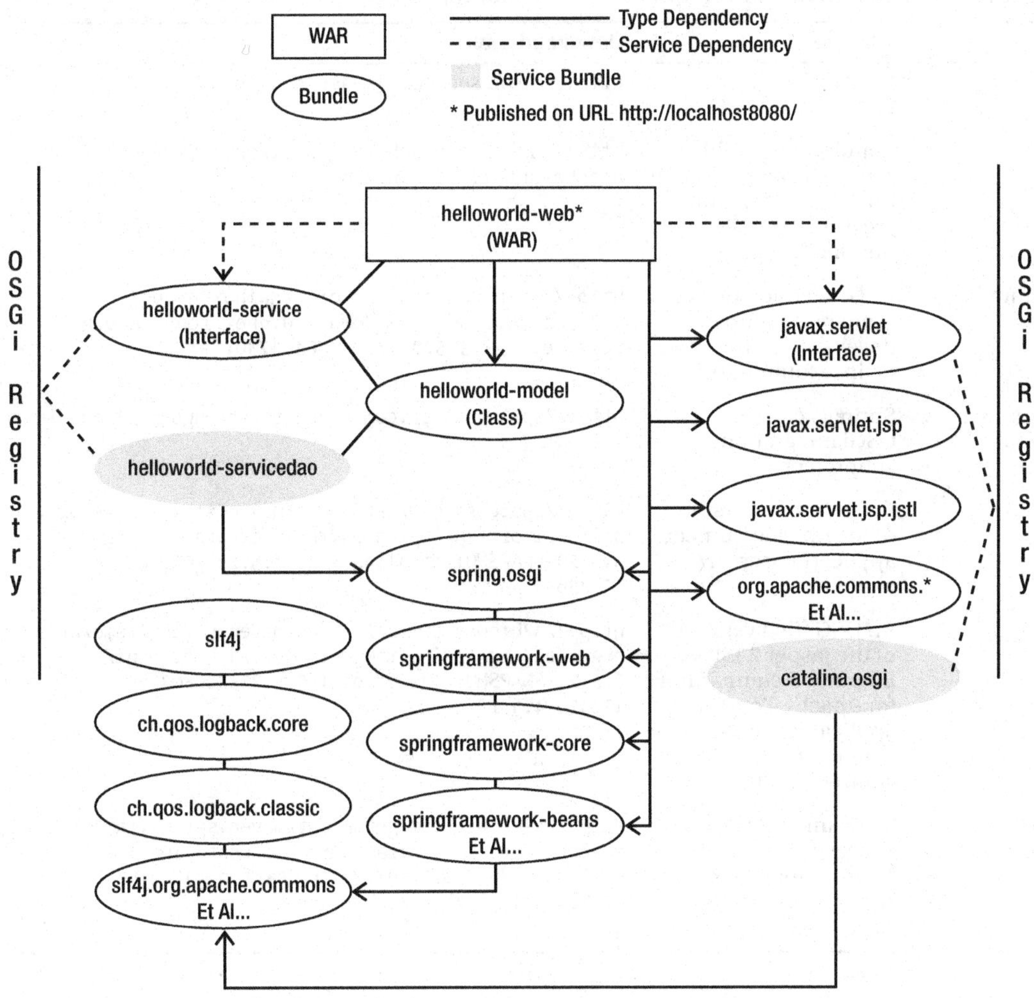

Figure 3-5. *Spring-DM Hello World application bundles and relationships*

Even though Figure 3-5 illustrates various bundles, don't let the number startle you. Many of the bundles in the application correspond to prepackaged bundles, such as those belonging to Apache Tomcat, SLF4J's logging facilities, and the Spring Framework itself. You will create only four of the bundles illustrated in Figure 3-5 in the upcoming sections.

Prerequisites and Downloads

Table 3-1 lists the software you will need to download and install prior to embarking on your first Spring-OSGi project.

Table 3-1. *Spring-OSGi Hello World Prerequisites and Downloads*

Software	Function	Download Site
Java SE 5 or higher	Java's runtime environment	`http://java.sun.com/javase/downloads/index.jsp`
Java Ant 1.6 or higher	Popular Java build project, used for easing the compilation and creation of OSGi bundles	`http://archive.apache.org/dist/ant/binaries/apache-ant-1.7.0-bin.zip`
Eclipse Equinox	OSGi 4.0 reference implementation developed by the Eclipse foundation	`http://download.eclipse.org/equinox/drops/S-3.5M1-200808071402/download.php?dropFile=org.eclipse.osgi_3.5.0.v20080804-1730.jar`
Spring Dynamic Modules for OSGi 1.2 (Spring-DM)	Spring's central OSGi integration subproject	`http://springsource.com/products/springdynamicmodules`
Tomcat 5.5.23 (OSGi'fied)	An OSGi'fied version of the Apache Tomcat application server/container	`http://s3browse.com/getObject/maven.springframework.org/osgi/org/springframework/osgi/catalina.osgi/5.5.23-SNAPSHOT/catalina.osgi-5.5.23-20080425.154256-4.jar`
Jasper 5.5.23 (OSGi'fied)	An OSGi'fied version of the Jasper 2 JSP Engine—a companion for Apache Tomcat's application server/container for compiling JSPs	`http://s3browse.com/getObject/maven.springframework.org/osgi/org/springframework/osgi/jasper.osgi/5.5.23-SNAPSHOT/jasper.osgi-5.5.23-20080305.122359-4.jar`
Tomcat OSGi Service Bootstrapper	Program that allows an OSGi'fied Apache Tomcat application server to be published as an OSGi service	`http://s3browse.com/getObject/maven.springframework.org/osgi/org/springframework/osgi/catalina.start.osgi/1.0-SNAPSHOT/catalina.start.osgi-1.0-20080425.161832-4.jar`

It's very likely you may have some of this software already installed on your workstation. If so, just ensure that you have the suggested versions, as minor version variations may hold you back in getting through the outlined steps.

Additionally, since some of this software was already used in the OSGi and Spring Hello World applications presented in Chapter 1 and Chapter 2, installation instructions for those packages will not be presented here, so please refer to the cited chapters for detailed installation instructions.

To complete the download list, Table 3-2 contains the OSGi'fied bundle dependencies needed in this Hello World project, all of which can be downloaded from the SpringSource Enterprise Bundle Repository.

Table 3-2. *OSGi'fied Bundles Used in the Hello World application—From the SpringSource Enterprise Bundle Repository*

OSGi Bundle	Download URL*
Logging	
LOGback Core	`http://www.springsource.com/repository/app/bundle/version/detail?name=com.springsource.ch.qos.logback.core&version=0.9.9`
LOGback Classic	`http://www.springsource.com/repository/app/bundle/version/detail?name=com.springsource.ch.qos.logback.classic&version=0.9.9`
SLF4J API	`http://www.springsource.com/repository/app/bundle/version/detail?name=com.springsource.slf4j.api&version=1.5.0`
Jakarta Commons Logging over SLF4J	`http://www.springsource.com/repository/app/bundle/version/detail?name=com.springsource.slf4j.org.apache.commons.logging&version=1.5.0`
Log4J Logging over SLF4J	`http://www.springsource.com/repository/app/bundle/version/detail?name=com.springsource.slf4j.org.apache.log4j&version=1.5.0`
Apache Tomcat	
Java Expression Language API	`http://www.springsource.com/repository/app/bundle/version/detail?name=com.springsource.javax.el&version=1.0.0`
Java JSP API	`http://www.springsource.com/repository/app/bundle/version/detail?name=com.springsource.javax.servlet.jsp&version=2.1.0`
Java Servlet API	`http://www.springsource.com/repository/app/bundle/version/detail?name=com.springsource.javax.servlet&version=2.5.0`
Apache Standard Tag Libraries	`http://www.springsource.com/repository/app/bundle/version/detail?name=com.springsource.org.apache.taglibs.standard&version=1.1.2`
Java JSP Standard Tag Library	`http://www.springsource.com/repository/app/bundle/version/detail?name=com.springsource.javax.servlet.jsp.jstl&version=1.1.2`
Apache Commons Expression Language	`http://www.springsource.com/repository/app/bundle/version/detail?name=com.springsource.org.apache.commons.el&version=1.0.0`
Spring	
Spring Core	`http://www.springsource.com/repository/app/bundle/version/detail?name=org.springframework.core&version=2.5.4.A`
Spring Beans	`http://www.springsource.com/repository/app/bundle/version/detail?name=org.springframework.beans&version=2.5.4.A`

Table 3-2. *OSGi'fied Bundles Used in the Hello World application—From the SpringSource Enterprise Bundle Repository (Continued)*

OSGi Bundle	Download URL*
Spring Context	`http://www.springsource.com/repository/app/bundle/version/detail?name=org.springframework.context&version=2.5.4.A`
Spring Context Support	`http://www.springsource.com/repository/app/bundle/version/detail?name=org.springframework.context.support&version=2.5.4.A`
Spring AOP	`http://www.springsource.com/repository/app/bundle/version/detail?name=org.springframework.aop&version=2.5.4.A`
AOP Alliance	`http://www.springsource.com/repository/app/bundle/version/detail?name=com.springsource.org.aopalliance&version=1.0.0`
Java Common Annotations	`http://www.springsource.com/repository/app/bundle/version/detail?name=com.springsource.javax.annotation&version=1.0.0`
Spring Web Servlet	`http://www.springsource.com/repository/app/bundle/version/detail?name=org.springframework.web.servlet&version=2.5.4.A`
Spring Web	`http://www.springsource.com/repository/app/bundle/version/detail?name=org.springframework.web&version=2.5.4.A`
CGLIB Code Generation Library	`http://www.springsource.com/repository/app/bundle/version/detail?name=com.springsource.net.sf.cglib&version=2.1.3`
Apache Commons Collections	`http://www.springsource.com/repository/app/bundle/version/detail?name=com.springsource.org.apache.commons.collections&version=3.2.0`
Backport Util Concurrent	`http://www.springsource.com/repository/app/bundle/version/detail?name=com.springsource.edu.emory.mathcs.backport&version=3.0.0`

* *See the book's source code download, which contains these bundles, on the Apress web site in the Book Extras section at http://www.apress.com/book/view/9781430216124. It will save you time instead of downloading each bundle separately. Additionally, Chapter 7 contains a short introduction to Apache Ivy, a dependency manager that facilitates downloading OSGi bundles with interdependencies.*

Installing Spring Dynamic Modules for OSGi

The process for installing Spring Dynamic Modules for OSGi, or Spring-DM, consists of just one step: unzipping the downloaded file into a directory of your choice. Since you will only be using the various libraries contained in this file, there is nothing more to do with respect to using Spring-DM right now; when the need arises I will indicate where to copy files from this download.

Installing Eclipse Equinox

The process for installing Eclipse Equinox is very straightforward, given it's a self-contained JAR file. In the directory where you downloaded Eclipse Equinox's JAR file, invoke the following command: `java -jar org.eclipse.osgi_3.5.0.v20080804-1730.jar -console`.

This last step will start an OSGi shell session, similar to Apache Felix's shell session illustrated in Chapter 1. The commands available in Eclipse Equinox's shell are strikingly similar to Apache Felix's shell, since they're both OSGi environments. You can enter **help** to obtain a detailed list of commands or press Ctrl+C to exit the shell session.

Additionally, starting this shell will also generate a directory named `configuration` under the working directory of Eclipse Equinox's JAR file. This directory serves various purposes: to contain Eclipse Equinox's main configuration file, to contain its log files, and to maintain Eclipse Equinox's application bundle states. If you move to the `configuration` directory at this juncture, you will see the `org.eclipse.osgi` directory and a log file.

The `org.eclipse.osgi` directory is very important in the sense that it's here that Eclipse Equinox keeps track of bundles between sessions. No matter how many times you start or stop an Eclipse Equinox shell, it will always perform a search in this directory to replicate the last session's actions. The `org.eclipse.osgi` directory functions like the profile concept used in Apache Felix, in which a directory is used to maintain copies of installed bundles and their states.

The log file appearing at this initial stage contains an error message. The reason for this error message is because Eclipse Equinox is designed to work in tandem with Eclipse's flagship platform, and therefore it attempts to bootstrap other JAR files in the process. In order to avoid this error message, you will need to create an Eclipse Equinox configuration file.

Eclipse Equinox's main configuration file is a simple text file that needs to be placed under the `configuration` directory by the name `config.ini`. For the moment, add the line `eclipse.ignoreApp=true` inside this file to avoid Eclipse Equinox from attempting to start Eclipse's flagship platform at startup.

If you restart an Eclipse Equinox shell session with this configuration file, you will note that no more log files are generated at startup. Next, you will install Apache Tomcat aided by this same Eclipse Equinox configuration file.

WHY CHANGE FROM APACHE FELIX TO ECLIPSE EQUINOX?

Like many other products based on standards, OSGi framework implementations vary by the number of features they support at any given time. At the time this book went to press, Apache Felix lacked support for what is known as **OSGi fragments**—a concept that will be formally introduced in Chapter 4—on which application bundles like Apache Tomcat rely.

Therefore, given the need to use Apache Tomcat in this chapter's application—and with it OSGi fragments—it was necessary to switch over to Eclipse Equinox, which already supports this OSGi feature.

Progress on support for fragments in Apache Felix can be found at `https://issues.apache.org/jira/browse/FELIX-29`.

Installing Apache Tomcat (OSGi'fied)

The process for installing Apache Tomcat (OSGi'fied) consists of colocating its OSGi'fied JAR and required bundle dependencies alongside Eclipse Equinox, the latter of which will serve as the underlying OSGi environment. In order to simplify the startup sequence of an

OSGi'fied Apache Tomcat, the first thing you will need to do is modify Eclipse Equinox's configuration file to bring up Apache Tomcat without needing to go into an OSGi shell.

Inside Eclipse Equinox's `configuration` directory, reedit the `config.ini` file to automatically load Apache Tomcat upon startup. Listing 3-1 contains a snapshot of how the `config.ini` file should look to initiate Apache Tomcat at startup.

Listing 3-1. *Eclipse Equinox `config.ini` Bootstrapping OSGi'fied Apache Tomcat App Server*

```
osgi.bundles=logging/com.springsource.ch.qos.logback.core-0.9.9.jar@start, \
logging/com.springsource.ch.qos.logback.classic-0.9.9.jar, \
logging/com.springsource.slf4j.api-1.5.0.jar@start, \
logging/com.springsource.slf4j.org.apache.commons.logging-1.5.0.jar@start, \
logging/com.springsource.slf4j.org.apache.log4j-1.5.0.jar@start, \
tomcat/com.springsource.javax.servlet-2.5.0.jar@start, \
tomcat/com.springsource.javax.el-1.0.0.jar@start, \
tomcat/com.springsource.javax.servlet.jsp-2.1.0.jar@start, \
tomcat/com.springsource.org.apache.commons.el-1.0.0.jar@start, \
tomcat/jasper.osgi-5.5.23-20080305.122359-4.jar, \
tomcat/com.springsource.org.apache.taglibs.standard-1.1.2.jar@start, \
tomcat/com.springsource.javax.servlet.jsp.jstl-1.1.2.jar@start, \
tomcat/catalina.osgi-5.5.23-SNAPSHOT.jar@start, \
tomcat/catalina.start.osgi-1.0-20080425.161832-4.jar@start
eclipse.ignoreApp=true
```

Caution All statements added to Eclipse Equinox's `osgi.bundles` parameter require a trailing backslash (\), except for the last one—prior to `eclipse.ignoreApp=true`. Ensure this syntax is enforced; otherwise Eclipse Equinox will not load these files at startup.

The first five bundles added to the Eclipse Equinox configuration file are those pertaining to logging, which will allow you to observe debugging information for Apache Tomcat and any other bundle deployed onto OSGi relying on either Jakarta Commons, Log4J, or SLF4J for logging purposes. Place each of these bundles under a subdirectory named `logging` in the same directory as Eclipse Equinox's JAR file, consulting Table 3-2 for the corresponding download links for these bundles.

The remaining bundles are those related to the OSGi'fied version of Apache Tomcat, hence their location under a subdirectory named `tomcat`, which also needs to be created alongside Eclipse Equinox's main JAR file.

WHEN LOGGING IN OSGI, WHY SLF4J?

Logging in Java applications is one of those subjects that often stirs endless debates, given the many approaches that are available to go about it. In the particular case of OSGi, there are two reasons why SLF4J is the recommended approach: tighter class loading and no control over preexisting logging approaches used in bundles.

SLF4J, or Simple Logging Facade for Java, is OSGi friendly in the sense that other Java logging libraries—like Jakarta commons—rely on class-loading inspection to operate properly, a process that does not bode well with OSGi's more stringent approach to class loading.

Additionally, in any deployment—OSGi or not—a Java logging approach is already ingrained in Java classes, whether it's Jakarta Commons or Log4J, creating an additional need to configure each logging mechanism prior to deployment. In this case, SLF4J can also serve as an aiding bridge for these other logging libraries, where all logging output is managed exclusively by SLF4J, without the need to load any non-OSGi-friendly libraries or configure separate logging handlers.

The first bundle is Java EE's OSGi'fied servlet implementation, which allows the execution of such components.

Next, you will find six supporting libraries also needed by Apache Tomcat that include those supporting JavaServer Pages (JSP), Java Standard Tag Libraries (JSTL), and the expression language used in these last two front-end Java technologies. See Table 3-2 for the corresponding download links on these OSGi bundles.

The second-to-last line is Apache Tomcat's OSGi bundle itself, with the last line providing the bootstrapping bundle necessary to publish Apache Tomcat as an OSGi service. See Table 3-1 for the corresponding download links on these OSGi bundles.

Once you copy all these OSGi'fied JARs into a subdirectory named `tomcat` in the same directory of Eclipse Equinox main JAR file, perform the following test to ensure Apache Tomcat's correct operation:

1. Execute `java -jar org.eclipse.osgi_3.5.0.v20080804-1730.jar -console` to start an OSGi session. At this point you will be placed inside an OSGi shell that, prior to presenting a final prompt, will display a list with all the installed OSGi bundles running in the system, including those related to Apache Tomcat.

2. If you open a browser and point it to `http://localhost:8080/`, you should see an empty page served by Tomcat; the empty page is on account of there being no applications running on the server.

3. In case this test fails, consult the error messages in Eclipse Equinox's configuration directory. Check under the `configuration` directory of Eclipse Equinox for files with a `log` extension—these will contain detailed information on errors.

Installing the Remaining Downloads

The remaining downloads are OSGi bundles that will aid you in the creation of the Hello World Spring-OSGi application. For now, just take note of their location; you will move them around when the need arises.

Setting Up the Hello World "Playground" Directory Structure

Now that you've got the tools working, it's time to create the proper workspace in which to maneuver. Building on a similar approach to earlier chapters, create a directory structure like the one illustrated in Figure 3-6.

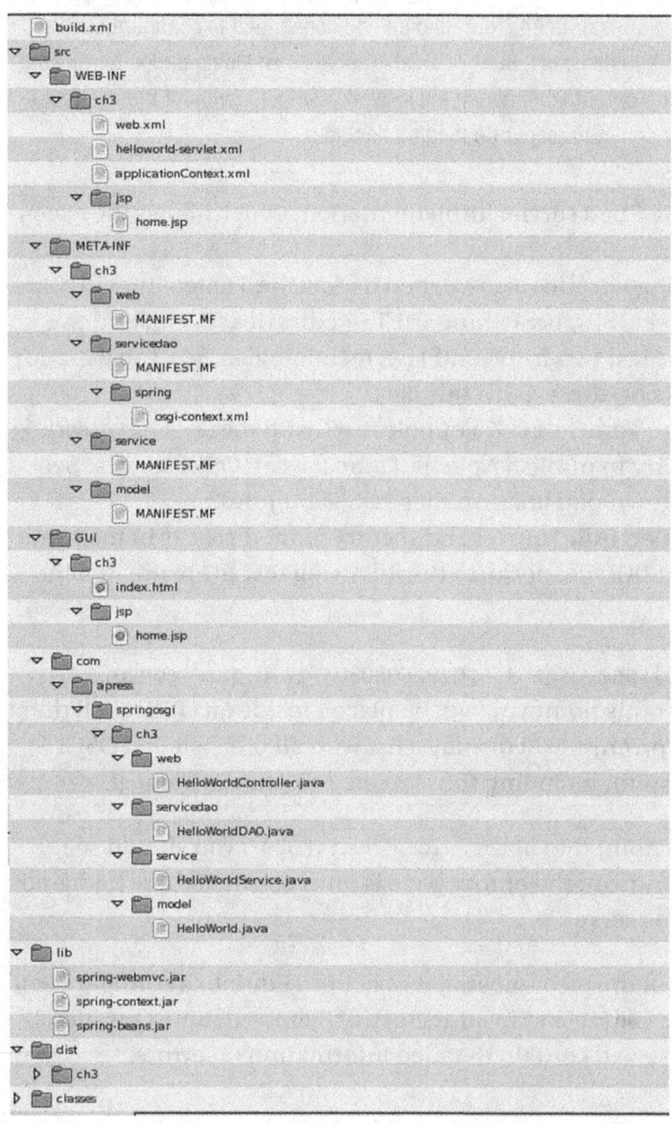

Figure 3-6. *Directory structure for Hello World "playground"*

The directory structure functions as follows:

- `build.xml`: This is the main Java Ant configuration file containing the necessary tasks to build the application.
- `classes`: All compiled Java classes are placed in this directory.
- `dist`: All built bundles are placed in this directory.
- `lib`: All JARs needed to compile Java sources are placed in this directory.
- `src`: All Java sources files composing the application are placed accordingly in subdirectories inside this directory, including the application descriptor used in the web-tier bundle inside `WEB-INF/ch3` and the corresponding OSGi manifests for each bundle placed inside `META-INF/ch3/<bundle_type>`.

The Domain Model

The domain model you are about to create will be composed of a single class, and it will serve the Data Access Object (DAO) that you will create later on. Unlike the domain model presented in Chapter 2, this domain model will be employed only by a DAO using in-memory access and not a RDBMS; the reasons for this will become more apparent later on in Chapter 5 and Chapter 7 when you explore Java persistence in the context of OSGi, which is considered a little more elaborate to set up than a Hello World example.

Listing 3-2 contains the `HelloWorld` class used as the domain model in this introductory Spring-OSGi application.

Listing 3-2. *`HelloWorld` Model Class*

```
package com.apress.springosgi.ch3.model;

import java.util.Date;

public class HelloWorld {

    private String message;
    private Date currentTime;
    private double modelVersion;

    public void setMessage(String message) {
        this.message = message;
    }
```

```
    public String getMessage() {
        return message;
    }

    public void setCurrentTime(Date currentTime) {
        this.currentTime = currentTime;
    }

    public Date getCurrentTime() {
        return currentTime;
    }

    public void setModelVersion(double modelVersion) {
        this.modelVersion = modelVersion;
    }

    public double getModelVersion() {
        return modelVersion;
    }

    public HelloWorld(String message, Date currentTime, double modelVersion) {
        this.message = message;
        this.currentTime = currentTime;
        this.modelVersion = modelVersion;
    }

    public HelloWorld() {
    }
}
```

As you can observe, the model is a standard POJO with three getter/setter methods and corresponding constructor methods; the actual data, though, will never make it beyond memory and will only be actioned one-way through the data service used by the application.

The domain class will be contained in its own OSGi bundle, making it the first of four bundles in which the Hello World application will be partitioned. Since this bundle will possess only one class, the requirements for the accompanying OSGi manifest, which can be observed in Listing 3-3, are simple.

Listing 3-3. *MANIFEST.MF for the Application Model*

```
Bundle-Version: 1.0
Bundle-SymbolicName: com.apress.springosgi.ch3.model
Bundle-Name: HelloWorld Spring-OSGi Model
```

```
Bundle-Vendor: Pro Spring-OSGi
Export-Package: com.apress.springosgi.ch3.model;version="1.0.0"
Bundle-ManifestVersion: 2
```

Most of the key-value pairs used in this OSGi manifest should be familiar to you from your initial OSGi exploration. They are used for indicating versioning and naming characteristics for the bundle, as well as the packages a bundle makes available to other bundles in the system.

As far as creating the actual bundle, you will once again rely on Apache Ant to output a package containing the model class and OSGi manifest. Copy the `MANIFEST.MF` file in Listing 3-3 to the `/META-INF/ch3/model/` subdirectory of your Hello World "playground." Next, modify the main `build.xml` file located in your Hello World "playground" to include the Ant task presented in Listing 3-4.

■ **Note** If you skipped the example presented in Chapter 1, you will not have a preexisting `build.xml` file to modify. If this is the case, you will need to copy the `build.xml` file presented in Listing 1-6, which is the base Apache Ant file needed by Listing 3-4.

Listing 3-4. *Ant Task for Building the OSGi Model Bundle*

```
<target name="ch3" depends="compile" description="Build Chapter 3 Spring-OSGi Appl➥
ication">

  <echo message="-------------- Building Chapter 3 Spring-OSGi Application ➥
for Pro Spring-OSGi --------------"/>

     <property name="ch3.dir"          value="${dist.dir}/ch3/"/>
     <mkdir dir="${ch3.dir}"/>

    <jar destfile="${ch3.dir}/helloworld-model.jar" manifest="${src.dir}/➥
META-INF/ch3/model/MANIFEST.MF">
         <fileset  dir="${build.dir}">
           <include name="com/apress/springosgi/ch3/model/*"/>
         </fileset>
        <metainf dir="${src.dir}/META-INF/ch3/model/"/>
     </jar>
</target>
```

This Ant task starts by defining a dependency on the `compile` target, guaranteeing that all classes are compiled prior to creating a bundle, followed by the creation of a subdirectory in which the application bundles are placed.

Next is the actual `<jar>` definition that creates the bundle; it will equip the bundle with the manifest file located in `${src.dir}/META-INF/ch3/model/`, as well as include the class files located under the `com/apress/springosgi/ch3/model` subdirectory—the domain model package—and inclusively copy any files located in the subdirectory `${src.dir}/META-INF/ch3/model/` to the bundle's `META-INF` directory.

Ensuring you have copied all the necessary bundles files to the appropriate "playground" directories, execute the command `ant ch3`, and the model bundle should be generated with the name `helloworld-model.jar` and placed under the `dist/ch3` subdirectory.

For the moment, you will leave the deployment of the model bundle until you have a little more to work with. The text that follows will continue describing the packaging of the service bundle.

Following the same pattern as the stand-alone Spring application presented in Chapter 2, the data service used in this Hello World application will be composed of an interface describing the various actions performed on the model, as well as an implementation class containing the actual DAO. Listing 3-5 and Listing 3-6 contain the classes corresponding to the `HelloWorld` service.

Listing 3-5. *`HelloWorldService` Service Interface*

```
package com.apress.springosgi.ch3.service;

import com.apress.springosgi.ch3.model.HelloWorld;

public interface HelloWorldService {

    public HelloWorld find();

    public HelloWorld update(HelloWorld hw);

    public void save(HelloWorld hw );

    public void delete(HelloWorld hw);

}
```

Listing 3-6. *`HelloWorldService` Service Implementation Class*

```
package com.apress.springosgi.ch3.servicedao;

import com.apress.springosgi.ch3.service.HelloWorldService;

import java.util.Date;
```

```
import com.apress.springosgi.ch3.model.HelloWorld;

public class HelloWorldDAO implements HelloWorldService {

    public HelloWorld find() {
        // Model object will be create here
        HelloWorld hw = new HelloWorld("Hello World",new Date(),1.0);
        return hw;
    }

    public HelloWorld update(HelloWorld hw) {
        hw.setCurrentTime(new Date());
        return hw;
    }

    public void save(HelloWorld hw) {
        throw new UnsupportedOperationException("Can't save anything, no RDBMS ➥
back here");
    }

    public void delete(HelloWorld hw) {
      throw new UnsupportedOperationException("Can't delete anything, no RDBMS ➥
back here");
    }

}
```

The first thing to note about these last listings is that both belong to different Java packages. Since OSGi grants access to a bundle's classes on a package basis, this ensures that other bundles are capable of accessing a service only by its interface, thereby protecting the DAO implementation from being accessed directly by other bundles.

The service in theory supports the standard CRUD (Create, Read, Update, Delete) operations performed on most data models—though technically two are supported, since two explicitly throw an exception given the lack of a data store: the `find()` method, which instantiates an inline `HelloWorld` object via the class's constructor method, and the `update()` method, which modifies a `HelloWorld` object's `currentTime` field.

Armed with these code listings, let's explore how each one needs to be packaged in order to be deployed in an OSGi environment.

Unlike the model bundle, the packaging for the application's service is a little more interesting, since it will not only rely on the model bundle, but also need to eventually provide functionality to the web bundle in order to expose data. Following the recommended practice of separating interface and implementing class into different bundles, the application's service will be split into a service implementation (DAO) bundle and an accompanying service interface bundle.

Listing 3-7 contains the service implementation (DAO) bundle manifest, and Listing 3-8 contains the service interface bundle manifest.

Listing 3-7. *`MANIFEST.MF` for the Application Service Implementation (DAO)*

```
Bundle-Version: 1.0
Bundle-SymbolicName: com.apress.springosgi.ch3.servicedao
Bundle-Name: HelloWorld Spring-OSGi Service DAO
Bundle-Vendor: Pro Spring-OSGi

Import-Package: com.apress.springosgi.ch3.model;version="1.0.0",
 com.apress.springosgi.ch3.service;version="1.0.0",

 org.springframework.util;version="2.5.4",
 org.springframework.beans.factory.xml;version="2.5.4",
 org.springframework.aop;version="2.5.4",
 org.springframework.aop.framework;version="2.5.4",

 org.springframework.osgi.service.exporter.support;version="2.5.4",

Bundle-ManifestVersion: 2
```

Listing 3-8. *`MANIFEST.MF` for the Service Interface*

```
Bundle-Version: 1.0

Bundle-SymbolicName: com.apress.springosgi.ch3.service

Bundle-Name: HelloWorld Spring-OSGi Service

Bundle-Vendor: Pro Spring-OSGi

Import-Package: com.apress.springosgi.ch3.model;version="1.0.0"

Export-Package: com.apress.springosgi.ch3.service;version="1.0.0"

Bundle-ManifestVersion: 2
```

As with the model bundle, both manifests import and export packages, including the model's package and several other Spring packages on which the service implementation (DAO) relies. However, merely exporting the class as in the earlier bundle is not all that's required for the service implementation (DAO) bundle. Since the service bundle contains a bean, this particular bean needs to be placed in the OSGi service registry in order for it to be actionable from other bundles.

This registration process relies on the use Spring descriptors, which are employed for both wiring a bean in the standard DI Spring manner—as you did in Chapter 2—and registering a bean in OSGi's central registry as a service. Listing 3-9 contains the Spring descriptor used by the service bundle to fulfill these purposes.

Listing 3-9. *`osgi-context.xml` Spring Descriptor*

```
<?xml version="1.0" encoding="UTF-8"?>
<beans xmlns="http://www.springframework.org/schema/beans"
  xmlns:xsi="http://www.w3.org/2001/XMLSchema-instance"
  xmlns:osgi="http://www.springframework.org/schema/osgi"
  xsi:schemaLocation="http://www.springframework.org/schema/beans http://www.spri➥
ngframework.org/schema/beans/spring-beans.xsd
                      http://www.springframework.org/schema/osgi http://www.spri➥
ngframework.org/schema/osgi/spring-osgi.xsd">

  <!-- Create the helloWorldDAO bean -->
  <bean id="helloWorldDAO" class="com.apress.springosgi.ch3.servicedao.Hello➥
WorldDAO"/>

  <!-- Export helloWorldDAO as a service to OSGi via its interface -->
  <osgi:service ref="helloWorldDAO" interface="com.apress.springosgi.ch3.servi➥
ce.HelloWorldService"/>
</beans>
```

The descriptor in Listing 3-9 is identical to those used in stand-alone Spring applications in one aspect: it instantiates a bean and assigns it an `id` so other Spring artifacts used in the descriptor can make reference to it. The second declaration is used to register this latter bean as a service using Spring-DM.

At this juncture, there are two points worth emphasizing. The OSGi service registration is made using an interface just like you did in Chapter 1. And the service's underlying object is an actual Spring bean with all the connotations this implies, contrary to a standard Java class that might be intertwined with explicit dependencies.

As to where this descriptor has to be placed, it has to be packaged inside a special subdirectory named `spring` within a bundle's `META-INF` directory, allowing Spring-DM to validate and execute such instructions. Don't worry if the explanation behind this descriptor seems a little scant, for the moment this will do; the next chapter is dedicated to describing all the elements available in such a descriptor.

Moving along, and in order to build the application's service bundles, place yourself back at the HelloWorld "playground." Copy the `MANIFEST.MF` file in Listing 3-7 to `/META-INF/ch3/servicedao/`, the one in Listing 3-8 to `/META-INF/ch3/service/`, and the osgi-context.xml file in Listing 3-9 to the subdirectory /META-INF/ch3/servicedao/spring/ of the same “playground.” Next, add the instructions presented in Listing 3-10 to the ch3 Ant task of your build.xml file.

Listing 3-10. *Ant Instruction for Building the OSGi Service Bundle*

```
<jar destfile="${ch3.dir}/helloworld-service.jar" manifest="${src.dir}/META-INF/➥
ch3/service/MANIFEST.MF">
         <fileset  dir="${build.dir}">
           <include name="com/apress/springosgi/ch3/service/*"/>

         </fileset>
        <metainf dir="${src.dir}/META-INF/ch3/service/"/>
</jar>
<jar destfile="${ch3.dir}/helloworld-servicedao.jar" manifest="${src.dir}/➥
META-INF/ch3/servicedao/MANIFEST.MF">

         <fileset  dir="${build.dir}">

           <include name="com/apress/springosgi/ch3/servicedao/*"/>

         </fileset>

        <metainf dir="${src.dir}/META-INF/ch3/servicedao/"/>

</jar>
```

The first <jar> Ant instruction in this listing is charged with creating a bundle with the classes contained under the com/apress/springosgi/ch3/service/subdirectory and the manifest file located at ${src.dir}/META-INF/ch3/service/. Additionally, the second <jar> Ant instruction creates a bundle with the classes contained under the com/apress/springosgi/ch3/servicedao/ directory and the manifest file located at ${src.dir}/META-INF/ch3/servicedao/, as well as copying the file inside ${src.dir}/META-INF/ch3/servicedao/spring/ to the bundle's /META-INF/spring/ directory, which corresponds to the special spring subdirectory containing the descriptor outlined in Listing 3-9.

If you execute the ant ch3 instruction from the main Hello World “playground” directory once again, the service implementation (DAO) bundle and its corresponding service interface bundle should be generated with the names helloworld-servicedao.jar and helloworld-service.jar and placed under the dist/ch3 subdirectory.

You now have three OSGi bundles ready to be deployed; however, you're still short one bundle, the one pertaining to the user interface. So up next, you will set out on the task of creating the last bundle needed by the Hello World application, the same one that will provide a web-bound interface.

Web Application

For the web bundle, you will be making use of Spring's MVC project in order to tap into the application bundles created in the last section. I will spare you from discussion of a few of the more Spring MVC-centric subjects to concentrate on Spring-DM/Spring MVC integration issues, so if you are unfamiliar with Spring MVC, I advise you to look over Chapter 2, which details the use of Spring MVC in stand-alone fashion.

The first order of business for the web bundle is creating a controller to broker requests between an application's views and its data services. Listing 3-11 contains the controller used for the Spring OSGi application.

Listing 3-11. *Spring MVC Controller for Building the OSGi Web Bundle*

```
package com.apress.springosgi.ch3.web;

import java.util.List;
import java.util.Date;

import org.springframework.beans.factory.annotation.Autowired;
import org.springframework.stereotype.Controller;
import org.springframework.web.bind.annotation.RequestMapping;
import org.springframework.web.bind.annotation.RequestMethod;
import org.springframework.web.bind.annotation.RequestParam;
import org.springframework.web.bind.annotation.ModelAttribute;
import org.springframework.ui.ModelMap;

import com.apress.springosgi.ch3.model.HelloWorld;
import com.apress.springosgi.ch3.service.HelloWorldService;

@Controller
public class HelloWorldController {

    private HelloWorldService helloWorldService;

    public void setHelloWorldService(HelloWorldService helloWorldService) {
        this.helloWorldService = helloWorldService;
    }

    public HelloWorldService getHelloWorldService() {
        return helloWorldService;
    }
```

```
    @RequestMapping(method = RequestMethod.GET)
    @ModelAttribute("helloworld")
    public HelloWorld home() {
        return this.helloWorldService.find();
    }
}
```

The first interesting thing to note about this `Controller` class is how it gets ahold of the `HelloWorldService` through the `setHelloWorldService()` method that will serve as an injection point for the service. By using this approach, the service is injected when the controller bean is instantiated in a Spring descriptor. In this case, Spring-DM performs the injection of services into classes, just like Spring performs the injection of beans.

Besides the service's getter/setter methods, the `Controller` class has one more method, named `home()`, that returns a `HelloWorld` object obtained from the `HelloWorldService`, which according to Spring MVC annotations is invoked when a request to a URL named `home` is made, placing the returned data inside a variable name `helloworld` to manipulate within a view template possessing a logical view named `home`.

The remaining parts of the web bundle are strictly application descriptors. Listing 3-12 contains the first one in the form of `web.xml`, which is the standard descriptor used in Java web applications.

Listing 3-12. *`web.xml` Descriptor for the Web Bundle*

```
<?xml version="1.0" encoding="ISO-8859-1"?>
<web-app xmlns="http://java.sun.com/xml/ns/j2ee"
        xmlns:xsi="http://www.w3.org/2001/XMLSchema-instance"
        xsi:schemaLocation="http://java.sun.com/xml/ns/j2ee http://java.sun.com/➥
xml/ns/j2ee/web-app_2_4.xsd"
        version="2.4">
        <display-name>Simple Osgi WebApp Bundle</display-name>
        <description>Simple OSGi War</description>

        <context-param>
          <param-name>contextClass</param-name>
          <param-value>org.springframework.osgi.web.context.support.OsgiBundleXml➥
WebApplicationContext</param-value>
        </context-param>

        <listener>
          <listener-class>
           org.springframework.web.context.ContextLoaderListener
          </listener-class>
        </listener>
```

```
        <servlet>
           <description>
             Pro Spring-OSGi MVC Dispatch Servlet
           </description>
           <display-name>DispatcherServlet</display-name>
           <servlet-name>helloworld</servlet-name>
           <servlet-class>
              org.springframework.web.servlet.DispatcherServlet
           </servlet-class>
            <load-on-startup>1</load-on-startup>
           <init-param>
            <param-name>contextClass</param-name>
            <param-value>org.springframework.osgi.web.context.support.OsgiBundle➥
XmlWebApplicationContext</param-value>
           </init-param>
        </servlet>

        <servlet-mapping>
                <servlet-name>helloworld</servlet-name>
                <url-pattern>/spring/*</url-pattern>
        </servlet-mapping>

        <welcome-file-list>
                <welcome-file>index.html</welcome-file>
        </welcome-file-list>
</web-app>
```

This Spring MVC `web.xml` descriptor is practically the same as any non-OSGi counterpart, with one exception: the use of `OsgiBundleXmlWebApplicationContext`, a class designed to let a web bundle access OSGi resources.

Recall that you won't be deploying the MVC application to a standard Java EE server designed to access resources from directories like `/WEB-INF/lib` or `/WEB-INF/classes`, but rather to an OSGi'fied application server that needs to locate resources under an OSGi environment, hence the need for this class provided by Spring-DM.

Notice that both Spring's context listener used in standard WARs and the servlet itself are assigned to this special context. This is done so both can resolve class and resource lookups from OSGi's administered classpath. Copy the `web.xml` file in Listing 3-12 to the `/src/WEB-INF/ch3/` directory of your Hello World "playground."

Next, you need to define the initial artifacts brought into the bundle's context. For this you will rely on the default `applicationContext.xml` file used in Spring applications. Listing 3-13 contains a snapshot of this file.

Listing 3-13. *applicationContext.xml Descriptor for the Web Bundle*

```
<?xml version="1.0" encoding="UTF-8"?>
<beans xmlns="http://www.springframework.org/schema/beans"
       xmlns:xsi="http://www.w3.org/2001/XMLSchema-instance"

       xmlns:context="http://www.springframework.org/schema/context"
       xsi:schemaLocation="http://www.springframework.org/schema/beans
                           http://www.springframework.org/schema/beans/➥
spring-beans.xsd
                           http://www.springframework.org/schema/context
                           http://www.springframework.org/schema/context/➥
spring-context-2.5.xsd
">

    <context:component-scan base-package="com.apress.springosgi.ch3.web"/>
</beans>
```

The only statement scans for the presence of annotations in the package corresponding to the controller servlet, a process that will instantiate the servlet with all its MVC annotations, and a declaration that is identical to the one used in Chapter 2. You will need to copy the applicationContext.xml file in Listing 3-13 to the /src/WEB-INF/ch3/ directory of your Hello World "playground." Given the controller servlet is named helloworld, you need to define a descriptor used by the servlet itself that by convention would be named helloworld-servlet.xml. Listing 3-14 illustrates such a descriptor.

Listing 3-14. *helloworld-servlet.xml Descriptor for the Web Bundle*

```
<?xml version="1.0" encoding="UTF-8"?>
<beans xmlns="http://www.springframework.org/schema/beans"
       xmlns:xsi="http://www.w3.org/2001/XMLSchema-instance"
       xmlns:osgi="http://www.springframework.org/schema/osgi"
       xmlns:context="http://www.springframework.org/schema/context"
       xsi:schemaLocation="http://www.springframework.org/schema/beans
                           http://www.springframework.org/schema/beans/➥
spring-beans.xsd
                           http://www.springframework.org/schema/context
                           http://www.springframework.org/schema/context/➥
spring-context-2.5.xsd
                           http://www.springframework.org/schema/osgi
                           http://www.springframework.org/schema/osgi/➥
spring-osgi.xsd">
```

```
  <osgi:reference id="helloWorldService" interface="com.apress.springosgi.ch3.ser➥
vice.HelloWorldService"/>

<bean id="helloWorldController" class="com.apress.springosgi.ch3.web.HelloWorld➥
Controller">
 <property name="helloWorldService" ref="helloWorldService"/>
</bean>

<bean id="urlMapper" class="org.springframework.web.servlet.handler.SimpleUrl➥
HandlerMapping">
        <property name="mappings">
         <props>
          <prop key="/**">helloWorldController</prop>
         </props>
        </property>
</bean>

<bean id="jspViewResolver" class="org.springframework.web.servlet.view.Internal➥
ResourceViewResolver">
      <property name="viewClass" value="org.springframework.web.servlet.view.Jstl➥
View"/>
              <property name="prefix" value="/jsp/"/>
              <property name="suffix" value=".jsp"/>
</bean>

</beans>
```

The first statement corresponds to Spring-DM's way of referencing a service present in OSGi's central registry; via this declaration alone, the service registered in the last bundle is brought into this bundle's context with an id value of helloWorldService. The reference ID is important in the sense that the controller servlet in Listing 3-11 is expecting to inject a service by this particular name, given its getter/setter method.

The remaining statements are strictly in line with those of any other Spring MVC project, indicating the following:

- The creation of the helloWorldController bean corresponding to the appropriate controller class, which also *injects* the helloWorldService as a bean property.
- A URL mapper statement, indicating that all requests, -- <prop key="/**"> --, for the Dispatcher servlet be managed by the helloWorldController bean.

- A view resolver, indicating that all logical views returned by the servlet be mapped to files under the /jsp/ directory and with a .jsp extension. In this application's case, the servlet returns a logical view named home, and will in turn attempt to render a file named home.jsp located under a bundle's /jsp/ subdirectory. Listing 3-15 shows this JSP.

Once you copy the Spring-MVC servlet descriptor in Listing 3-14 to the /src/WEB-INF/ch3/ directory of the Hello World "playground," you will need to define the actual graphical user interface for the application. Listing 3-15 presents the JSP used by the application, which you need to place in the src/GUI/ch3/jsp/ directory of the Hello World "playground."

Listing 3-15. *JSP for the Web Bundle*

```
<!DOCTYPE HTML PUBLIC "-//W3C//DTD HTML 4.01//EN"
        "http://www.w3.org/TR/html4/strict.dtd">
<%@ taglib prefix="c" uri="http://java.sun.com/jsp/jstl/core" %>
<html>
<head>
  <title> Spring DM HelloWorld </title>
</head>
<body>
<p> Results from accessing Spring-DM service bundle: </p>
<p> Message: <c:out value="${helloworld.message}"/> </p>
<p> Current Time: <c:out value="${helloworld.currentTime}"/> </p>
<p> Model Version: <c:out value="${helloworld.modelVersion}"/> </p>
</body>
```

The template shown in Listing 3-15 is nothing more than a JSP displaying the values returned by the controller servlet, per instructions used in the servlet's view resolver, located in a bundle's absolute directory /jsp/home.jsp.

Since Java web applications rely on the presence of an index.html file as their primary entry point, you also need to define this file. Listing 3-16 illustrates the index.html file used by the web bundle.

Listing 3-16. *index.html File for Web Bundle*

```
<html>
<head>
  <meta http-equiv="Refresh" content="0; URL=spring/home.jsp">
</head>
</html>
```

This index.html file simply redirects control over to Spring's MVC controller present at the application's /spring/ directory—see Listing 3-12's servlet mapping. Further, it makes a call to `home.jsp`, which per Spring-MVC behavior invokes the `home()` controller method, finally returning control and results to the `home.jsp` JSP presented earlier. Place the `index.html` file in Listing 3-16 directly inside the `src/GUI/ch3/` directory of the Hello World "playground."

Next, you need to create the OSGi manifest used by the web bundle. Listing 3-17 contains a snapshot of this file.

Listing 3-17. *`MANIFEST.MF` for the Web Bundle*

```
Bundle-Version: 1.0
Bundle-SymbolicName: com.apress.springosgi.ch3.web
Bundle-Name: HelloWorld Spring-OSGi Web
Bundle-Vendor: Pro Spring-OSGi
Bundle-Classpath: WEB-INF/classes

Import-Package: com.apress.springosgi.ch3.model;version="1.0.0",
 com.apress.springosgi.ch3.service;version="1.0.0",

 javax.servlet;version="2.5.0",
 javax.servlet.http;version="2.5.0",
 javax.servlet.resources;version="2.5.0",

 javax.servlet.jsp;version="2.0.0",

 javax.servlet.jsp.jstl.core;version="1.1.2",

 javax.servlet.jsp.jstl.fmt;version="1.1.2",

 javax.servlet.jsp.jstl.tlv;version="1.1.2",

 org.apache.taglibs.standard.functions;version="1.1.2",

 org.apache.taglibs.standard.resources;version="1.1.2",

 org.apache.taglibs.standard.tag.common.core;version="1.1.2",

 org.apache.taglibs.standard.tag.common.fmt;version="1.1.2",

 org.apache.taglibs.standard.tag.rt.core;version="1.1.2",

 org.apache.taglibs.standard.tag.rt.fmt;version="1.1.2",
```

```
 org.apache.taglibs.standard.tei;version="1.1.2",
 org.apache.taglibs.standard.tlv;version="1.1.2",
 org.springframework.aop;version="2.5.4",
 org.springframework.core;version="2.5.4",
 org.springframework.ui;version="2.5.4",
 org.springframework.stereotype;version="2.5.4",
 org.springframework.context.support;version="2.5.4",
 org.springframework.web.context;version="2.5.4",
 org.springframework.web.context.support;version="2.5.4",
 org.springframework.web.servlet;version="2.5.4",
 org.springframework.web.servlet.handler;version="2.5.4",
 org.springframework.web.servlet.mvc;version="2.5.4",
 org.springframework.web.servlet.view;version="2.5.4",
 org.springframework.web.bind.annotation;version="2.5.4",
 org.springframework.osgi.service.importer;version="1.2.0",
 org.springframework.osgi.web.context.support;version="1.2.0",
 org.springframework.osgi.service.importer.support;version="1.2.0"
Web-ContextPath: /
Bundle-ManifestVersion: 2
```

Besides the usual suspects used for naming and versioning, this bundle manifest makes extensive declarations in the `Import-Package` line and uses the `Bundle-Classpath` OSGi statement. The reason behind the extensive imports—even though the bundle contains one class—is that all these packages are needed to support Spring's MVC, JSP, and JSTL in a bundle, hence they need to be localized and activated by OSGi prior to starting this bundle. It's essentially OSGi's dynamic behavior at work telling the environment "I need to make use of the packages x, y, z. Please load them into memory now."

The `Bundle-Classpath` OSGi value is simply used as a convenience. Notice how its value is pointing to the `/WEB-INF/classes` directory, which is a standard location used by Java web applications to find classes. In this situation, you are indicating to OSGi that it instead should load its classes from that specific directory, allowing you to maintain the standard location used by Java web applications and yet still load the classes into the OSGi environment.

Finally, the `Web-ContextPath` header is a Spring-DM parameter used to indicate on what context path the web bundle (WAR) will be deployed on the OSGi'fied Apache Tomcat. In this case, the value / indicates the web bundle will be deployed on the root context (e.g., `http://localhost:8080/`). By default, if no `Web-ContextPath` header is declared, Spring-DM will deploy a web bundle (WAR) based on its name (e.g., a web bundle named `helloworld-web` would be deployed by default to `http://localhost:8080/helloworld-web/`).

As a last step, copy the OSGi manifest in Listing 3-17 to the `src/META-INF/ch3/` directory of the Hello World "playground." This does it as far as descriptors are concerned for the web bundle. It's time to put it all together and package our last application bundle.

The layout for our web bundle will look something like a hybrid between an OSGi bundle and a standard WAR. Listing 3-18 contains the additional instructions you need to add to your `ch3` Ant task in order to create this type of bundle.

Listing 3-18. *Ant Instructions for the Web Bundle*

```
<war destfile="${ch3.dir}/helloworld-web.war" webxml="${src.dir}/WEB-INF/ch3/➥
web.xml" manifest="${src.dir}/META-INF/ch3/web/MANIFEST.MF">
        <metainf dir="${src.dir}/META-INF/ch3/web/"/>
        <webinf dir="${src.dir}/WEB-INF/ch3/"/>
        <zipfileset dir="${src.dir}/GUI/ch3/" prefix=""/>
        <classes dir="${build.dir}">
           <include name="com/apress/springosgi/ch3/web/*"/>
        </classes>
</war>
```

■ **Caution** You need to ensure all compile dependencies for the web bundle are placed in the `lib` directory of your Hello World "playground," since a web bundle requires that its classes be compiled prior to packaging. If you skipped Chapter 2, you will need to copy the `spring-beans.jar`, `spring-webmvc.jar`, and `spring-context.jar` files, available in the `dist/modules` subdirectory of the Spring Framework's download, to the `lib` directory of the Hello World "playground."

These last Ant instructions make use of the `<war>` statement, indicating that a WAR package should be created using the `web.xml` and manifest files specified in the corresponding attributes, as well as placing all the contents located inside `${src.dir}/META-INF/ch3/web/` into the package's `META-INF` directory, all the contents inside `${src.dir}/META-INF/ch3/web/` into the package's `WEB-INF` directory, and all the contents inside `${src.dir}/GUI/ch3/` into the package's root directory, and finally copying all the classes inside the subdirectory `com/apress/springosgi/ch3/web/` to the package's `/WEB-INF/classes/` directory.

Initially you might be taken by surprise at the use of a `<war>` statement; after all, you will be deploying this as an OSGi bundle. As it turns out, there is nothing special about a WAR file in itself, it's simply a JAR file with a particular layout. And since an OSGi bundle is a JAR file equipped with special manifest, there is nothing wrong with using this Ant instruction for building purposes, because a WAR file is fully compatible as an OSGi bundle so long as it has its corresponding manifest.

If you place yourself in the Hello World "playground" root directory and execute `ant ch3`, the web bundle should be generated with the name `helloworld-web.war` and placed under the `dist/ch3` subdirectory.

With all three OSGi bundles composing the entire application on hand, it's time to take the final step in the form of deployment.

Deploying Spring-OSGi Bundles

With a running OSGi'fied Apache Tomcat container, as outlined in the section "Installing Apache Tomcat (OSGi'fied)" presented earlier in the chapter, deploying an application consists of two simple steps: loading the application's dependency bundles and later loading the actual application bundles.

Besides the dependencies required by applications themselves, using Spring and OSGi together always requires the presence of a certain set of bundles in order to operate correctly, many of which are simply OSGi'fied versions of the same libraries used in standard Spring applications, as well as those bundles that make up the Spring-DM.

The easiest approach to loading such libraries is by defining them in the startup sequence for the OSGi environment, a process that you already explored when you set up your OSGi'fied Apache Tomcat instance. Listing 3-19 shows the additional library bundles required by most Spring/OSGi applications.

Listing 3-19. *Spring-OSGi Dependencies Defined in the Eclipse Equinox* `config.ini`

```
tomcat/catalina.osgi-5.5.23-SNAPSHOT.jar@start, \

tomcat/catalina.start.osgi-1.0-20080425.161832-4.jar@start, \

springcore/com.springsource.edu.emory.mathcs.backport-3.0.0.jar@start, \
```

```
springcore/com.springsource.org.apache.commons.collections-3.2.0.jar@start, \

springcore/com.springsource.net.sf.cglib-2.1.3.jar@start, \

springcore/com.springsource.org.aopalliance-1.0.0.jar@start, \

springcore/org.springframework.core-2.5.4.A.jar@start, \

springcore/org.springframework.beans-2.5.4.A.jar@start, \

springcore/org.springframework.aop-2.5.4.A.jar@start, \

springcore/org.springframework.context-2.5.4.A.jar@start, \

springcore/org.springframework.context.support-2.5.4.A.jar@start, \

springcore/org.springframework.web-2.5.4.A.jar@start, \

springcore/org.springframework.web.servlet-2.5.4.A.jar@start, \

springcore/spring-osgi-io-1.2.0.jar@start, \

springcore/spring-osgi-core-1.2.0.jar@start, \

springcore/spring-osgi-extender-1.2.0.jar@start, \

springcore/spring-osgi-web-1.2.0.jar@start, \

springcore/spring-osgi-web-extender-1.2.0.jar@start

eclipse.ignoreApp=true

....
```

Caution All statements added to Eclipse Equinox's `osgi.bundles` parameter require a trailing backslash (\), except for the last one—prior to `eclipse.ignoreApp=true`. Ensure this syntax is enforced; otherwise Eclipse Equinox will not load these files at startup.

The listing starts off with four bundles supporting the operation of the Spring Framework, followed by seven bundles that form part of the Spring distribution (see Table 3-2 earlier in the chapter for the corresponding download links) with the five remaining bundles belonging to Spring-DM, libraries that can be located in the `dist` directory of this last package's download.

The last two loaded bundles in this sequence are special in the sense that they provide the functionality needed to inspect and process all bundles containing Spring-DM descriptors. If these two bundles are not active at the time a Spring-DM bundle is installed, a bundle will simply be loaded as a run-of-the-mill OSGi package with no Spring bean activation or service registration taking place.

Strictly speaking, the `spring-osgi-extender` bundle looks for a `spring` directory inside a bundle's `META-INF` directory, while the `spring-osgi-web-extender` bundle looks for a `.war` extension to recognize whether a bundle is to be wired with the underlying OSGi'fied application server/container (OSGi's `HttpService`); the next chapter will detail this particular process in depth.

Once you add these files to a subdirectory named `springcore` in the same directory as Eclipse Equinox's JAR file, and modify the `config.ini` file to reflect the new additions in Listing 3-19, execute `java -jar org.eclipse.osgi_3.5.0.v20080804-1730.jar -console`, and you will automatically initiate an Eclipse Equinox instance ready to accept and deploy Spring-OSGi bundles.

DON'T FORGET OSGI'S ROOTS!

A very important takeaway from this whole deployment process is that you can deploy many applications (bundles) relying on particular packages and have just one copy of each bundle take up system resources. Contrast this to the typical deployment of two or more standard WAR files in an application server. In all likelihood such files contain duplicate packages of some type, each consuming system resources equally, not to mention they leave the door completely open to potential class clashes if operating in the same WAR file.

It is also important that you recall that all bundles begin in an *installed* state that doesn't take up resources immediately either. It's only after another bundle requires a particular package that a bundle enters its *active* state and in turn takes up system resources.

In order to install the Hello World application bundles while inside an Eclipse Equinox session, simply perform the following instructions:

```
> install file:<dir_to_bundles>/helloworld-model.jar
> start <model bundle number assigned in last step>
> install file:<dir_to_bundles>/helloworld-service.jar
> start <service bundle number assigned in last step>
> install file:<dir_to_bundles>/helloworld-servicedao.jar
> start <servicedao bundle number assigned in last step>
> install file:<dir_to_bundles>/helloworld-web.war
> start <web bundle number assigned in last step>
```

Alternatively, you could also add four more declarations to Eclipse Equinox's `config.ini` file containing the application's bundles, allowing the Hello World application to be started automatically upon an Apache Felix session.

With all four Spring-OSGi Hello World application bundles started in the system, open up a browser and point it toward the URL `http://localhost:8080/`.

Once you do this, you will then be able to see an end-to-end application designed completely on Spring-OSGi principles.

Summary

In this chapter you learned how Spring and OSGi address complementary issues in the Java ecosystem, with both OSGi standing to gain from Spring's IoC/DI approach, and Spring benefiting from OSGi's dynamic-loading and versioning capabilities for the Java platform.

To support the integration of Spring and OSGi, you also learned about the various application layers that need to be attended to in order to support the integration of both platforms, which include application design, application packaging, and application server layers. The chapter further discussed how certain initiatives serve as aids in each corresponding layer, including Spring-DM, SpringSource Enterprise Bundle Repository, and SpringSource dm Server.

Additionally, you explored firsthand how to partition an application into numerous bundles, specifically model, service, and web bundles, learning how to package each one leveraging Spring-DM in order to expose each unit with the behavioral patterns present in both Spring and OSGi.

Finally, you learned how to deploy bundles in an OSGi environment accompanied by an OSGi'fied application server/container, therefore gaining experience on the process of deploying an end-to-end web-enabled OSGi application using Spring technology as the underlying Java framework.

CHAPTER 4

Spring Dynamic Modules for OSGi

Though you've already taken the Spring Dynamic Modules for OSGi (Spring-DM) for a test run in the last chapter, there is much more to be learned about the way this Spring subproject operates. In this chapter we will take the first big dive through the core parts that compromise Spring-DM.

You will likely come back here for future reference, since many of the remaining chapters that deal with more specific Spring-DM areas build on the concepts explained in the coming pages.

Extenders and Fragments in Spring-DM

Extenders and fragments are central pieces in Spring-DM. Though the terms sound somewhat esoteric, they really aren't, especially when you consider that you've already used one approach in the introductory Hello World Spring-DM application in Chapter 3.

The extender model[1] refers to the process of a bundle scanning another bundle's contents and performing an action on the scanned bundle's behalf. In the particular case of Spring-DM, the extender model signifies that when a certain extension is present in an OSGi manifest or a bundle's contents, Spring-DM should automatically trigger a chain of events.

The chain of events or action in Spring-DM is simple. In fact there is only one type of event: creating a Spring context, one that will serve a bundle throughout its life cycle for managing any Spring-related artifacts a bundle may possess, including a context that is designed around the special class type `OsgiBundleXmlApplicationContext`.

Any bundle deployed into an OSGi environment running Spring-DM will always be inspected for the presence of a Spring-DM trigger point. If such a trigger point is found, a bundle will automatically be assigned a Spring context of the `OsgiBundleXmlApplicationContext` class. If, on the other hand, no Spring-DM trigger

1. Peter Kriens, OSGi blog, "The OSGi Extender Model," `http://www.osgi.org/blog/2007/02/osgi-extender-model.html`

point is found in the bundle, Spring-DM logging will show the message "No application context created for bundle <bundle_name>"; scanning is still performed, but since no trigger point is found, no Spring context is created for the bundle.

In Spring-DM there are two types of extenders, those applicable to bundles using standard Spring artifacts, and those having to do with bundles using Spring web artifacts. The differences are subtle, but nevertheless very important, since in the web-bound case it implies the underlying bundle needs to be deployed as a web application.

But let's not digress just yet on these subtleties; let's explore the actual extensions in Spring-DM. Table 4-1 lists Spring-DM's extensions and the default trigger points that invoke the creation of a Spring `OsgiBundleXmlApplicationContext` context for a bundle.

Table 4-1. *Spring-DM Default Triggers for Creating Spring Context**

Trigger Point	Notes
Spring-DM Core Extender	
`/META-INF/spring/*.xml`	One or more XML files inside a bundle's `META-INF/spring` directory initiate the creation of a Spring context.
`Spring-Context` manifest value	This allows more granular control over the properties assigned to a Spring context. Table 4-2 contains such values.
Spring-DM Web Extender	
`.war` bundle extension	The presence of the `.war` extension to package a bundle indicates that it will be deployed as a web application.

* *CAUTION: It's critical to note that the corresponding Spring-DM extender bundles—*`spring-osgi-extender.jar` *and* `spring-osgi-web-extender.jar`*—need to be running in a system in order for these triggers to be detected.*

As you can now appreciate, you've already made use of the first and third type of Spring-DM trigger points when you placed Spring application descriptors inside the `/META-INF/spring` directory and made use of a `.war` extension in the introductory Spring-DM application in Chapter 3.

There is, however, a more powerful Spring-DM extender trigger point, one that allows you to override the default behaviors used to create a Spring application context and indicate alternative locations in which to locate Spring application descriptors. This trigger point comes in the form of a special OSGi manifest value named `Spring-Context`, which has the highest precedence of any Spring-DM trigger.

Table 4-2 describes the values available for the Spring-Context header, which has a syntax in the form Spring-Context:<alternate_spring_context_configuration_files>; <configuration_properties>.

Table 4-2. *Spring-Context OSGi Header Values*

Value	Description	Default Value	Example
<alternate_spring_context_configuration_files><alternate_spring_context_configuration_files>	Indicates a comma-separated list of bundle locations or files in which Spring-DM should attempt to locate Spring configuration files to build its context	Bundle-Context:*; Spring-Context:*; (meaning inspect the default Spring-DM location—/META-INF/spring/—for Spring configuration files)	Spring-Context:config/mycontext.xml; (meaning build a context from the Spring configuration file located in config/mycontext.xml)
create-asynchronously	Indicates the creation pattern—asynchronous or synchronous—for initializing Spring's context	Spring-Context:*; create-asynchronously:=true; (meaning create a context asynchronously with configuration files in the default location)	Spring-Context:*; create-asynchronously:=false; (meaning create a context synchronously with configuration files in the default location)
wait-for-dependencies	Specifies whether to wait for any service dependencies to be fulfilled before a Spring context is created	Spring-Context:*;wait-for-dependencies:=true; (meaning create a Spring context until all service dependencies have been fulfilled)	Spring-Context:config/*.xml; wait-for-dependencies:=false; (meaning create the context from files located under a bundle's config directory, without waiting for service dependencies to be fulfilled)
timeout	Indicates the time to wait (in seconds) for dependencies to be fulfilled, prior to giving up on the creation of a Spring context (Note: If wait-for-dependencies is false, this value is ignored.)	Spring-Context:*; timeout:=300; (meaning wait 5 minutes before giving up on locating dependencies and building the Spring context)	Spring-Context:*;timeout:=60; (meaning wait 1 minute before giving up on locating dependencies and building the Spring context)
publish-context	Specifies whether to publish the Spring context to the OSGi registry	Spring-Context:*; publish-context:=true; (meaning publish the actual Spring context as a service in the OSGi registry)	Spring-Context:config/*.xml;publish-context:=false; (meaning create the context from files located under a bundle's config directory, and don't publish the Spring context as a service in the OSGi registry)

While Table 4-2 presents the various values that can be overridden for creating a bundle's Spring context, you should be aware of certain design implications these values have. The following list contains a more exhaustive look at each option:

- **Alternative context configuration files**: If you're not keen on placing configuration files for Spring's context inside a bundle's `/META-INF/spring` directory, you are allowed to define alternative bundle locations from which a Spring context should take its configuration values. Note: If you define alternative configuration locations through `Spring-Context`, the default `/META-INF/spring` directory is ignored, unless explicitly specified.

- **Asynchronous vs. synchronous behavior**: By default, asynchronous behavior is used to instantiate a Spring context, allowing the generation to take place without blocking OSGi's event thread. Specifying synchronous behavior blocks OSGi's event thread until the creation of a bundle's Spring context is terminated. Though this behavior is often merited if a bundle has many Spring artifacts needed by other bundles, it's discouraged given its potential for deadlocks with bundles having interdependencies.

- **Dependency waiting**: This refers to whether the creation of a Spring context should await the resolution of OSGi services specified in Spring configuration context files. By default, Spring-DM always awaits dependency resolution. Further note that since asynchronous behavior is used by default when creating a Spring context, waiting for dependent services never locks a system.

- **Timeout**: The `timeout` value is used to set the timeout period before Spring-DM gives up on the localization of mandatory OSGi services and reports a failure creating a Spring context. In cases where Spring-DM bundles depend on services that are deployed in the same batch of bundles, or are services that take considerable time to be bootstrapped and registered, it's recommended to increment Spring-DM's default timeout.

- **Context publication**: Though a bundle's Spring context is always published as a service in OSGi's central registry, you may opt to avoid this process, thereby requiring context values to always be accessed through individually published services and not through the context itself.

With this I conclude describing the subject of Spring-DM extenders used to create Spring contexts. The remainder of this chapter will focus on the Spring configuration files associated with a bundle's context, which are primarily used for registering and locating services in OSGi's central registry. But before doing so, there is one more high-level OSGi concept worth elaboratingon: fragments.

A fragment's purpose in OSGi was originally to support internationalization (i18n) by allowing a bundle to introduce different country locales at deployment time, and thus avoiding the need to have multiple localized versions of the same bundle. In essence, a fragment is a bundle that is attached to a host bundle and is treated as part of the host, including any permitted headers.

This makes fragments an ideal solution for situations when a bundle's internal logic can't be modified or when a complete bundle upgrade is not an option. However, while *a fragment is itself a bundle*, there are certain limitations to using them in an OSGi environment.

For starters, a fragment can only add configuration information, classes, or resources to a host bundle; it cannot, however, have its own activator class or class loader like any standard bundle, giving fragments a second-class-citizen nature in OSGi. Nevertheless, they do provide an important function in Spring-DM, as will be illustrated at the end of this chapter in the section "OSGi fragments with Spring-DM" and in other sections of the book.

The way in which a fragment bundle is attached to a bundle is by means of an OSGi manifest header: `Fragment-Host`. If an OSGi environment encounters such a value at deployment time, it will immediately recognize it is dealing with a fragment bundle, and will attempt to attach the fragment in question to a host bundle, all based on matching the value specified in `Fragment-Host` to a host bundle's symbolic name.

In this manner, say you wanted to attach a fragment bundle to a bundle with a symbolic name `com.apress.osgi.ch4.service`. The way you would go about this process is by creating an OSGi bundle in the regular fashion and adding the OSGi manifest value `Fragment-Host:com.apress.osgi.ch4.service`; in this way the bundle would automatically become a fragment of the former bundle at deployment time. Note that a bundle's symbolic name is specified using the OSGi manifest header `Bundle-SymbolicName`.

Next, we will move on to exploring Spring-DM's process for registering services in OSGi's central registry, services that are made up of Spring artifacts created once a bundle's context is instantiated, and which will be made available to other OSGi bundles running in a system.

Registering OSGi Services Through Spring-DM

You can forget about the programmatic process of registering OSGi services illustrated in Chapter 1. Though programmatic registration is still an option in Spring-DM, the preferred process is using Spring context definitions, which are executed at the time a bundle's Spring context is created and are taken from Spring-DM's predefined or default trigger point locations.

In the last section, you learned that Spring-DM automatically processes any XML file located under a bundle's `/META-INF/spring/` directory. It turns out that located here are not only standard Spring configuration files containing beans and other artifacts that are eventually placed in a bundle's context, but also specific Spring-DM configuration files needed to register these same Spring artifacts as OSGi services.

Much like other Spring descriptors containing bean definitions, the process for registering OSGi services relies on the use of a specific namespace declared in the root element of an XML configuration file, which is illustrated in Listing 4-1.

Listing 4-1. *Spring-DM osgi Namespace Used in Spring Configuration Files*

```
<beans:beans
      xmlns="http://www.springframework.org/schema/osgi"
      xmlns:xsi="http://www.w3.org/2001/XMLSchema-instance"
      xmlns:beans="http://www.springframework.org/schema/beans"
      xsi:schemaLocation="http://www.springframework.org/schema/osgi http://www.s➥
pringframework.org/schema/osgi/spring-osgi.xsd
http://www.springframework.org/schema/beans
http://www.springframework.org/schema➥
/beans/spring-beans.xsd">

       <!-- OSGi service registration statements -->
</beans:beans>
```

Listing 4-1 demonstrates the use of Spring-DM's osgi namespace as a default namespace within a Spring configuration file, with the top-level beans namespace being further qualified through the beans prefix. Though you could easily add any other Spring namespace to support many more Spring artifacts in the same configuration file, it's a recommended practice to create separate configuration files for values pertaining to Spring and those for Spring-DM.

Given these conventions, having the Spring configuration files module-context.xml and osgi-context.xml inside a bundle's /META-INF/spring directory is standard practice. This process works because Spring-DM's extender automatically processes every file present in this last directory. Note that the naming convention used in these configuration files is open-ended, with each and every file with an .xml extension independent of its name being processed if it's present in a bundle's /META-INF/spring directory. See Table 4-2 on the use of Spring-Context to override this location.

Now that you are aware of the primary OSGi namespace used in Spring-DM configuration files, let's take a look at one of its first elements. Listing 4-2 contains an example of the service element used to register services.

Listing 4-2. *Basic Registration of an OSGi Service in Spring-DM*

```
<service ref="serviceBean" interface="com.apress.springosgi.FlightService"/>
```

This is the simplest declaration for registering a service in OSGi's central registry using Spring-DM. This statement registers a Spring bean with the ID `serviceBean` and associates its access through the `com.apress.springosgi.FlightService` interface.

In this case, it should be evident that in order for this process to take place, a bean with an ID value of `serviceBean` should be created using the traditional Spring approach and available in a bundle's Spring context. Additionally, the corresponding interface should also be available either in the bundle itself or for import from another bundle running in the system.

Even though this last service declaration implies the use of an interface to register a Spring bean's logic in an OSGi registry, you can also use an actual class representing a bean inside the `interface` attribute. However, be advised that this requires the use of CGLIB (Code Generation Library)[2] in a bundle in order to generate the corresponding interfaces at runtime—a process that may not work under certain circumstances, so it's best to use explicit interfaces whenever possible.

Under the hood, this Spring-DM registration process also has a few characteristics worth mentioning: a service is always registered with the property `org.springframework.osgi.bean.name` set to the value corresponding to the reference bean value, `ref`, and the defined bean itself is a `ServiceRegistration` object of the type `org.osgi.framework.ServiceRegistration`.

These are of course the basics behind the `<service>` element. Other variations allow more finer-grained registration processes to take place. Listing 4-3 illustrates one such variation used to register a multiple-interface service in Spring-DM.

Listing 4-3. *Multiple-Interface Registration of an OSGi Service in Spring-DM*

```
<service ref="serviceBean">
  <interfaces>
     <value>com.apress.springosgi.FlightService</value>
     <value>com.apress.springosgi.InFlightOperations</value>
     <value>com.apress.springosgi.GroundCrewOperations</value>
   </interfaces>
</service>
```

Since OSGi operates on the premise of interfaces, and Spring-DM creates a proxy via a `ServiceRegistration` object, which in turn delegates to the Spring bean itself. Some actions in a Spring bean may be inaccessible using a single interface. A multiple interface registration allows a service to expose operations contained in various interfaces that may belong to a backing Spring bean; though for the moment multiple interface registration may not seem significant, it will become so once you learn the lookup process for registered services. Figure 4-1 illustrates this concept.

---

2. CGLIB home page, `http://cglib.sourceforge.net/`. CGLIB OSGi bundle, `http://www.springsource.com/repository/app/search?query=cglib`

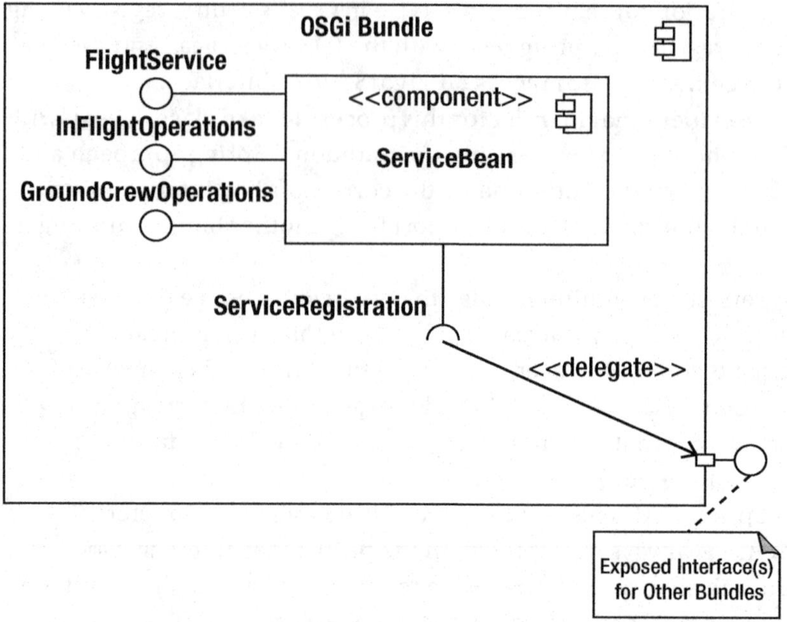

Figure 4-1. *Spring-DM proxy exposing service interface(s) for backing a Spring bean*

Additionally, on the same subject of published interfaces, Spring-DM also provides autodetection of interfaces through the use of the `auto-export` attribute. Table 4-3 contains the various values available for this `<service>` element attribute.

Table 4-3. *Spring-DM `auto-export` Attribute Values for the `<service>` Element*

auto-export Value	Behavior
`disabled`	(Default value) Indicates that no interface auto-detection will take place. Instead Spring-DM will rely on the use of an `interface` or `interfaces` declaration.
`interfaces`	Registers a service using the interfaces implemented by a bean.
`class-hierarchy`	Registers a service using its class and supertypes (if any).
`all-classes`	Registers a service using its class, supertypes (if any), plus all implemented interfaces by a bean.

Table 4-4 shows a grid with the different `auto-export` values and the service registration behaviors these values produce on a series of interface/class hierarchies.

While the use of `auto-export` facilitates the registration of services, you should be aware that there is a reason why this attribute is disabled by default. The main drawback to using autodetection is that it may unintentionally expose operations not intended to be registered or lack the proper registration of operations if the correct level is not chosen.

Table 4-4. *Spring-DM* `auto-export` *Registration Behaviors for Different Interface/Class Hierarchies*

Interface/Class Hierarchy	Disabled	Interfaces	class-hierarchy	all-classes
Stand-alone Interface A	None	Registers Interface A	None	Registers Interface A
Interface B extends Interface A	None	Registers Interface A and Interface B	None	Registers Interface A and Interface B
Stand-alone Class A	None	None	Registers Class A	Registers Class A
Class B extends Class A	None	None	Registers Class A and Class B	Registers Class A and Class B
Class C implements Interface B and extends Class B	None	Registers Interface A and Interface B	Registers Class C, Class B, and Class A	Registers Class C, Class B, Class A, and Interface A and Interface B

If you look at the grid illustrated in Table 4-4, you will note that the use of different `auto-export` values produces varying registration results depending on the underlying interface/class hierarchy used by a bean. For this reason, using explicit interface declarations is the preferred method since it provides much tighter control over what is exposed via OSGi's central registry.

Moving along to another `<service>` element variation, Spring-DM also supports the use of multiple service properties, this in addition to the default property assigned to a service via its reference name. Service properties, of course, become essential once a service needs to be located in an OSGi registry; nonetheless, they need to be declared at the moment a service is registered. Listing 4-4 illustrates how to associate additional service properties in Spring-DM.

Listing 4-4. *Additional Service Properties Used in the Registration of an OSGi service in Spring-DM*

```
<service ref="serviceBean" interface="com.apress.springosgi.FlightService">
 <service-properties>
    <beans:entry key="flight" value="ACMEAirlines"/>
    <beans:entry key="aports" value-ref="airportsBean"/>
 </service-properties>
</service>
```

In this listing, besides including the default `serviceBean` property created by Spring-DM, two more properties are declared using Spring's `<entry>` bean—notice the `beans:` prefix indicating these properties are not the default Spring-DM namespace used by `<service>`. The first is a service property in the form of a string using the `value` attribute, and the second a service property in the form of a Spring bean using the `value-ref` attribute, with both properties possessing a corresponding key for later reference.

It should be noted that the statements inside `<service-properties>` are not performing Dependency Injection (DI) like most nested declarations inside Spring declarations. The use of Spring's `<entry>` statements inside `<service-properties>` are just that, properties used to filter a service at the time it's looked up. The use of filtering and service lookup is addressed in the next section of the chapter.

On certain occasions, besides adding properties to a service that will be used in other bundles, you may need to reference a service locally for the purpose of DI. This allows the service to be used in some other Spring artifact declared in the same configuration file or Spring-DM context. Under these circumstances, you would go with the standard Spring practice of using an `id` attribute. Listing 4-5 shows this scenario.

Listing 4-5. *Registration of OSGi Service in Spring-DM with ID for Further Reference*

```
<service ref="serviceBean" id="flightServiceDM" interface="com.apress.springosgi.F➥
lightService"/>
```

This statement will make the service bound to the reference `serviceBean` Spring bean available under a value of `flightServiceDM`, making it further available for injection in other Spring constructs used in the same application context or configuration file; note that the `id` in this case will correspond to a `ServiceRegistration` object of the type `org.osgi.framework.ServiceRegistration`.

Using a reference for a service exported by the same bundle can cause application context creation to fail, due to either deadlock or timeout. Such behaviors—if presented—can be solved by overriding Spring-DM's default context characteristics using Spring-DM's directive `Spring-Context` presented earlier in Table 4-2.

The `<service>` element also allows a service to be registered using an anonymous bean. Instead of using the `ref` attribute as in all the previous listings to associate a backing Spring bean to an OSGi service, you could use an anonymous bean as illustrated in Listing 4-6.

Listing 4-6. *Registration of an OSGi Service in Spring-DM Using an Anonymous Bean*

```
<service interface="com.apress.springosgi.FlightService">
   <bean:bean class="com.apress.springosgi.FlightServiceDAO">
   </bean>
</service>
```

As you can see, anonymous beans simply provide a shortcut for linking a bean to a service, and this is the preferred approach when a bean instance will be of use to one and only one service.

Another variation to the `<service>` element, which given the asynchronous nature of Spring-DM can prove to be essential, is the `depends-on` attribute. As its name implies, `depends-on` is used to indicate prerequisite elements needed before registering a service, ensuring that any explicit bean dependencies required by a service are fully constructed prior to registering a service. Listing 4-7 shows the use of this attribute.

Listing 4-7. *Spring-DM depends-on Attribute Used in Registration of an OSGi Service*

```
<service ref="serviceBean" interface="com.apress.springosgi.FlightService" ➥
depends-on="groundCrewBean"/>
```

Further adding to the <service> element's attributes we find ranking, whose value is used to indicate a priority grade among OSGi services. The ranking attribute, which takes an integer value, is used as a qualifier when two or more services possessing the same interfaces are looked up in OSGi's central registry. Under such circumstances, an OSGi registry will return whatever service was registered with the highest ranking value.

The ranking attribute is fully supported according to the OSGi specification. But generally speaking, when it's known that two or more services will be registered using the same interface, a more robust approach would be to use service properties—as outlined in Listing 4-4.

Continuing to explore the <service> element, you'll find the context-class-loader attribute, which is used to define the visibility available through a class loader. By default, the context-class-loader attribute in a <service> element has a value of unmanaged, indicating that only those resources available in a class loader will be utilized.

The relevance to altering context-class-loader's default value to that of service-provider—which is the other available value—arises when a service makes special use of resources that may become invisible to a consuming bundle given OSGi's more stringent class-loading approach. By using the service-provider value, Spring-DM ensures that the consuming bundle has full access to all the resources available in the host bundle—the one providing the service—without the consuming bundle requiring extra provisions.

Finally, on the matter of registering services in Spring-DM, we will discuss two more subjects, one related to the way backing Spring beans are created in Spring-DM, and the other to the actual registration and unregistration phases undergone by a Spring-DM service.

By default, all backing Spring beans supporting an OSGi service are created with a global scope, global in the sense that there is only one bean instance for all clients making use of a service. In order to support a more granular approach though, Spring-DM also provides access to the widely known Factory pattern used in enterprise software.

In essence, what the Factory pattern in Spring-DM provides is a way to associate an individual Spring bean instance to each client bundle accessing an underlying service. In order to use this technique, a Spring bean needs to be scoped within a bundle, as illustrated in Listing 4-8.

Listing 4-8. *Spring-DM Bundle-Scoped Bean Used in Registration of an OSGi Service*

```
<bean:bean id="serviceBean" scope="bundle" class="com.apress.springosgi.Flight➥
ServiceImpl"/>
<service ref="serviceBean" interface="com.apress.springosgi.FlightService"/>
```

Notice how the underlying Spring bean used within the <service> statement employs the attribute scope="bundle". Under this scenario, a Spring bean instance would be created for each client bundle accessing a service, with the same bean being destroyed once a client bundle is stopped.

While we're on the subject of creating and destroying artifacts, Spring-DM also offers hooks into the standard OSGi listeners used to execute instructions when a service is registered and unregistered. Registration and unregistration of services is linked to the activation and stoppage of bundles, which are two of the life-cycle states an OSGi bundle goes through; OSGi's bundle life cycle is described in Chapter 1 and illustrated in that chapter's Figure 1-2.

Providing such support is the `<registration-listener>` element, which needs to be nested within a `<service>` element itself.

The `<registration-listener>` specifies the execution of certain Spring bean methods through the attributes `registration-method` and `unregistration-method`, with the values for each attribute corresponding to methods contained in either a referenced or anonymous bean within a Spring-DM configuration file. Listing 4-9 demonstrates the former approach, while Listing 4-10 shows the latter.

Listing 4-9. *Spring-DM Listener Used in the Registration of an OSGi Service*

```
<service ref="serviceBean" interface="com.apress.springosgi.FlightService">
<registration-listener ref="runwayBean"
registration-method="preTakeoff"
unregistration-method="postTakeoff">
</service>
```

Listing 4-10. *Spring-DM Listener with an Anonymous Bean Used in the Registration of an OSGi Service*

```
<service ref="serviceBean" interface="com.apress.springosgi.FlightService">
<registration-listener
registration-method="preTakeoff"
unregistration-method="postTakeoff">
 <bean class="com.apress.springosgi.FlightServiceRunway"/>
</registration-listener>
</service>
```

Notice how each `<service>` element nests a `<registration-listener>` element with a corresponding method to be executed once a service is registered and unregistered. These methods, in order to preserve OSGi compatibility, need to possess a signature like either one presented in Listing 4-11.

Listing 4-11. *Spring-DM Signatures for Listeners in the Registration of an OSGi Service*

```
public void methodName(ServiceType serviceInstance, Map serviceProperties);
public void methodName(ServiceType serviceInstance, Dictionary serviceProperties);
```

In this last listing, ServiceType represents a compatible element with the interface belonging to the service being registered or unregistered, and Map and Dictionary represent basic Java constructs containing properties used inside the registration/unregistration method.

This concludes coverage of all the service registration issues related to Spring-DM. Up next, we will explore the complementary process of locating registered services using Spring-DM.

Locating OSGi Services Through Spring-DM

Much like the registration process for OSGi services in Spring-DM, the localization process for OSGi services can be done programmatically; nevertheless, the preferred method in Spring-DM is to use application descriptor elements.

While Spring-DM registration relies on the use of a single element named <service>, Spring-DM localization makes use of three elements: <reference>, <list>, and <set>. Let's start by exploring the most basic lookup sequence available in Spring-DM, the one illustrated in Listing 4-12.

Listing 4-12. *Spring-DM Lookup of an OSGi Service*

```
<reference id="serviceBean" interface="com.apress.springosgi.FlightService"/>
```

This sequence looks up a service backed by an interface with the value defined in the corresponding attribute, and instantiates a backing Spring bean in a bundle's context with an ID value of serviceBean. Note that this is an exact reversal of the registration sequence presented in Listing 4-2 and Figure 4-1.

Similarly, the <reference> element also supports the use of multiple interfaces for locating and importing a service into another bundle. Listing 4-13 shows the use of multiple interfaces for locating an OSGi service using Spring-DM.

Listing 4-13. *Spring-DM Lookup of an OSGi Service with Multiple Interfaces*

```
<reference id="serviceBean">
  <interfaces>
      <value>com.apress.springosgi.FlightService</value>
      <value>com.apress.springosgi.InFlightOperations</value>
      <value>com.apress.springosgi.GroundCrewOperations</value>
   </interfaces>
</service>
```

In this scenario, a Spring bean named serviceBean is created within a bundle's context supporting the declared interfaces, which of course need to be found as registered OSGi services. It's important to note that communication between a bundle looking up a Spring bean—the consumer—and a bundle providing such a backing bean—the provider—is always done via proxy, which then delegates to the actual Spring bean. This proxy concept was illustrated earlier in Figure 4-1.

On a related note, the same use of interface statements in a `<service>` element apply to those in a `<reference>` element. The `<interfaces>` tag cannot be used in conjunction with the `interface` attribute, and in case the imported service is bound to an actual class, the presence of CGLIB is required within a bundle so the interfaces can be generated at runtime.

If you prefer a finer-grained approach to querying an OSGi service by its interfaces, you can rely on the use of the actual name employed by a backing bean, as well as any other properties assigned to a service upon registration.

Recall that Spring-DM automatically registers a service with a property type `org.springframework.osgi.bean.name` set to the value corresponding to the reference bean, making such a value a valid lookup property. Listing 4-14 illustrates this process via the `bean-name` attribute.

Listing 4-14. *Spring-DM Lookup of an OSGi Service Using* `bean-name`

```
<reference id="lookedUpserviceBean" interface="com.apress.springosgi.Flight➥
Service" bean-name="serviceBean"/>
```

This declaration will create a proxy to a Spring bean backed by a service with the `FlightService` interface, having been created with a bean named `serviceBean`. However, don't be misled by what is a shortcut notation in Spring-DM: `bean-name` is simply an abbreviated version for looking up a specific service property in the form of a bean's name.

Using the `bean-name` property is often discouraged, since it introduces tight coupling between the bundles. The preferred method is to use a service's explicit properties, like those illustrated and assigned previously in Listing 4-4. In order to look up such properties, you require a more general approach offered by the `filter` attribute, which is presented in Listing 4-15.

Listing 4-15. *Spring-DM Lookup of an OSGi Service Using* `filter` *Based on Properties*

```
<reference id="serviceBean" interface="com.apress.springosgi.FlightService">
 filter="(flight=ACMEAirlines)"/>
```

This statement will instantiate a Spring bean backed by a service reference possessing the `FlightService` interface that has a property named `flight` with a value named `ACMEAirlines`.

Having explored the use of interfaces and filters in the `<reference>` element, you may have one obvious question regarding Spring-DM's lookup process: what happens if the OSGi registry has more than one registered service matching the specified query?

According to the OSGi specification, Spring-DM returns the service with the highest `ranking` attribute value matching a lookup, and if more than two services possess the same interface as well as `ranking` value, then the one with the lowest service ID, which will likely always be the first registered service, in the OSGi registry is returned. Although using a unique service property for each registered service is sufficient to guarantee that one and only one service is returned on a Spring-DM lookup, the Spring-DM elements `<list>` and `<set>` are used precisely for circumstances in which a lookup sequence will knowingly return and require two or more matching services. However, before delving into the use of `<list>` and `<set>`, let's finish looking at the available attributes in the `<reference>` element.

Like its registration counterpart, the `<reference>` element also has `depends-on` and `context-class-loader` attributes. The `depends-on` attribute functions in pretty much the same way, guaranteeing that a certain Spring bean is already present in a bundle's context prior to performing a service lookup; however, the `context-class-loader` attribute has a small variation from how it's used in a `<service>` element.

When used in the context of looking up a service, the `context-class-loader` attribute can take any one of the values `client`, `service-provider` and `unmanaged`, with the default value being `client`. This is in contrast to the Spring-DM service registration process, where the same attribute has a default value of `unmanaged` and only one alternative value of `service-provider`.

The addition of the `client` attribute value for this particular instance is required because a service lookup entails the coordination of resources that may be present in both a consuming bundle and a providing bundle. Thus the `client` attribute guarantees that the context class loader is able to see types on the class path of the invoking bundle during the service invocation

Rounding off the attributes available in the `<reference>` element, we come to the `cardinality` attribute. If you're not too familiar with the term "cardinality," in Spring-DM it has a very simple meaning: cardinality indicates either a service is mandatory or optional.

By default, a `<reference>` element has a cardinality value of `1..1`, indicating a service lookup must be successful prior to creating a Spring bean with the associated service. On the other hand, a cardinality value of `0..1` indicates that a service reference is optional and that a Spring bean may be created immediately without fulfilling its service dependencies.

Complementing the `cardinality` attribute, you will find the `timeout` attribute, which is used to indicate the time in seconds that Spring-DM should wait before giving up on resolving a service reference for creating a Spring bean. By default this timeout is set to 300 seconds (5 minutes).

A few of the attributes just described can be configured globally for every statement pertaining to Spring-DM lookup elements. Listing 4-16 illustrates how this process works in a Spring-DM configuration file.

Listing 4-16. *Spring-DM Global Default Values for Lookup of an OSGi Service*

```
<beans xmlns="http://www.springframework.org/schema/beans"
       xmlns:xsi="http://www.w3.org/2001/XMLSchema-instance"
       xmlns:osgi="http://www.springframework.org/schema/osgi"
           osgi:default-timeout="5000"
           osgi:default-cardinality="0..X">

  <reference id="flightService" interface="com.apress.springosgi.FlightService"/>

  <reference id="nightlyFlightService" interface="com.apress.springosgi.Nightly➥
FlightService"
        timeout="1000"/>

<list id="cargoFlightServices" interface="com.apress.springosgi.CargoFlight➥
Service" cardinality="1..N"/>

</beans:beans>
```

■ **Note** Default cardinality for all OSGi references (singular or collection) elements that do not explicitly specify one, are the following: The default value is `1..X` (resolved to `1..1` for `osgi:reference` and `1..N` for `osgi:list/set`), which means that a backing service must exist (this is a mandatory service reference). A value of `0..X` (resolved to `0..1` for `osgi:reference` and `0..N` for `osgi:list/set`) indicates that it is acceptable to have no backing service (an optional service reference).

This listing declares Spring-DM's lookup properties using the `osgi` namespace inside the configuration file's root element, overriding the default timeout value to `5000` seconds and changing the default cardinality to an optional service value of `0..X`. By using such statements, these values will take effect for every Spring-DM lookup statement made in the configuration file, unless further overridden by their in-line attributes, in which case the attribute values take precedence.

Moving along through Spring-DM's element arsenal, you will find the `<list>` and `<set>` elements, both of which are closely related to the `<reference>` element. Whereas all three elements are used to locate OSGi services using Spring-DM, it's the `<list>` and `<set>` elements that are designed to retrieve more than one service matching a predetermined interface or filter.

`<list>` and `<set>` support the same attributes used by the `<reference>` element, which include `interface`, `filter`, `bean-name`, `cardinality`, and `context-class-loader`. Each of these attributes behaves in exactly the same manner as its single service matching counterpart; however, the dynamics to using `<list>` and `<set>` are somewhat different, and I'll elaborate why.

Let's start off by exploring the differences between `<list>` and `<set>`—after all, if both support the retrieval of multiple services, when should you use one rather than the other? The semantics behind the `<list>` and `<set>` elements are rooted in the Java Collections Framework interfaces of the same names, which makes the selection process in tune with the same behavior of the former framework.

In very simplified terms, the `<set>` element should be used when a group of retrieved services needs to be pruned of elements possessing object equality, a characteristic of the `Set` interface in the Java Collections Framework, in which no two equal objects can form part of the same `Set`. On the other hand, the `<list>` element should be used under circumstances in which all retrieved services need to be accounted for, whether they possess object equality or not. (See the sidebar "<list>, <set>, and the Java Collections Framework" for more background on the Java Collections Framework.)

<LIST>, <SET>, AND THE JAVA COLLECTIONS FRAMEWORK

The `<list>` and `<set>` elements are based on the principles of the Java Collections Framework, a general-purpose framework introduced in Java SE 1.4 (`http://java.sun.com/docs/books/tutorial/collections/index.html`).

The Java Collections Framework sets forth a series of well-known interfaces and classes, each with its own set of specific behaviors, all designed to easily manage groups of objects in the Java language. It's an extensive topic to say the least, with some books written entirely on this subject alone, so I won't even attempt to elaborate on its workings.

In Spring-DM, though, you really need to familiarize yourself with two aspects of the Java Collections Framework. One involves the `List` and `Set` interfaces—understanding how these interfaces behave and how object equality is determined in sets, giving way to the shedding of certain elements in sets and not necessarily in lists.

The second aspect is the ordering of objects in the Java Collections Framework, a subject that proves to be important since Spring-DM services can be sorted either in their natural order or using a special comparator class, a topic rooted in the Java Collections Framework itself.

The Spring beans generated by both the `<list>` and `<set>` elements are different from those instantiated by the unitary `<reference>` element, with one bean having a `java.util.List` type and the other a `java.util.Set` type. Additionally, both rely on the use of other Java Collections constructs like `Iterator` to access specific services within a collection, with this latter manipulation taking place inside the Java Beans that will make use of such services.

Still, without resorting to Java code and within the confines of Spring-DM's configuration file, it's possible to apply a sorting strategy for a collection of services using the `<comparator>` element. Listing 4-17 illustrates the first case scenario for this element.

Listing 4-17. *Spring-DM Sorting Services in Natural Order for Lookup of OSGi Services*

```
<list id="flightServices" interface"com.apress.springosgi.FlightService">
  <comparator><natural-ordering basis="services"/></comparator>
</list>

<set id="nightlyFlightServices" interface="com.apress.springosgi.FlightService">
  <comparator><natural-ordering basis="service-references"/></comparator>
</set>
```

The first-case scenario for the `<comparator>` element makes further use of the `<natural-ordering>` element, which as its name implies uses the natural ordering algorithm employed by the Java Collections Framework. Further, notice that Spring-DM can perform the natural ordering of services based on two values, one on `service-references` and the other on the `services` themselves.

The second-case scenario for the `<comparator>` element relies on the creation of a special class of the type `java.util.Comparator`, which is used as the basis for sorting a collection of services. Though you will need to refer to the Java Collections Framework for building such a class, Listing 4-18 illustrates how to use the `<comparator>` element through this approach.

Listing 4-18. *Spring-DM Sorting Services Based on the* `Comparator` *Class for Lookup of OSGi Services*

```
<set id="flightServices" interface="com.apress.springosgi.FlightService"
  comparator-ref="flightComparator"/>

<list id="nightlyFlightServices"
  interface="com.apress.springosgi.NightlyFlightService">
  <comparator>
     <beans:bean class="nightlyFlightComparator"/>
  </comparator>
</list>
```

Much like the natural ordering mechanism, which has two variations, using a custom-made comparator class also has two alternatives: one in which a comparator class is instantiated as a Spring bean and associated through the `comparator-ref` attribute directly inside a `<set>` or `<list>` element, and a second option in which the comparator is instantiated anonymously inside the `<comparator>` element.

The benefit to using the `<comparator>` element in any capacity is that the desired sorting strategy for a group of services is performed without the need to do so with in-line code inside a POJO.

Additionally, both the `<set>` and `<list>` elements provide another special Spring-DM attribute named `greedy-proxying`, one that grants access to all the underlying classes and interfaces used by a group of services; this is specially important in the context of a collection of services, given the various interfaces that may be supported.

Take for example Listing 4-19, which illustrates the use of the greedy-proxying attribute.

Listing 4-19. *Spring-DM Greedy Proxying for Lookup of OSGi Services*

```
<set id="flightServices" interface="com.apress.springosgi.FlightService"
  greedy-proxying="true"/>
```

At first sight, the use of greedy-proxying might seem inconsequential, but take a look at Listing 4-20, which illustrates what can be done inside a POJO using such a collection of service-backed beans.

Listing 4-20. *Spring-DM Greedy Proxying Consuming a POJO Iterator*

```
for (Iterator iterator = services.iterator(); iterator.hasNext();) {
        FlightService service = (FlightService) iterator.next();
        service.runwayOperation();
        // If the service implements additional type, execute more logic
        if (service instanceof ACMEFlight) {
                ((ACMEFlight)service).sendRunwayClearance();
        }
}
```

Were it not for the use of the greedy-proxying attribute, the iterator over the set of services would have no knowledge of any other service interface, hence the utility of such an attribute when looking up multiple services via Spring-DM.

With this, I've practically covered all the variations used in the primary elements for looking up services in Spring-DM; however, I have yet to cover one important aspect specifically linked to OSGi, the event listeners related to services referenced via <reference>, <set>, and <list>.

Similar to the <registration-listener> element used to execute instructions once an OSGi service is registered or unregistered, Spring-DM offers the same capability when a service is bound or unbound through any of its lookup elements.

A binding operation in Spring-DM takes place when a Spring bean reference is initially bound to a backing service, as well as when such a backing service is replaced by a new service. Similarly, in the context of service collections—<set> or <list>—a binding operation takes place each time a service is added to a group.

On the other hand, an unbinding operation in Spring-DM takes place each time a backing service is unregistered and no replacement service is available. Similarly, in the context of service collections—<set> or <list>—an unbinding operation takes place each time a service is unregistered and removed from the group.

In order to respond to such events in Spring-DM, a special bean needs to be created and associated through the `<listener>` element, which then has to be nested in either a `<reference>`, `<set>`, or `<list>` element. Listing 4-21 shows this process.

Listing 4-21. *Spring-DM Event Listener for Binding and Unbinding of a Service*

```
<reference id="flightService" interface="com.apress.springosgi.FlightService">
  <listener ref="flightListenerBean"/>
</reference>
```

In this last listing the bean `flightListenerBean` represents a bean implementing the Spring-DM interface `org.springframework.osgi.service.importer.OsgiServiceLifecycleListener`, which by doing so will contain the methods `bind` and `unbind`. These methods will be invoked when a backing Spring bean is bound to and unbound from its underlying service, respectively.

Additionally, Spring-DM also supports the use of custom `bind` and `unbind` methods as an alternative mechanism to this last interface; under these circumstances, the listener methods need to be declared through attributes inside the `<listener>` element, with the associated bean nested inside this latter element. Listing 4-22 shows this process.

Listing 4-22. *Spring-DM Custom Event Listener Methods for Binding and Unbinding of a Service*

```
<reference id="flightService" interface="com.apress.springosgi.FlightService">
  <listener bind-method="onBind" unbind-method="onUnbind">
   <beans:bean class="flightListenerBean"/>
  </listner>
</reference>
```

In this case, the `bind-method` and `unbind-method` attributes point toward the method names that will be invoked once the binding and unbinding process take place, methods that are contained in the bean referenced within the nested `<bean>` statement. It should also be pointed out that such custom method listeners need to conform to certain signatures set forth by OSGi, signatures that are illustrated in Listing 4-23.

Listing 4-23. *Spring-DM Signatures for Listeners in Lookup of OSGi Services*

```
public void methodName(ServiceType serviceInstance, Map serviceProperties);
public void methodName(ServiceType serviceInstance, Dictionary serviceProperties);
public void methodName(ServiceType serviceInstance);
```

Like the listener signatures described for Spring-DM's service registration process, the `ServiceType` class represents an interface for a matching service interface, while the `Map` and `Dictionary` instances are used to pass properties to the underlying method's logic.

Finally, there is one more technique that needs to be addressed while on the subject of accessing a registered service in OSGi via Spring-DM: annotations.

Instead of instantiating a Spring bean through the use of a `<reference>`, `<list>`, or `<set>` element inside a Spring configuration file and later injecting it into a `<bean>` statement, a Spring-DM-backed OSGi service can be instantiated and injected directly inside a POJO using annotations, Listing 4-24 presents this approach.

Listing 4-24. *Injecting a Spring-DM Service Reference Using Annotations*

```
import org.springframework.osgi.extensions.annotation.ServiceReference

public class AirportBeanClass {

  @ServiceReference
  public void setFlightService(FlightService airService) {

  }

}
```

When Spring-DM encounters the annotation `@ServiceReference` in a bundle class, it automatically attempts to locate a service with an interface corresponding to the setter method decorated with the annotation. In the case of Listing 4-24, it will attempt to locate a service with the `FlightService` interface and inject it directly into the Java class representing a Spring bean.

If required, the `@ServiceReference` annotation also supports the same attributes as its XML counterparts used to alter the default lookup process; values like `cardinality`, `contextClassLoader`, `filter`, `serviceBeanName`, `serviceTypes`, and `timeout` can all be specified as parameters inside parentheses alongside the annotation.

This concludes the subject of locating services in OSGi using Spring-DM. The next section will discuss one more area related to Spring-DM: the management of bundles themselves.

OSGi Bundle Activities with Spring-DM

Just as you explored the registration and lookup of services in OSGi, Spring-DM also has support for interacting directly with the higher-level units in the OSGi framework: bundles. Through Spring-DM statements, you can also perform all the standard OSGi actions available to bundles, such as installing or updating them at any given time.

Supporting the interaction of bundles in Spring-DM configuration files is the `<bundle>` element. Listing 4-25 shows the most basic statement making use of this element.

Listing 4-25. *Spring-DM Bundle Reference*

```
<bundle id="acmeBundle" symbolic-name="com.apress.springosgi.ACMEAirlines"/>
```

This statement will instantiate a Spring bean of the type `org.osgi.framework.Bundle`, taken from a system bundle having a symbolic name `com.apress.springosgi.ACMEAirlines` (recall that a bundle's symbolic name is defined in its OSGi manifest).

By itself, the declaration in Listing 4-25 only serves to inject a given bundle into another Spring statement in the configuration file; however, the `<bundle>` element also supports other attributes.

One such attribute is `action`, which is used to change a bundle's state when a host bundle's Spring context is created. In Spring-DM the same bundle actions as employed in any other OSGi environment are supported: `start`, `update`, `stop`, and `uninstall`.

Additionally, Spring-DM also supports an attribute named `destroy-action`, which takes the same values as its `action` counterpart; however, `destroy-action`'s changes in state are processed once a host bundle's Spring context is destroyed.

And last but not least, the `<bundle>` element makes use of the `location` attribute, whose value is used to indicate the physical location of a bundle and which is necessary to perform both installation and update actions on a bundle. Listing 4-26 shows a more comprehensive example of Spring-DM's `<bundle>` element.

Listing 4-26. *Spring-DM Bundle Installation*

```
<bundle id="acmeBundle"
location="http://www.apress.com/springosgi/bundles/ACMEAirlines.jar"
symbolic-name="com.apress.springosgi.ACMEAirlines"
action="start"/>
```

This statement installs and starts the bundle located in the corresponding `location` value, and assigns it an ID of `acmeBundle` for further reference within the Spring configuration file.

Next, we will explore another concept related to Spring-DM that has close ties to the management of bundle: fragments.

OSGi Fragments with Spring-DM

At the start of the chapter, you learned about OSGi fragments and how they are used to add information to a bundle without disturbing its preexisting structure. Additionally, at the outset you also learned about OSGi extenders, which are patterns used to automatically fire off a chain of events and on which Spring-DM relies to process a bundle's Spring-DM configuration files.

As it turns out, the two bundles that provide Spring-DM with its extender capabilities—`spring-osgi-extender.jar` and `spring-osgi-web-extender.jar`—can easily be modified using fragments.

Using OSGi fragments to modify Spring-DM's extender bundles requires that a fragment bundle follow certain rules. However, before exploring such rules, it's important to know the actual Spring-DM values that can be modified through fragments.

Spring-DM's extenders make use of beans to expose values that can be modified via fragments, and since there are two Spring-DM extenders, you need to familiarize yourself with two sets of bean values. Table 4-5 presents the first set corresponding to the core `spring-osgi-extender.jar`.

Table 4-5. *`spring-osgi-extender.jar` Bean Values Exposed for Fragments*

Bean Name	Type	Function	Default Value
`task-executor`	`org.springframework.core.task.TaskExecutor`	Creates and runs the Spring application contexts associated with each bundle. The task executor is responsible for managing its own pool of threads used by the application contexts.	`org.springframework.core.task.SimpleAsyncTaskExecutor`
`shutdownTaskExecutor`	`org.springframework.core.task.TaskExecutor`	Destroys managed Spring application contexts associated with each bundle. The task executor is responsible for managing its own pool of threads used by the application contexts.	`org.springframework.scheduling.timer.TimerTaskExecutor`
`applicationEventMulticaster`	`org.springframework.context.event.ApplicationEventMulticaster`	Propagates Spring-DM events to third parties.	`org.springframework.context.event.SimpleApplicationEventMulticaster`
`applicationContextCreator`	`org.springframework.osgi.extender.OsgiApplicationContextCreator`	Allows customization of the application context created by the extender. This includes changing the application context class type or additional processing. (See info on `OsgiBeanFactoryPostProcessor` in the next entry.)	The extender default behavior applies.

Table 4-5. *spring-osgi-extender.jar Bean Values Exposed for Fragments (Continued)*

Bean Name	Type	Function	Default Value
N/A	org.springframework.osgi.extender.OsgiBeanFactoryPostProcessor	Similar to Spring's BeanFactoryPostProcessor interface, beans of type OsgiBeanFactoryPostProcessor are automatically detected and applied to all contexts created by the extender (whether user defined or not). This type of post processor is useful as it allows customization of the bean factory such as adding/removing/changing existing bean definitions or adding new bean instances.	The extender default behavior applies.
extenderProperties	java.util.Properties	Defines simple properties.	See the following property names.
Property Name for extenderProperties	**Type**	**Function**	**Default Value**
shutdown.wait.time	java.lang.Number	The amount of time the extender will wait for each application context to shut down gracefully. Expressed in milliseconds.	10000 ms (10 seconds)
process.annotations	java.lang.Boolean	Flag indicating whether or not the extender will process Spring-DM annotations.	false

Additionally, the spring-osgi-web-extender.jar extender has its own set of beans, presented in Table 4-6.

Knowing what bean values can be modified in both Spring-DM's extender bundles using fragments, let's explore the actual structure a bundle fragment needs to adhere to in order to modify these bean values.

Upon deployment of a bundle fragment, Spring-DM will automatically inspect a bundle's /META-INF/spring/extender/ folder for the presence of a descriptor containing any declaration with the beans outlined in Table 4-5 or Table 4-6. And upon processing such a configuration file, Spring-DM will automatically use the new bean values for its extenders.

Table 4-6. *`spring-osgi-web-extender.jar` Bean Values Exposed for Fragments*

Bean Name	Type	Function	Default Value
`warDeployer`	`org.springframework.osgi.web.deployer.WarDeployer`	Installs OSGi bundles as web applications. The deployer takes care of locating the required web container and installing and uninstalling web applications.	`org.springframework.osgi.web.deployer.tomcat.TomcatWarDeployer`
`contextPathStrategy`	`org.springframework.osgi.web.deployer.ContextPathStrategy`	Determines the context path associated with an OSGi bundle/WAR. The returned path is used by the war deployer to install the war application.	`org.springframework.osgi.web.deployer.support.DefaultContextPathStrategy`

To illustrate this concept further, let's create two fragments to modify Spring-DM's extender bundles, one to activate the processing of Spring-DM annotations and another to modify the default target web container used by Spring-DM.

Listing 4-24 illustrated that Spring-DM could make use of annotations to inject service references into POJOs; however, by default this behavior is disabled in Spring-DM's extender, `spring-osgi-extender.jar`, to avoid the scanning overhead. In order to modify this behavior, a fragment or inclusively a dedicated bean post processor could be used. Next I will illustrate the fragment approach.

The first thing that needs to be created is a `MANIFEST.MF` file that will accompany the bundle fragment. Listing 4-27 illustrates the syntax for a `MANIFEST.MF` file used to create a fragment targeting Spring-DM's core extender.

Listing 4-27. *OSGi Manifest for a Fragment Used on Spring-DM's `spring-osgi-extender.jar`*

```
Manifest-Version: 1.0
Bundle-ManifestVersion: 2
Fragment-Host: org.springframework.bundle.osgi.extender
Bundle-SymbolicName: com.apress.springosgi.ch4.fragment
Bundle-Name: HelloWorld Spring-OSGi Fragment
Bundle-Description: Spring-DM Fragment for activating OSGi annotation scanning
```

The most important part of this `MANIFEST.MF` file is the `Fragment-Host` directive, which tells the OSGi environment it's dealing with bundle fragment. The value `org.springframework.bundle.osgi.extender` indicates the fragment is targeted at a bundle with that symbolic name, which in this case corresponds to Spring-DM's `spring-osgi-extender.jar` bundle.

This same MANIFEST.MF file would be used for any fragment attempting to modify the bean values presented in Table 4-5. But what about the bean values? Where are they located? Listing 4-28 shows the descriptor used in a fragment to activate Spring-DM's annotation processing.

Listing 4-28. *Spring-DM Descriptor for Activating Annotation Processing*

```
<?xml version="1.0" encoding="UTF-8"?>
<beans xmlns="http://www.springframework.org/schema/beans"
   xmlns:xsi="http://www.w3.org/2001/XMLSchema-instance"
   xsi:schemaLocation="http://www.springframework.org/schema/beans
       http://www.springframework.org/schema/beans/spring-beans.xsd">

   <bean id="extenderProperties">
      <property name="process.annotations" value="true"/>
   </bean>
</beans>
```

Notice this last listing is a standard Spring descriptor using the bean namespace to define the extenderProperties bean and assign it a property named process.annotations with a value of true. Such values are Spring-DM's exposed bean values, which were presented previously in Table 4-5. The only thing special about this descriptor is where it needs to be placed, which is under a bundle's /META-INF/spring/extender/ directory.

Listing 4-29 illustrates the final layout for the bundle fragment targeting Spring-DM's spring-osgi-extender.jar bundle.

Listing 4-29. *Spring-DM Extender Layout*

```
+META-INF+
         |--MANIFEST.MF
         |
         +-spring-+
                  |
                  +-extender-+
                             |--annotation-activator.xml
```

The bundle's layout simply contains the MANIFEST.MF file (Listing 4-27) and the corresponding descriptor used to modify Spring-DM's core extender bundle (Listing 4-28). Once this bundle fragment is deployed, Spring-DM will be capable of performing annotation scanning for service references.

Caution Apache Felix, used in Chapter 1 and Chapter 3, ***does not support fragments***. If your Spring-DM projects require fragments as outlined here or in other parts of this book, you will need to use another OSGi environment like Eclipse Equinox or Knopflerfish. Progress on support for fragments in Apache Felix can be found at `https://issues.apache.org/jira/browse/FELIX-29`.

Using a fragment to modify Spring-DM's other extender, `spring-osgi-web-extender.jar`, is very similar. Listing 4-30 illustrates the `MANIFEST.MF` file used in fragments targeting this last extender.

Listing 4-30. *OSGi Manifest for Fragments Used on Spring-DM's `spring-osgi-web-extender.jar`*

```
Manifest-Version: 1.0
Bundle-ManifestVersion: 2
Fragment-Host: org.springframework.bundle.osgi.web.extender
Bundle-SymbolicName: com.apress.springosgi.ch4.fragment
Bundle-Name: HelloWorld Spring-OSGi Fragment
Bundle-Description: Spring-DM Fragment for activating OSGi annotation scanning
```

Similar to the earlier extender `MANIFEST.MF` file, the `Fragment-Host` directive is the most important part. However, note that the value in this last listing points toward `org.springframework.bundle.osgi.web.extender`, which is the symbolic name corresponding to Spring-DM's `spring-osgi-web-extender.jar` bundle.

This same `MANIFEST.MF` file would be used for any fragment attempting to modify the bean values presented in Table 4-6. Listing 4-31 shows the descriptor used in a fragment to modify the underlying OSGi'fied application server used by Spring-DM to deploy WAR files.

Listing 4-31. *Spring-DM Descriptor for Using the Jetty Web Container As Spring-DM's OSGi'fied Application Server*

```
<?xml version="1.0" encoding="UTF-8"?>
<beans xmlns="http://www.springframework.org/schema/beans"
   xmlns:xsi="http://www.w3.org/2001/XMLSchema-instance"
   xsi:schemaLocation="http://www.springframework.org/schema/beans
      http://www.springframework.org/schema/beans/spring-beans.xsd">

    <bean id="warDeployer">
        class="org.springframework.osgi.web.deployer.jetty.JettyWarDeployer" />
    </bean>
</beans>
```

Notice the same use of Spring's standard bean namespace to define the warDeployer bean and assign it a class named org.springframework.osgi.web.deployer.jetty.JettyWarDeployer. This bean value is taken from Table 4-6, which contains Spring-DM's web extender bean values. Identical to the earlier fragment, this descriptor needs to be placed inside a bundle's /META-INF/spring/extender/ directory.

Listing 4-32 illustrates the final layout for a bundle fragment targeting Spring-DM's org.springframework.bundle.osgi.web.extender bundle.

Listing 4-32. *Spring-DM Extender Layout*

```
+META-INF+
         |--MANIFEST.MF
         |
         +-spring-+
                  |
                  +-extender-+
                             |--jetty-deployer.xml
```

The bundle's layout simply contains the MANIFEST.MF file (Listing 4-30) and the corresponding descriptor used to modify Spring-DM's web extender bundle (Listing 4-31). Once this fragment bundle is deployed, Spring-DM will use the Jetty web container as the underlying OSGi'fied application server to deploy its WAR files.

Summary

In this chapter you learned the core concepts behind Spring-DM, starting off with the meaning and functionality offered by extenders and fragments, with the former allowing the inspection and processing of Spring configuration files inside OSGi bundles and the latter providing the necessary mechanisms to add extra logic to preexisting bundles.

You also explored how each Spring-DM-powered bundle makes use of a special context throughout its life cycle, in which it manages all its related Spring artifacts, which can range from a bundle's own local Spring beans, to any Spring beans instantiated from OSGi services imported via Spring-DM.

Additionally, you also learned all the valid Spring-DM statements that can be used inside Spring configuration files, including how a Spring bean can be registered as an OSGi service for consumption by other bundles, how these same services can be reincarnated as Spring beans inside bundles, as well as statements related to the management of bundles themselves via Spring-DM.

Finally, you learned how to use fragments targeting both Spring-DM extender bundles, creating fragments to activate the use Spring-DM annotation processing and to override the default web container used by Spring-DM to process WAR files.

CHAPTER 5

SpringSource dm Server

So far you've experienced the benefits of building Spring applications using the Spring-DM framework, taking advantage of things like versioning and cleaner tier separation between the components that make up an application.

The adaptation process for using Spring-DM has required you to incorporate new design techniques for enterprise applications. This process is probably something you've become accustomed to, since continuous design enhancements are normal in the software industry. However, there is one aspect to using Spring-DM that, whatever your individual design efforts, falls outside your control: deployment.

Though an OSGi'fied servlet container has served as a deployment solution up to this point, using such an environment can be problematic. The first and foremost difficulty with an OSGi'fied application server/container is that you need to put it together, unlike Java EE servlet containers that can be installed in a few clicks.

Since an OSGi'fied servlet container works in coordination with an OSGi environment, this requires additional steps beyond those needed to install each part—steps you took in the Spring-DM Hello World application presented in Chapter 3.

Even assuming you achieved dexterity in putting together an OSGi'fied servlet container, it still leaves other issues you have to contend with, such as the following: What happens to all those old WAR files? Do you OSGi'fy them just to run on a new environment? Or do you run a parallel Java EE servlet container just for this purpose?

We pondered a few of these questions in Spring-DM's integration layers back in Chapter 3. It's time to further explore the answers to these questions, familiarizing yourself with the most versatile option for deploying Spring-DM applications: the SpringSource dm Server.

Benefits

Created by the company behind the Spring Framework, the SpringSource dm Server makes Spring-DM work in a more streamlined fashion with the established practices used in Java EE application servers/containers and OSGi technology. This includes integrated deployment and monitoring for Java applications using OSGi, backward compatibility for applications using the standard WAR servlet container format, and a company to support the formal development of a joint Java/OSGi platform, among other things.

Still, with products driven by standards like Java EE and OSGi, it can be hard to make a switch to a new product, since many products are rightfully marketed as Java EE *compatible* servlet containers or OSGi v.4.0 *compatible*. So what are the benefits of using the SpringSource dm Server? Let's explore them one by one.

OSGi Deployment in the Enterprise

OSGi technology presents new challenges to the way Java EE applications are deployed. Simply using bundles as a deployment format is the beginning of a long road that needs to be traveled to give OSGi applications the same feature set offered in Java EE applications.

You will recall that OSGi environments are used to underpin things as small as a smartphone, IDE, or some other Java application. This creates a void for a particular set of features that have become the norm in Java EE applications and which the SpringSource dm Server addresses:

- **Shared repository**: Java EE applications mostly depend on the same set of staple JARs, with application servers/containers providing a location in which these JARs can be shared across applications. The SpringSource dm Server offers a similar approach for OSGi bundles, providing a shared repository visible to all bundles running in a system, allowing these same shared bundles to fulfill JAR dependencies present in WAR files. Additionally, the SpringSource dm Server's shared repository also reduces the need to manually install every single bundle in a system, since each repository bundle is automatically installed at startup and activated once another bundle requires it for dependency fulfillment.

- **OSGi library definitions**: Java EE application libraries tend to be made up of various JAR files—think web frameworks or ORMs made up of five to ten JAR files. However, when these JAR files undergo OSGi'fication, their use requires a bundle to import library packages or bundles individually. The SpringSource dm Server supports a special bundle library statement, simplifying the way libraries are imported into consuming OSGi bundles. So instead of importing packages or bundles through multiple `Import-Package` or `Require-Bundle` headers, the same results can be achieved using a single library import statement supported by the SpringSource dm Server.

- **OSGi application packaging and service scoping**: OSGi's bundle and class loader approach may seem like it can do no wrong, but it can become unmanageable under certain circumstances. Java EE's application deployment units—Enterprise Archives (EARs) or Web Archives (WARs)—provide good cues for what can become unmanageable in OSGi as explained next.

EAR and WAR files package entire applications, making each of them a single-step deployment unit. OSGi applications, on the other hand, are made up of numerous bundles, each one requiring individual deployment. This lack of aggregation format in OSGi can make the management of more than one application difficult, requiring all bundles to be processed one by one, for either installing, uninstalling, or updating an application.

Similarly, EAR and WAR files provide class isolation for running multiple applications on the same application server/container. While it's true that OSGi's class-loading approach supersedes the need for this type of isolation, OSGi introduces its own isolation problem with services.

Since a majority of OSGi bundles either publish or use services, there is potential for service conflicts when more than one application is deployed on the same OSGi environment. If Application A uses a service named UserName, and Application B uses its own service named UserName, what happens then? If service scoping is not used, Application A can end up using Application B's service, or vice versa.

To solve these packaging and service scoping problems, the SpringSource dm Server defines a logical application unit named Platform Archive (PAR).

Next, we come to another set of benefits conferred by the SpringSource dm Server. These have to do with the integration issues related to Spring, OSGi, and Java.

Spring, OSGi, and Java Integration

The Spring Framework in combination with some of Java EE's parts requires certain integration support that doesn't sort well with OSGi environments in their out-of-the-box state. This makes the SpringSource dm Server a good provider for resolving such integration issues.[1]

Weaving is widely used with the Spring Framework and Java EE. In the introductory Spring application presented in Chapter 2, there were a few instances in which weaving classes were used to support the Java Persistence API and Apache Tomcat.

The problem with weaving in an environment like OSGi is that it tends to occur in groups of classes, especially in cases like those using JPA, which is common in enterprise applications. This creates a problem since it can't be guaranteed that every class requiring weaving is placed in the same bundle. If classes requiring weaving are placed in different bundles, cross-bundle weaving, as well as update propagation, is troublesome since each bundle has its own class loader.

Weaving modifies all classes that match a given pointcut. In a non-OSGi environment this has no major consequences, since applications use a single class loader. But what happens in OSGi, where applications are partitioned into bundles, each having its own class loader?

1. Rob Harrop, *Running Spring Applications on OSGi with the SpringSource Application Platform*, `http://blog.springsource.com/main/2008/05/02/running-spring-applications-on-osgi-with-the-spring-source-application-platform/`

In such cases, weaving cannot be applied easily, requiring OSGi's default class loader to be equipped to handle this type of cross-bundle weaving.

The SpringSource dm Server takes care of these weaving issues, guaranteeing that a refresh performed on a bundle that contains an aspect is propagated to all those bundles needing weaving (e.g., if more than one bundle makes up a design using JPA, which requires weaving, propagation is taken care of by the SpringSource dm Server). The SpringSource dm Server also comes preconfigured with an OSGi environment supporting weaving.

Another problem with out-of-the-box OSGi environments is their lack of support for certain resource protocols common in Java EE applications. A resource protocol is the prefix added to a configuration file or Java class, qualifying a resource of a certain type.

Resource protocols like `file:` or `jar:` are not detected in OSGi environments by default. This makes applications, JARs, or classes relying on such conventions inoperable in OSGi. The SpringSource dm Server uses a special adapter that makes an OSGi environment's classpath aware of such resources.

Another thing that gives problems in OSGi is Java's thread-context class loader. Many Java EE applications rely on Java's thread-context class loader to inspect class types or resources. In OSGi, this scenario can create a problem due to how Java's context class loader operates.

Java's context class loader is always associated with a thread; therefore, a context class loader might fail to load classes from packages that are not directly imported into a calling bundle. This is a *very subtle* problem that tends to occur when any bundle class uses a construct like `Class.forName()` that employs Java's context class loader for localization.

As a consequence, if a bundle attempts to locate class types or resources via Java's thread-context class loader, it will only be able to do so in the bundle itself. The SpringSource dm Server addresses this by creating a special thread-context class loader that imports all packages used in an application, and then replacing it with the original thread-context loader. This process makes all class types and resources visible—whether located in the bundle itself or in other bundles that form part of an application's PAR file.

■ **Note** In addition to the SpringSource dm Server addressing this context class loader issue in OSGi, the Eclipse foundation—producers of the Equinox OSGi framework—also offer a solution to this process via *buddy class loading*. However, it should be mentioned that this is a custom-made solution usable only in Eclipse Equinox. More information on buddy class loading can be found at `http://wiki.eclipse.org/index.php/Context_Class_Loader_Enhancements`.

Other features supported in the SpringSource dm Server to make the integration of Spring, OSGi, and Java easier include JavaServer Pages (JSP) support, Tag Library Descriptor (TLD) scanning, which is used in the JSP Standard Tag Library (JSTL), annotation matching, and resource lookups.

Next, we will take a look at another SpringSource dm Server benefit, this one related to legacy Java EE applications.

Java EE Native and Shared Library WAR Support

The SpringSource dm Server offers native WAR support, just like any other Java EE server/container. This backward compatibility with older WAR files is beneficial since it allows preexisting Java EE applications to coexist with OSGi applications.

For example, the standard WAR file containing a Spring application, presented in Chapter 2, can simply be executed on the SpringSource dm Server and be accessible instantly. There is no need to incorporate OSGi or Spring-DM, or make any other changes. All details are taken care of by the SpringSource dm Server, including Spring's load-time weaving support, which is a requirement for Java EE native WAR files.

Getting a little closer to the full advantages of OSGi technology, the SpringSource dm Server also supports Shared Library WARs. A Shared Library WAR allows the SpringSource dm Server to use its shared bundle repository to fulfill a WAR's dependencies.

Instead of a WAR loading its library dependencies (JARs) from the standard `/WEB-INF/lib` directory, libraries are taken from the SpringSource dm Server shared bundle repository. This makes a WAR file not only smaller in size, but also a contributor to reducing overall memory usage, since a WAR uses Shared Library instances.

There is one other small variation to a Shared Library WAR, as well as another web packaging format exclusive to the SpringSource dm Server. These subjects, including a more detailed look at WARs in the SpringSource dm Server, will be discussed in the "Deployment Units" section of the chapter.

Next, we will explore the last group of benefits offered by the SpringSource dm Server.

Tooling and Administration Support

Creating OSGi bundles in a simple text editor can be tedious. Tracking dependencies needed by various bundles in a similar environment can be downright complicated. Add to this the constant back-and-forth process of writing, testing, and then deploying bundles onto an OSGi'fied servlet container, and you're looking at a very time-consuming process. All these steps can be speeded up using the right tools.

The SpringSource dm Server can be integrated through a set of plug-ins with the Eclipse IDE. This not only supports the development of bundles due to the fact that classpath dependencies are resolved based on the manifest entries, but also automates the deployment of bundles into an OSGi'fied servlet container to a few simple clicks in applications undergoing development, allowing developers to stay within their tool of choice.

OSGI IDE SUPPORT

The SpringSource dm Server aside, making use of an IDE for OSGi development can be a very good investment toward reducing development time. Currently, the primary Java IDE supporting OSGi is the Eclipse IDE (`http://www.eclipse.org/downloads/`).

The Eclipse IDE includes Equinox—the OSGi environment you used in other parts of the book. In Eclipse's case, Equinox is used to *build and run* the IDE; however, this does not preclude using Equinox to develop OSGi applications.

Additionally, you may find some plug-ins offered for the same Eclipse IDE useful in the development of your Spring and OSGi applications:

- **Spring IDE plug-in**: Spring IDE is a graphical interface for editing and managing the configuration files used by applications designed around the Spring Framework (`http://springide.org/`).
- **Eclipse Knopflerfish plug-in**: Knopflerfish is an OSGi environment, like Eclipse Equinox or Apache Felix. This plug-in allows OSGi development in Eclipse using Knopflerfish as the backing OSGi environment (`http://www.Knopflerfish.org/eclipse_install.html`).
- **Eclipse ProSyst plug-in**: ProSyst provides additional support for developing OSGi applications on Eclipse (`http://dz.prosyst.com/oss/`).

All Java EE application servers/containers have a central location where you can install and monitor the state of applications. The SpringSource dm Server provides a similar solution focused on applications using OSGi.

The SpringSource dm Server's administrative interface offers a central location in which to manage all deployed bundles, WARs, Shared Library WARs, Web Modules, and PARs. Additionally, it includes support for managing diagnostic information generated by applications, including logging, trace, and dump files.

Having covered the benefits of the SpringSource dm Server, let's move a little deeper into the subject and discuss the main concepts you will encounter in the platform, as well as its overall architecture.

Concepts and Architecture

The first thing you need to realize about the SpringSource dm Server is that it's not an entirely new product written from scratch. The SpringSource dm Server is a *stack* made up of parts that would otherwise be present in many Spring, Java EE, and OSGi projects. These parts are presented in Table 5-1.

Table 5-1. *SpringSource Application Platform Parts*

Software	Function
Spring	Provides the Spring Framework's core functionality
Apache Tomcat	Serves as the Java servlet container
OSGi (Eclipse Equinox)	Serves as the OSGi environment
Spring-DM	Provides the capabilities to use Spring with OSGi features
SpringSource Tool Suite	Provides an Eclipse (as in the IDE) powered development environment for the platform
SpringSource Application Management Suite	Provides a centralized location to manage and monitor all applications running on the platform

With the exception of the last two entries in Table 5-1, all the parts that make up the SpringSource dm Server are components used in either Spring, OSGi, or Java EE applications. So what makes the SpringSource dm Server special if it's just a collection of parts? That can be answered by looking at Figure 5-1.

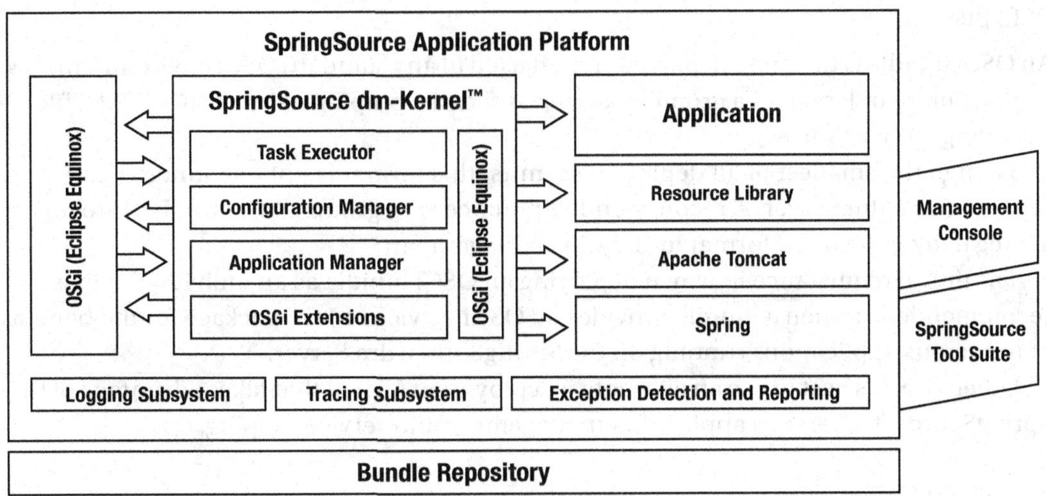

Figure 5-1. *SpringSource Application Platform architecture*

In this figure, notice how the same parts mentioned in Table 5-1 are present; however, also notice those additional features, under the SpringSource dm-Kernel, that lie between the parts enumerated in the table. These squares are specially designed pieces that make the SpringSource dm Server deliver on all the benefits presented at the start of the chapter, and this is what makes the platform convenient compared to putting in these same parts yourself.

As a user of the SpringSource dm Server, you will never have to deal directly with any of the individual parts that make up the platform, much less any of these features that hold the platform together. Nevertheless, it's important to know how the SpringSource dm Server is composed prior to performing actions from its administrative console.

In fact, that's all you will do upon using the SpringSource dm Server: deploy and manage everything through web-based interfaces—or through a command-line interface.

But let's not get ahead of ourselves; you will see and use these interfaces in the Hello World application presented later in the chapter. Right now, it's important for you to understand the terminology used in the SpringSource dm Server, so let's start by expanding the deployment unit concepts used in the SpringSource dm Server.

Deployment Units

The SpringSource dm Server supports four major deployment unit formats. They range from the minimum common denominator OSGi bundle, capable of being deployed on any stand-alone OSGi environment, to the PAR format, which takes full advantage of the SpringSource dm Server's architecture.

OSGi Bundle

An OSGi bundle is the same deployment unit used in any standard OSGi environment. It's nothing more or less than a group of Java class files accompanied by a `MANIFEST.MF` file including OSGi headers.

Though the smallest of all deployment units, this format is not encouraged in the SpringSource dm Server. A recommended practice is to group OSGi bundles into an aggregated deployment format to simplify management.

The only circumstance in which deploying an OSGi bundle as an individual unit is recommended is when a bundle provides an OSGi service or Java package for the benefit of numerous applications running on the SpringSource dm Server.

Otherwise, it's best to use an alternative deployment format that takes advantage of the SpringSource dm Server's application management and service scoping.

Java EE WAR

Java EE's WAR format is supported in two different forms in the SpringSource dm Server: a completely backward-compatible Java EE version and a more OSGi-friendly version.

Standard Java EE WAR

This deployment unit is completely backward compatible with Java EE servlets/containers. This means the SpringSource dm Server creates a space consisting of a separate application class loader, loading classes from a WAR's `/WEB-INF/lib` and `/WEB-INF/classes/` directories, and performing all the other bootstrapping tasks undergone by application servers/containers.

Support for this format is good since it allows you to keep deploying Java EE and Spring applications the way you always have. However, this format makes you lose out on all the benefits offered by OSGi, since this type of unit is deployed in its own sandbox, isolated from every other class running in the system.

Using WARs in such a way should be strictly reserved for cases in which it's not possible to migrate applications to the more OSGi-friendly WAR format illustrated next.

Shared Library/Services WAR

Easing the transition to a more OSGi-friendly WAR format is the Shared Library/Services WAR. This deployment unit is identical to the WAR format used in Chapter 3 to illustrate the use of Spring-DM.

By "shared," I mean that this type of WAR is capable of leveraging both OSGi bundles and services. Not only does this reduce the size and memory footprint of a standard WAR, it also grants a WAR's classes access to services present in an OSGi environment.

The first difference from a standard WAR is that this deployment unit has a `MANIFEST.MF` file with OSGi directives. This allows it to import packages from other OSGi bundles using the `Import-Package` manifest header, thus ceasing to use isolated classes located in the standard `/WEB-INF/lib` and `/WEB-INF/classes` directories inside WARs.

The second functionality offered by this deployment unit is its ability to access OSGi services via Spring-DM. This eliminates the sandbox in which standard WARs operate, allowing the contents of a WAR to access logic outside of its packaging confines.

This deployment unit is no doubt a step forward toward OSGi. However, it still contains remnants used in WAR files, which is why the SpringSource dm Server also defines its own Web Module deployment format.

Web Modules

A Web Module is the recommended approach for deploying web-enabled units in the SpringSource dm Server. For all practical purposes, a Web Module is the next best thing to a Shared Library WAR, just as a Shared Library WAR is better than a standard Java EE WAR.

Even in a Shared Library/Services WAR, there are certain configuration aspects like servlet mappings, JSTL libraries, context paths, filters, and Spring Model-View-Controller (MVC) values that need to be placed in the descriptors like `web.xml` and `*-servlet.xml` used in WARs.

A Web Module is the SpringSource dm Server's answer to configuring a web-bound unit entirely through a `MANIFEST.MF` file with OSGi directives. This eliminates the last trace of a WAR structure in the form of XML configuration files.

Therefore, in a SpringSource dm Server Web Module you can expect to see the same configuration values used in configuration files like `web.xml`, `*-servlet.xml`, or others placed in a WAR's `/WEB-INF/` directory, directly supported inside a bundle's manifest.

Next, I will describe the last deployment unit in the SpringSource dm Server: Platform Archive.

Platform Archive

Platform Archive serves as the building block for deploying entire applications in the SpringSource dm Server. A PAR not only facilitates the grouping of bundles to streamline application installation, but also offers application isolation. Application isolation is critical for various cases outlined earlier, such as service name clashes, weaving, bundle refreshes, and Java's thread-context class loader.

A PAR scopes OSGi services, making them visible only in the same deployment unit. This eliminates any possibility of name clashes, if more than two applications using the same service name, but different logic, are deployed on the platform.

A PAR also forms a boundary, applying load-time weaving and bundle refreshes to all bundles contained in the deployment unit. This guarantees that weaving and refreshes aren't performed indiscriminately to all bundles running a system.

Additionally, all bundles contained in a PAR have their exported packages assigned to a synthetic bundle, which is used for thread-context class loading. This ensures that any lookup for class types or resources—for example, `Class.forName()`—is found across any bundles belonging to an application.

The composition of a PAR is made of bundles—referred to as *modules* in the platform—and a special `MANIFEST.MF` file that includes OSGi headers just like the ones presented in Listing 5-1.

Listing 5-1. *Platform Archive `MANIFEST.MF` File*

```
Manifest-Version: 1.0
Application-SymbolicName: com.apress.springosgi.ch5.HelloWorld
Application-Version: 1.0
Application-Name: HelloWorld SpringSource dm Server
Application-Description: A Hello World Platform Archive for Pro-Spring OSGi
```

The use of this OSGi manifest allows a PAR to have its own identity, both in terms of versioning and naming, similar to all OSGi bundles. The directory structure of a PAR will be explored in the Hello World application presented later in the chapter.

Next, we will take a look at another feature offered by the SpringSource dm Server: libraries.

Libraries

A library is a common concept in Java EE applications, but in a non-OSGi environment, using libraries is never given much thought. All JARs that make up a library are declared in Java's `CLASSPATH` variable, and any class needing the library automatically has access to it.

In an OSGi application these same JARs belonging to a library need to undergo OSGi'fication—adding a `MANIFEST.MF` file with OSGi headers—thereby splitting up a library to benefit from OSGi's dynamic loading. This process unfortunately creates overhead for classes needing libraries.

For a class contained in an OSGi bundle to use a library, it needs to import its packages to bundles individually via OSGi's `Import-Package` or `Require-Bundle` manifest header. While this import granularity is beneficial in some circumstances, it can become overwhelming if a bundle requires multiple libraries. Listing 5-2 shows a bundle manifest importing part of the Spring Framework library.

Listing 5-2. *OSGi Manifest Using `Import-Package` to Import a Library*

```
Import-Package: org.springframework.util,org.springframework.beans.factory.xml,➥
org.springframework.aop,org.springframework.aop.framework,org.aopalliance.aop
```

Note that this manifest is only *part* of the Spring Framework library. Extrapolate this to a bundle requiring the entire Spring Framework library, an Object-Relational Mapping (ORM) library, or some other library, and you have a very long and error-prone process given the sheer number of values.

The SpringSource dm Server optimizes this process by supporting a special library manifest header in an OSGi environment. Therefore, a bundle—or module as it is referred to in the SpringSource dm Server—would only require a one-line statement as illustrated in Listing 5-3.

Listing 5-3. *OSGi Manifest Using the `Import-Library` Header Interpreted by the SpringSource Application Platform*

```
Import-Library: org.springframework.spring
```

Isn't this easier than using OSGi's `Import-Package` or `Require-Bundle` manifest? A library in the SpringSource dm Server is a *logical grouping of bundles,* so it's not something that you need to package separately. A library takes its contents from OSGi'fied JARs deployed as stand-alone bundles.

The way to define a SpringSource dm Server library is through a simple text file with a `.libd` extension, using OSGi type headers. Listing 5-4 shows a SpringSource dm Server library definition.

Listing 5-4. *SpringSource Application Platform Library Definition*

```
Library-SymbolicName: org.springframework.spring
Library-Version: 2.5.4
Library-Name: Spring Framework
Import-Bundle: org.springframework.core;version="[2.5.4,2.5.5)",
 org.springframework.beans;version="[2.5.4,2.5.5)",
 org.springframework.context;version="[2.5.4,2.5.5)",
```

```
org.springframework.aop;version="[2.5.4,2.5.5)",
org.springframework.web;version="[2.5.4,2.5.5)",
org.springframework.web.servlet;version="[2.5.4,2.5.5)",
org.springframework.jdbc;version="[2.5.4,2.5.5)",
org.springframework.orm;version="[2.5.4,2.5.5)",
org.springframework.transaction;version="[2.5.4,2.5.5)",
org.springframework.context.support;version="[2.5.4,2.5.5)",
org.springframework.aspects;version="[2.5.4,2.5.5)",
com.springsource.org.aopalliance;version="1.0"
```

Notice how `Library-Symbolic-Name` is employed to assign the key identifier for other bundles using the `Import-Library` header. Additionally, notice how a library has its own versioning header, as well as a common name used as a more friendly identifier.

Note as well the special `Import-Bundle` manifest header—also unique to the SpringSource dm Server—which is used to declare bundles that make up a library. In this case, all the bundles declared in Listing 5-4 correspond to the Spring Framework library, with each part deployed as an individual bundle.

Next, the discussion will turn toward the last conceptual subject on the SpringSource dm Server, its directory structure.

SPRINGSOURCE DM SERVER IMPORT-BUNDLE VS. OSGI'S REQUIRE-BUNDLE

Library definitions for the SpringSource dm Server use a custom header named `Import-Bundle`, which associates the contents of an entire bundle in a single statement to a library. At first glance, this last header might look strikingly similar in functionality to OSGi's standard `Require-Bundle` header; nevertheless they are different.

The semantics behind OSGi's standard `Require-Bundle` allow it to support split packages, whereas the SpringSource dm Server `Import-Bundle` header avoids the complexities of split packages.

Additionally, given the foreseeable evolution of the SpringSource dm Server, it was decided to create the custom `Import-Bundle` header to support any future enhancements required by the SpringSource dm Server—a process that also allows OSGi's standard header `Require-Bundle` to maintain its same semantics, whether used in bundles deployed inside or outside the SpringSource dm Server.

You can find more information on the reasoning behind this design and other custom manifest headers used by the SpringSource dm Server at `http://blog.springsource.com/2008/05/08/springsource-application-platform-manifest-headers/`.

Directory Structure

The layout for the SpringSource dm Server consists of various subdirectories, each with a specific purpose as outlined in the following list:

- `bin`: Contains the SpringSource dm Server's scripts to start and stop the platform on Unix and Windows environments, as well as set the system's Java `CLASSPATH`.
- `config`: Contains all the configuration files affecting the SpringSource dm Server, which include those for Apache's Tomcat container, Eclipse's OSGi Equinox environment, and the SpringSource dm Server itself.
- `docs`: Contains both a users and programmers guide for using the SpringSource dm Server.
- `lib`: Contains Java libraries required to bootstrap the SpringSource dm Server.
- `licenses`: Contains the various licenses applicable to components used in the SpringSource dm Server.
- `pickup`: Is used as a "hot" location in which to place WARs, Shared Library WARs, Web Modules, or PARs, and have the SpringSource dm Server automatically deploy each unit at startup.
- `serviceability`: Contains diagnostic information generated by the SpringSource dm Server, which is further collocated in the following directories:
    - `dump`: Contains data snapshots occurring when a failure in SpringSource dm Server code or thread deadlock is detected. Note: This information is not intended for end-user consumption but for SpringSource dm Server service personnel.
    - `logs`: Contains low-volume logs of important events in the SpringSource dm Server—like startup, shutdown, and application deployment—as well as the application visitor logs generated by Apache Tomcat inside the `access` subdirectory.
    - `trace`: Contains application-generated output. This includes output generated by logging and tracing APIs, as well as output generated by calls to Java's `System.out` and `System.err`.

- `work`: Is used by the SpringSource dm Server to place its running application classes and configuration file snapshots. The naming convention and purpose is identical to the directory by the same name used in stand-alone Apache Tomcat installations and is not intended to be modified by end users.

- `repository`: Contains the various bundles and libraries used by the SpringSource dm Server, providing a complementary role to the top-level `pickup` and `lib` directories. The `repository` directory is further split to accommodate resources into either the `bundles`, `libraries`, or `installed` directories, which in themselves are subdivided according to the following list:

  - `repository/bundles/ext`: Contains OSGi bundles provided by the SpringSource dm Server, which include the Spring Framework, Spring-DM, and other Java EE utilities

  - `repository/bundles/subsystems`: Contains OSGi bundles used internally by the SpringSource dm Server

  - `repository/bundles/usr`: Contains OSGi bundles provided by the user, either tailor-made or obtained from the SpringSource Enterprise Bundle Repository[2]

  - `repository/libraries/ext`: Contains libraries provided by the SpringSource dm Server, which include the Spring Framework and Spring Web Flow

  - `repository/libraries/usr`: Contains libraries provided by the user

  - `repository/installed`: Used at runtime by the SpringSource dm Server and should not contain either bundles or libraries

This concludes coverage of the directory structure that makes up the SpringSource dm Server, and with it the concepts you need to embark on your first application using the SpringSource dm Server.

SpringSource dm Server Hello World Application

The Hello World application you are about to start will take you through the SpringSource dm Server's most basic steps, such as accessing its administrative interface, to more advanced topics like harnessing an RDBMS, creating an application's bundles to make a PAR, and deploying PARs onto the platform.

2. `http://www.springsource.com/repository/`

If you've been following along chapter by chapter, the application here is ported from the Hello World application presented in Chapter 2, which demonstrated Spring's stand-alone framework. Given this fact, the example will also help you grasp the steps needed to migrate stand-alone Spring applications to use Spring-DM and run on the SpringSource dm Server.

Finally, it should also be noted the following application is not a complete port from the one in Chapter 2. In order to simplify deployment, this chapter's application forgoes the use of Apache Tiles and Spring's AJAX support. Figure 5-2 illustrates the bundles that will make up the application and the relationship between each one.

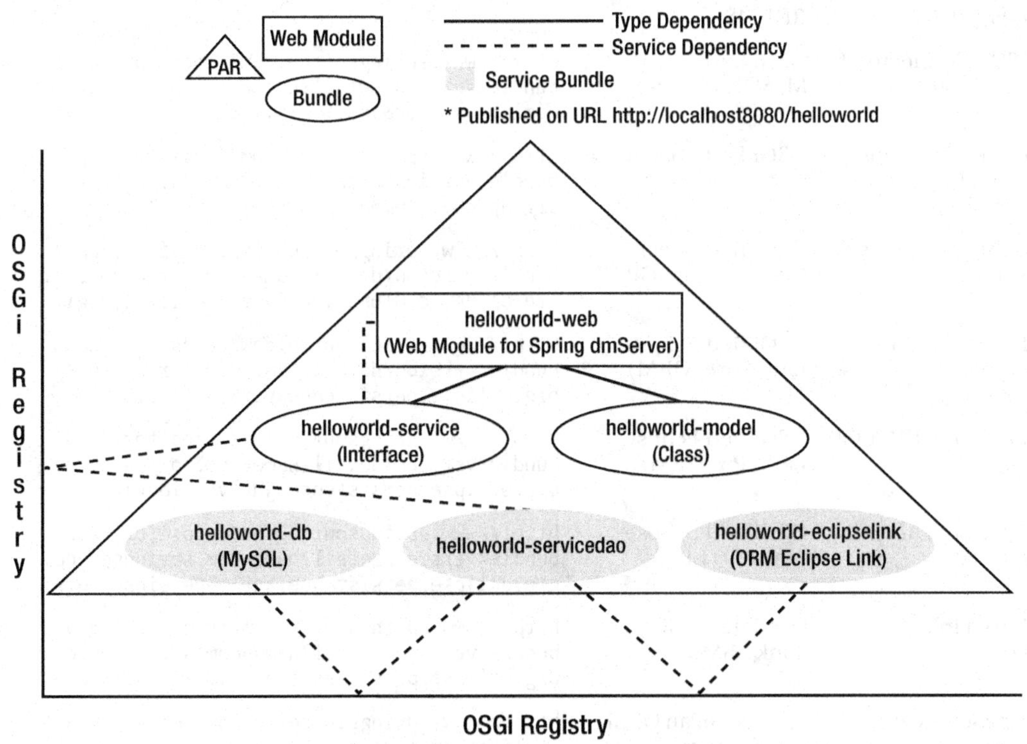

Figure 5-2. *SpringSource dm Server Hello World application bundles*

Note that Figure 5-2 only illustrates the bundles you will create that form part of the actual application. Additional bundle dependencies required by the application that are either included by default in the SpringSource dm Server or need to be installed in the server's repository are not illustrated.

Prerequisites and Downloads

Table 5-2 contains the software you will need to download and install prior to embarking on your first SpringSource dm Server project.

Table 5-2. *SpringSource dm Server Hello World Prerequisites and Downloads**

Software	Function	Download Site
Java SE 5 or higher	Java's runtime environment	`http://java.sun.com/javase/downloads/index.jsp`
MySQL Community Server 5.0	An open source RDBMS	`http://dev.mysql.com/downloads/mysql/5.0.html`
MySQL Connector/J Driver 5.1.6	OSGi'fied MySQL-Java driver	`http://www.springsource.com/repository/app/bundle/version/detail?name=com.springsource.com.mysql.jdbc&version=5.1.6`
Apache Commons Pool 1.4.0	OSGi'fied Apache Commons Pool	`http://www.springsource.com/repository/app/bundle/version/detail?name=com.springsource.org.apache.commons.pool&version=1.4.0`
Apache Commons DBCP 1.2.2	OSGi'fied Apache Commons DBCP	`http://www.springsource.com/repository/app/bundle/version/detail?name=com.springsource.org.apache.commons.dbcp&version=1.2.2.osgi`
Eclipse Link Core 1.0.0	OSGi'fied Eclipse Link Core (ORM)	`http://www.springsource.com/repository/app/bundle/version/detail?name=com.springsource.org.eclipse.persistence&version=1.0.0`
Eclipse Link JPA 1.0.0	OSGi'fied Eclipse Link JPA (ORM)	`http://www.springsource.com/repository/app/bundle/version/detail?name=com.springsource.org.eclipse.persistence.jpa&version=1.0.0`
Eclipse Link ANTLR 1.0.0	OSGi'fied Eclipse Link ANTLR	`http://www.springsource.com/repository/app/bundle/version/detail?name=com.springsource.org.eclipse.persistence.antlr&version=1.0.0`
Eclipse Link ASM 1.0.0	OSGi'fied Eclipse Link ASM	`http://www.springsource.com/repository/app/bundle/version/detail?name=com.springsource.org.eclipse.persistence.asm&version=1.0.0`
SpringSource dm Server 1.0	Provider of an OSGi environment, OSGi'fied servlet container, monitoring interfaces, and other resources	`http://www.springsource.com/products/suite/applicationplatform`

* *Note the limited number of downloads compared to Chapter 2 and Chapter 3; this is because the SpringSource dm Server includes many components needed to run Spring and OSGi out of the box.*

It's very likely you may have some of this software already installed on your workstation. If so, just ensure that you have the suggested versions, as minor version variations may hold you back in getting through the outlined steps.

Additionally, since some of this software was already used in earlier chapters, installation instructions for those packages will not be presented here, so please refer to the earlier chapters for detailed installation instructions.

Finally (unlike many other downloads presented in the book), the SpringSource dm Server download requires you to fill a registration form with personal information and a few questions regarding the technical environment you currently use. This process should not take you more than 5 minutes.

Installing the SpringSource dm Server

The process for installing the SpringSource dm Server consists of just one step: unzipping the downloaded file into a directory of your choice. Next, descend into the `bin` subdirectory of the SpringSource dm Server, and, depending on your operating system, execute `startup.sh` on Unix or `startup.bat` on Windows.

Upon executing one of these scripts, you will see the startup sequence for the SpringSource dm Server, starting the platform on port 8080. Next, open a browser and attempt to access the address `http://localhost:8080/`. You should see the SpringSource dm Server's Welcome page. In case this test fails, verify that port 8080 is not busy: check that no other application is running on the same default port (8080).

In this Welcome page, in the top-left corner you will see an Admin Console icon that will take you to the address `http://localhost:8080/admin/`. Click this last icon or paste the address into a browser.

You will then be prompted for an ID and password. Give the platform's default values, which are ID `admin` and password `springsource`. Once verified, you will see the main administrative interface for the SpringSource dm Server, as illustrated in Figure 5-3.

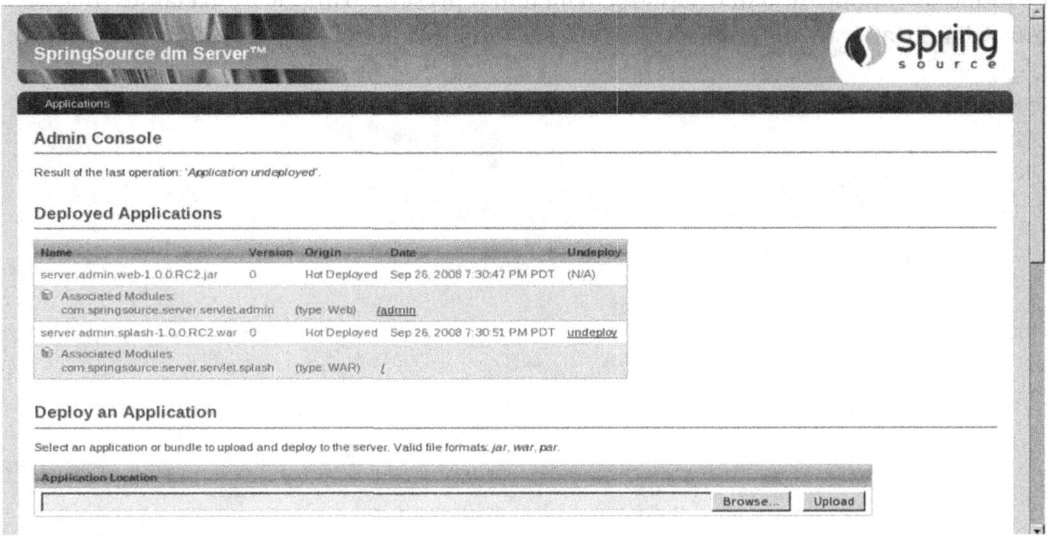

Figure 5-3. *SpringSource dm Server administrative interface*

The Admin Console is the platform's main interface for managing applications; it is here that you will deploy the application created in the remainder of the chapter.

Setting Up the Hello World "Playground" Directory Structure

You've now got the tools working, so it's time to create the proper workspace in which to maneuver, a directory structure like the one illustrated in Figure 5-4.

The directory structure functions as follows:

- `build.xml`: This is the main Apache Ant configuration file containing the necessary tasks to build the application.
- `classes`: All compiled Java classes are placed in this directory.
- `dist`: All built bundles are placed in this directory.
- `lib`: All JARs or OSGi bundles needed to compile Java sources are placed in this directory.
- `src`: All Java sources files composing the application are placed accordingly in subdirectories inside this directory, including the corresponding OSGi manifests for each bundle placed inside `META-INF/ch5/<bundle_type>` and the web interface used by the application in `GUI/ch5/`.

Since application packaging is central to understanding the benefits of the SpringSource dm Server, I will divide the exploration of classes that make up the application and the packaging of bundles into separate sections. This will be in contrast to the Spring-DM introductory application in Chapter 3, which first presented application classes followed immediately after by the packaging of classes into bundles.

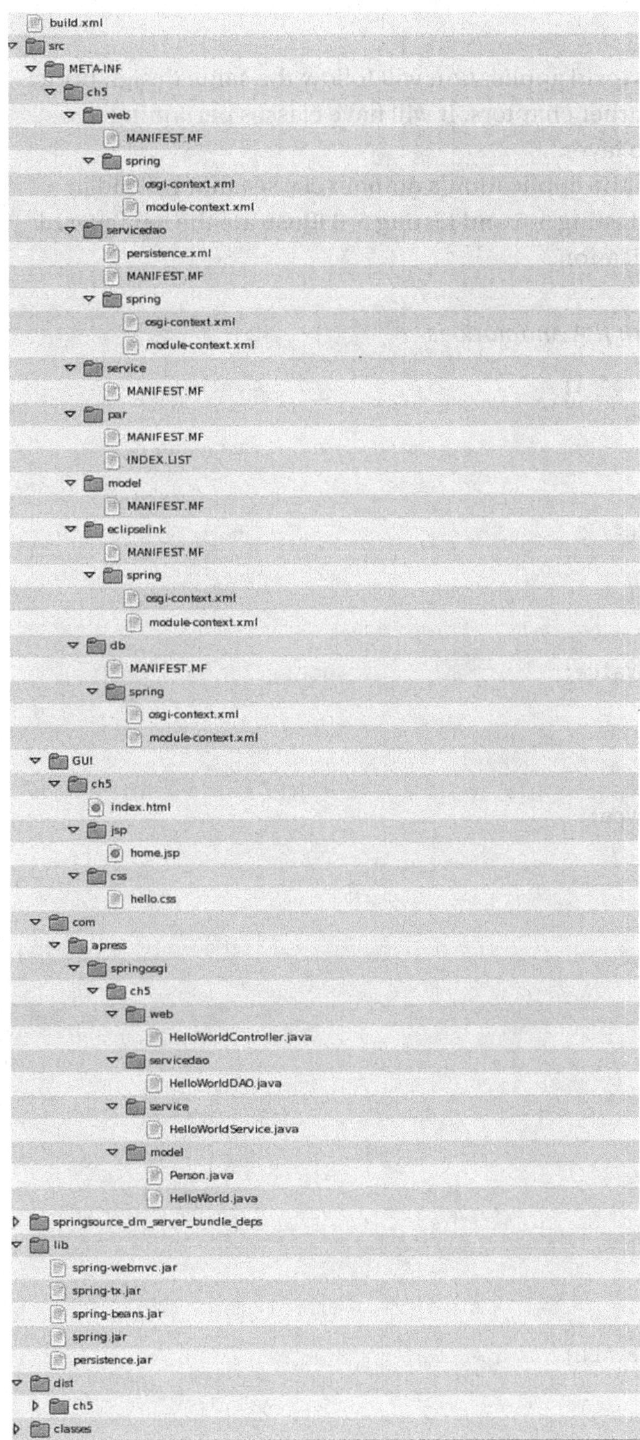

Figure 5-4. *Directory structure for the Hello World "playground"*

Application Classes

The SpringSource dm Server Hello World application will follow the same design principles as the examples presented in earlier chapters. It will have classes pertaining to a domain layer, service layer, and web layer.

Let's start things off by looking at the application's domain classes that will aid in persisting its objects to an RDBMS. Listing 5-5 and Listing 5-6 illustrate the `HelloWorld` and `Person` classes used by the application.

Listing 5-5. *`HelloWorld.java` POJO with JPA Annotations*

```
package com.apress.springosgi.ch5.model;

import java.util.Date;

import javax.persistence.CascadeType;
import javax.persistence.Column;
import javax.persistence.Entity;
import javax.persistence.Table;
import javax.persistence.GeneratedValue;
import javax.persistence.Id;
import javax.persistence.OneToOne;
import javax.persistence.Temporal;
import javax.persistence.TemporalType;

@Entity
@Table(name="HelloWorld")
public class HelloWorld {

    @Id
    @GeneratedValue
    private long id;
    @Column
    private String language;
    @Column
    private String message;
    @Temporal(TemporalType.DATE)
    private Date transdate;
    @OneToOne(cascade = CascadeType.ALL)
    private Person translator;
    public void setId(long id) {
        this.id = id;
    }
```

```
    public long getId() {
        return id;
    }

    public void setLanguage(String language) {
        this.language = language;
    }

    public String getLanguage() {
        return language;
    }

    public void setMessage(String message) {
        this.message = message;
    }

    public String getMessage() {
        return message;
    }

    public void setTransdate(Date transdate) {
        this.transdate = transdate;
    }
    public Date getTransdate() {
        return transdate;
    }

    public Person getTranslator() {
        return translator;
    }

    public void setTranslator(Person translator) {
        this.translator = translator;

    }

    public HelloWorld(String language, String message, Date transdate, ➥
Person translator) {
        this.language = language;
        this.message = message;
        this.transdate = transdate;
        this.translator = translator;
    }
```

```
    public HelloWorld() {
    }
}
```

Listing 5-6. *Person.java POJO with JPA Annotations*

```
package com.apress.springosgi.ch5.model;

import javax.persistence.Column;
import javax.persistence.Entity;
import javax.persistence.Table;
import javax.persistence.GeneratedValue;
import javax.persistence.GenerationType;
import javax.persistence.Id;

@Entity
@Table(name="Person")
public class Person {

    @Id
    @GeneratedValue
    private long id;
    @Column(name = "FNAME")
    private String firstName;
    @Column(name = "LNAME")
    private String lastName;
    @Column(precision=4, scale=2)
    private double hourlyRate;

    public double getHourlyRate() {
        return hourlyRate;
    }

    public void setHourlyRate(double hourlyRate) {
        this.hourlyRate = hourlyRate;
    }
    public String getLastName() {
        return lastName;
    }
```

```
    public void setLastName(String lastName) {
        this.lastName = lastName;
    }

    public String getFirstName() {
        return firstName;
    }

    public void setFirstName(String firstName) {
        this.firstName = firstName;
    }

    public void setId(long id) {
        this.id = id;
    }

    public long getId() {
        return id;
    }

    public Person(String firstName, String lastName, double hourlyRate) {
        this.firstName = firstName;
        this.lastName = lastName;
        this.hourlyRate = hourlyRate;
    }

    public Person() {
    }
}
```

Both of the application's model classes make use of JPA annotations in order to define a persistence strategy for each domain class. If you're unfamiliar with JPA, Chapter 2 contains a detailed description on the origins of JPA and the meaning of these JPA annotations.

The classes in Listings 5-5 and 5-6 are identical to those presented in Listings 2-6 and 2-7 back in Chapter 2, with the exception of the `@Table` annotation. Here it's important to note that this minor difference is not due to the use of the SpringSource dm Server, but rather because the application will use a different JPA provider, Eclipse Link, than the one used in Chapter 2, which was OpenJPA.

If this application were to have used OpenJPA as its JPA provider, the domain classes could have remained the same. However, by using Eclipse Link, the default RDBMS table mapping strategy differs. Eclipse Link attempts to map a class by the convention

<database_name>.<class_name>, compared to OpenJPA's default mapping strategy of <class_name>.

Therefore, by using the JPA annotation @Table, Eclipse Link will attempt to map a class to a specific table name in accordance with the same RDBMS schema created back in Chapter 2 by OpenJPA. As a consequence, this will allow you to reuse the same database. See the sidebar "JPA Providers and OSGi" for the reasons behind this JPA provider switch.

JPA PROVIDERS AND OSGI

Persistence in OSGi is a thorny subject, so much so that Chapter 7 addresses this topic in further detail. However, I will elaborate a little on the issue of JPA providers in this, your first encounter with persistence in the context of OSGi.

Persistence using JPA in stand-alone Spring applications can be done through any of the following three JPA providers: OpenJPA, Hibernate, and Eclipse Link (the latter being the new name for what was once Oracle TopLink).

With the emergence of OSGi, these same JPA providers have undergone parallel developments to support the class-loading paradigms brought forth by OSGi. In this area, though, Eclipse Link is the clear frontrunner, having developed the first OSGi-compatible JPA provider.

This is not to say Eclipse Link is better than OpenJPA or Hibernate for developing Spring-DM/OSGi applications, a statement that would be equally analogous and unfair as saying it for non-OSGi JPA versions. But Eclipse Link is the most mature of the three Spring JPA providers used in OSGi environments at the time of this writing.

Moving along, we come to the service interface that will perform operations against an application's domain classes. Listing 5-7 shows the application's service interface.

Listing 5-7. *HelloWorldService.java Interface*

```
package com.apress.springosgi.ch5.service;

import com.apress.springosgi.ch5.model.HelloWorld;

import java.util.List;

public interface HelloWorldService {

    public HelloWorld findById(long id);

    public List<HelloWorld> findAll();

    public HelloWorld update(HelloWorld hw);
```

```
    public void save(HelloWorld hw);

    public void delete(HelloWorld hw);

    public void deleteMessage(long id);

    public List<HelloWorld> findByTranslatorFirstName(String firstName);

    public List<HelloWorld> findByTranslatorLastName(String lastName);

    public List<HelloWorld> findByTranslatorHourlyRateOver(double hourlyRate);

    public List<HelloWorld> findByLanguage(String language);

    public List<HelloWorld> findByMessage(String message);

}
```

This service interface is identical to the one used in Chapter 2 (Listing 2-5) and provides the various signatures needed to update, save, and delete objects corresponding to the domain model, as well as perform searches on these same objects using criteria like language, message, and translator.

However, this interface by itself doesn't do much. To perform persistence operations against objects, a DAO using JPA is needed. Listing 5-8 illustrates the DAO used by the SpringSource dm Server Hello World application.

Listing 5-8. *`HelloWorldDAO.java` DAO Class*

```
package com.apress.springosgi.ch5.servicedao;

import java.util.List;

import com.apress.springosgi.ch5.service.HelloWorldService;
import com.apress.springosgi.ch5.model.HelloWorld;

import org.springframework.transaction.annotation.Propagation;
import org.springframework.transaction.annotation.Transactional;
import org.springframework.stereotype.Repository;

import javax.persistence.EntityManager;
import javax.persistence.PersistenceContext;
import javax.persistence.Query;
```

```
@Repository
@Transactional
public class HelloWorldDAO implements HelloWorldService {

    @PersistenceContext
    private EntityManager em;

    public HelloWorld findById(long id) {
        return this.em.find(HelloWorld.class, id);
    }

    public List<HelloWorld> findAll() {
        return this.em.createQuery("select e from HelloWorld e").getResultList();
    }
   public HelloWorld update(HelloWorld hw) {
        return this.em.merge(hw);
    }

    public void save(HelloWorld hw) {
        this.em.persist(hw);
    }

    public void delete(HelloWorld hw) {
        this.em.remove(hw);
    }

    public List<HelloWorld> findByTranslatorFirstName(String firstName) {
        Query query = this.em.createQuery("select e from HelloWorld e where➥
 e.translator.firstName like :firstName");
        query.setParameter("firstName", firstName + "%");
        return query.getResultList();
    }

    public List<HelloWorld> findByTranslatorLastName(String lastName) {
        Query query = this.em.createQuery("select e from HelloWorld e where➥
 e.translator.lastName like :firstName");
        query.setParameter("lastName", lastName + "%");
        return query.getResultList();
    }
```

```
    public List<HelloWorld> findByTranslatorHourlyRateOver(double hourlyRate) {
        Query query = this.em.createQuery("select e from HelloWorld e where➥
e.translator.hourlyRate > :hourlyRate");
        query.setParameter("hourlyRate", hourlyRate + "%");
        return query.getResultList();
    }

    public List<HelloWorld> findByLanguage(String language) {
        Query query = this.em.createQuery("select e from HelloWorld e where➥
e.language like :language");
        query.setParameter("language", language + "%");
        return query.getResultList();
    }
  public List<HelloWorld> findByMessage(String message) {
        Query query = this.em.createQuery("select e from HelloWorld e where➥
e.message like :message");
        query.setParameter("message", message + "%");
        return query.getResultList();
    }

    @Transactional(propagation = Propagation.REQUIRED)
    public void deleteMessage(long id) {
        HelloWorld hw = this.em.find(HelloWorld.class, id);
        this.em.remove(hw);
    }
}
```

If you look closely at this last listing, you will once again find similarities to the `HelloWorldDAO` class used in Chapter 2 (Listing 2-8). Yet, there is one glaring difference between the cited reference and the class presented here: this chapter's class does not use inheritance to support a JPA DAO.

By forgoing the inheritance of the Spring Framework's support class `org.springframework.orm.jpa.support.JpaDaoSupport`, this chapter's DAO class must incorporate equivalent JPA behaviors by other means.

So it is that in this last DAO class, you will notice the explicit presence of JPA's `EntityManager`—which is injected by the JPA annotation `@PersistenceContext`—used inside each of the DAO's service methods to get hold of JPA's `EntityManager` and perform the corresponding queries against an RDBMS. Additionally, the DAO class is decorated with the `@Repository` and `@Transactional` annotations, which stipulate that persistence exceptions should be autotranslated and that a DAO's methods should be transactional.

For all intents and purposes, *the logic in the* `HelloWorldDAO` *class presented in Listing 5-9 is identical to that in Listing 2-8 of Chapter 2; their differences have nothing to do with the SpringSource dm Server, but are rather different styles of implementing the same thing.* The only difference is that one uses annotations and makes explicit use of JPA's `EntityManager`, while the other inherits its JPA DAO behavior from the Spring Framework support class `org.springframework.orm.jpa.support.JpaDaoSupport`.

Continuing with the classes that make up the application, we come to the controller that will broker incoming web requests to the application's service layer. Listing 5-9 illustrates the `HelloWorldController` class.

Listing 5-9. *HelloWorldController.java*

```
package com.apress.springosgi.ch5.web;

import java.util.List;
import java.util.Date;

import org.springframework.beans.factory.annotation.Autowired;
import org.springframework.stereotype.Controller;
import org.springframework.web.bind.annotation.RequestMapping;
import org.springframework.web.bind.annotation.RequestMethod;
import org.springframework.web.bind.annotation.RequestParam;
import org.springframework.web.bind.annotation.ModelAttribute;
import org.springframework.ui.ModelMap;

import com.apress.springosgi.ch5.model.HelloWorld;
import com.apress.springosgi.ch5.model.Person;
import com.apress.springosgi.ch5.service.HelloWorldService;

@Controller
public class HelloWorldController {

    private HelloWorldService helloWorldService;

   public void setHelloWorldService(HelloWorldService helloWorldService) {
        this.helloWorldService = helloWorldService;
    }
```

```
    public HelloWorldService getHelloWorldService() {
        return helloWorldService;
    }

    @RequestMapping(method = RequestMethod.GET)
    @ModelAttribute("helloworlds")
    public List<HelloWorld> home() {
        return this.helloWorldService.findAll();
    }

    @RequestMapping(method = RequestMethod.GET)
    public String translator(@RequestParam("id") Long id, ModelMap model) {
     Person translator = helloWorldService.findById(id).getTranslator();
     List<HelloWorld> hws = helloWorldService.findAll();
     model.addAttribute("helloworlds",hws);
     model.addAttribute("translator",translator);
     return "home";
    }

    @RequestMapping(method = RequestMethod.GET)
    public String deleteMessage(@RequestParam("id")
    Long id) {
        helloWorldService.deleteMessage(id);
        return "redirect:home";
    }
}
```

Once again, by way of comparison, this last controller has one minor difference from the one used in the stand-alone Spring application in Listing 2-15. The `helloWorldService` value is not injected using the `@Autowired` annotation that facilitates the injection of Spring beans into a class. Instead, the controller in Listing 5-9 uses a setter/getter approach in which the injection takes place at the time a bean is instantiated in a Spring descriptor.

In this scenario, the `@Autowired` annotation was not used because the application's `helloWorldService` is not available as a Spring bean initially, but rather as an OSGi service. This requires that the bundle containing this controller first look up a service's reference in OSGi's registry—using Spring-DM statements—and then inject the value through Spring descriptors when the controller is instantiated. See the sidebar "Injecting OSGi Services Using Annotations" for more on this process.

INJECTING OSGI SERVICES USING ANNOTATIONS

Like the @Autowired annotation used to inject Spring beans directly inside classes, Spring-DM supports the annotation @ServiceReference for the purpose of injecting OSGi services inside classes.

The @ServiceReference would have allowed this last controller class to forgo the use of setter/getter methods to perform the injection inside Spring descriptors, instead delegating the injection of the service directly to an annotation.

However, this was not done because Spring-DM annotations—like @ServiceReference—are disabled by default in Spring-DM's standard release. In order to activate Spring-DM annotations, it's necessary to use OSGi fragments, a process that would sidetrack us from the chapter's main focus on the SpringSource dm Server.

Consult Chapter 4 for more background on the use of fragments. And specifically take a look at Listing 4-24, which illustrates the use of the @ServiceReference annotation, as well as Listings 4-27 and 4-28, which contain the necessary code listings to create the fragment for activating Spring-DM annotations.

Next, we come to the application's GUI and the JSP that will be presented to end users. Listing 5-10 illustrates the application's main page.

Listing 5-10. *Home Page (home.jsp)*

```
<!DOCTYPE HTML PUBLIC "-//W3C//DTD HTML 4.01//EN"
        "http://www.w3.org/TR/html4/strict.dtd">
<%@ taglib prefix="c" uri="http://java.sun.com/jsp/jstl/core" %>
<%@ taglib prefix="fmt" uri="http://java.sun.com/jsp/jstl/fmt" %>
<html>
<head>
        <title>SpringSource Application Platform - Pro Spring-OSGi </title>
        <link href="../css/hello.css" rel="stylesheet" type="text/css">
</head>
<body>

<div id="wrap">
         <div id="header">
         <h1>SpringSource Application Platform - Pro Spring-OSGi</h1>
         </div>

         <div id="content">
           <div id="main">
                <h2>Hello World Messages </h2>
<div id="helloMessages">
 <c:forEach var="hello" items="${helloworlds}">
```

```
   <div style="border:red 2px dashed;margin:10px;padding:5px">
       <b><c:out value="${hello.language}"/></b>
       <c:out value="${hello.message}"/> - Translated on:  <fmt:formatDate➥
 value="${hello.transdate}" dateStyle="long" /> <br/>
       <a id="deleteMessage_${hello.id}" href="deleteMessage?id=${hello.id}">➥
Delete Message </a>
       <br/>

   </div>
     </c:forEach>
 </div>
      </div>
          <div id="sidebar">
            <h2>Translators </h2>
<div id="helloTranslators">
 <ul>
  <c:forEach var="hello" items="${helloworlds}">
       <li><c:out value="${hello.language}"/>
       <a id="showTranslator_${hello.id}" href="translator?id=${hello.id}">➥
Translator Details </a>
  </c:forEach>
 </ul>
</div>
 <div id="person">
  <div style="border:red 2px dashed;margin:10px;padding:5px;">
   <b>Name</b> :<c:out value="${translator.firstName}"/>➥
 <c:out value="${translator.lastName}"/><br/>
   <b>Hourly Rate</b> : $<c:out value="${translator.hourlyRate}"/><br/>
  </div>
</div>
           </div>
         </div>

         <div id="footer">
         <h3>Pro SpringOSGi by Daniel Rubio - Published by Apress</h3>
         </div>
</div>
</body>
</html>
```

Building off the GUI used in Chapter 2, Listing 5-10 is a composition of the JSP files used in that earlier chapter. The difference is that Apache Tiles and Spring's AJAX support are omitted in order to simplify the application. The only side effect to this change is that actions taken by a user will require complete screen refreshes, unlike in Chapter 2's example, which used AJAX updates backed by the use of Apache Tiles.

With all the application's classes and GUI code illustrated, place each of these listings in the corresponding folders inside the Hello World "playground":

- Place the application's classes inside the appropriate `src/com/apress/springosgi/ch5/` subfolder, according to each class's `package` statement.
- Copy the JSP presented in Listing 5-10 to the directory `src/GUI/ch5/jsp/`.
- Copy the `index.html` page presented in Chapter 2's Listing 2-24 to the directory `src/GUI/ch5/`.
- Copy the CSS file presented in Chapter 2's Listing 2-25 to the directory `src/GUI/ch5/css/`.

Now that the application's code is staged and ready to be packaged, let's move on to the more interesting subject of creating the application's bundles, the OSGi manifests that will accompany each bundle, and the Spring-DM and Spring descriptors used in each bundle.

Application Bundles, Manifests, and Descriptors

The SpringSource dm Server Hello World application will be partitioned into six bundles—yes that's right, six! The reason behind this design for a typical three-tier application will become more apparent once you see what each bundle accomplishes. The following list contains a brief description of the functionality offered by each bundle:

- `db`: Contains the service for the data source connecting to the RDBMS
- `eclipselink`: Contains the service for the JPA provider Eclipse Link
- `model`: Contains the application's model classes
- `service`: Contains the service interface to access the application's DAO class
- `servicedao-jpa`: Contains the DAO class using JPA (Eclipse Link) to access the application's model classes
- `web`: Contains the web component to access the application's DAO service
- `par`: Contains all the previous bundles packaged into the SpringSource dm Server's recommended deployment unit

Knowing the various bundles needed by the application, let's tackle the first one, which is charged with connecting to the application's data source.

Database Bundle

The database bundle will be somewhat different from the bundles you've created so far in the book, in the sense that it will have no Java classes. The contents of this bundle will consist of a `MANIFEST.MF` file and Spring descriptors processed from a bundle's default Spring-DM extender directory `/spring/`.

The purpose of the database bundle is to offer other bundles access to a data source via an OSGi service. Therefore, this bundle will contain all the necessary logic needed to connect to an RDBMS, including data connection strategies like pooling, as well as specific parameters needed to connect from Java to a particular brand of RDBMS.

Listing 5-11 illustrates the database bundle's `MANIFEST.MF` file.

Listing 5-11. *Database Bundle `MANIFEST.MF` File*

```
Manifest-Version: 1.0
Bundle-ManifestVersion: 2
Bundle-SymbolicName: com.apress.springosgi.ch5.db
Bundle-Version: 1.0.0
Bundle-Name: HelloWorld SpringSource dm Server Database
Bundle-Vendor: Pro Spring-OSGi
Import-Library: org.springframework.spring;version="[2.5,2.6)"
Import-Bundle: com.springsource.org.apache.commons.dbcp;version="[1.2.2.osgi,➥
1.2.2.osgi]",
 com.springsource.com.mysql.jdbc;version="[5.1.6,5.1.6]"
Import-Package: javax.sql
```

Among the most noteworthy OSGi directives in the last `MANIFEST.MF` file you will find

- `Import-Library`: Grants the bundle access to the entire Spring Framework library, which is available by default in the SpringSource dm Server
- `Import-Bundle`: Grants the bundle access to the Apache Commons DBCP bundle used as the database pooling library, as well as MySQL's Java driver bundle used to connect to a MySQL RDBMS
- `Import-Package`: Grants the bundle access to Java's standard `javax.sql` package, used in RDBMS connectivity

---

■ **Note** The bracketed numbers appearing next to the `version` value are version ranges, specifying the particular range needed by either library, bundle, or package. Chapter 6 explores the use of versioning and this particular syntax.

Like any other `MANIFEST.MF` file containing OSGi directives, these values only indicate the Java packages—bundles or libraries—that will be accessible in a bundle. The next important question is how an RDBMS connection is bootstrapped inside this bundle. Listing 5-12 illustrates the `module-context.xml` file used for this purpose.

Listing 5-12. *`module-context.xml` for the Database Bundle*

```
<?xml version="1.0" encoding="UTF-8"?>
<beans xmlns="http://www.springframework.org/schema/beans"
        xmlns:xsi="http://www.w3.org/2001/XMLSchema-instance"
        xmlns:context="http://www.springframework.org/schema/context"
        xmlns:p="http://www.springframework.org/schema/p"
        xsi:schemaLocation="
                        http://www.springframework.org/schema/beans➥
 http://www.springframework.org/schema/beans/spring-beans-2.5.xsd
                        http://www.springframework.org/schema/context➥
 http://www.springframework.org/schema/context/spring-context-2.5.xsd">

        <bean id="dataSource"
              class="org.apache.commons.dbcp.BasicDataSource"
              p:url="jdbc:mysql://localhost:3306/springosgi"
              p:username="hello"
              p:password="world"
              p:driverClassName="com.mysql.jdbc.Driver"
              init-method="createDataSource"
              destroy-method="close"/>
</beans>
```

■ **Note** The loading of the JDBC driver is one case where classes are loaded using the thread-context class loader.

This last `module-context.xml` file is nothing more than a standard Spring descriptor. It's used to instantiate a Spring bean with the RDBMS parameters to establish a connection to MySQL using the Apache Commons DBCP library.

In fact, this descriptor is strikingly similar to Chapter 2's Listing 2-13 and Listing 2-27, which created Spring beans for accessing MySQL and HSQLDB data sources. The twist in this chapter, however, is that the `dataSource` bean will be published as an OSGi service. Listing 5-13 illustrates the `osgi-context.xml` file used to publish the `dataSource` bean as a service.

Listing 5-13. *`osgi-context.xml` for the Database Bundle*

```
<?xml version="1.0" encoding="UTF-8"?>
<beans:beans
   xmlns="http://www.springframework.org/schema/osgi"
   xmlns:xsi="http://www.w3.org/2001/XMLSchema-instance"
   xmlns:beans="http://www.springframework.org/schema/beans"
   xsi:schemaLocation="http://www.springframework.org/schema/osgi
       http://www.springframework.org/schema/osgi/spring-osgi.xsd
       http://www.springframework.org/schema/beans
       http://www.springframework.org/schema/beans/spring-beans.xsd">

    <service ref="dataSource" interface="javax.sql.DataSource"/>
</beans:beans>
```

This last listing makes use of the Spring-DM element `<service>` to register the `dataSource` bean and expose it using Java's standard database interface `javax.sql.DataSource`.

In order for this `dataSource` bean creation and service registration to take place, you will need to place both the `osgi-context.xml` and `module-context.xml` files inside a bundle's `/spring/` directory so Spring-DM may process these descriptors once a bundle is activated.

We will leave the building of the database bundle for the "Building and Deploying the Application" section of this chapter. For now, copy each of the bundle's files to the following Hello World "playground" directories: the `MANIFEST.MF` file in Listing 5-11 to the subdirectory `/src/META-INF/ch5/db/`, and the descriptors in Listings 5-12 and 5-13 to the subdirectory `/src/META-INF/ch5/db/spring/`.

Next, we will tackle a close companion to the database bundle, the one containing the JPA provider Eclipse Link.

Eclipse Link Bundle

The Eclipse Link bundle follows a similar strategy to the database bundle, since it will only be composed of a `MANIFEST.MF` file and Spring descriptors. As far as the purpose of the Eclipse Link bundle is concerned, it's simply to offer other application bundles access to Eclipse Link's JPA adapter via an OSGi service.

Listing 5-14 shows the Eclipse Link's bundle `MANIFEST.MF` file.

Listing 5-14. *Eclipse Link Bundle MANIFEST.MF File*

```
Manifest-Version: 1.0
Bundle-ManifestVersion: 2
Bundle-SymbolicName: com.apress.springosgi.ch5.eclipselink
Bundle-Version: 1.0.0
Bundle-Name: HelloWorld SpringSource dm Server EclipseLink
Bundle-Vendor: Pro Spring-OSGi
Import-Library: org.springframework.spring;version="[2.5,2.6)"
Import-Bundle: com.springsource.org.eclipse.persistence;version="1.0.0";➥
import-scope:=application
```

This last manifest makes use of the `Import-Library` header to grant the bundle access to the Spring Framework's library, as well as the `Import-Bundle` directive to give the bundle access to Eclipse Link's *distribution* bundle.

■ Note By "Eclipse Link's distribution bundle," I mean the one you downloaded from the link presented in Table 5-2. "Eclipse Link bundle" refers to the Hello World application's bundle providing Eclipse Link's OSGi service.

One important aspect of the `Import-Bundle` directive is the use of the `import-scope:=application` property, which is a special feature of the SpringSource dm Server. By adding this property to the `Import-Bundle` directive, the imported bundle is *dynamically* added—imported—to all bundles (a.k.a. modules) comprising an application.

This last process is *critical* when applied to something like persistence. Let me take a brief sidestep and elaborate why. When another application bundle requires using the JPA adapter service provided by the Eclipse Link bundle, accessing the service is only part of the issue, for using a service like Eclipse Link entails weaving and introducing new dependencies into the bundle consuming the service.

For example, take the application's model bundle—introduced next—that will contain the `Person` and `HelloWorld` classes and will require using Eclipse Link's JPA service to persist these objects to an RDBMS. Upon using this service, Eclipse Link will attempt to weave both the `Person` and `HelloWorld` classes, therefore requiring access to the Eclipse Link *distribution* bundle. The interesting question is, how will the model bundle get this access?

The simple answer would be by importing the Eclipse Link *distribution* bundle into the model bundle itself; however, this is not advisable because it breaks the application's modularity and introduces a hard dependency on the consuming bundle.

Why shouldn't the model bundle use some non-JPA persistence strategy or some other JPA provider? The issue is that using an OSGi service doesn't necessarily mean the consuming bundle will automatically have access to the class dependencies needed to run a service.

And persistence fits this special case, since it introduces dependencies required for weaving classes on consuming bundles.

So using the **import-scope:=application** property on the Import-Bundle value for the Eclipse Link *distribution* bundle will make Eclipse Link's *distribution* classes available *dynamically* to all bundles that make up an application. This allows any bundle to use Eclipse Link's JPA service, without introducing hard import dependencies on consuming bundles.

Having elaborated on the use of the import-scope:=application property, I will now continue describing the Spring-DM and Spring descriptors needed by the Eclipse Link bundle. Listing 5-15 illustrates the module-context.xml used by the Eclipse Link bundle.

Listing 5-15. *module-context.xml for the Eclipse Link Bundle*

```
<?xml version="1.0" encoding="UTF-8"?>
<beans xmlns="http://www.springframework.org/schema/beans"➥
 xmlns:xsi="http://www.w3.org/2001/XMLSchema-instance"
               xmlns:p="http://www.springframework.org/schema/p"➥
xmlns:aop="http://www.springframework.org/schema/aop"
               xmlns:context="http://www.springframework.org/schema/context"➥
 xmlns:jee="http://www.springframework.org/schema/jee"
               xmlns:tx="http://www.springframework.org/schema/tx"
               xsi:schemaLocation="
                       http://www.springframework.org/schema/aop➥
 http://www.springframework.org/schema/aop/spring-aop-2.5.xsd
                       http://www.springframework.org/schema/beans➥
 http://www.springframework.org/schema/beans/spring-beans-2.5.xsd
                       http://www.springframework.org/schema/context➥
 http://www.springframework.org/schema/context/spring-context-2.5.xsd
                       http://www.springframework.org/schema/jee➥
 http://www.springframework.org/schema/jee/spring-jee-2.5.xsd➥

                       http://www.springframework.org/schema/tx➥
 http://www.springframework.org/schema/tx/spring-tx-2.5.xsd">

<bean id="jpaVendorAdapter"➥
 class="org.springframework.orm.jpa.vendor.EclipseLinkJpaVendorAdapter"
      p:databasePlatform="org.eclipse.persistence.platform.database.MySQLPlatform"
      p:showSql="true"/>
</beans>
```

This last module-context.xml file contains Eclipse Link's target JPA mapping strategy pegged to the MySQL RDBMS via the class org.eclipse.persistence.platform.database.MySQLPlatform, as well as the JPA property showSql="true".

Here again, a look back at Listing 2-27 in Chapter 2 will confirm that a similar Spring bean was used to instantiate a jpaVendorAdapter bean to access a MySQL RDBMS using the OpenJPA JPA adapter.

As with this chapter's database bundle, however, the jpaVendorAdapter bean must be published as an OSGi service. Listing 5-16 illustrates the osgi-context.xml file used for just this task.

Listing 5-16. *osgi-context.xml for the Database Bundle*

```
<?xml version="1.0" encoding="UTF-8"?>
<beans:beans
   xmlns="http://www.springframework.org/schema/osgi"
   xmlns:xsi="http://www.w3.org/2001/XMLSchema-instance"
   xmlns:beans="http://www.springframework.org/schema/beans"
   xsi:schemaLocation="http://www.springframework.org/schema/osgi
        http://www.springframework.org/schema/osgi/spring-osgi.xsd
        http://www.springframework.org/schema/beans
        http://www.springframework.org/schema/beans/spring-beans.xsd">

    <service ref="jpaVendorAdapter"➥
  interface="org.springframework.orm.jpa.JpaVendorAdapter"/>
</beans:beans>
```

This last listing makes use of the Spring-DM element <service> to register the jpaVendorAdapter bean and expose it using Spring's JPA vendor adapter interface org.springframework.orm.jpa.JpaVendorAdapter.

In order for this jpaVendorAdapter bean creation and service registration to take place, you will need to place both the osgi-context.xml and module-context.xml files inside a bundle's /spring/ directory, so that Spring-DM can process these descriptors once a bundle is activated.

We will leave the building of the Eclipse Link bundle for the "Building and Deploying the Application" section of this chapter. For now, copy each of the bundle's files to the following Hello World "playground" directories: the MANIFEST.MF file in Listing 5-14 to the subdirectory /src/META-INF/ch5/eclipselink/, and the descriptors in Listings 5-15 and 5-16 to the subdirectory /src/META-INF/ch5/eclipselink/spring/.

Next, we will explore the third bundle for the application, the first one that will contain a set of application classes created earlier.

Model Bundle

The model bundle will contain the JPA annotated model classes created earlier, as well as a MANIFEST.MF file. This bundle, however, will not contain any Spring-DM or Spring descriptor used to look up or register services.

Listing 5-17 shows the model bundle MANIFEST.MF file.

Listing 5-17. *Model Bundle MANIFEST.MF File*

```
Manifest-Version: 1.0
Bundle-ManifestVersion: 2
Bundle-SymbolicName: com.apress.springosgi.ch5.model
Bundle-Version: 1.0.0
Bundle-Name: HelloWorld SpringSource dm Server Model
Bundle-Vendor: Pro Spring-OSGi
Import-Library: org.springframework.spring;version="[2.5,2.6)"
Import-Bundle: com.springsource.javax.persistence;version="[1.0.0,1.0.0]"
Export-Package: com.apress.springosgi.ch5.model;version="1.0.0"
```

This last manifest makes use of the Import-Library header to grant the bundle access to the Spring Framework's library, as well as the Import-Bundle directive to give the bundle access to Java's persistence javax.persistence classes used in the model classes. Additionally, the manifest uses Export-Package to make the bundle's model classes available to other bundles.

Having described the model bundle's **MANIFEST.MF** file, there is not much more to say. We will leave the building of the model bundle for an upcoming section. For now, just copy the bundle's MANIFEST.MF file in Listing 5-17 to the subdirectory /src/META-INF/ch5/model/ of the Hello World "playground."

Next, we will explore the bundles pertaining to the service layer of the application, which are the most extensive but equally the most interesting ones.

Service Bundles

Following the same bundle partitioning strategy as in Chapter 3, the service layer will be split into two bundles: one bundle designed to contain the application's DAO class using JPA, in which actions are performed against the application's model classes, and the other containing the necessary interface to access this service. These service operations include querying and updating model objects from an RDBMS, as well as offering these same operations as a service to other bundles in the application.

All this functionality makes the service implementation (DAO-JPA) bundle more extensive, since it will use JPA, perform weaving on application classes, access services from other bundles, and publish its own service for other bundles.

Let's start things off by looking at the two service bundles' MANIFEST.MF files. Listing 5-18 contains the MANIFEST.MF file for the service interface bundle and Listing 5-19 the MANIFEST.MF file for the service implementation (DAO-JPA) bundle.

Listing 5-18. *Service Interface Bundle`MANIFEST.MF` File*

```
Manifest-Version: 1.0

Bundle-ManifestVersion: 2

Bundle-SymbolicName: com.apress.springosgi.ch5.service

Bundle-Version: 1.0.0

Bundle-Name: HelloWorld SpringSource dm Server Service Interface

Bundle-Vendor: Pro Spring-OSGi

Import-Package: com.apress.springosgi.ch5.model;version="1.0.0"

Export-Package: com.apress.springosgi.ch5.service;version="1.0.0"
```

Listing 5-19. *Service Implementation (DAO-JPA) Bundle`MANIFEST.MF` File*

```
Manifest-Version: 1.0
Bundle-ManifestVersion: 2
Bundle-SymbolicName: com.apress.springosgi.ch5.servicedao
Bundle-Version: 1.0.0
Bundle-Name: HelloWorld SpringSource dm Server JPA Backed DAO Service
Bundle-Vendor: Pro Spring-OSGi
Import-Library: org.springframework.spring;version="[2.5,2.6)"
Import-Bundle: com.springsource.javax.persistence;version="[1.0.0,1.0.0]",
 com.springsource.org.aspectj.runtime;version="1.6.0",
 com.springsource.org.aspectj.weaver;version="1.6.0"
Import-Package: com.apress.springosgi.ch5.model="1.0.0",
 com.apress.springosgi.ch5.service;version="1.0.0",
 javax.sql
```

The `MANIFEST.MF` file in Listing 5-18 is very straightforward; it simply imports the application's model package and exports the application interface package granting external access to the bundle's `com.apress.springosgi.ch5.service` package, which contains the DAO's service interface

Listing 5-19, as with the other bundle's `MANIFEST.MF` files, starts off by importing Spring's library into the bundle using the `Import-Library` directive. Then it declares three values in the manifest's `Import-Bundle` directive, Java's persistence `javax.persistence` classes used in the DAO class, as well as AspectJ's runtime and weaver bundle, which will aid in weaving the application's persistence classes.

Additionally, the Import-Package directive is used to bring in the application's model package com.apress.springosgi.ch5.model and service package com.apress.springosgi.ch5.service into the scope of the bundle—since the DAO persists against classes in this package and also requires the service interface. The Import-Package directive also imports Java's javax.sql package, used in RDBMS operations.

Listing 5-19 is a more extensive MANIFEST.MF file than the other bundles given the operations it will perform, but notice that even though persistence and weaving bundles are imported, there is no sign of importing a JPA provider to support the persistence process. So what's happening? Where is the service bundle gaining access to a JPA's classes?

For starters, the service implementation (DAO-JPA) bundle will gain access to a JPA provider by accessing the jpaVendorAdapter service published by another bundle. However, the service alone is not enough. Since classes in the service bundle need to be weaved with the aid of a particular JPA *distribution*, the service bundle also must import such a JPA *distribution*.

As outlined earlier, it is considered bad practice to import a package or bundle into a consuming bundle that is not known to be used until runtime. Therefore, the service bundle abstains from importing a particular JPA distribution and instead relies on *dynamic* import support provided by the SpringSource dm Server.

The reason the service implementation (DAO-JPA) bundle will be able to weave classes using a JPA provider is because the JPA provider used in the application (as a whole) is imported through the import-scope:=application property. This allows the SpringSource dm Server to *dynamically* propagate the import scope of the JPA provider to all bundles contained in the application, the PAR file, allowing the service bundle to access the same JPA *distribution* bundle used by the application.

On the same subject of persistence, the service implementation (DAO-JPA) bundle will also need to include the standard persistence.xml file used in JPA applications. However, unlike the file used in Chapter 2 (Listing 2-9), this application's persistence.xml file will differ as can be observed in Listing 5-20.

Listing 5-20. *persistence.xml File Used in the Service Implementation (DAO-JPA) Bundle*

```
<persistence xmlns="http://java.sun.com/xml/ns/persistence"
             xmlns:xsi="http://www.w3.org/2001/XMLSchema-instance"
             xsi:schemaLocation="http://java.sun.com/xml/ns/persistence➥
 http://java.sun.com/xml/ns/persistence/persistence_1_0.xsd"
             version="1.0">

      <persistence-unit name="proSpringOSGiJpaSpringSourceAppPlatform"➥
 transaction-type="RESOURCE_LOCAL">

             <class>com.apress.springosgi.ch5.model.HelloWorld</class>
             <class>com.apress.springosgi.ch5.model.Person</class>
```

```
            <exclude-unlisted-classes>true</exclude-unlisted-classes>
        </persistence-unit>

</persistence>
```

The difference in this last persistence.xml file is that it explicitly states which classes are JPA entities. Unlike in Chapter 2, where we used the Spring Framework to automatically scan JPA entities, *classpath scanning for annotated JPA entities is not supported in the SpringSource dm Server*, so it is necessary to explicitly declare JPA entities.

Next, let's take a look at the service implementation (DAO-JPA) bundle descriptor containing standard Spring artifacts. Listing 5-21 illustrates the service implementation (DAO-JPA) bundle's module-context.xml file.

Listing 5-21. *module-context.xml for the Service Implementation (DAO-JPA) Bundle*

```
<?xml version="1.0" encoding="UTF-8"?>
<beans xmlns="http://www.springframework.org/schema/beans"➥
 xmlns:xsi="http://www.w3.org/2001/XMLSchema-instance"
                xmlns:p="http://www.springframework.org/schema/p"➥
 xmlns:aop="http://www.springframework.org/schema/aop"
                xmlns:context="http://www.springframework.org/schema/context"➥
 xmlns:jee="http://www.springframework.org/schema/jee"
                xmlns:tx="http://www.springframework.org/schema/tx"
                xmlns:osgi="http://www.springframework.org/schema/osgi"
                xsi:schemaLocation="
                        http://www.springframework.org/schema/aop➥
 http://www.springframework.org/schema/aop/spring-aop-2.5.xsd
                        http://www.springframework.org/schema/beans➥
 http://www.springframework.org/schema/beans/spring-beans-2.5.xsd
                        http://www.springframework.org/schema/context➥
 http://www.springframework.org/schema/context/spring-context-2.5.xsd
                        http://www.springframework.org/schema/jee➥
 http://www.springframework.org/schema/jee/spring-jee-2.5.xsd
                        http://www.springframework.org/schema/tx➥
 http://www.springframework.org/schema/tx/spring-tx-2.5.xsd
                        http://www.springframework.org/schema/osgi➥
 http://www.springframework.org/schema/osgi/spring-osgi.xsd">

 <context:load-time-weaver aspectj-weaving="on"/>
```

```
<bean id="entityManagerFactory"➥
class="org.springframework.orm.jpa.LocalContainerEntityManagerFactoryBean"
              p:dataSource-ref="dataSource">
   <property name="jpaVendorAdapter" ref="jpaVendorAdapter"/>
       </bean>

     <bean id="transactionManager"➥
class="org.springframework.orm.jpa.JpaTransactionManager"
                     p:entityManagerFactory-ref="entityManagerFactory"/>

   <context:annotation-config/>

   <tx:annotation-driven mode="aspectj"/>

   <bean class="org.springframework.dao.annotation.➥
PersistenceExceptionTranslationPostProcessor"/>

   <bean id="helloWorldServiceBean"➥
class="com.apress.springosgi.ch5.servicedao.HelloWorldDAO"/>

</beans>
```

■ **Note** If you are curious to see how this Spring descriptor differs from the one used in the stand-alone Spring application in Chapter 2, consult Listing 2-27. The bean names and injection values are strikingly similar.

This listing's first statement activates AspectJ's load-time weaver on the bundle. The next statement instantiates the `entityManagerFactory` bean, injecting it with both a `dataSource` and `jpaVendorAdapter` bean. Further note that both these beans are backed by OSGi services in other bundles—services that are looked up using Spring-DM's `<reference>` element in the bundle's `osgi-context.xml` file, presented next.

Continuing with the `module-context.xml` file, though, you will find the creation of the `transactionManager` bean, which is itself injected with the `entityManagerFactory` bean. Next is the `<context:annotation-config/>` statement, used to activate the inspection of annotations like `@PersistenceContext`, employed in the bundle's DAO class.

Next, the statement `<tx:annotation-driven mode="aspectj"/>` instructs Spring to automatically perform declarative transaction management on annotated classes, such as the bundle's DAO class. Immediately after is the `PersistenceExceptionTranslation PostProcessor` bean, used for performing exception translation on classes annotated with `@Repository`, like the bundle's DAO class.

Finally, you can find the instantiation of the helloWorldServiceBean that will be published as an OSGi service for consumption by other application bundles. The publication of this last service is delegated to Spring-DM elements, which by default are placed in a bundle's osgi-context.xml file. Listing 5-22 illustrates the service's bundle osgi-context.xml file.

Listing 5-22. *osgi-context.xml for the Database Bundle*

```
<?xml version="1.0" encoding="UTF-8"?>
<beans:beans
   xmlns="http://www.springframework.org/schema/osgi"
   xmlns:xsi="http://www.w3.org/2001/XMLSchema-instance"
   xmlns:beans="http://www.springframework.org/schema/beans"
   xsi:schemaLocation="http://www.springframework.org/schema/osgi
       http://www.springframework.org/schema/osgi/spring-osgi.xsd
       http://www.springframework.org/schema/beans
       http://www.springframework.org/schema/beans/spring-beans.xsd">

    <service id="helloWorldService"
             ref="helloWorldServiceBean"
             interface="com.apress.springosgi.ch5.service.HelloWorldService" />

    <reference id="dataSource" interface="javax.sql.DataSource"/>
    <reference id="jpaVendorAdapter"➥
 interface="org.springframework.orm.jpa.JpaVendorAdapter"/>

</beans:beans>
```

This last listing makes use of Spring-DM's <service> and <reference> elements. The <service> declaration registers the helloWorldServiceBean as an OSGi service under the name helloWorldService using the service bundle's interface com.apress.springosgi.ch5.service.HelloWorldService.

On the other hand, the <reference> statements are used to look up services by the interfaces javax.sql.DataSource and org.springframework.orm.jpa.JpaVendorAdapter, assigning them to the identifiers dataSource and jpaVendorAdapter. Note that these last identifiers are injected into the beans declared in the bundle's module-context.xml file (Listing 5-21).

Now that you are familiar with both the service interface bundle and service implementation (DAO-JPA) bundle configuration files, copy each of the earlier files to the following locations in the Hello World "playground": the service bundle's MANIFEST.MF file in Listing 5-18 to the subdirectory /src/META-INF/ch5/service/, the service implementation (DAO-JPA) MANIFEST.MF file in Listing 5-19 and persistence.xml file in Listing 5-20 to the subdirectory `/src/META-INF/ch5/servicedao/`, and the descriptors in Listings 5-21 and 5-22 to the subdirectory `/src/META-INF/ch5/servicedao/spring/`.

Next, we will explore the last bundle belonging to the application, which is bound to the Web.

LOOSE COUPLING—OSGI STYLE!

In the process of partitioning an application into different OSGi bundles, a highly desirable trait in software emerges: loose coupling, a process often defined as making minimal assumptions about the resources used by an application's parts.

Simply look at this application's service bundle, which uses a `dataSource` and `jpaVendorAdapter` reference. This makes the service implementation (DAO-JPA) bundle loosely coupled with respect to its resources. If this concept isn't too clear yet, ask yourself the following questions: Does the service bundle assume the application uses MySQL? No. Does the service bundle assume the application uses Eclipse Link? No it doesn't. Does the service bundle assume anything? Well yes, but only the minimal assumptions of using a `dataSource` and `jpaVendorAdapter` reference.

This confers tremendous advantages, protecting software investments and encouraging software reuse. Say you wanted to use OpenJPA or Hibernate instead of Eclipse Link, or use Oracle instead of MySQL. What changes would you need to make to an application?

By having a loosely coupled application using OSGi bundles, the only thing you would need to do is publish a `dataSource` service backed by Oracle and a `jpaVendorAdapter` service backed by either OpenJPA or Hibernate. The remaining application bundles would continue to work with no changes whatsoever, because they are loosely coupled with respect to their resources—data source and JPA provider—having minimal assumptions.

This is one of the reasons why OSGi is often categorized as an SOA-enabling technology; it fosters one of the primary tenets behind this architectural style, which is loose coupling.

Web Bundle

The web bundle will contain the user interface for the application in the form of a JSP (Listing 5-10), as well as a Spring MVC controller (Listing 5-9) to broker requests onto the application's service DAO class and obtain data to populate the user interface.

This web bundle, though, will differ from the other web deployment units you've used so far in this book. In Chapter 2 you created a standard WAR file, and in Chapter 3 you created a shared services WAR. Here you will make use of the SpringSource dm Server's deployment unit dubbed a Web Module.

As outlined in the "Deployment Units" section of this chapter, a Web Module is completely devoid of any configuration file present in Java EE's standard WAR format and is configured entirely in a bundle's `MANIFEST.MF` file. Given this file's importance, let's take a look at it in Listing 5-23.

Listing 5-23. *The Web Bundle (Module)* `MANIFEST.MF` *file*

```
Manifest-Version: 1.0
Bundle-ManifestVersion: 2
Bundle-SymbolicName: com.apress.springosgi.ch5.web
Bundle-Version: 1.0
Bundle-Name: HelloWorld SpringSource Application Platform Web Module
Bundle-Vendor: Pro Spring-OSGi
Import-Library: org.springframework.spring;version="[2.5,2.6)"
Import-Bundle: com.springsource.org.apache.taglibs.standard;version="[1.1.2,1.1.2]"
Import-Package: com.apress.springosgi.ch5.model;version="1.0.0",
 com.apress.springosgi.ch5.service;version="1.0.0"
Module-Type: Web
Web-ContextPath: helloworld
Web-DispatcherServletUrlPatterns: /spring/*
```

Like the other application `MANIFEST.MF` files, this file makes use of the `Import-Library`, `Import-Bundle`, and `Import-Package` directives. Among the imports you will find the Spring Framework library, the Apache Taglibs library, which is used to compile the user interface JSP, and the application packages included in the model and service bundles.

However, the last three directives in this `MANIFEST.MF` file deserve special attention. The `Module-Type: Web` directive is used to mark the bundle as a Web Module, telling the SpringSource dm Server to take the necessary steps to deploy the bundle's logic onto the OSGi'fied Apache Tomcat container. Given that this bundle will be deployed as a web application, it's necessary to further specify some standard properties used by this type of application.

In a standard WAR or shared service WAR like those you created in Chapter 2 and Chapter 3, the `web.xml` file serves to specify things like servlet mappings and filter mappings, as well as context paths that serve to indicate an application's deployment URL. In a Web Module this file does not exist; taking its place are directives like `Web-ContextPath` and `Web-DispatcherServletUrlPatterns`.

The `Web-ContextPath: helloworld` Spring-DM header indicates that the web bundle should be deployed under the URL `<hostname>/helloworld/`, while the `Web-DispatcherServletUrlPatterns: /spring/*` directive indicates that all requests matching the URL pattern `<hostname>/helloworld/`**`spring`**`/` be processed by the bundle's Dispatcher servlet (Listing 5-9). As a further point of comparison with Chapter 2's application, you can look at Listing 2-26 and see the similarities between a `web.xml` file and these last two directives.

Moving along we come to the web bundle's `module-context.xml` file, which contains the standard Spring artifacts. Listing 5-24 shows this file.

Listing 5-24. *module-context.xml for the Web Bundle (Module)*

```
<?xml version="1.0" encoding="UTF-8"?>
<beans xmlns="http://www.springframework.org/schema/beans"➥
 xmlns:xsi="http://www.w3.org/2001/XMLSchema-instance"
               xmlns:context="http://www.springframework.org/schema/context"➥
 xmlns:jee="http://www.springframework.org/schema/jee"
               xmlns:tx="http://www.springframework.org/schema/tx"
               xsi:schemaLocation="
                       http://www.springframework.org/schema/beans➥
 http://www.springframework.org/schema/beans/spring-beans-2.5.xsd
                       http://www.springframework.org/schema/context➥
 http://www.springframework.org/schema/context/spring-context-2.5.xsd
                       http://www.springframework.org/schema/jee➥
 http://www.springframework.org/schema/jee/spring-jee-2.5.xsd
                       http://www.springframework.org/schema/tx➥
 http://www.springframework.org/schema/tx/spring-tx-2.5.xsd">

        <context:component-scan base-package="com.apress.springosgi.ch5.web"/>

<bean id="helloWorldController"➥
 class="com.apress.springosgi.ch5.web.HelloWorldController">
 <property name="helloWorldService" ref="helloWorldServiceBean"/>
</bean>

<bean id="urlMapper"➥
 class="org.springframework.web.servlet.handler.SimpleUrlHandlerMapping">
        <property name="mappings">
         <props>
          <prop key="/**">helloWorldController</prop>
         </props>
        </property>
</bean>

<bean id="jspViewResolver"➥
 class="org.springframework.web.servlet.view.InternalResourceViewResolver">
      <property name="viewClass"➥
 value="org.springframework.web.servlet.view.JstlView"/>
               <property name="prefix" value="/jsp/"/>
               <property name="suffix" value=".jsp"/>
</bean>

</beans>
```

This last module-context.xml file starts off with the <context:component-scan> element, used to trigger the scanning of the package containing the bundle's servlet mapping annotations. The next statement is used to instantiate the helloWorldController bean, which in itself is injected with the helloWorldService bean, which is backed by an OSGi service that is looked up in this same bundle's osgi-context.xml file (illustrated next).

Continuing with the module-context.xml file, note the instantiation of the urlMapper bean, which indicates that all requests (pkey="**") should be processed by the helloWorldController bean. And finally, you will encounter the jspViewResolver bean, which indicates that Spring's InternalResourceViewResolver class will be used for rendering the application's view, and that it attempts to locate the corresponding view files under the /jsp/ directory (<property name="prefix") with a .jsp extension (<property name="suffix").

You can compare this last listing to the one used in Chapter 2's stand-alone Spring application by consulting Listing 2-28. The differences you will find arise because the descriptor in Listing 5-24 does not use Apache Tiles or Spring's AJAX support.

Next, we come to the web bundle's descriptor containing Spring-DM artifacts. Listing 5-25 shows this descriptor, osgi-context.xml.

Listing 5-25. *osgi-context.xml for the Web Bundle (Module)*

```
<?xml version="1.0" encoding="UTF-8"?>
<beans:beans
   xmlns="http://www.springframework.org/schema/osgi"
   xmlns:xsi="http://www.w3.org/2001/XMLSchema-instance"
   xmlns:beans="http://www.springframework.org/schema/beans"
   xsi:schemaLocation="http://www.springframework.org/schema/osgi
       http://www.springframework.org/schema/osgi/spring-osgi.xsd
       http://www.springframework.org/schema/beans
       http://www.springframework.org/schema/beans/spring-beans.xsd">

    <reference id="helloWorldServiceBean"➥
 interface="com.apress.springosgi.ch5.service.HelloWorldService"/>
</beans:beans>
```

This last descriptor has only one statement, the Spring-DM <reference> element used to look up a service with the HelloWorldService interface—the one provided by the service bundle—which is injected into the controller bean declared in the bundle's osgi-context.xml file.

This concludes the description of the application's Web Module. Copy the `MANIFEST.MF` file in Listing 5-23 to the subdirectory `/src/META-INF/ch5/web/` of the Hello World "playground" and the descriptors in Listings 5-24 and 5-25 to the subdirectory `/src/META-INF/ch5/service/web/` in the same Hello World "playground."

Next, I will describe the last application bundle you will need to create for the Hello World application, which targets the SpringSource dm Server.

Platform Archive

The PAR will provide the Hello World application with supporting functionality like service scoping and dynamic import propagation, features that were assumed when designing the application and are among the most important offerings in the SpringSource dm Server.

Important as the PAR format is to harnessing the power of the SpringSource dm Server, it only requires the inclusion of a `MANIFEST.MF` file, as well as the packaged bundles that will make up an application.

Listing 5-26 illustrates the Hello World application's PAR `MANIFEST.MF` file.

Listing 5-26. *Platform Archive `MANIFEST.MF` File*

```
Manifest-Version: 1.0
Application-SymbolicName: com.apress.springosgi.ch5.HelloWorld
Application-Version: 1.0
Application-Name: HelloWorld SpringSource dm Server
Application-Description: A Hello World Platform Archive for Pro-Spring OSGi
```

This last `MANIFEST.MF` file does not contain the typical directives used by all bundles. With the exception of the `Manifest-Version: 1.0` directive, the remaining directives are exclusive to the SpringSource dm Server. However, the naming conventions should be sufficient to clarify their purpose, giving a PAR a symbolic name, version, name, and description.

Copy the `MANIFEST.MF` file in Listing 5-26 to the `src/META-INF/ch5/service/par/` subdirectory of the Hello World "playground."

Next, we will finish the application by building and deploying it.

Building and Deploying the Application

Using the same tools as other chapters in the book, the build process for the SpringSource dm Server application will use Apache Ant. To start the build process for the SpringSource dm Server Hello World application, place yourself in the Hello World "playground" root directory and modify the `build.xml` file to include the Apache Ant task illustrated Listing 5-27.

Note If you skipped the example presented in Chapter 1, you will not have a preexisting `build.xml` file to modify. In that case, you will need to copy the `build.xml` file presented in Listing 1-6, which is the base Apache Ant file needed by Listing 5-27.

Listing 5-27. *Apache Ant Task for Building the SpringSource dm Server Hello World Application*

```
   <target name="ch5" depends="compile" ➥
description="Build Chapter 5 Spring-OSGi Application">

    <echo message="-------------- Building Chapter 5 Spring-OSGi Application for ➥
Pro Spring-OSGi --------------"/>

     <property name="ch5.dir"          value="${dist.dir}/ch5/"/>
     <mkdir dir="${ch5.dir}"/>

     <jar destfile="${ch5.dir}/helloworld-db.jar" ➥
manifest="${src.dir}/META-INF/ch5/db/MANIFEST.MF">
         <fileset  dir="${build.dir}">
           <include name="com/apress/springosgi/ch5/db/*"/>
         </fileset>
        <metainf dir="${src.dir}/META-INF/ch5/db/"/>
     </jar>

     <jar destfile="${ch5.dir}/helloworld-model.jar" ➥
manifest="${src.dir}/META-INF/ch5/model/MANIFEST.MF">
         <fileset  dir="${build.dir}">
           <include name="com/apress/springosgi/ch5/model/*"/>
         </fileset>
        <metainf dir="${src.dir}/META-INF/ch5/model/"/>
     </jar>

     <jar destfile="${ch5.dir}/helloworld-eclipselink.jar" ➥
manifest="${src.dir}/META-INF/ch5/eclipselink/MANIFEST.MF">
        <metainf dir="${src.dir}/META-INF/ch5/eclipselink/"/>
     </jar>

     <jar destfile="${ch5.dir}/helloworld-service.jar" ➥
manifest="${src.dir}/META-INF/ch5/service/MANIFEST.MF">
         <fileset  dir="${build.dir}">
           <include name="com/apress/springosgi/ch5/service/*"/>
```

```
        </fileset>
       <metainf dir="${src.dir}/META-INF/ch5/service/"/>
   </jar>
     <jar destfile="${ch5.dir}/helloworld-servicedao-jpa.jar" ➥
manifest="${src.dir}/META-INF/ch5/servicedao/MANIFEST.MF">

        <fileset  dir="${build.dir}">

          <include name="com/apress/springosgi/ch5/servicedao/*"/>

        </fileset>

       <metainf dir="${src.dir}/META-INF/ch5/servicedao/"/>

     </jar>

   <jar destfile="${ch5.dir}/helloworld-web.jar" ➥
manifest="${src.dir}/META-INF/ch5/web/MANIFEST.MF">
        <fileset  dir="${build.dir}">
          <include name="com/apress/springosgi/ch5/web/*"/>
        </fileset>
       <metainf dir="${src.dir}/META-INF/ch5/web/"/>
       <zipfileset dir="${src.dir}/GUI/ch5/" prefix="MODULE-INF"/>
     </jar>

    <jar destfile="${ch5.dir}/helloworld.par" ➥
manifest="${src.dir}/META-INF/ch5/par/MANIFEST.MF">
        <fileset  dir="${ch5.dir}">
          <include name="helloworld-db.jar"/>
          <include name="helloworld-model.jar"/>
          <include name="helloworld-eclipselink.jar"/>
          <include name="helloworld-service.jar"/>
          <include name="helloworld-servicedao-jpa.jar"/>

          <include name="helloworld-web.jar"/>
        </fileset>
    </jar>

   </target>
```

Caution You need to ensure all compile dependencies for the application are placed in the `lib` directory of your Hello World "playground." If you skipped the previous chapters, you will need to copy the following JARs to the `lib` directory of your Hello World "playground."

`persistence.jar`: Located in the `lib/j2ee` directory of the Spring Framework with dependencies download

`spring-beans.jar`: Located in the `dist/modules` directory of the Spring Framework with dependencies download

`spring-tx.jar`: Located in the `dist/modules` directory of the Spring Framework with dependencies download

`spring-webmvc.jar`: Located in the `dist/modules` directory of the Spring Framework with dependencies download

`spring.jar`: Located in the `dist` directory of the Spring Framework with dependencies download

---

This Ant task starts by defining a dependency on the `compile` target, ensuring that all application classes are compiled prior to being packaged. Immediately after, a build directory is created in which the application's bundles are placed. The remaining statements perform the packaging of the application's bundles.

The first five bundle creation statements follow an identical approach, taking the appropriate `MANIFEST.MF` file from a bundle's designated Hello World "playground" directory and packaging it with the corresponding compiled classes for each bundle.

The next-to-last statement is used to create the web bundle. This statement, though, differs slightly from the previous ones in that it has a SpringSource-AP Web Module format. This requires placing an application's GUI files—JSP, HTML, and CSS—inside a special bundle directory named `MODULE-INF`, hence the use of the additional declaration `<zipfileset dir="${src.dir}/GUI/ch5/" prefix="MODULE-INF"/>`.

Finally, you can observe the last statement used to create the application's PAR file. This sequence simply takes the PAR `MANIFEST.MF` file located in the subdirectory `src/META-INF/ch5/par/MANIFEST.MF` and groups it with all the application's bundles.

With this entire Ant task placed inside the `build.xml` file of the "playground," execute the command `ant ch5`. On completion, you will have the following bundles under the `src/dist/ch5/` directory: `helloworld-db.jar`, `helloworld-model.jar`, `helloworld-eclipselink.jar`, `helloworld-service.jar`, `helloworld-servicedao-jpa.jar`, `helloworld-web.jar`, and `helloworld.par`.

The `helloworld.par` file is the only one required for deploying the application in the SpringSource dm Server. Having the application's PAR file, the next step is to ensure that the application and the SpringSource dm Server have all of their external dependencies in check.

Having a running MySQL RDBMS is the first prerequisite before PAR deployment. Recall, however, that this application is based on the same database schema used in Chapter 2, so if you followed along, you will already be set.

If you skipped Chapter 2, you can find instructions on setting up MySQL in that chapter, as well as instructions on creating the database schema and prepopulating the application with data in Listing 2-31.

Even though the SpringSource dm Server comes with many built-in bundles, you will need to copy the bundles you downloaded in Table 5-2 to the SpringSource dm Server's repository. So with MySQL up and running, the next step is copying the application's external bundle dependencies to the SpringSource dm Server's `/repository/bundles/usr/` directory.

The bundles' names, which are shown earlier in Table 5-2, are

```
com.springsource.com.mysql.jdbc-5.1.6.jar
com.springsource.org.eclipse.persistence.antlr-1.0.0.jar
com.springsource.org.apache.commons.dbcp-1.2.2.osgi.jar
com.springsource.org.eclipse.persistence.asm-1.0.0.jar
com.springsource.org.apache.commons.pool-1.4.0.jar
com.springsource.org.eclipse.persistence.jpa-1.0.0.jar
com.springsource.org.eclipse.persistence-1.0.0.jar
```

With the application's PAR file in hand, MySQL running, and the application's external bundle dependencies installed, log in to the SpringSource dm Server Admin Console as outlined at the start of the example and illustrated in Figure 5-2.

Once there, navigate to the Deploy an Application section and click the Browse button to search for the application's PAR file. A typical location would be `<playground_home>/dist/ch5/helloworld.par`. Next, click Upload.

Upon processing you should see a screen like the one in Figure 5-5.

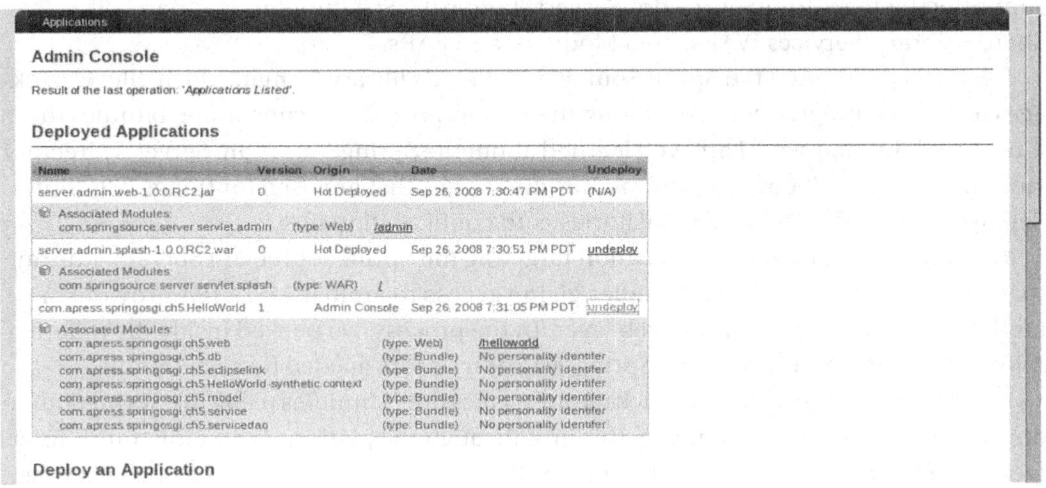

Figure 5-5. *SpringSource dm Server administrative interface with the deployed Hello World application*

Congratulations! You've just deployed your first application in the SpringSource dm Server. If you click the /helloworld link or point your browser to the URL `http://localhost:8080/helloworld/`, you will be able to see the application's main page.

You're done, but before moving on to the next chapter, there is an interesting thing to note about the deployment information presented in Figure 5-5. Look at the Associated Modules summary of Hello World PAR. Besides the bundles you created, there is another bundle by the name `com.apress.springosgi.ch5.HelloWorld-synthetic.context`.

This last bundle, generated by the SpringSource dm Server upon deployment of the PAR, is what makes the property `import-scope:=application` function. As you will recall, it's precisely this property that allows a bundle to share a package—or bundle—with all of the application's bundles via a shared thread-context class loader.

It may seem inconsequential, but its value is a critical factor in easing the use of techniques like persistence in the context of Spring-DM and OSGi.

Summary

In this chapter you learned how the SpringSource Application Platform (SpringSource dm Server) helps to deploy OSGi applications in enterprise settings. You saw that a standalone OSGi environment lacks many of the facilities associated with Enterprise Java applications. It turns out that SpringSource dm Server supports such features—for instance, native Java EE web applications, weaving, and monitoring support in the context of OSGi.

You then learned about the SpringSource dm Server's architecture, and how it's built on the foundations of Apache Tomcat as its Java OSGi'fied container and Eclipse Equinox as its OSGi environment. Additionally, you saw the various deployment unit formats supported by the SpringSource dm Server: standard OSGi bundles, standard WARs, Shared Library/Services WARs, Web Modules, and PARs.

Next, you discovered the SpringSource dm Server's library format, which allows packages to be logically grouped, facilitating the import process for consuming bundles to more simpler statements. Later you learned about the SpringSource dm Server's directory structure, and how it possesses numerous directories that are used for things like "hot" deployment, log files, bundle repositories, and configuration files.

You went on to design an application targeting the SpringSource dm Server platform that consisted of five separate bundles giving access to an RDBMS, a JPA provider, a model layer, a service layer, and web layer. In the process, we peeked inside the different `MANIFEST.MF` files, and Spring and Spring-DM descriptors needed by each bundle.

Finally, you found out how to package an application's bundles using the SpringSource dm Server's PAR format and deploy this unit through the platform's administrative interface. The final result is a live end-to-end OSGi application running on the SpringSource dm Server, using Eclipse Link as the JPA provider, Spring's MVC, and MySQL as the RDBMS.

CHAPTER 6

■■■

Versioning with OSGi and Spring

Java compilers can forewarn you of many flaws present in an application, but when it comes to versioning, compilers know little except the underlying Java platform version being used. This can make class versioning conflicts one of the hardest problems to correct, since they can be discovered only when an application enters Java's runtime.

A compiler can ensure an application has access to Class A, but it is only Java's runtime that will detect that an application relies on two or more versions of Class A. Often version conflicts are so subtle only *you* can detect them, like minor business logic modifications between versions that are only discoverable after an application is put to use.

Similarly, Java applications using well-known libraries can be difficult to deploy given the number of versions (a.k.a. releases) these libraries tend to have. With the exception of the classical README file indicating "This application requires version 2.5 of the Y library," it is *you* who needs to ensure the appropriate library version is used at runtime.

OSGi handles a lot of these versioning conflicts for you, warning you about them right at deployment. Next, I will discuss the overall benefits and concepts of versioning and how these are applied to OSGi and Spring.

Benefits and Concepts

Versioning is a process ingrained in any software's life cycle. Product releases use versions to distinguish between milestones, source code repositories use versioning to keep track of advances in development, and the list goes on.

However, enforcing versioning when a Java application enters its runtime proves difficult. As outlined in the OSGi introduction back in Chapter 1, Java *by itself* possesses a very simple class-loading mechanism that does not allow it to support more robust features like versioning.

Still, you may question what you gain by using versioning at runtime in your applications. The following list details some of these benefits:

- Ability to deploy packages/classes using the same namespace simultaneously on a JVM (e.g., Class A requires Class B, and a newer version of Class B is required by Class C in the same application).

- No need to use Java class loaders designed through APIs to enforce package/class isolation. Package/class clashes can be avoided by using version numbers on multiple packages by the same name.

- Ability to enforce minimum or range version requirements at runtime (e.g., Package A requires a minimum version 1.1 of Library X or Package B requires a version between 1.0 to 2.0 of Library Y).

Application designers often try to avoid being boxed into such versioning "corners" at all costs, putting upgrades or new application functionality on hold for fear of disturbing what already works.

For others, introducing a new class or library version into an application can cause angst, as it entails either the painstaking task of retesting an entire application to ensure everything works as expected or simply taking a leap of faith ("Let's hope it all works").

Introducing new class or library versions doesn't have to be such a pain. OSGi allows your applications to use multiple versions without many worries, not only allowing you to run different versions in the same JVM, but also advising you at deployment time whether an application is lacking certain dependencies right down to specific versions.

Like any other versioning strategy, OSGi has its own characteristics:

- Versioning is based on a three-digit notation and optional alphanumeric string (e.g., 1.3.0, 2.0.0.RC1, 1.4.0.Beta).

- Versioning can be range bound (e.g., from 1.1.0 to 2.5.0, from 1.0.0.RC to 3.0.0).

- Versioning can be enforced at the Java package level.

- Versioning can be enforced at the Java bundle (JAR) level.

One of the biggest benefits of OSGi's versioning strategy is that it's performed in the `MANIFEST.MF` file that accompanies bundles (JARs). This simplifies the versioning process since it's not tangled up with code, but rather left to the last step in the development process, which is grouping classes into deployable units or OSGi bundles.

A `MANIFEST.MF` file can contain various OSGi headers that use versions values. Table 6-1 illustrates the different OSGi headers that support versioning.

Table 6-1. *OSGi Headers Supporting Versioning*

Directive	Purpose
OSGi Manifest Headers	
`Manifest-Version`	Indicates manifest version. NOTE: This value is always set to `1.0` for OSGi bundles.
`Bundle-ManifestVersion`	Indicates bundle-manifest version. Note that this value is always set to `2` for bundles targeting OSGi framework v.4.0 or higher. Future OSGi versions may use a different number.
OSGi Bundle Headers	
`Bundle-Version`	Assigns a bundle's version.
`Bundle-SymbolicName`	Serves as an identifier along with `Bundle-Version`. (`Bundle-Version` provides the number against `Bundle-SymbolicName` values; they both work together.)
`Require-Bundle`	Imports the exported packages of a Java bundle into another bundle.
OSGi Package Headers	
`Export-Package`	Exports a bundle's Java packages for the benefit of other bundles.
`Import-Package`	Imports Java packages from another bundle.
`DynamicImport-Package`	Dynamically imports Java packages from another bundle.
OSGi Fragment Header	
`Fragment-Host`	Assigns a fragment to a host bundle.
OSGi Spring-DM Header	
`SpringExtender-Version`	Assigns a target version of a Spring extender to a host bundle.
OSGi SpringSource dm Server Header	
`Library-Version`	Assigns a library's version.
`Library-SymbolicName`	Serves as an identifier along with `Library-Version`.
`Import-Bundle`	Imports a bundle using SpringSource dm Server semantics.
`Import-Library`	Imports a library using SpringSource dm Server semantics.
`Application-Version`	Assigns an application's version.
`Application-SymbolicName`	Serves as an identifier along with `Application-Version`.

OSGi's manifest headers `Manifest-Version` and `Bundle-ManifestVersion` always use a single-digit version value, which is the same for all applications targeting OSGi framework v4.0 or higher. As an application developer, you usually don't have to deal with these two version values, but since I am on the topic of OSGi versioning, it's important you be aware of their existence. The remaining OSGi headers use a three-digit/two-dot notation version value in the form `0.0.0`.

From this group of OSGi headers, only those appended with `-Version` require the explicit use of version values. Version assignments for the remaining headers are optional. OSGi headers requiring explicit version values use a syntax like `<Header_Name>: 0.0.0`, and those with optional version values use a syntax like `<Header_Name>: <package/bundle/library>;version ="0.0.0"`.

There is not much to say about headers requiring explicit version values, since a version value is the only piece of information assigned to this type of header. But the remaining headers rely on a special syntax to assign version values on a case-by-case basis.

In this last group of OSGi headers—those with optional version values—a comma (`,`) is used to delimit a list of values corresponding to packages, bundles, or libraries (e.g., `Import-Package: com.apress.ch1,com.apress.ch2,com.apress.ch3`). However, a semicolon (`;`) can be used to assign properties to each value in a comma-separated header list.

One of these properties is `version`, indicating the assignment of a version delimited by quotes (") (e.g., `Import-Package: com.apress.ch1;version="1.0.0"`). By using this `version` property, you are telling the OSGi environment at the moment a bundle is installed "Please *wire* the package `com.apress.ch1` with version 1.0.0 to this bundle." If the package cannot be found, the OSGi environment will warn you in addition to leaving the bundle in an installed state instead of changing it to a resolved state. Chapter 1's Figure 1-2 illustrates a bundle's states and transitions.

■ **Note** *Wire* is a widely used term in OSGi. It indicates a "link," or association, between installed packages and bundles in an OSGi environment. It's common to see phrasing like "Bundle A has a wire to package X" or "Bundle B has a wire to package Y." This generally means one bundle uses a package in another bundle, and there is said to be a wire between them.

The `version` property is optional. However, if it is omitted, OSGi always interprets the version property as `version=[0.0.0,)"`. This last notation indicates a version range from 0 to infinity; in other words, it's interpreted by an OSGi environment as "Any version for the package/bundle/library declared prior to ; will do." Version ranges are not applicable for exports (you can't include them in the `Export-Package` header); you can only use version ranges to **import** packages or bundles.

This version range notation can also be used to indicate specific values, with the syntax following the mathematical conventions of brackets (`[]`) to indicate inclusive values or parentheses (`()`) for noninclusive values. For example, a range definition `version="[1.0.0,2.0.0)"` would indicate from version 1.0.0 inclusively (as indicated by the opening bracket, [) up to but not including (as indicated by the closing parenthesis,)) 2.0.0. A range `version="(5.0.0,10.0.0)"` would indicate a version higher than, but not including, version 5.0.0 (as indicated by the opening parenthesis, () up to, but not including, version 10.0.0.

Now that you are aware of OSGi's versioning syntax and the headers that support it, I will break down and illustrate the specific behaviors for each header based on its area of influence.

Each of the versioning behaviors presented next is taken from the context of the application presented in Chapter 3, unless otherwise specified. Therefore, this chapter will not require you to set up a new application, but rather only present a series of `MANIFEST.MF` and accompanying files that you can substitute from this earlier example.

OSGi Package Versioning Behaviors

Package headers are by far the most common type of header used in OSGi applications, comprising `Export-Package`, `Import-Package`, and `DynamicImport-Package`. These headers control what each bundle's class loader is able to access and expose to other bundles running in an OSGi environment.

Let's start things off by looking at the `Export-Package` package behavior. Let's assume the service layer for the application presented in Chapter 3 requires an upgrade to support new functionality. Listing 6-1 illustrates what the application's new service interface would look like.

Listing 6-1. *`HelloWorldService` Modified Service Interface*

```
package com.apress.springosgi.ch3.service;

import com.apress.springosgi.ch3.model.HelloWorld;

public interface HelloWorldService {

    public HelloWorld find();

    public HelloWorld qualify(HelloWorld hw);

    public boolean validate(HelloWorld hw);

    public HelloWorld update(HelloWorld hw);

    public void save(HelloWorld hw );

    public void delete(HelloWorld hw);

}
```

This last interface adds two new service methods to the application's service layer. However, incorporating this new interface into the application does not mean you need to replace the earlier interface by the same name or even make modifications to other parts of the application that relied on the older version.

Two different interfaces—or classes for that matter—with the same name can perfectly co-inhabit the same JVM instance if an OSGi framework is used to manage them. In this case, the interface presented in Listing 6-1 would need to be packaged in its own bundle using a `MANIFEST.MF` file like the one illustrated Listing 6-2.

Listing 6-2. *`MANIFEST.MF` for the Modified Service Bundle*

```
Bundle-Version: 2.0
Bundle-SymbolicName: com.apress.springosgi.ch3.service
Bundle-Name: HelloWorld Spring-OSGi Service
Bundle-Vendor: Pro Spring-OSGi
Import-Package: com.apress.springosgi.ch3.model;version="1.0.0"
Export-Package: com.apress.springosgi.ch3.service;version="2.0.0"
Bundle-ManifestVersion: 2
```

Note this last `MANIFEST.MF` file now uses `version="2.0.0"` to qualify the `Export-Package` header value, which corresponds to the service interface package. At this juncture, if you took these last two listings and packaged them as a bundle, the bundle could be deployed alongside the original bundle designed in Chapter 3 containing version 1.0.0 of the interface.

Let's assume you've now installed these two bundles with different versions of the `HelloWorldService` interface. How do you access them? The process consists of using either the `Import-Package` header or the `DynamicImport-Package` header in a consuming bundle. Listing 6-3 illustrates the header statement that you would need to add to the `MANIFEST.MF` file of a consuming bundle.

Listing 6-3. *`Import-Package` Statement for the Versioned Package*

```
Import-Package: com.apress.springosgi.ch3.service;version="2.0.0"
```

Note this last statement qualifies the imported package into a bundle's class loader by appending the `version="2.0.0"` property. By doing so, resolution of the consuming bundle will only be successful if this version of the package is installed.

IMPORT-PACKAGE OR DYNAMICIMPORT-PACKAGE?

Both `Import-Package` and `DynamicImport-Package` allow a bundle to import packages into a bundle's class loader, but when should you choose one over the other? If you are uncertain whether a bundle will require a particular class in a package, use `DynamicImport-Package`; otherwise, you should use `Import-Package`. For importing optional packages, either header will do.

Being uncertain whether a bundle requires a certain package might sound strange, but it specifically fits the case for classes using constructs like `Class.forName()`. Under these circumstances, class dependencies tend to be more difficult to detect, since such dependencies are interspersed throughout a class's structure, unlike Java's `import` statements, which can easily be read at the top of a class's body. So a bundle builder might not know in advance the class name a bundle may be requested to load.

As its name implies, `DynamicImport-Package` imports a package dynamically. In other words, it doesn't require the package to be resolved at the time a bundle is installed, but can be resolved dynamically at a later time. Additionally, given this behavior, ***`DynamicImport-Package` supports wildcard (*) imports*** (e.g., `com.apress.ch3.*`), which ease importing multiple packages at once.

`Import-Package`, on the other hand, requires that a package be resolved at the time a bundle is resolved, not to mention it does not support `wildcard` (*) imports.

The `DynamicImport-Package` header is often associated with importing optional packages; however, the `Import-Package` header can also import optional packages using the `resolution:=optional` directive. For example, `DynamicImport-Package:acme` and `Import-Package:acme;resolution:=optional` would both attempt to wire the `acme` package *if available* at the time a bundle is resolved.

There is, however, one subtle difference for importing optional packages using these last two approaches. `DynamicImport-Package` will try to *wire a package every time there is an attempt to load a class for that package,* whereas the `Import-Package` header with the `resolution:=optional` directive will *only try to wire a package when a bundle is resolved.*

Still, it's important to mention what the behavior is for either `Export-Package` or `Import-Package`/`DynamicImport-Package` if one header uses the `version` property while the other does not.

If a package assigned to an `Export-Package` header does not have a `version` property, recall that OSGi automatically assigns the range `version="0.0.0`, which indicates "This is package version 0.0.0." In such cases, any `Import-Package` header—whether using the `version` property or not—would import such a package.

On the other hand, is an `Import-Package` header has no `version` property, and there are multiple exported package versions using the `version` property, the imported package will be the highest version available. (For example, if Listing 6-3 is reduced to a statement like `Import-Package: com.apress.springosgi.ch3.service`, OSGi would still import version 2.0.0 of the package, on account of its being the highest version exported by any installed bundle.) It's important to emphasize that even though one bundle can export version 1.0.0 of a package and another bundle export version 2.0.0 of the same package—thus having them coexist in the same OSGi environment—*a bundle can never see different versions of the same package.*

Therefore, if only certain classes of a bundle require a newer package version while others need to maintain backward compatibility, such classes would need to be partitioned into different bundles in order to use different package versions.

As you can see, using package versions is very straightforward in OSGi. In the next section you will learn about service versioning. See the sidebar "Package Versions or Service Versions?" for more background on why package versioning and service versioning are often closely related.

PACKAGE VERSIONS OR SERVICE VERSIONS?

With any change made to a class's code—which in turn belongs to a package—it can be natural to assume this will always require creating a new package version to support multiple versions. However, in OSGi this is not always the case due to how OSGi deals with class types and services.

Recall that it's a recommended practice for OSGi to register and locate services using interfaces, a process that causes services to be decoupled from consuming bundles. As a consequence, changes made to classes backing a service's logic are not subject to the same OSGi package versioning `MANIFEST.MF` header semantics presented earlier.

If you look at previous chapters and the figures used for illustrating each sample application—such as Figure 3-5 in Chapter 3—you will note there are both service dependencies and type dependencies. Changes made in type dependencies are subject to the versioning semantics of OSGi headers like `Export-Package` and `Import-Package`. On the other hand, changes to service dependencies are dependent on using a versioning strategy based on OSGi registration and lookup procedures.

As a rule of thumb, changes in *method signature* generally require the use of versioning through OSGi headers like `Export-Package` and `Import-Package`, whereas changes in a *method logic* are generally supported through registering multiple versions of the affected service's logic—illustrated next.

OSGi Service Versioning Behaviors

Service versioning is not based on the same semantics as OSGi's multiple headers that use the `version` property. Nevertheless, service versioning can be a very common practice once OSGi applications start to grow.

Take the case of Chapter 3's HelloWorld service, which is used to return a message to a web-based application. This last service's backing class—HelloWorldDAO—returns a message containing "Hello World" and "1.0." In order for the application to return a new message like "Braver New World" and "2.0" without losing the older version, it's not package versions that you need, but rather service versions.

The first step in creating a new service version is of course creating a modified version of the backing class. Listing 6-4 illustrates what this new service implementation class would look like.

Listing 6-4. *Modified HelloWorldDAO Service Implementation Class*

```
package com.apress.springosgi.ch3.servicedao;

import com.apress.springosgi.ch3.service.HelloWorldService;

import java.util.Date;

import com.apress.springosgi.ch3.model.HelloWorld;

public class HelloWorldDAO implements HelloWorldService {

    public HelloWorld find() {
        // Model object will be create here
        HelloWorld hw = new HelloWorld("Braver New World",new Date(),2.0);
        return hw;
    }

    public HelloWorld update(HelloWorld hw) {
        hw.setCurrentTime(new Date());
        return hw;
    }

    public void save(HelloWorld hw) {
        throw new UnsupportedOperationException("Can't save anything, ➥
no RDBMS back here");
    }

    public void delete(HelloWorld hw) {
      throw new UnsupportedOperationException("Can't delete anything, ➥
no RDBMS back here");
    }

}
```

This last listing isn't very different from the one in Chapter 3, except for the hard-coded values, which now reflect a newer version. If you rebuild the service implementation bundle using this new service class and the same MANIFEST.MF file used in Chapter 3, and then attempt to install it alongside Chapter 3's service implementation bundle, the OSGi framework will generate an error.

The error message will indicate a bundle by the same name is already installed. In this case, OSGi is protecting your application from an inadvertent update. In order to bypass this error, you will need to either rename the bundle or assign the bundle a new version, steps that are done using OSGi manifest headers. Listing 6-5 illustrates the MANIFEST.MF file needed by the new service implementation bundle.

Listing 6-5. *Modified MANIFEST.MF for the Service Implementation Bundle*

```
Bundle-Version: 1.5
Bundle-SymbolicName: com.apress.springosgi.ch3.servicedao
Bundle-Name: HelloWorld Spring-OSGi Service DAO
Bundle-Vendor: Pro Spring-OSGi
Import-Package: com.apress.springosgi.ch3.model;version="1.0.0",
 com.apress.springosgi.ch3.service;version="1.0.0",
 org.springframework.util;version="2.5.4",
 org.springframework.beans.factory.xml;version="2.5.4",
 org.springframework.aop;version="2.5.4",
 org.springframework.aop.framework;version="2.5.4",
 org.springframework.osgi.service.exporter.support;version="1.2.0"
Bundle-ManifestVersion: 2
```

This last MANIFEST.MF file modifies the Bundle-Version header to a value of 1.5 and leaves the bundle's name—Bundle-SymbolicName header—the same. If you repackage the service implementation bundle using this last MANIFEST.MF file, the installation of the bundle will now be successful.

Still, you may be left wondering why OSGi reported success. Two bundles are now publishing the same service name—which you haven't modified—yet both have different backing implementation classes. What is happening?

The initial errors for the new service implementation bundle are *type-dependency checks*, specifically on the bundle name and version, which are enforced through OSGi manifest headers. In this case, the Bundle-Version and Bundle-SymbolicName headers are inspected at installation, and OSGi notifies you if a bundle using the same Bundle-Version and Bundle-SymbolicName values is already installed.

By changing the Bundle-Version header value, OSGi is satisfied with the type-dependency check. Equally, you could have used another Bundle-SymbolicName header value to successfully install this new bundle. In the next section, I will describe these last OSGi headers in more detail, but for now one important question remains: how will OSGi behave with two services published under the same name?

By activating both bundles, via each bundle's Spring-DM configuration file, a service using the `HelloWorldService` interface will be registered and made available to consuming bundles. So what service will consuming bundles have access to—the one returning "HelloWorld" and "1.0" or the one returning "Braver New World" and "2.0"? It will be the one with the lowest service ID, which generally belongs to the first installed service implementation bundle.

As you can probably imagine, having access to the first installed service implementation is not a good way to support different versions of an OSGi service. In order to support different service versions in a more robust fashion, there are two approaches that can be incorporated when a *service is registered.*

One is to use the `ranking` attribute and the other to use service properties. Both approaches were briefly described in Chapter 4 along with Spring-DM's `<service>` element, which registers OSGi services using Spring type configuration files.

I'll start by describing the use of the `ranking` attribute. This is an integer assigned to an OSGi service at the time it is registered, which serves as a precedence value for services using the same interface. This mechanism fits nicely with the two service implementations presented in this chapter, since both use the `HelloWorldService` interface.

Listing 6-6 illustrates the `osgi-context.xml` file needed by the new service implementation bundle to register a service via Spring-DM using a `ranking` attribute.

Listing 6-6. *Modified `osgi-context.xml` File Service Implementation Bundle Using the `ranking` Attribute*

```
<?xml version="1.0" encoding="UTF-8"?>
<beans xmlns="http://www.springframework.org/schema/beans"
  xmlns:xsi="http://www.w3.org/2001/XMLSchema-instance"
  xmlns:osgi="http://www.springframework.org/schema/osgi"
  xsi:schemaLocation="http://www.springframework.org/schema/beans➥
 http://www.springframework.org/schema/beans/spring-beans.xsd
                      http://www.springframework.org/schema/osgi➥
 http://www.springframework.org/schema/osgi/spring-osgi.xsd">

  <!-- Create the helloWorldDAO bean -->
  <bean id="helloWorldDAO" class="com.apress.springosgi.ch3.servicedao.Hello➥
WorldDAO"/>

  <!-- Export helloWorldDAO as a service to OSGi via its interface -->
  <osgi:service ref="helloWorldDAO" ranking="100" interface=➥
"com.apress.springosgi.ch3.service.HelloWorldService"/>

</beans>
```

Note the `ranking="100"` value accompanying the `<service>` element. Using this last file in the new service implementation bundle will guarantee that every lookup for a service with the `HelloWorldService` interface will always return this particular version, irrespective of the service ID, which often correlates with the installation order.

The ranking attribute has two advantages. It takes the guesswork out of what service will be returned to bundles looking up a service; if more than one service using the same interface is registered, OSGi will return whichever one was registered with the highest ranking value. And the second advantage is the `ranking` attribute does not require any changes to the lookup sequence of a service used in consuming bundles.

From an OSGi point of view, `ranking` is just a predefined and standard service property. This means service properties are the more general-purpose and robust approach to using multiple versions of the same service. However, unlike `ranking`, using service properties require incorporating not only a new approach to registering services, but also one for looking them up.

Listing 6-7 illustrates the `osgi-context.xml` file needed by the new service implementation bundle to register a service via Spring-DM using service properties.

Listing 6-7. *Modified `osgi-context.xml` File Using Service Properties for the Service Implementation Bundle*

```
<?xml version="1.0" encoding="UTF-8"?>
<beans xmlns="http://www.springframework.org/schema/beans"
  xmlns:xsi="http://www.w3.org/2001/XMLSchema-instance"
  xmlns:osgi="http://www.springframework.org/schema/osgi"
  xsi:schemaLocation="http://www.springframework.org/schema/beans➥
 http://www.springframework.org/schema/beans/spring-beans.xsd
                      http://www.springframework.org/schema/osgi➥
 http://www.springframework.org/schema/osgi/spring-osgi.xsd">

  <!-- Create the helloWorldDAO bean -->

  <bean id="helloWorldDAO"➥
 class="com.apress.springosgi.ch3.servicedao.HelloWorldDAO"/>

  <!-- Export helloWorldDAO as a service to OSGi via its interface -->
  <osgi:service ref="helloWorldDAO"➥
  interface="com.apress.springosgi.ch3.service.HelloWorldService">
 <osgi:service-properties>
    <entry key="version" value="2.0"/>
    <entry key="greeting" value="Braver World"/>
 </osgi:service-properties>
   <osgi:service>
</beans>
```

Note this last listing uses Spring-DM's `<service-properties>` element nested inside the `<service>` element. By doing so, the OSGi service will be registered using key/value pairs that will serve as identifiers for bundles looking up the service. The values assigned through Spring-DM's `<service-properties>` element, which in themselves are contained in Spring `<entry>` elements, are pretty much open ended.

In this case, I opted to use a key named `version` with a string value of `2.0`, as well as a key named `greeting` with a string value of `Braver World`. But any key/value combination is possible. It is also valid to use the `value-ref` attribute—instead of `ref`—to point to a Spring bean value. See Chapter 4 and its Listing 4-4 for more details on registering services using properties.

Registering a service using properties is only one part of the process; the other part consists of looking up a service with these properties. In order to look up a service using properties, you need to use the `filter` attribute in conjunction with Spring-DM's `<reference>` element, both of which were also discussed in Chapter 4.

Listing 6-8 illustrates how a Spring-DM `<reference>` statement using the `filter` attribute would resemble for looking up the previously registered service.

Listing 6-8. *Spring-DM `<reference>` Element Using the `filter` Attribute*

```
<osgi:reference id="helloWorldService"➥
        interface="com.apress.springosgi.ch3.service.HelloWorldService" ➥
filter="(version=2.0)"/>
```

Note this last listing's `filter` attribute has a value of `(version=2.0)`, which is exactly the key/value pair assigned when the service was registered with the interface `HelloWorldService` using Spring-DM's `<service>` and `<service-properties>` elements.

A statement like the one in Listing 6-8 would need to be placed in a service-consuming bundle's Spring-DM configuration file, such as Chapter 3's shared service WAR bundle, which makes use of this service.

When using the `filter` attribute to look up service versions using the same interface, keep in mind two things:

- The filter matching pattern is based on *string values*. In this example, I opted to use the key/value property `(version=2.0)` as a convention on the topic of versions. However, using a filter value of `(version=2.0)` is not equal to one declared as `(version=2)` or `(version=2.0.0)`.

- There is no default service; either the filter is matched or no service is returned. If a filter value does not match the exact pattern for a service property, it doesn't matter whether there are other registered services using the same interface—no service will be returned.

This concludes our review of using multiple OSGi service versions. Next, I will return to discussing OSGi headers that make use of the version property. This time though, the focus will not be on individual package versioning but rather bundle versioning.

OSGi Bundle Versioning Behaviors

Bundle versioning offers a coarser-grained alternative to the package-based approach presented earlier. This does not mean, though, that package versioning can be totally supplanted by bundle versioning. In fact, most well-thought-out OSGi versioning approaches use a combination of the two.

Bundle versioning is supported through the headers Bundle-Version, Bundle-SymbolicName, and Require-Bundle, with the first two headers—Bundle-Version and Bundle-SymbolicName—always working in tandem.

By "tandem," I mean that Bundle-Version values are based on the value assigned to the Bundle-SymbolicName header. In the previous section, "OSGi Service Versioning Behaviors," you learned OSGi protects against installing bundles using the same Bundle-Version and Bundle-SymbolicName values.

But what happens when multiple versions of a bundle using the same Bundle-SymbolicName value are installed? Nothing much really; both bundles continue to operate with the same package and service semantics. Whatever potential clashes might exist between two different bundle versions are only of the package or service kind and are thus resolved according to each of these cases.

In essence, different versions of a bundle using the same Bundle-SymbolicName name are treated as if they were different bundle names altogether. So is the point of versioning bundles that simple? Not exactly—there is a more important reason for versioning bundles that is related to the Require-Bundle header and fragments, which are addressed later. So I will first discuss the purpose of the Require-Bundle header.

The Require-Bundle header is used as a shortcut for importing packages exported by other bundles. Let's first take a look at how the Require-Bundle header would look like in a bundle. Listing 6-9 shows a modified MANIFEST.MF file for the application web bundle (shared services WAR) used in Chapter 3 that leverages the Require-Bundle header.

Listing 6-9. *MANIFEST.MF Using Require-Bundle for a Shared WAR Bundle*

```
Bundle-Version: 1.0
Bundle-SymbolicName: com.apress.springosgi.ch3.web
Bundle-Name: HelloWorld Spring-OSGi Web
Bundle-Vendor: Pro Spring-OSGi
Bundle-Classpath: WEB-INF/classes
Import-Package: com.apress.springosgi.ch3.model;version="1.0.0",
 com.apress.springosgi.ch3.service;version="1.0.0"
```

```
Require-Bundle: com.springsource.javax.servlet;version="2.5.0",
 com.springsource.javax.servlet.jsp;version="2.1.0",
 com.springsource.org.apache.taglibs.standard;version="1.1.2",
 org.springframework.aop;version="2.5.4",
 org.springframework.core;version="2.5.4",
 org.springframework.context;version="2.5.4",
 org.springframework.web;version="2.5.4",
 org.springframework.web.servlet;version="2.5.4",
 org.springframework.bundle.osgi.core;version="1.2.0",
 org.springframework.bundle.osgi.web;version="1.2.0"
Web-ContextPath: /
Bundle-ManifestVersion: 2
```

Though this last `MANIFEST.MF` file still makes use of the `Import-Package` header, notice how the listing is shorter than the one used in Chapter 3 (Listing 3-17) on account of the `Require-Bundle` header.

The values assigned to a `Require-Bundle` header are equivalent to `Bundle-SymbolicName` and `Bundle-Version` values. For example, the value `com.springsource.javax.servlet;version="2.5.0"` indicates a version range `[2.5.0,)`, which specifies importing the packages exported by the bundle with a `Bundle-SymbolicName` value of `com.springsource.javax.servlet` and a `Bundle-Version` value of `2.5.0`. or greater.

In the same manner as unsatisfied OSGi package header values, if OSGi cannot find a bundle by the name and version declared in the `Require-Bundle` header, it will warn you of a type-check error and leave the bundle in an installed state instead of changing the state to resolved.

To illustrate exactly what packages are imported using the `Require-Bundle` header, Listing 6-10 shows the `MANIFEST.MF` file used by the `com.springsource.javax.servlet` bundle, which contains packages related to Java servlets.

Listing 6-10. *`MANIFEST.MF` Using the `com.springsource.javax.servlet` Bundle*

```
Manifest-Version: 1.0
Bundle-Name: Java Servlet API
Created-By: 1.5.0_06-b05 (Sun Microsystems Inc.)
Ant-Version: Apache Ant 1.6.5
Bundle-ManifestVersion: 2
Bundle-Vendor: SpringSource
Bundle-SymbolicName: com.springsource.javax.servlet
Export-Package: javax.servlet;version="2.5.0",
 javax.servlet.http;version="2.5.0";uses:="javax.servlet",
 javax.servlet.resources;version="2.5.0"
Bundle-Version: 2.5.0
```

All packages declared in this last listing's `Export-Package` header are made available to any bundle using a `Require-Bundle` header that matches the values for `Bundle-SymbolicName` and `Bundle-Version`. As you can see, the `Require-Bundle` header is an effective shortcut to using multiple `Import-Package` statements, but you need to be aware of some other issues with it.

One of the more obvious drawbacks to using the `Require-Bundle` header is that the consuming and providing bundles become dependent on one another—being coupled by a bundle's name. This is unlike the more granular `Import-Package` header, where you can pick and choose individual packages irrespective of a bundle.

The effects of this become more obvious once you start versioning. If a providing bundle contains numerous packages, and many consuming bundles rely on the `Require-Bundle` header to use it, each new package version will also require you to create an entirely new bundle version to guarantee backward compatibility, since the `Require-Bundle` header is an "all or nothing" affair.

This last process can quickly become unmanageable if enough packages in a providing bundle require versioning. Using the `Import-Package` header in consuming bundles won't require you to fork new bundle versions each time a package is changed—given this last header's granularity.

Still, if you don't see this previous `Require-Bundle` header behavior as a drawback, you will likely even see a greater benefit to using this header's optional `visibility` directive. By default, if a consuming bundle uses the `Require-Bundle` header, the imported packages will be made available to that bundle alone, but it's possible to extend this availability.

For example, if Bundle B uses a statement like `Require-Bundle:A`, Bundle A's exported packages will only be available to Bundle B. But if Bundle B uses a statement like `Require-Bundle:A ;visibility:=reexport`, this allows any consuming bundle requiring Bundle B—`Require-Bundle:B`—to automatically see the same packages exported by Bundle A. By default, this behavior is not active since the default value for this directive is `visibility:=private`.

The topic of using `Require-Bundle` headers also leads inevitably to the subject of *split packages*, which can only occur if a bundle uses this particular header. Though not related to versioning, split packages are an interesting topic, so the next section will describe them in more detail. If you wish to stick to versioning issues exclusively, you can skip ahead to the section "OSGi Fragment Versioning Behaviors."

REQUIRE-BUNDLE AND IMPORT-PACKAGE MISCONCEPTIONS

The following content is taken from Peter Krien's blog post entitled "Misconceptions about OSGi Headers," `http://www.osgi.org/blog/2006/04/misconceptions-about-osgi-headers.html`, April 2006:

- `Require-Bundle` ensures that the required bundles are initialized before you can use them.
  - False. `Require-Bundle` and `Import-Package` only relate to resolving. Resolving is the process where different bundles are wired to each other on the package level. From the perspective of a bundle, this is an atomic process. The start/stop primitives are completely independent from this resolving process. The only difference between `Require-Bundle` and `Import-Package` is granularity. `Require-Bundle` is internally transformed to the same wires as `Import-Package` uses (except when the more esoteric split packages are desired).
- **Any bundle can contribute classes to imported packages.**
  - False. The framework must select a single exporter for a package that is imported. We call the case where a package can come from multiple sources a split package. This is a common case with the traditional Java class path and a potential source for errors because a package should contain highly cohesive classes; there are also security implications. To address this problem Java added sealed packages. On top of this, the OSGi Specifications added the constraint that a package must have a single source.
  - This said, there is an exception because in certain cases (Java localization, for example), split packages are a necessity. *`Require-Bundle` can therefore be used as a façade to multiple bundles that are aggregated.* From the outside it looks like the bundle exports a single package, but it gets the content from its bundle classpath or other required bundles. Fragments can also be used to provide split packages. However, split packages should be exceptions because of the related security and confusion problems.
- **With `Require-Bundle` you are ensured all packages come from the same source.**
  - True. But the same result can be better achieved with `Import-Package` and the `uses` directive. When packages are not cohesive and are aware of each other's implementation details, then it is paramount that they actually import the same package. In those cases packages cannot be substituted independently. `Import-Package` solves this problem with a package directive that lists the referred (used) packages. For example, Bundle A has Package P that uses Package Q. The Framework ensures that A, and all its wired bundles, shares the same class loader for Package Q.
  - `Require-Bundle` can actually worsen the problem because it can use packages that are internal. The requiree can easily get into trouble if it imports these private packages. For example, a bundle requiring Xerces could separately import `javax.xml.parsers`. If this package is also available privately to the Xerces bundle, then a class cast exception will occur.

- **You must import all packages of an exporter.**
  - False. A bundle should only import the packages that it actually uses. This list is easy to generate from the class files (next-generation Eclipse PDE will track this), and it is usually shorter than most people think. Well-designed libraries have a few access points. These access points must be exported to use the library; however, all the packages that can be referred from the exported package do not have to be exported or imported. Once you have an object from a library, any classes that are linked from this object are automatically loaded from the same class loader. Most Java standards limit the use of a library to a single package that is shared between all implementations. For example, if you use the Apache Derby database, you should not have to import any packages from that library; importing `java.sql` from the Java runtime should be sufficient.
- **Bundles are versioned, packages not**.
  - False. Both bundles and packages are versioned. It is true that most programmers tend to ignore versions altogether, but good developers version both their bundles and packages.
- **A required bundle is a closed collection of code**
  - False. A bundle can be extended by fragments.

Split packages in OSGi occur when a Java package is contained in more than one bundle. For example, Bundle A contains *part* of Package P, and Bundle B *another part* of Package P. Even though OSGi's specification dictates that a package can come only from a single bundle, on certain occasions split packages are inevitable.

So what would be a real-life scenario for using split packages? One case could be related to internationalization (i18n), where the same package name (e.g., `com.apress.springosgi.lang`) is split out into various bundles, with each one supporting a different language (e.g., English, Spanish, French, etc.). Another case could be related to refactoring—the process of enhancing a code base—with one bundle providing the original package (e.g., `com.apress.springosgi.util`) while another bundle provides a series of new classes for the same package.

At first glance, you might think there is no problem installing two bundles using a header like `Export-Package:com.apress.springosgi.lang`, and you would actually be partially correct. An OSGi environment won't balk at installing two bundles exporting the same package; what it will have trouble with is importing the split packages into one bundle.

If a consuming bundle uses `Import-Package:com.apress.springosgi.lang`, and there are two bundles exporting this package, only one will get wired. So how do you support split packages? Easy—*split packages can only work with the use of the* `Require-Bundle` *header.*

Since the `Require-Bundle` header accesses all `Export-Package` values of a declared bundle, its semantics allows it to join split packages. This behavior by the `Require-Bundle` header accompanied by its `visibility:=reexport` directive can serve as facade for split packages.

Figure 6-1 illustrates this scenario of split packages and a facade bundle using the `Require-Bundle` header.

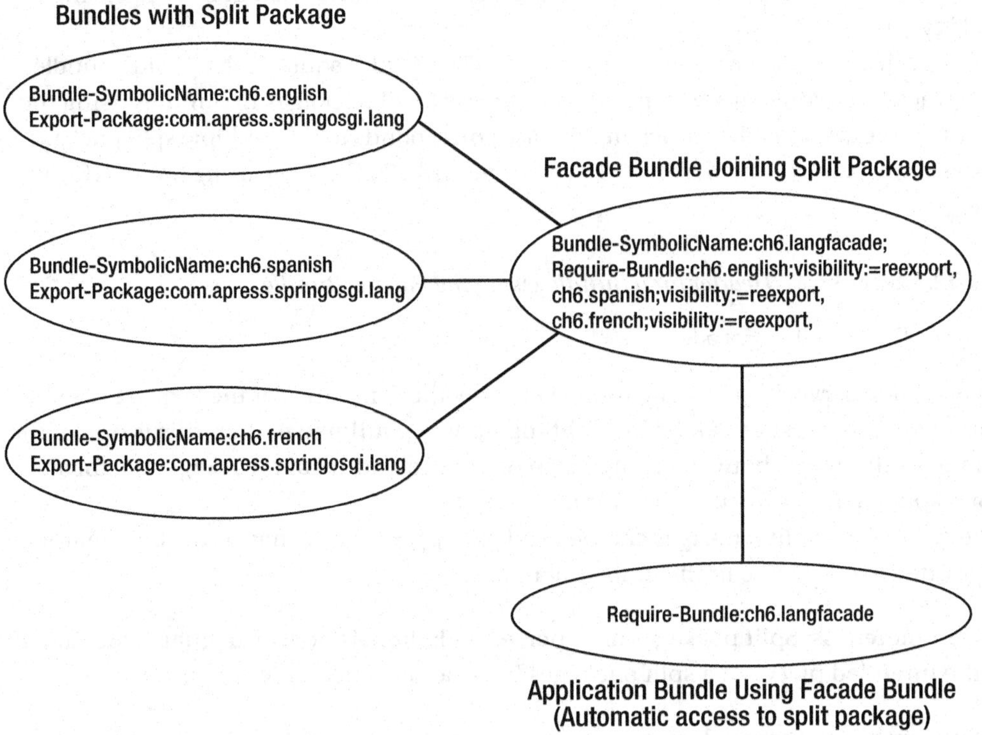

Figure 6-1. *Split packages using a facade with* `Require-Bundle`

Figure 6-1 shows various bundles using the package `com.apress.springosgi.lang`, with each of these bundles having a `Bundle-SymbolicName` in the form `ch6.english`, `ch6.spanish`, and `ch6.french`. In order to bring these split packages together, a new facade bundle is created that leverages the `Require-Bundle` header. Listing 6-11 illustrates the `MANIFEST.MF` file for the facade bundle.

Listing 6-11. *`MANIFEST.MF` Headers for the Facade Bundle `langfacade`*

```
Bundle-SymbolicName: ch6.langfaced;
Require-Bundle: ch6.english;visibility:=reexport,
 ch6.spanish;visibility:=reexport,
 ch6.french;visibility:=reexport
```

Note the values in this listing's `Require-Bundle` header point to each of the bundles containing *a part* of the `com.apress.springosgi.lang` package, while also using the `visibility:=reexport` directive. This means that any other bundle using this facade bundle will automatically have access to all the packages contained in bundles using `visibility:=reexport`.

Therefore, if an application bundle used a `MANIFEST.MF` file requiring this facade bundle, `ch6.langfacade`, it would automatically have access to all packages in bundles using the `visibility:=reexport` header, which in this case corresponds to the multiple split package `com.apress.springosgi.lang`. Listing 6-12 illustrates a `MANIFEST.MF` file using the `langfacade` bundle.

Listing 6-12. *`MANIFEST.MF` Header for a Bundle Using the Facade Bundle*

```
Require-Bundle: ch6.langfacade
```

As you can observe, it's only due to the very specific semantics of the `Require-Bundle` header that a split package can be brought together. As outlined earlier, this is one of the other major differences between using `Require-Bundle` and `Import-Package`: the former supports split packages, while the latter does not.

But even though split packages can be used to support the scenarios outlined earlier, they are often avoided due to the following issues:[1]

- **Completeness**: Split packages are open ended; there is no way to guarantee that all the intended pieces of a split packages have actually been included.

- **Ordering**: If the same classes are present in more than one required bundle, the ordering of `Require-Bundle` is significant. A wrong ordering can cause hard-to-trace errors, as with the Java classpath model.

- **Performance**: A class must be searched in all providers when packages are split. This increases the number of times that a `ClassNotFoundException` must be thrown, which can introduce significant overhead.

- **Confusing**: It is easy to create a very contrived structure of dependencies if a package is spread out in multiple bundles.

---

1. Note that the following list is taken from the OSGi Service Platform Release 4 Specification, Section 3.13.3, `http://www.osgi.org/Specifications/HomePage`.

- **Mutable exports:** The feature of `visibility:=reexport` can unexpectedly change depending on the export signature of the required bundle.
- **Shadowing:** The classes in the requiring bundle that are shadowed by those in a required bundle depend on the export signature of the required bundle and the classes the required bundle contains. (In contrast, `Import-Package`, except with `resolution:=optional`, shadows whole packages regardless of the exporter.)
- **Unexpected signature changes:** The `Require-Bundle` directive `visibility:=private` (the default) may be unexpectedly overridden in some circumstances.

Now that you know the pros and cons of split packages and how they relate to the `Require-Bundle` and `Import-Package` headers, I will switch over to discussing versioning in relation to fragments.

OSGi Fragment Versioning Behaviors

As mentioned in Chapter 4, fragments are bundles that are attached to a host bundle and are treated as part of the host. Similar to the package and bundle versioning approaches explored earlier, fragment versioning is supported through the OSGi header `Fragment-Host`.

If you recall the discussion on fragments, a fragment bundle always possesses a `Fragment-Host` header value, which is compared to installed bundles' `Bundle-SymbolicName` header values. If a match occurs, the fragment is attached to the host with the matching header value; if not, the fragment fails to be installed.

Since a fragment itself is a bundle, it can have its own `Bundle-Version` header; however, this continues to be a bundle versioning header that has little to do with fragment dynamics. The versioning dynamics for fragments are assigned through the `version` property of the `Fragment-Host` header.

For example, if a fragment used a header in the form `Fragment-Host:com.apress.spinrgosgi.ch6;version="2.0.0"`, this would indicate a version range `[2.0.0,)`, which attempts to attach the fragment to a host bundle with a `Bundle-SymbolicName` value of `com.apress.spinrgosgi.ch6` and a `Bundle-Version` of `2.0.0.` or greater.

Similar to other OSGi version header behaviors, the lack of a `version` property on a `Fragment-Host` statement is automatically translated into `version=[0.0.0,)"`—in plain English this means "From 0 to infinity"—indicating this fragment should be attached to any version of a bundle with a matching `Bundle-SymbolicName` value.

So what happens to a fragment if there is more than one bundle using the same `Bundle-SymbolicName` value? The host for the fragment will become the bundle with the highest `Bundle-Version` value. And recall, since there can't be two bundles using the same `Bundle-SymbolicName` value (unless they have a different `Bundle-Version` value), there will always be a bundle that has a highest version value.

As far as fragments and their versioning behavior are concerned, there is nothing more to elaborate on. Next, I will finish off the subject and this chapter on versioning by discussing the dynamics behind Spring-DM's and SpringSource dm Server's proprietary OSGi headers.

OSGi Spring-DM and SpringSource dm Server Versioning Behaviors

As you've learned in previous chapters, not all the necessary functionality to support Spring and OSGi applications is provided by the OSGi standard. To fill this gap, both Spring-DM (discussed in Chapter 4) and the SpringSource dm Server (discussed in Chapter 5) make use of their own proprietary headers.

But proprietary as these headers are, when it comes to versioning and when it's applicable to any of these headers, they use the same syntax and semantics as the standard OSGi headers that support versioning.

The first proprietary header supporting versioning corresponds to Spring-DM's `SpringExtender-Version` header used in application bundles. Revisiting the topic of Spring-DM extenders presented in Chapter 4, recall that once Spring-DM extenders are installed in an OSGi environment, they will always inspect every subsequently installed bundle for the presence of trigger points to execute Spring-DM instructions.

By default, once Spring-DM extenders are installed, they will inspect each and every bundle. The `SpringExtender-Version` header allows an application bundle to override this behavior and indicate that it should only be inspected and processed if a certain version of Spring-DM extender is present.

For example, suppose you want an application to be processed only by Spring-DM's extender version 1.1.0. Listing 6-13 illustrates the header you would need to add to an application bundle.

Listing 6-13. *`MANIFEST.MF` Header for `SpringExtender-Version`*

```
SpringExtender-Version: 1.1.0
```

Note that like every header appended with `Version`, this header requires an explicit three-digit/two-dot value. By using this last header in an application bundle, at the time any Spring-DM extender initiates its scanning process, this header will indicate not to continue or attempt to process any trigger points, unless the Spring-DM extender bundle version is 1.1.0.

The only reason you would use the `SpringExtender-Version` header is for cases when an application bundle requires functionality present only in certain Spring-DM extenders. Given the short lifespan of Spring-DM and its extender versions, for practical purposes this header can be considered esoteric. Nevertheless, once future versions of Spring-DM extenders become available, it can serve to enforce that only certain versions of Spring-DM extenders process application bundles.

Moving through the set of proprietary headers supporting versioning, we come to SpringSource dm Server's set, which includes `Application-Version`, `Library-SymbolicName`, `Library-Version`, `Import-Bundle`, and `Import-Library`.

The `Application-Version` header is only used in `MANIFEST.MF` files that accompany Platform Archives (PARs), which are the preferred format for deploying applications in SpringSource dm Server. Similar to the `Bundle-Version` header, the `Application-Version` header is always used in tandem with the `Application-SymbolicName` header, thus guaranteeing that no two PARs using the same symbolic name and version are deployed simultaneously.

Following the same conventions as other headers appended with `Version`, the `Application-Version` header requires an explicit three-digit/two-dot value. Listing 6-14 illustrates a sample `MANIFEST.MF` file added to a PAR.

Listing 6-14. *`MANIFEST.MF` Headers for `Application-Version` and `Application-SymbolicName`*

```
Application-SymbolicName: com.apress.springosgi.ch6

Application-Version: 1.0.0
```

As you will note, the sole purpose of the `Application-Version` header is to avoid two PARs with the same `Application-SymbolicName` header being deployed simultaneously.

Currently, there are no further implications to using the `Application-Version` header. Which is to say it's not like the `Bundle-Version` header, with its influence on fragments and headers like `Require-Bundle`, though this could change with future versions of the SpringSource dm Server.

Next, we come to the `Library-SymbolicName` and `Library-Version` headers, which serve to declare libraries according to the SpringSource dm Server—see the "Libraries" section in Chapter 5 for more background on the use of libraries.

Applying versions to SpringSource dm Server libraries works in the same way as bundles and applications (PARs). It's necessary to use both a `Library-SymbolicName` and `Library-Version` to avoid two libraries using the same symbolic name and version being deployed inadvertently. Listing 6-15 illustrates a SpringSource dm Server library definition using these two headers.

Listing 6-15. *SpringSource dm Server Library Definition Using `Import-Bundle`*

```
Library-SymbolicName: org.aspectj

Library-Version: 1.6.1

Library-Name: AspectJ

Import-Bundle:
```

```
com.springsource.org.aspectj.runtime;version="[1.6.1 ,1.6.1]",

com.springsource.org.aspectj.weaver;version="[1.6.1, 1.6.1]"
```

Note the `Library-Version` header follows the same conventions as others appended with `Version`, requiring an explicit three-digit/two-dot value, whereas the `Library-SymbolicName` header is a simple text field just like other `SymbolicName`-appended headers.

But before I get to importing such a library, notice the `Import-Bundle` header in the library definition. The `Import-Bundle` header allows a library to import the whole set of packages exported by a particular bundle, in a very similar fashion to `Require-Bundle`, though they do have different semantics. (See Chapter 5's sidebar "SpringSource dm Server Import-Bundle vs. OSGi's Require-Bundle" for the differences.) For example, the statement `com.springsource.org.aspectj.runtime;version="[1.6.1 ,1.6.1]"` in Listing 6-15 indicates to wire the exported packages from the bundle with a `Bundle-SymbolicName` value of `com.springsource.org.aspectj.runtime` and an exact `Bundle-Value` of `1.6.1` into bundles that import this library.

The same versioning syntax and behaviors as `Require-Bundle` and `Import-Package` apply to the `Import-Bundle` header. If no `version` attribute is specified, it will automatically be interpreted as `version=[0.0.0,)`", or from 0 to infinity, meaning any version of a bundle matching `Bundle-SymbolicName`. Equally, noninclusive ranges or exact values can be used.

Next, we come to the `Import-Library` header used directly inside the `MANIFEST.MF` file of application bundles, which is used to grant a bundle access to the entire contents of a SpringSource dm library. Listing 6-16 illustrates a sample `Import-Library` header.

Listing 6-16. *SpringSource dm Server* `Import-Bundle`

```
Import-Library: org.aspectj;version="1.6.1"
```

By using this last statement in an application bundle, you are indicating to the underlying SpringSource dm Server environment that it should load the library with a `Library-SymbolicName` value of `org.aspectj` and a `Library-Version` value of `1.6.1` or greater (e.g., `[1.6.1,)`) into this bundle's class loader.

Similarly, if the `version` property is omitted in this header, it's automatically interpreted as `Import-Library;org.aspectj ;version=[0.0.0,)`, meaning any version of such library should be imported. And following the same versioning semantics as other OSGi headers, if there are two libraries with the same `Library-SymbolicName` value, the one with the highest version will take precedence.

This concludes our review of the different proprietary headers used by Spring-DM and SpringSource dm Server in which versioning can be applied.

Summary

In this chapter you started by learning how OSGi compensates for Java's lack of runtime versioning, allowing you to easily deploy multiple versions of the same class in the same JVM instance, as well as enforce that only certain versions of JAR files (bundles) are used to run an application.

You then read about OSGi's various `MANIFEST.MF` file headers that support versioning, including the notation and conventions used to version packages, bundles, fragments, and more specific Spring-DM and SpringSource dm Server headers.

Next, you explored the dynamics of package versioning using the OSGi headers `ExportPackage` and `Import-Package`/`DynamicImport-Package` to rework the same application created in Chapter 3. Immediately after, you learned about OSGi service versioning, and how to apply service properties and ranking values to allow the deployment of multiple services using the same interface in the same OSGi environment.

Next, you found out about bundle versioning and how the `Bundle-SymbolicName`, `Bundle-Version`, and `Require-Bundle` headers are used to provide a coarser-grained approach to versioning than packages. You also learned about the `Require-Bundle` header and the split packages that are supported thanks to this header.

Finally, you discovered something about the versioning dynamics applied to OSGi fragments, as well as the proprietary headers used by both Spring-DM and SpringSource dm Server to support special behaviors outside of OSGi's scope.

CHAPTER 7

Data Access and Bundle Management Without SpringSource dm Server

Applications usually need some type of external data source, from a Relational Database Management System (RDBMS) to the classical "quick-and-dirty" approach of using text files to store data.

Suitable mechanisms to access many of these data sources from Java have been widely documented. But some Java frameworks require special treatment, depending on the access strategy and data source being used.

Such is the case with the Java Persistence API (JPA) in the context of the Spring Framework accessing an RDBMS, which as illustrated in Chapter 2 requires the use of special weaving classes.

In Chapter 5 you also used JPA, but in the context of OSGi using the SpringSource dm Server, a product that is equipped to handle weaving and other factors needed to use JPA with OSGi. But what happens if you want to access an RDBMS in the context of OSGi and don't want to use the SpringSource dm Server?

This chapter will focus on the peculiarities of using Java's most common approach for accessing data sources in the context of Spring and OSGi without the aid of the SpringSource dm Server.

Further, and to add to your growing toolbox for Spring and OSGi projects, it will introduce you to Apache's Ivy dependency management tool and the BND tool used to inspect and modify JAR files into OSGi bundles. These two tools can aid you in the deployment of Spring and OSGi applications, especially if you don't want to rely on the SpringSource dm Server to provide out-of-the-box application dependencies or the SpringSource Enterprise Bundle Repository to obtain OSGi'fied JARs.

Access to RDBMSs

RDBMSs are the preferred way of storing large amounts of data in the enterprise, so learning the ins and outs of accessing this type of data store in the context of OSGi is vital.

The RDBMS itself is not the main issue for an application leveraging OSGi, but rather the strategy used to access it from Java. As explained in Chapter 2, Java has a wide range of data access strategies extending from JDBC, JDO, and Entity EJBs to Object-Relational Mappers (ORMs).

Using some of these strategies to access an RDBMS is transparent even with the presence of OSGi, but others require special measures to work properly with OSGi's more stringent class-loading approach.

In fact, in Chapter 5 you saw how the SpringSource dm Server is specially equipped to deal with some of the nuisances of using the JPA, Java's de facto ORM API, in applications using both Spring and OSGi.

What you will explore next is a detailed look at accessing an RDBMS without the need of a specialized product like the SpringSource dm Server.

JDBC was the first, and still one of the most important, building blocks for accessing RDBMS from Java. However, many of its advantages can look more like disadvantages, depending on your vantage point.

JDBC is capable of performing low-level operations against an RDBMS using Structured Query Language (SQL). Using SQL directly in Java classes, however, is where this approach shows its pros and cons.

Having the power to use SQL in Java gives a developer the flexibility to invoke any SQL operation imaginable. SQL statements ranging from simple queries to more sophisticated things like stored procedures can be declared in line with Java classes.

On the other hand, this approach can become unwieldy due to the differing nature of Java classes and relational database tables. This set of differences is often described as the *object-relational impedance mismatch*,[1] and this is what ORM products seek to overcome (or at least hide).

However, even though ORM products in the Java market have come a long way with initiatives like JPA, using ORM technology entails thinking more deeply about an application's design, as well as dealing with additional configuration issues. Given this fact, JDBC is unlikely to lose appeal anytime soon, and should thus continue to be used as a data access strategy even with emerging technologies like OSGi and Spring-DM.

So what do you need to employ JDBC in an application using Spring and OSGi? For someone already using JDBC with the Spring Framework, the only additional steps are incorporating OSGi headers into a JAR's `MANIFEST.MF` file. This applies to those JARs containing the classes with JDBC access code, as well as those corresponding to the JDBC driver provided by an RDBMS vendor.

1. Wikipedia, "Object-relational impedence mismatch," `http://en.wikipedia.org/wiki/Object-Relational_impedance_mismatch`

You've already created an application accessing an RDBMS in this book, first in Chapter 2, where you used the Spring Framework, and then in Chapter 5, where you learned how to redesign the same application to run on the SpringSource dm Server. With the intent of not writing everything from scratch, I've built the JDBC design presented next on the same application.

The bundle partitioning scheme laid out in Chapter 5 took special care to separate the service interface and the service implementation (DAO) class into different bundles. This design will make it easier to incorporate a new service implementation (DAO) bundle based on JDBC.

Listing 7-1 contains the first part of the service implementation (DAO) bundle, the service class using JDBC.

Listing 7-1. *Service DAO Class Using JDBC*

```
package com.apress.springosgi.ch7.servicedaojdbc;

import java.util.List;

import javax.sql.DataSource;

import com.apress.springosgi.ch7.service.HelloWorldService;
import com.apress.springosgi.ch7.model.HelloWorld;
import com.apress.springosgi.ch7.model.Person;

import org.springframework.jdbc.core.simple.SimpleJdbcTemplate;

import org.springframework.jdbc.core.simple.ParameterizedBeanPropertyRowMapper;

import org.springframework.jdbc.core.namedparam.BeanPropertySqlParameterSource;

import org.springframework.dao.EmptyResultDataAccessException;

import java.util.Date;

public class HelloWorldDAO implements HelloWorldService {

 private SimpleJdbcTemplate simpleJdbcTemplate;
```

```
    public void setDataSource(DataSource dataSource) {

        this.simpleJdbcTemplate = new SimpleJdbcTemplate(dataSource);

    }

    // JDBC-backed implementations of the methods on HelloWorld Service

    public HelloWorld findById(long id) {

        HelloWorld hw;

        try {

            hw = (HelloWorld) this.simpleJdbcTemplate.queryForObject("select * ➥
from HelloWorld where id = ?", ParameterizedBeanPropertyRow➥
Mapper.newInstance(HelloWorld.class),id);

            long personIdToAdd = this.simpleJdbcTemplate.queryForLong("select➥
 translator_id from HelloWorld where id= ?", new Object[]{new Long(id)});

            hw.setTranslator(this.simpleJdbcTemplate.queryForObject("select * ➥
from Person where id = ?", ParameterizedBeanPropertyRowMapper.new➥
Instance(Person.class),personIdToAdd));

        } catch (EmptyResultDataAccessException ex) {

            throw new EmptyResultDataAccessException("No HelloWorld by the➥
 provided id - " + ex,0);

        }

        return hw;

    }

    public List<HelloWorld> findAll() {

        return this.simpleJdbcTemplate.query("select * from HelloWorld",➥
 ParameterizedBeanPropertyRowMapper.newInstance(HelloWorld.class));

    }
```

```
    public HelloWorld update(HelloWorld hw) {

        this.simpleJdbcTemplate.update("update HelloWorld set language=:language, ➥
message=:message, transdate=:transdate where id=:id", new BeanProperty➥
SqlParameterSource(hw));

        return findById(hw.getId());

    }

    public void save(HelloWorld hw) {

        this.simpleJdbcTemplate.update("insert into Person(FNAME,LNAME,hourlyRate)➥
 values(:firstName, :lastName, :hourlyRate)", new BeanPropertySqlParameter➥
Source(hw.getTranslator()));

        long personIdToInsert = this.simpleJdbcTemplate.queryForLong("select id➥
 from Person where FNAME= ? and LNAME = ?", new Object[]{new String(hw.get➥
Translator().getFirstName()), new String(hw.getTranslator().getLastName())});

        this.simpleJdbcTemplate.update("insert into HelloWorld(language,message,➥
transdate,translator_id) values(?,?,?,?)", new Object[]{hw.getLanguage(), ➥
hw.getMessage(), hw.getTransdate(), new Long(personIdToInsert)});

    }

   public void delete(HelloWorld hw) {

        long personIdToDelete = this.simpleJdbcTemplate.queryForLong("select➥
 translator_id from HelloWorld where id= ?", new Object[]{new Long(hw.getId())});

        this.simpleJdbcTemplate.update("delete from HelloWorld where id= ?",➥
 new Object[]{new Long(hw.getId())});

        this.simpleJdbcTemplate.update("delete from Person where id= ?", new➥
 Object[]{new Long(personIdToDelete)});

    }

    public List<HelloWorld> findByTranslatorFirstName(String firstName) {

        Person translator;
```

```
        try {

            translator = this.simpleJdbcTemplate.queryForObject("select * from➥
 Person where FNAME= ?",ParameterizedBeanPropertyRowMapper.new➥
Instance(Person.class),firstName);

        } catch (EmptyResultDataAccessException ex) {

            throw new EmptyResultDataAccessException("No Person by the provided➥
 firstName - " + ex,0);

        }

        return this.simpleJdbcTemplate.query("select * from HelloWorld where➥
 translator_id = ?", ParameterizedBeanPropertyRowMapper.new➥
Instance(HelloWorld.class),translator.getId());

    }

    public List<HelloWorld> findByTranslatorLastName(String lastName) {

        Person translator;

        try {

            translator = this.simpleJdbcTemplate.queryForObject("select * from➥
 Person where LNAME= ?",ParameterizedBeanPropertyRowMapper.new➥
Instance(Person.class),lastName);

        } catch (EmptyResultDataAccessException ex) {

            throw new EmptyResultDataAccessException("No Person by the provided➥
 lastName - " + ex,0);

        }

        return this.simpleJdbcTemplate.query("select * from HelloWorld where➥
 translator_id = ?", ParameterizedBeanPropertyRowMapper.new➥
Instance(HelloWorld.class),translator.getId());

    }
```

```
    public List<HelloWorld> findByTranslatorHourlyRateOver(double hourlyRate) {

        return this.simpleJdbcTemplate.query("select * from HelloWorld where➥
 translator_id = ( select id from Person where hourlyRate > ?)", Parameterized➥
BeanPropertyRowMapper.newInstance(HelloWorld.class),hourlyRate);

    }

    public List<HelloWorld> findByLanguage(String language) {

        return this.simpleJdbcTemplate.query("select id, language, message,➥
 transdate, translator_id from HelloWorld where language = ?", Parameterized➥
BeanPropertyRowMapper.newInstance(HelloWorld.class),language);

    }

    public List<HelloWorld> findByMessage(String message) {

        return this.simpleJdbcTemplate.query("select id, language, message,➥
 transdate, translator_id from HelloWorld where message = ?", Parameterized➥
BeanPropertyRowMapper.newInstance(HelloWorld.class),message);

    }

 public void deleteMessage(long id) {

        long personIdToDelete = this.simpleJdbcTemplate.queryForLong("select➥
 translator_id from HelloWorld where id= ?", new Object[]{new Long(id)});

        this.simpleJdbcTemplate.update("delete from HelloWorld where id= ?",➥
 new Object[]{new Long(id)});

        this.simpleJdbcTemplate.update("delete from Person where id= ?", new➥
 Object[]{new Long(personIdToDelete)});

    }

}
```

First of all, notice that the class inherits from the `HelloWorldService` interface, requiring it to use the signatures defined by the application's service interface. Next, an overall scan of the listing will show the various SQL statements interspersed throughout the class's methods, in line with the application's RDBMS table names and columns.

The in-line SQL statements represent an alternative approach to the one used earlier in the form of JPA, but notice the use of the Spring Framework's `SimpleJdbcTemplate` class.

This class is like the Spring `JpaDaoSupport` class employed to design the application's earlier service DAO class using JPA, except that in this case the Spring `SimpleJdbcTemplate` class reduces the amount of boilerplate code needed to perform data access using JDBC.

Next in the listing is the `setDataSource()` method. This method is used by the Spring Framework to inject the RDBMS data source into an instance of the DAO class. Note that upon calling this setter method, an instance of the `SimpleJdbcTemplate` class is associated with the data source and assigned to a class's field. It is precisely this last field that is used throughout the class's methods to fulfill the service implementation methods.

Though this JDBC service DAO implementation class might seem verbose—especially when viewed alongside its JPA counterpart in Chapter 2's Listing 2-8—it is important to keep in mind the support the Spring Framework brings to the table under these circumstances.

This class is not only shorter compared to one using stand-alone JDBC API functions, but also devoid of in-line dependencies. The dependency on the external data source is fulfilled by the Spring Framework injecting a reference, thus keeping the class a POJO.

The next step consists of creating the Spring configuration files to inject the data source into the DAO class and publish the service implementation (DAO) as an OSGi service for consumption of another application bundle.

Listing 7-2 illustrates the Spring configuration file needed to deploy a bundle using JDBC in a Spring and OSGi application.

Listing 7-2. *Spring* `osgi-context.xml` *File for Service DAO-JDBC Bundle*

```
<?xml version="1.0" encoding="UTF-8"?>
<beans xmlns="http://www.springframework.org/schema/beans"
  xmlns:xsi="http://www.w3.org/2001/XMLSchema-instance"
  xmlns:osgi="http://www.springframework.org/schema/osgi"
  xsi:schemaLocation="http://www.springframework.org/schema/beans➥
 http://www.springframework.org/schema/beans/spring-beans.xsd
                      http://www.springframework.org/schema/osgi➥
 http://www.springframework.org/schema/osgi/spring-osgi.xsd">

  <!-- Import the Data source service -->
  <osgi:reference id="dataSource" interface="javax.sql.DataSource"/>

  <!-- Create the helloWorldDAO bean -->
  <bean id="helloWorldDAO"➥
 class="com.apress.springosgi.ch7.servicedaojdbc.HelloWorldDAO">
     <property name="dataSource" ref="dataSource"/>
  </bean>
```

```
  <!-- Export helloWorldDAO as a service to OSGi via its interface -->
  <osgi:service ref="helloWorldDAO"➥
 interface="com.apress.springosgi.ch7.service.HelloWorldService"/>
</beans>
```

The first thing this listing does is look up and import an OSGi service using the interface `java.sql.DataSource` via the Spring-DM element `<reference>`. In case you don't recall or skipped Chapter 5 altogether, in line with the application's design, another bundle is charged with publishing an OSGi service pointing to the application's data source, which in itself has the necessary connection parameters to the RDBMS.

Once a reference to this last service is found, it will be associated with the `dataSource` ID. You will then encounter the `<bean>` element used to instantiate the service implementation JDBC class `com.apress.springosgi.ch7.servicedaojdbc.HelloWorldDAO`. Note also that a reference to the `dataSource` is *injected* into the bean via the `<property>` element.

Finally, the service implementation (DAO) bean employing JDBC is published as an OSGi service—using the `HelloWorldService` interface—through the Spring-DM element `<service>`. Again in line with the application's design, another bundle will be charged with accessing this published OSGi service pointing to the application's service implementation (DAO) and presenting results to end users via a web interface.

To complete the contents of this bundle using JDBC, it's also necessary to create the `MANIFEST.MF` file that will accompany the bundle. Listing 7-3 illustrates this file.

Listing 7-3. *`MANIFEST.MF` for the Service DAO-JDBC Bundle*

```
Bundle-Version: 1.0
Bundle-SymbolicName: com.apress.springosgi.ch7.servicejdbc
Bundle-Name: HelloWorld Spring-OSGi Service JDBC
Bundle-Vendor: Pro Spring-OSGi
Import-Package: com.apress.springosgi.ch7.model;version="1.0.0",
 com.apress.springosgi.ch7.service;version="1.0.0",

 org.springframework.jdbc.core.simple;version="2.5.4",

 org.springframework.jdbc.core.namedparam;version="2.5.4",

 org.springframework.dao;version="2.5.4",

 javax.sql
Bundle-ManifestVersion: 2
```

Since I have described numerous OSGi `MANIFEST.MF` files in the book, the meaning of this last file probably requires little explanation. The only notable point is the inclusion of Spring's JDBC package, `org.springframework.jdbc.core.simple`; the application's service interface, `com.apress.springosgi.ch7.service`; and Java's core SQL package, `javax.sql`.

For the moment, put these last three listings aside. The service DAO-JDBC bundle—including the entire application—will be built in the last section of the chapter. Next, you will perform one more step in order to use JDBC with OSGi: OSGi'fying a JDBC driver for an RDBMS.

WHAT ABOUT JPA IN AN OSGI BUNDLE?

The JPA counterpart for this DAO-JDBC bundle was already illustrated in Chapter 5—Listings 5-8, 5-19, 5-20, and 5-21 show its parts. But even though OSGi's modularity allows you to swap between JDBC and JPA with ease in a service bundle, there are certain differences you need to be aware of.

First the obvious. A DAO-JPA bundle requires a JPA implementation bundle (Eclipse Link, OpenJPA, or Hibernate) to offer persistence services. Configuring and running a JPA implementation bundle is where the differences in using JDBC become more evident.

Chapter 5 made the addition of a JPA implementation bundle relatively straightforward on account of the SpringSource dm Server. But what happens if you can't (or don't want to) use SpringSource dm Server? I will elaborate on what made this process straightforward in Chapter 5 and the alternative steps you would need to take if you don't use it.

The JPA implementation bundle (Eclipse Link) used in Chapter 5 relied on the *Import-Scope:=application* directive (Listing 5-14), a proprietary SpringSource dm Server value. What this last value does is import the JPA implementation bundle classes to every bundle belonging to an application.

This last step is critical due to how JPA works. With JPA an application's model classes require access to a JPA's implementation packages since they are annotated with JPA values (using @). This creates a visibility problem in OSGi, since an application's model classes are in their own bundle.

This requires an application's model bundle to *explicitly* import JPA implementation packages. The recommended practice for this is to use an optional `import` statement, so as to not make a model bundle rely on a particular JPA provider. See the sidebar "Import-Package or DynamicImport-Package?" in Chapter 6 for optionally importing packages into a bundle.

In addition, a DAO-JPA bundle also needs to be configured with a Spring load-time weaver (Listing 5-21) in order to fulfill JPA's duties. This is also a critical step due to how JPA works. Recall that even in Chapter 2, deploying a non-OSGi JPA application required configuring Apache Tomcat to use the weaver `spring-tomcat-weaver.jar`.

The SpringSource dm Server used in Chapter 5 already comes preconfigured with an OSGi environment capable of handling Spring aspect weaving. Therefore, if the SpringSource dm Server is not used, it is necessary to start up an OSGi environment with the necessary weaving provisions.

This last step can be achieved through Java's Virtual Machine (via the `-javaagent` flag) and Spring's general-purpose weaver at the time an OSGi environment is started (e.g., `java -javaagent:spring-agent.jar -jar org.eclipse.osgi_3.5.0.jar`). You can find more information on using load-time weaving with Spring here: `http://static.springframework.org/spring/docs/2.5.x/reference/aop.html#aop-aj-ltw-spring`.

Whether you are using a DAO-JDBC bundle or a DAO-JPA bundle, a JDBC driver is central to achieving connectivity to an RDBMS. Provided by an RDBMS vendor, a JDBC driver provides the necessary "hooks" to connect from a Java environment to a particular RDBMS brand.

In our OSGi application design, this driver (bundle) is used by a bundle to register a Java data source as an OSGi service that can later be used by other bundles requiring RDBMS connectivity.

In Chapter 5, Listings 5-12 and 5-13 illustrate the contents of a bundle that harness the MySQL RDBMS driver and publish a Java data source as an OSGi service. Specifically, Listing 5-12 uses various `import` statements to access this RDBMS's JDBC driver, a driver that you obtained from the SpringSource Enterprise Bundle Repository.[2]

This, however, raises an interesting question. What happens if the RDBMS driver you require is not available at the SpringSource Enterprise Bundle Repository? While the site has made considerable progress OSGi'fying commonly used JARs, this doesn't mean it will have every OSGi'fied JAR bundle in existence, especially something like JDBC drivers, which are plentiful given the number of RDBMS vendors and versions.

Do you ask an RDBMS vendor for an OSGi'fied version of a JDBC driver? Well, good luck with that. OSGi has only recently gained a wider audience in the Java world, and it will likely take a few more years for mainstream vendors to start distributing their JAR files with OSGi headers.

So what other choice do you have? OSGi'fying the JDBC driver JAR file yourself is one possibility. After all, it is just a matter of finding out what packages a JAR file needs and makes available to other bundles. But before you cringe at the mere thought of inspecting a JAR's code and what may well be hundreds of classes for dependencies, there is a tool that can aid you in this process: BND (`http://www.aqute.biz/Code/Bnd`).

So next, in order to continue with the purpose at hand, OSGi'fying a JDBC driver, I will introduce you to the BND tool.

Introducing the BND Tool

The BND tool is a Java utility that inspects the contents of a *compiled* JAR and attempts to construct the `MANIFEST.MF` file necessary to deploy the JAR in an OSGi environment. In essence, it attempts to convert a JAR into an OSGi bundle.

BND may prove to be a far more useful tool than the following OSGi'fication process of a JDBC driver. The reason is that BND can migrate JARs to OSGi bundles without source code, which can become critical as you migrate preexisting projects to an OSGi-based architecture, in which determining a class's import/export relationship may be impossible without source code.

---

2. `http://www.springsource.com/repository/`

BND can run using a variety of tools that include Ant, Maven, and Eclipse, and there is also a command-line version. To simplify the exploration process, I will use the command-line version in this section.

Once you download BND from `http://www.aqute.biz/Code/Download#bnd` and a JDBC driver like PostgreSQL from `http://jdbc.postgresql.org/download/postgresql-8.3-603.jdbc2.jar`, you can go straight to the command line of your workstation and invoke BND's most basic operation, illustrated in Listing 7-4.

Listing 7-4. *BND JAR Inspection*

```
java -jar bnd-0.0.249.jar postgresql-8.3-603.jdbc2.jar
```

BND's command-line invocation always starts with the instruction `java -jar bnd-0.0.249.jar`, indicating "execute the `bnd-0.0.249.jar` JAR." As illustrated in Listing 7-4, BND requires at least one argument. This example argument corresponds to the JDBC driver for the PostgreSQL RDBMS `postgresql-8.3-603.jdbc2.jar`. Upon executing the instruction in Listing 7-4, a detailed output of a JAR's contents is generated. Listing 7-5 illustrates this information.

Listing 7-5. *BND JAR Inspection Results.*

```
[MANIFEST postgresql-8.3-603.jdbc2.jar]

Ant-Version                 Apache Ant 1.5.4
Created-By                  1.2.2 (Sun Microsystems Inc.)
Manifest-Version        1.0
[IMPEXP]
[USES]
org.postgresql                      java.sql
                                            org.postgresql.core
                                            org.postgresql.fastpath
                                            org.postgresql.jdbc2
                                            org.postgresql.largeobject
                                            org.postgresql.util
org.postgresql.core             java.sql
                                            org.postgresql
                                            org.postgresql.core.v2
                                            org.postgresql.core.v3
                                            org.postgresql.jdbc2
                                            org.postgresql.util
org.postgresql.core.types     java.sql
                                            org.postgresql.util
```

```
org.postgresql.core.v2          java.sql
                                          org.postgresql
                                          org.postgresql.core
                                          org.postgresql.util
org.postgresql.core.v3          java.sql
                                          org.postgresql
                                          org.postgresql.core
                                          org.postgresql.util
org.postgresql.fastpath        java.sql
                                          org.postgresql.core
                                          org.postgresql.util
org.postgresql.geometric       java.sql
                                          org.postgresql.util
org.postgresql.jdbc2             java.sql
                                          org.postgresql
                                          org.postgresql.core
                                          org.postgresql.core.types
                                          org.postgresql.fastpath
                                          org.postgresql.geometric
                                          org.postgresql.largeobject
                                          org.postgresql.util
org.postgresql.largeobject     java.sql
                                          org.postgresql
                                          org.postgresql.core
                                          org.postgresql.fastpath
                                          org.postgresql.util
org.postgresql.translation     org.postgresql.util
                                          java.sql
                                          org.postgresql
[USEDBY]
java.sql                                org.postgresql
                                          org.postgresql.core
                                          org.postgresql.core.types
                                          org.postgresql.core.v2
                                          org.postgresql.core.v3
                                          org.postgresql.fastpath
                                          org.postgresql.geometric
                                          org.postgresql.jdbc2
                                          org.postgresql.largeobject
                                          org.postgresql.util
```

```
org.postgresql                    org.postgresql.core
                                           org.postgresql.core.v2
                                           org.postgresql.core.v3
                                           org.postgresql.jdbc2
                                           org.postgresql.largeobject
                                           org.postgresql.util
org.postgresql.core             org.postgresql
                                           org.postgresql.core.v2
                                           org.postgresql.core.v3
                                           org.postgresql.fastpath
                                           org.postgresql.jdbc2
                                           org.postgresql.largeobject
org.postgresql.core.types     org.postgresql.jdbc2
org.postgresql.core.v2          org.postgresql.core
org.postgresql.core.v3          org.postgresql.core
org.postgresql.fastpath         org.postgresql
                                            org.postgresql.jdbc2
                                            org.postgresql.largeobject
org.postgresql.geometric      org.postgresql.jdbc2
org.postgresql.jdbc2               org.postgresql
                                            org.postgresql.core
org.postgresql.largeobject     org.postgresql
                                            org.postgresql.jdbc2
org.postgresql.util                  org.postgresql
                                            org.postgresql.core
                                            org.postgresql.core.types
                                            org.postgresql.core.v2
                                            org.postgresql.core.v3
                                            org.postgresql.fastpath
                                            org.postgresql.geometric
                                            org.postgresql.jdbc2
                                            org.postgresql.largeobject

[LIST]
META-INF
  MANIFEST.MF
META-INF/services
  java.sql.Driver
org
org <no contents>
org/postgresql
  Driver$1.class
  Driver$ConnectThread.class
```

```
  Driver.class
  PGConnection.class
  PGNotification.class
  PGRefCursorResultSet.class
  PGResultSetMetaData.class
  PGStatement.class
org/postgresql/core
  BaseConnection.class
  BaseResultSet.class
  BaseStatement.class
  ConnectionFactory.class
  Encoding.class
  Field.class
  Logger.class
  Notification.class
  Oid.class
  PGBindException.class
  PGStream$1.class
  PGStream.class
  ParameterList.class
  Parser.class
  ProtocolConnection.class
  Query.class
  QueryExecutor.class
  ResultCursor.class
  ResultHandler.class
  UTF8Encoding.class
  Utils.class
  VisibleBufferedInputStream.class
org/postgresql/core/types
  PGBigDecimal.class
  PGBoolean.class
  PGByte.class
  PGDouble.class
  PGFloat.class
  PGInteger.class
  PGLong.class
  PGNumber.class
  PGShort.class
  PGString.class
  PGType.class
  PGUnknown.class
```

```
org/postgresql/core/v2
  ConnectionFactoryImpl$SimpleResultHandler.class
  ConnectionFactoryImpl.class
  FastpathParameterList.class
  ProtocolConnectionImpl.class
  QueryExecutorImpl$1.class
  QueryExecutorImpl$2.class
  QueryExecutorImpl$3.class
  QueryExecutorImpl.class
  SimpleParameterList.class
  V2Query.class
org/postgresql/core/v3
  CompositeParameterList.class
  CompositeQuery.class
  ConnectionFactoryImpl$UnsupportedProtocolException.class
  ConnectionFactoryImpl.class
  Portal.class
  ProtocolConnectionImpl.class
  QueryExecutorImpl$1.class
  QueryExecutorImpl$2.class
  QueryExecutorImpl$3.class
  QueryExecutorImpl$ErrorTrackingResultHandler.class
  QueryExecutorImpl.class
  SimpleParameterList.class
  SimpleQuery.class
  V3ParameterList.class
  V3Query.class
org/postgresql/fastpath
  Fastpath.class
  FastpathArg.class
org/postgresql/geometric
  PGbox.class
  PGcircle.class
  PGline.class
  PGlseg.class
  PGpath.class
  PGpoint.class
  PGpolygon.class
org/postgresql/jdbc2
  AbstractJdbc2Array$PgArrayList.class
  AbstractJdbc2Array.class
  AbstractJdbc2Blob.class
```

```
  AbstractJdbc2BlobClob$LOIterator.class
  AbstractJdbc2BlobClob.class
  AbstractJdbc2Clob.class
  AbstractJdbc2Connection$TransactionCommandHandler.class
  AbstractJdbc2Connection.class
  AbstractJdbc2DatabaseMetaData.class
  AbstractJdbc2ResultSet$CursorResultHandler.class
  AbstractJdbc2ResultSet$NullObject.class
  AbstractJdbc2ResultSet$PrimaryKey.class
  AbstractJdbc2ResultSet.class
  AbstractJdbc2ResultSetMetaData.class
  AbstractJdbc2Statement$BatchResultHandler.class
  AbstractJdbc2Statement$CallableBatchResultHandler.class
  AbstractJdbc2Statement$StatementResultHandler.class
  AbstractJdbc2Statement.class
  EscapedFunctions.class
  Jdbc2Array.class
  Jdbc2Blob.class
  Jdbc2CallableStatement.class
  Jdbc2Clob.class
  Jdbc2Connection.class
  Jdbc2DatabaseMetaData.class
  Jdbc2PreparedStatement.class
  Jdbc2ResultSet.class
  Jdbc2ResultSetMetaData.class
  Jdbc2Statement.class
  ResultWrapper.class
  TimestampUtils$ParsedTimestamp.class
  TimestampUtils.class
  TypeInfoCache.class
org/postgresql/largeobject
  BlobInputStream.class
  BlobOutputStream.class
  LargeObject.class
  LargeObjectManager.class
org/postgresql/translation
  messages_cs.class
  messages_de.class
  messages_es.class
  messages_fr.class
  messages_it.class
  messages_nl.class
```

```
    messages_pl.class
    messages_pt_BR.class
    messages_ru.class
    messages_sr.class
    messages_tr.class
    messages_zh_CN.class
    messages_zh_TW.class
  org/postgresql/util
    Base64.class
    GT.class
    MD5Digest.class
    PGInterval.class
    PGbytea.class
    PGmoney.class
    PGobject.class
    PGtokenizer.class
    PSQLDriverVersion.class
    PSQLException.class
    PSQLState.class
    PSQLWarning.class
    ServerErrorMessage.class
    StreamWrapper.class
    UnixCrypt.class
```

The first section of the output, [MANIFEST], reproduces the existing MANIFEST.MF file of a JAR. As you will note, the inspected JAR, the JDBC driver, lacks OSGi headers. Next comes the [IMPEXP] section, which is further subdivided into three more sections containing a JAR's packages in different layouts.

The [USES] section is formatted into two columns. The right side represents a series of packages that are *required* by the package on the left side. The section [USEDBY] is a mirror image of the [USES] section. The right side represents a series of packages that *depend* on the package on the left side. Finally, the [LIST] section contains the entire layout—classes, packages, and other files—for the JAR as a list.

Inspecting a JAR for its package dependency structure is a nice start toward OSGi compatibility. But the process of manually copying and pasting these results into a new JAR structure is still error prone. BND offers a simple shortcut to create an OSGi'fied JAR version on the fly. Listing 7-6 illustrates the BND wrap command to achieve this.

Listing 7-6. *BND wrap—On-the-Fly OSGi Bundle Creation*

```
java -jar bnd-0.0.249.jar wrap -output postgresql-osgi-8.3.jar ➥
postgresql-8.3-603.jdbc2.jar
```

This listing invokes BND with the `wrap` command, creating a bundle with an OSGi-compatible `MANIFEST.MF` file. The additional snippet `-output postgresql-osgi-8.3.jar` is used to indicate an explicit name for the newly created JAR (bundle). However, this newly created JAR has the side effect of being a *best-guess* effort at generating an OSGi-compatible `MANIFEST.MF` file. Listing 7-7 illustrates what this newly created bundle's `MANIFEST.MF` file looks like.

Listing 7-7. *`MANIFEST.MF` After Applying BND `wrap`*

```
Ant-Version: Apache Ant 1.5.4
Bnd-LastModified: 1226028717542
Bundle-ManifestVersion: 2
Bundle-SymbolicName: postgresql-8.3-603.jdbc2
Bundle-Version:0
Created-By:1.5.0_16 (Sun Microsystems Inc.)
Export-Package:                    org.postgresql.largeobject;uses:="org.post➥
gresql.fastpath,org.postgresql.util,org.postgresql.core,org.postgresql",org.post➥
gresql.fastpath;uses:="org.postgresql.util,org.postgresql.core",org.post➥
gresql.geometric;uses:="org.postgresql.util",org.postgresql.util;uses:="org.post➥
gresql",org.postgresql.core.v2;uses:="org.postgresql.util,org.postgresql.core,➥
org.postgresql",org.postgresql.translation,org.postgresql.jdbc2;uses:="org.post➥
gresql.fastpath,org.postgresql.geometric,org.postgresql.util,org.postgresql,➥
org.postgresql.largeobject,org.postgresql.core.types,org.postgresql.core",org.post➥
gresql.core.types;uses:="org.postgresql.util",org.postgresql.core;uses:="org.post➥
gresql.util,org.postgresql.core.v2,org.postgresql.jdbc2,org.postgresql,org.post➥
gresql.core.v3",org.postgresql;uses:="org.postgresql.largeobject,org.post➥
gresql.fastpath,org.postgresql.util,org.postgresql.jdbc2,org.postgresql.core",➥
org.postgresql.core.v3;uses:="org.postgresql.util,org.postgresql.core,org.post➥
gresql"
Import-Package:                    org.postgresql;resolution:=optional,org.post➥
gresql.core;resolution:=optional,org.postgresql.core.types;resolution:=optional,➥
org.postgresql.core.v2;resolution:=optional,org.postgresql.core.v3;resolution:➥
=optional,org.postgresql.fastpath;resolution:=optional,org.postgresql.geometric;➥
resolution:=optional,org.postgresql.jdbc2;resolution:=optional,org.post➥
gresql.largeobject;resolution:=optional,org.postgresql.translation;resolution:➥
=optional,org.postgresql.util;resolution:=optional
Manifest-Version: 1.0
Originally-Created-By: 1.2.2 (Sun Microsystems Inc.)
Tool:Bnd-0.0.249
```

In short, this `MANIFEST.MF` file makes no assumptions about what packages a bundle needs or will make available to other bundles. It simply exports (and optionally imports) every package detected by BND. It is a nice step toward OSGi compatibility, but falls short of a correct and feature-rich OSGi `MANIFEST.MF` file like the ones used throughout this book.

Remember that a `MANIFEST.MF` file used in an OSGi bundle needs to take into account *everything*. This can range from nonessential packages a JAR might use, like those for logging, and packages that might have gone undetected by BND, to some other artifacts, like images or text files needed by a JAR's classes that would go undetected if not explicitly declared.

You might also want to use other OSGi headers like `DynamicImport-Package` or assign OSGi version values, not to mention the possibility of wanting to keep preexisting `MANIFEST.MF` file values instead of overwriting a JAR's original `MANIFEST.MF` file with a BND-generated one.

For all these tasks, BND relies on a properties file. A BND properties file consists of a series of processing instructions applied to a JAR when it is transformed using BND's `wrap` command. Here I will show you how to create a BND properties file with the necessary `Import-Package` header values for the JDBC driver.

As a starting point for your first BND properties file, I will define a series of packages typically used by JDBC drivers belonging to the Java Runtime Environment (JRE), such as `javax.sql` and `javax.xml`. OSGi's more stringent class-loading approach often blocks certain JRE packages unless an OSGi environment is globally configured to import such packages.

So assuming you're using an out-of-the-box OSGi environment, it's necessary to explicitly import certain packages into a bundle using the `Import-Package` header. In addition, I will also add the necessary logging packages so the JDBC driver is capable of producing debugging information.

Keep in mind that even though BND is likely to automatically detect such packages if used by a JAR, under certain circumstances it might not be able to do so. For this reason, it's best to start with this type of "safety net" when OSGi'fying a JDBC driver using BND. In addition, since these packages are part of the JRE, they do not introduce any external dependency on the JDBC driver, but simply ensure the OSGi'fied JDBC driver has access to these JRE packages.

Listing 7-8 illustrates the first iteration of the BND properties file applied to the JDBC driver.

■ **Warning** Though BND is an excellent tool for transforming JARs into OSGi bundles, be aware that this process might violate the terms of the licenses that govern certain JARs. The PostgreSQL JDBC driver is open source, so modification is not an issue, but this may not be the case for other JDBC drivers or JARs of another nature.

Listing 7-8. *BND Properties File for* `Import-Package` *Header*

```
Import-Package: javax.naming, \
  javax.naming.spi, \
  javax.net, \
  javax.net.ssl, \
  javax.sql, \
  javax.transaction.xa;version="[1.0.1, 2.0.0)";resolution:=optional, \
  javax.xml.parsers, \
  javax.xml.stream;version="[1.0.1, 2.0.0)";resolution:=optional, \
  javax.xml.transform, \
  javax.xml.transform.dom, \
  javax.xml.transform.sax, \
  javax.xml.transform.stax;resolution:=optional, \
  javax.xml.transform.stream, \
  org.apache.commons.logging;version="[1.1.1,2.0.0)", \
  org.apache.log4j;version="[1.2.15, 2.0.0)";resolution:=optional, \
  org.w3c.dom, \
  org.xml.sax, \
  org.xml.sax.helpers
```

If you place this listing in its own file—`iter1.bnd`—and invoke the BND command in Listing 7-9, a new JAR with these `Import-Package` values will be created.

Listing 7-9. *BND* `wrap` *On-the-Fly OSGi Bundle Creation with the Properties File*

```
java -jar bnd-0.0.249.jar wrap -output postgresql-osgi-8.3.jar -properties ➥
iter1.bnd postgresql-8.3-603.jdbc2.jar
```

Notice the addition of the `-properties` flag on the `wrap` command pointing to a file named `iter1.bnd` (Listing 7-8). If you inspect the newly created bundle after executing this instruction, you will see its `Import-Package` values now reflect those declared in Listing 7-8.

A BND properties file might seem like a copy of a `MANIFEST.MF` file that is put into a new bundle, but it has more capabilities than that of a simple placeholder. A BND properties file can also contain regular expressions to ease the inclusion or exclusion of packages, as well as macros.

Let's make a second iteration of a BND properties file for the JDBC driver, this time for the `Export-Package` header. Listing 7-10 illustrates this second iteration using regular expressions.

Listing 7-10. *BND Properties File with a* `Export-Package` *Header Using Regular Expressions*

```
<Import-Package values ommited for brevity>
Export-Package: org.postgresql.core.*
```

Notice the * at the end of the `Export-Package` value. The * is a wildcard regular expression specifying that every package should be exported under the name `org.postgresql.core`. As illustrated in Listing 7-6, BND's default behavior is to export every package detected in a JAR.

By using regular expressions in a BND properties file, you can control the visibility of a bundle's packages and limit some packages to private status. Listing 7-11 illustrates the `MANIFEST.MF` file generated by applying the BND properties file in Listing 7-10 to the PostgreSQL JDBC driver.

Listing 7-11. `MANIFEST.MF` *After Applying BND* `wrap` *with a Regular Expression*

```
Ant-Version: Apache Ant 1.5.4
Bnd-LastModified: 1226170593490
Bundle-ManifestVersion: 2
Bundle-Name: iter2
Bundle-SymbolicName: iter2
Bundle-Version: 0
Created-By: 1.5.0_16 (Sun Microsystems Inc.)
Export-Package: org.postgresql.core.v2;uses:="org.postgresql.core",
 org.postgresql.core.types,
 org.postgresql.core;uses:="org.postgresql.core.v2,org.postgresql.core.v3",
 org.postgresql.core.v3;uses:="org.postgresql.core"
Import-Package: javax.naming,
 javax.naming.spi,
 javax.net,
 javax.net.ssl,
 javax.sql,
 javax.transaction.xa;resolution:=optional;version="[1.0.1, 2.0.0)",
 javax.xml.parsers,
 javax.xml.stream;resolution:=optional;version="[1.0.1, 2.0.0)",
 javax.xml.transform,
 javax.xml.transform.dom,
 javax.xml.transform.sax,
 javax.xml.transform.stax;resolution:=optional,
 javax.xml.transform.stream,
 org.apache.commons.logging;version="[1.1.1,2.0.0)",
 org.apache.log4j;resolution:=optional;version="[1.2.15, 2.0.0)",
 org.w3c.dom,org.xml.sax,org.xml.sax.helpers
```

```
Manifest-Version: 1.0
Originally-Created-By: 1.2.2 (Sun Microsystems Inc.)
Private-Package: org.postgresql,
 org.postgresql.fastpath,
 org.postgresql.geometric,
 org.postgresql.jdbc2,
 org.postgresql.largeobject,
 org.postgresql.translation,
 org.postgresql.util
Tool:Bnd-0.0.249
```

Notice how the Export-Package values are now limited to the four packages under the name org.postgresql.core. Also notice how the remaining packages that were once exported by default are now assigned to the Private-Package header. If you look toward the top of this last MANIFEST.MF file, you will see the values for the headers Bundle-Name and BundleSymbolicName are assigned a value based on the BND properties file name.

These last default values can also be overridden by including the corresponding OSGi headers in a BND properties file. Listing 7-12 illustrates another iteration of the BND properties used on the PostgreSQL JDBC driver, this one using macros.

Listing 7-12. *BND Properties File with Bundle-Name and Bundle-SymbolicName Headers Using Macros and Comments*

```
<Import-Package values omitted for brevity>
Export-Package: org.postgresql.core.*
# Assign version
version=8.3
# Assign name
bundle_name=com.postgres
Bundle-Name: OSGi'fied JDBC Driver - ${bundle_name} ${version}
Bundle-SymbolicName: ${bundle_name}
Bundle-Version: ${version}
```

The first thing this BND properties file makes use of is comments and variables. A # sign represents a comment to describe the purpose of a BND statement. Also note the declarations bundle_version and bundle_name; these represent variables that are later used in the assignment of OSGi headers. The primary characteristic of comments and variables in BND properties files is that they are only used for processing purposes; they never go on to form part of a bundle's final MANIFEST.MF file.

The remaining three statements correspond to the OSGi headers Bundle-Name, Bundle-SymbolicName, and Bundle-Version, which do go on to form part of a bundle's final MANIFEST.MF file. However, notice how the assigned values contain syntax in the form ${}.

The ${} syntax represents BND macros. Upon processing, BND will replace these macro statements with the corresponding variable values by the same name. Therefore, in this case a bundle's final `MANIFEST.MF` file will contain headers in the form `Bundle-Version: 8.3` and `Bundle-SymbolicName: com.postgres`.

This concludes my introduction to how BND can aid you in migrating a JDBC driver—or any other JAR for that matter—toward OSGi compliance. Be advised there are numerous other options available in BND, including more regular expressions, macros, filters, and support for embedding resources like images or entire JARs. Consult BND's documentation for more information on these topics.

Next, I will move on to rebuilding the application using the JDBC-DAO bundle created earlier and using Apache Ivy to manage the application's dependencies.

NOT EVERYTHING CAN BE AN OSGI BUNDLE, OR CAN IT?

As tempting as it might be to think any JAR can be made an OSGi-compliant bundle with a tool like BND, this may not be the case if certain conditions are present in the Java classes.

Even knowing with a 100% certainty the packages a bundle requires to import and export—such as those hard-to-detect `Class.forName()` class/package dependencies—there are certain Java instructions that, while innocuous in non-OSGi environments, do not fit in well with OSGi's class-loading mechanisms.

These can range from `System.exit()` calls and static `main()` methods to code designed on the assumption of a single class loader. Though many of these Java instructions are rare, it is always best to perform the necessary tests to ensure migrated code does not contain these instructions and as a consequence have unintended behaviors in an OSGi environment.

On a related note, the Knopflerfish OSGi implementation offers a nonstandard way of dealing with these types of Java instructions. You can find more information on this proprietary approach in the following presentation, appropriately entitled "Everything can be a bundle": `http://www.osgi.org/wiki/uploads/CommunityEvent2008/30_knopflerfish-osgi-berlin-2008.pdf`.

Hello World Application Revisited Without the SpringSource dm Server: Data Access and Apache Ivy

The Hello World application you are about to start will be based on the application you created in Chapter 2, as well as the one in Chapter 5, which in itself was ported from Chapter 2 to use the SpringSource dm Server.

So what's new in this application? It will show you how to manage OSGi bundle dependencies—the staple libraries used by most applications—more easily using the Apache Ivy tool, how to deploy an OSGi bundle designed to access an RDBMS, and how to deploy everything without the aid of the SpringSource dm Server.

Figure 7-1 illustrates the bundles that will make up the application and the relationship between each one.

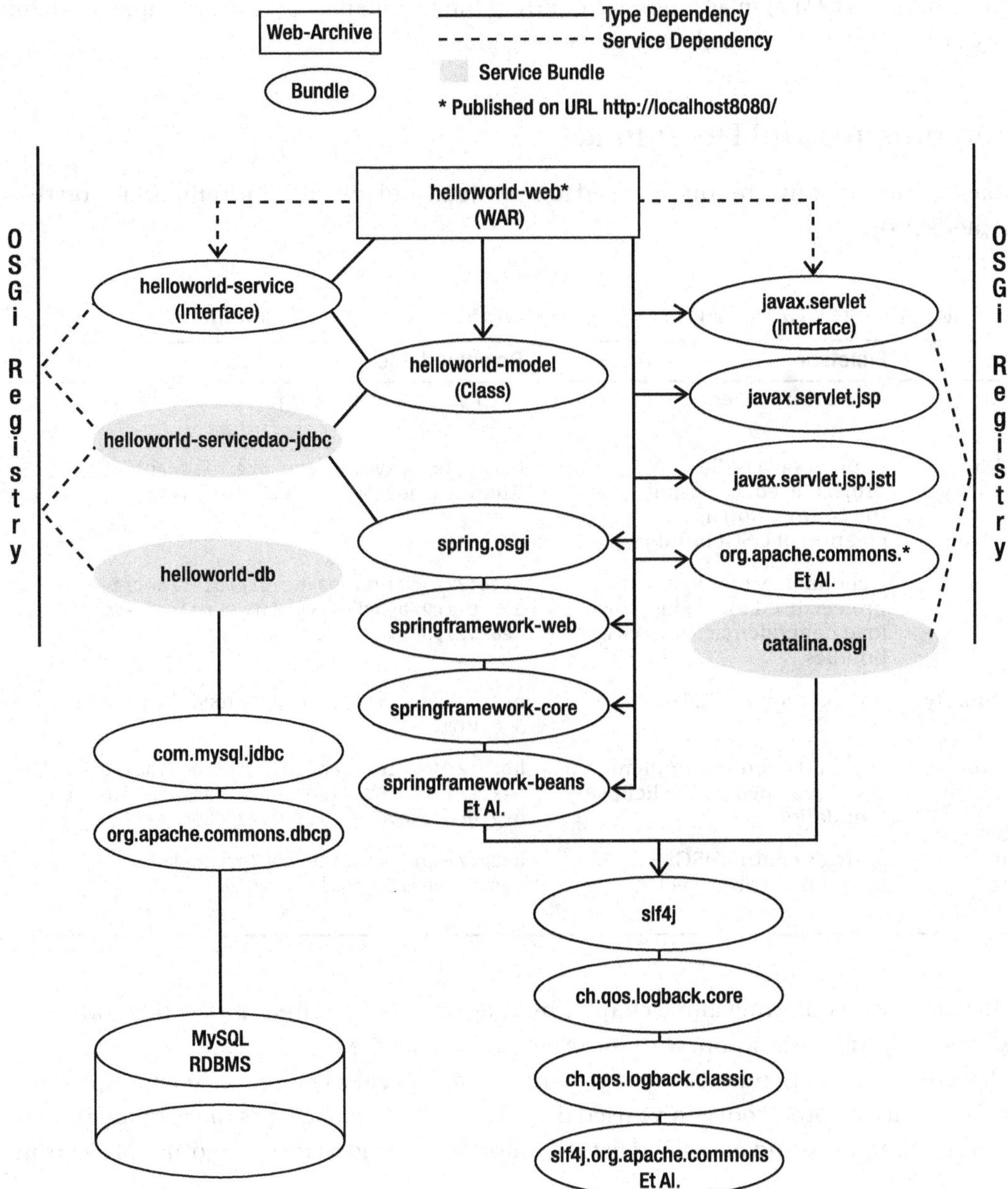

Figure 7-1. *Hello World application bundles without SpringSource dm Server*

There are a few things to note with respect to the applications in Chapter 2 and Chapter 5. With respect to Chapter 2's application, the service DAO bundle is now backed by an RDBMS via an OSGi data source bundle. With respect to Chapter 5, there are no application boundaries (PARs) in addition to requiring the installation of various staple bundles that in Chapter 5 were provided by the SpringSource dm Server.

Prerequisites and Downloads

Table 7-1 lists the software you will need to download and install before embarking on this chapter's project.

Table 7-1. *Revisited Spring OSGi Hello World Application Prerequisites and Downloads*

Software	Function	Download Site
Java SE 5 or higher	Java's runtime environment	`http://java.sun.com/javase/downloads/index.jsp`
Apache Ant 1.6 or higher	Popular Java build project, used for easing the compilation and creation of OSGi bundles	`http://archive.apache.org/dist/ant/binaries/apache-ant-1.7.0-bin.zip`
Apache Ivy 2.0 or higher	Dependency management project, used for easing download dependencies for OSGi bundles	`http://archive.apache.org/dist/ant/ivy/2.0.0-rc2/apache-ivy-2.0.0-rc2-bin-with-deps.zip`
MySQL Community Server 5.0	An open source RDBMS	`http://dev.mysql.com/downloads/mysql/5.0.html`
Eclipse Equinox	OSGi 4.0 reference implementation developed by the Eclipse foundation	`http://download.eclipse.org/equinox/drops/S-3.5M1-200808071402/download.php?dropFile=org.eclipse.osgi_3.5.0.v20080804-1730.jar`
Spring Dynamic Modules for OSGi 1.2(Spring-DM)	Spring's central OSGi integration subproject	`http://springsource.com/products/springdynamicmodules`

If you've been following along chapter by chapter, you will already have this software installed on your workstation, with the exception of Apache Ivy.

Apache Ivy is a dependency management tool that is closely integrated with Apache Ant—the primary build tool you've used thus far. In fact, Apache Ivy is the primary reason this last prerequisite and download list is so short compared to those for other projects in the book.

Through a few simple statements, Apache Ivy can automatically download the dependencies needed by an application. If an application requires a bundle named Vowels, Apache Ivy will automatically download all dependencies required by such a bundle (e.g., Bundle A, Bundle E, Bundle I, Bundle O, and Bundle U) in order to proceed with a streamlined compilation and runtime process, without the hassles of manually tracking dependencies.

Installing Apache Ivy

The process for installing Apache Ivy consists of the following steps:

1. Unzip the downloaded Apache Ivy file into a directory of your choice.

2. Copy Apache Ivy's JAR file, `ivy-2.0.0.jar` (located in the root directory of the download), to the `lib` directory of Apache Ant.

Next, perform the following test to ensure Apache Ivy is operating correctly: create an Apache Ant `build.xml` file like the one in Listing 7-13.

Listing 7-13. *Apache Ant `build.xml` Test File for Apache Ivy*

```
<?xml version="1.0"?>
<project xmlns:ivy="antlib:org.apache.ivy.ant" default="init" basedir=".">
  <target name="init" description="Apress - Pro Spring-OSGi">
    <ivy:retrieve/>
  </target>
</project>
```

This last listing declares the `ivy` namespace necessary to execute Ivy tasks in an Apache Ant project. Inside the only project target is the `<ivy:retrieve>` element used to trigger the retrieval of dependencies. What dependencies? Those defined in an Apache Ivy `ivy.xml` file like the one in Listing 7-14.

Listing 7-14. *Apache Ivy `ivy.xml` Test File*

```
<ivy-module version="2.0">
    <info organisation="apache" module="helloworld-ivy"/>
    <dependencies>
       <dependency org="commons-lang" name="commons-lang" rev="2.4"/>
    </dependencies>
</ivy-module>
```

This last `ivy.xml` file declares one dependency on the `commons-lang` JAR version `2.4`. If you place both these files in the same directory and invoke `ant`, you should see output like that in Listing 7-15.

Listing 7-15. *Apache Ivy Retrieval Sequence*

```
web@localhost:/tmp$ ant
Buildfile: build.xml
init:
No ivy:settings found for the default reference 'ivy.instance'.  A default➥
 instance will be used
```

```
no settings file found, using default...
[ivy:retrieve] :: Ivy 2.0.0-rc2 - 20081028224207 :: http://ant.apache.org/ivy/ ::
:: loading settings :: url = jar:file:/usr/local/ant/lib/ivy-2.0.0-rc2.jar!/➥
org/apache/ivy/core/settings/ivysettings.xml
[ivy:retrieve] :: resolving dependencies :: apache#helloworld-ivy;working@ubuntu
[ivy:retrieve]      confs: [default]
[ivy:retrieve]      found commons-lang#commons-lang;2.4 in public
[ivy:retrieve] downloading http://repo1.maven.org/maven2/commons-lang/➥
commons-lang/2.4/commons-lang-2.4.jar ...
[ivy:retrieve] ..........................
[ivy:retrieve] ................................................ (255kB)
[ivy:retrieve] .. (0kB)
[ivy:retrieve]      [SUCCESSFUL ] commons-lang#commons-lang;2.4!➥
commons-lang.jar (6941ms)
[ivy:retrieve] downloading http://repo1.maven.org/maven2/commons-lang/➥
commons-lang/2.4/commons-lang-2.4-javadoc.jar ...
[ivy:retrieve] ................
[ivy:retrieve] ........ (695kB)
[ivy:retrieve] .. (0kB)
[ivy:retrieve]      [SUCCESSFUL ] commons-lang#commons-lang;2.4!➥
commons-lang.jar(javadoc) (33960ms)
[ivy:retrieve] downloading http://repo1.maven.org/maven2/commons-lang/➥
commons-lang/2.4/commons-lang-2.4-sources.jar ...
[ivy:retrieve] ..................
[ivy:retrieve] ............ (331kB)
[ivy:retrieve] .. (0kB)
[ivy:retrieve]      [SUCCESSFUL ] commons-lang#commons-lang;2.4!➥
commons-lang.jar(source) (15081ms)
[ivy:retrieve] :: resolution report :: resolve 6639ms :: artifacts dl 56024ms
           ---------------------------------------------------------------------
           |                  |            modules             ||   artifacts   |
           |       conf       | number| search|dwnlded|evicted|| number|dwnlded|
           ---------------------------------------------------------------------
           |      default     |   1   |   1   |   1   |   0   ||   3   |   3   |
           ---------------------------------------------------------------------
[ivy:retrieve] :: retrieving :: apache#helloworld-ivy
[ivy:retrieve]      confs: [default]
[ivy:retrieve]      0 artifacts copied, 3 already retrieved (0kB/5ms)

BUILD SUCCESSFUL
Total time: 1 minute 4 seconds
```

This last listing indicates Apache Ivy successfully retrieved the `commons-lang` JAR in its `2.4` version. In this case, the downloaded dependencies correspond to three JARs, the binary, source, and javadoc for the `commons-lang` JAR. If the `commons-lang` library relied on another JAR to operate correctly, these instructions would be enough for Apache Ivy to retrieve such dependencies automatically—though it is clear from this listing there are no other outstanding dependencies for this JAR.

The default site from which Apache Ivy attempts to retrieve JARs is `http://repo1.maven.org/maven2/`, and the default local directory in which downloaded files are placed is the `.ivy2/cache/<jar_package_family>` directory under the home directory of the user who invoked Apache Ivy. These default values will be changed in the application to accommodate the project's structure and retrieve OSGi'fied bundles from the appropriate site (a.k.a. repository).

WHY NOT USE APACHE MAVEN? WHY APACHE IVY?

Maven was the first Apache dependency management project to come to fruition. It is the dependency management tool of choice for top-level Apache projects and many software development projects in general, and is inclusively used by Spring-DM to manage its build and example dependencies.

However, Maven is so feature rich that this is often its biggest drawback; it's too complex to set up for simple projects. By its definition: "Maven is essentially a project management and comprehension tool and as such provides a way to help with managing builds, documentation, reporting, dependencies, SCMs, releases, distribution" (`http://maven.apache.org/guides/getting-started/index.html#What_is_Maven`). It's many things besides a dependency management tool.

Apache Ivy, on the other hand, *is just* a dependency management tool tightly integrated with Apache Ant. By its definition: "Ant Ivy can be used to bring the dependency management feature of Maven to Ant build files, for those of you who already use Ant and who do not want to set up a maven project" (`http://ant.apache.org/ivy/features.html`), therefore it fits very nicely with what we've already used throughout the book.

A comprehensive comparison of Ivy to Maven can be found here: `http://ant.apache.org/ivy/m2comparison.html`.

Additionally, since the Spring-DM distribution contains various examples based on Maven, there is no point in repeating what you can already find in the distribution itself. Apache Ivy will provide you with an alternative route for dependency management, so you can choose whatever tool best suits your needs.

Revisiting the Hello World "Playground" Directory Structure

It is time once again to create the proper workspace in which to maneuver, a directory structure like the one illustrated in Figure 7-2.

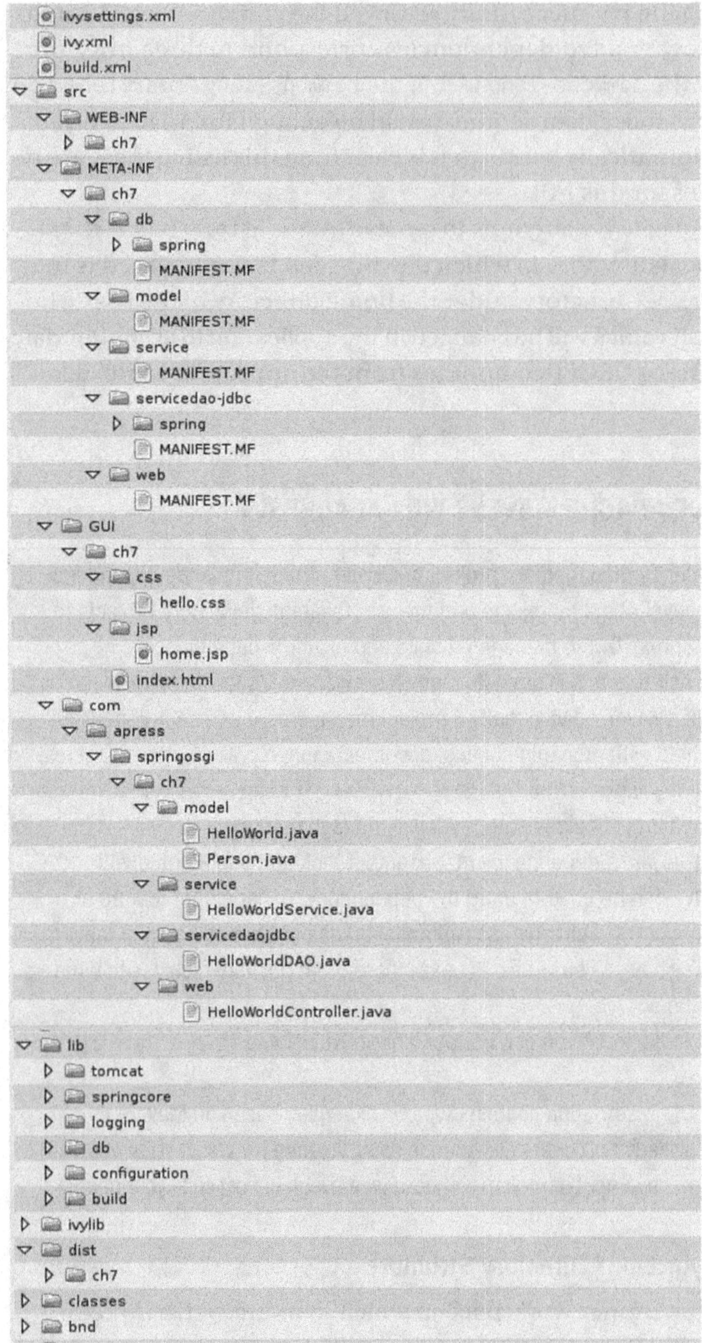

Figure 7-2. *Directory structure for the Hello World "Playground" Revisited*

The directory structure functions as follows:

- `build.xml`: This is the main Apache Ant configuration file containing the necessary tasks to build the application.
- `ivy.xml`: This is the main Apache Ivy configuration file containing the dependencies necessary to build and run the application.
- `ivysettings.xml`: This is the Apache Ivy settings file used to define dependency repositories and the local cache directory.
- `bnd`: BND tool and BND property files are placed in this directory.
- `classes`: All compiled Java classes are placed in this directory.
- `dist`: All built applications are placed in this directory.
- `ivylib`: All Apache Ivy dependency downloads are placed in this directory.
- `lib & subdirectories`: All JARs/bundles needed to compile Java sources and run the application are placed in this directory.
- `src`: All Java sources files composing the application are placed accordingly in subdirectories inside this directory, including application web descriptors in `WEB-INF`, metadata files in `META-INF`, and application user interfaces (like JSP files) in GUI.

Since you've already tackled this application in earlier chapters and should be familiar with the Hello World "playground" layout, I will only elaborate on the topics that are new to the present chapter.

Building and Deploying the Application

Moving directly to building and deploying the application is indeed fast-forwarding. But the only thing new for the application is the JDBC-DAO bundle presented in the first section of this chapter. So it is not necessary to dwell on the application's contents, especially when you've seen them in two earlier chapters. Listing 7-16 illustrates the main Apache Ant `build.xml` for this chapter's version.

Listing 7-16. *Apache Ant build.xml*

```
<?xml version="1.0"?>
<project xmlns:ivy="antlib:org.apache.ivy.ant" default="init" basedir=".">

  <target name="init" description="Apress - Pro Spring-OSGi">
  <tstamp/>
  <property name="projectname" value="Pro Spring-OSGi"/>
  <echo message="-------${projectname}------"/>

  <property name="debug"          value="on"/>
  <property name="optimize"       value="off"/>
  <property name="deprication"    value="off"/>
  <property name="build.compiler" value="modern"/>
  <property name="target.vm"      value="1.5"/>
  <property name="build.dir"      value="classes"/>
  <property name="dist.dir"       value="dist"/>
  <property name="src.dir"        value="src"/>
  <property name="lib.dir"        value="lib/build"/>

  <!-- Load JAR's onto the classpath, taken from lib subdir -->
  <path id="classpath">
   <fileset dir="${lib.dir}">
    <include name="*.jar"/>
   </fileset>
   <pathelement location="${build.dir}"/>
  </path>
 </target>

 <target name="compile" depends="init" description="Compile code">

  <ivy:retrieve pattern="lib/[conf]/[artifact]-[revision].[ext]" />

  <echo message="-------Compiling code for Pro-Spring OSGi------"/>
  <mkdir dir="${build.dir}"/>
  <mkdir dir="${dist.dir}"/>

  <javac srcdir="${src.dir}"
         destdir="${build.dir}"
         debug="${debug}"
         optimize="${optimize}"
```

```
        deprecation="${depreaction}"
        target="${target.vm}">
      <classpath refid="classpath"/>
  </javac>

<copy todir="${build.dir}">
          <fileset dir="${src.dir}">
<!-- Some of the following statements are relevant to Ch2 -->
<!-- They are present here because the same compile task is used -->
              <include name="**/*.properties"/>
              <include name="**/*.xml"/>
              <exclude name="**/*.java"/>
              <exclude name="META-INF/**"/>
              <exclude name="WEB-INF/**"/>
              <exclude name="GUI/**"/>
           </fileset>
  </copy>
  </target>

<target name="ch7" depends="compile" description="Build Chapter 7 Spring-OSGi➥
 Application">

  <echo message="-------------- Building Chapter 7 Spring-OSGi Application for➥
 Pro Spring-OSGi --------------"/>

     <property name="ch7.dir"          value="${dist.dir}/ch7/"/>
     <mkdir dir="${ch7.dir}"/>

     <jar destfile="${ch7.dir}/helloworld-db.jar" ➥
manifest="${src.dir}/META-INF/ch7/db/MANIFEST.MF">
        <metainf dir="${src.dir}/META-INF/ch7/db/"/>
     </jar>

    <jar destfile="${ch7.dir}/helloworld-model.jar" ➥
manifest="${src.dir}/META-INF/ch7/model/MANIFEST.MF">
         <fileset  dir="${build.dir}">
           <include name="com/apress/springosgi/ch7/model/*"/>
         </fileset>
        <metainf dir="${src.dir}/META-INF/ch7/model/"/>
     </jar>
```

```
<jar destfile="${ch7.dir}/helloworld-service.jar" ➥
manifest="${src.dir}/META-INF/ch7/service/MANIFEST.MF">
         <fileset  dir="${build.dir}">
           <include name="com/apress/springosgi/ch7/service/*"/>
         </fileset>
        <metainf dir="${src.dir}/META-INF/ch7/service/"/>
</jar>

<jar destfile="${ch7.dir}/helloworld-servicedao-jdbc.jar" ➥
manifest="${src.dir}/META-INF/ch7/servicedao-jdbc/MANIFEST.MF">
         <fileset  dir="${build.dir}">
           <include name="com/apress/springosgi/ch7/servicedaojdbc/*"/>
         </fileset>
        <metainf dir="${src.dir}/META-INF/ch7/servicedao-jdbc/"/>
</jar>

<war destfile="${ch7.dir}/helloworld-web.war" ➥
webxml="${src.dir}/WEB-INF/ch7/web.xml" manifest=➥
"${src.dir}/META-INF/ch7/web/MANIFEST.MF">
        <metainf dir="${src.dir}/META-INF/ch7/web/"/>
        <webinf dir="${src.dir}/WEB-INF/ch7/"/>
        <zipfileset dir="${src.dir}/GUI/ch7/" prefix=""/>
        <classes dir="${build.dir}">
           <include name="com/apress/springosgi/ch7/web/*"/>
        </classes>
</war>

</target>
</project>
```

The first thing to note about this Apache Ant project file is that it is Apache Ivy enabled. Notice the Apache Ivy namespace declared in the top-level <project> element. In addition, notice the <ivy:retrieve> element inside the compile target, which allows the build process to retrieve the application's dependencies and have them available for compilation and later for running the application.

The other marked section in this listing corresponds to the JDBC-DAO bundle named helloworld-servicedao, whose contents are Listings 7-1, 7-2, and 7-3. The remaining bundles created in this project file—helloworld-db.jar, helloworld-model.jar, helloworld-service.jar, and helloworld-web.war—are replicas of the bundles created in Chapter 5 by the same name. You can consult this chapter or the book's accompanying source code for their particular contents.

Since the Apache Ant file is already tied to Apache Ivy, the next step consists of configuring Apache Ivy to fulfill the application's dependencies.

Before I start describing Apache Ivy's configuration files, it is best to define exactly what we want to get out of Apache Ivy. What dependencies are needed by the application? The following list gives a broad classification of the application's dependencies:

- `build`: Bundles or standard JARs needed to compile the application's classes
- `db`: Bundles used by the application at runtime to enable RDBMS access
- `logging`: Bundles used by the application at runtime to enable logging
- `spring`: Bundles used by the application at runtime to enable Spring and Spring-DM support
- `tomcat`: Bundles used by the application at runtime to enable Tomcat (web container) support

In total you need to obtain over 40 bundles (JARs) to fulfill the application's five broad areas. The next obvious question is where to get these bundle dependencies. There are numerous places called repositories on the Internet where you can obtain bundles.

So the first step to configuring Apache Ivy is defining the repositories where you wish to obtain bundles. Listing 7-17 illustrates the `ivysettings.xml` file used for this purpose.

Listing 7-17. *Apache Ivy `ivysettings.xml` File*

```
<ivysettings>

  <settings defaultResolver="chain-springosgi"/>

  <caches defaultCacheDir="${basedir}/ivylib">
  </caches>

  <resolvers>
    <chain name="chain-springosgi">
        <filesystem name="my-repository">
            <ivy pattern="${basedir}/ivylib/[organisation]/[module]/ivys/➥
ivy-[revision].xml"/>
            <artifact pattern="${basedir}/ivylib/[organisation]/[module]/[type]s/➥
[artifact]-[revision].[ext]"/>
        </filesystem>
```

```
        <url name="spring-release-repo">
                <ivy pattern="http://repository.springsource.com/ivy/bundles/➥
release/[organisation]/[module]/[revision]/[artifact]-[revision].[ext]" />
                <artifact pattern="http://repository.springsource.com/ivy/bundles/➥
release/[organisation]/[module]/[revision]/[artifact]-[revision].[ext]" />
        </url>

        <url name="spring-external-repo">
                <ivy pattern="http://repository.springsource.com/ivy/bundles/➥
external/[organisation]/[module]/[revision]/[artifact]-[revision].[ext]" />
                <artifact pattern="http://repository.springsource.com/ivy/bundles/➥
external/[organisation]/[module]/[revision]/[artifact]-[revision].[ext]" />
        </url>

        <url name="spring-milestone-repo" m2compatible="true">
                <artifact pattern="http://s3.amazonaws.com/➥
maven.springframework.org/milestone/[organisation]/[module]/[revision]/➥
[artifact]-[revision].[ext]"/>
        </url>

        <ibiblio name="ibiblio"/>

        <url name="default-repo" m2compatible="true">
                <artifact pattern="http://repo1.maven.org/maven2/[organisation]/➥
[module]/[revision]/[artifact]-[revision].[ext]"/>
        </url>

      </chain>
    </resolvers>

</ivysettings>
```

Apache Ivy repositories are configured inside the `<resolvers>` element of an `ivysettings.xml` file. For this application we will rely on Apache Ivy's concept of a *chain*, which is a list of repositories for locating dependencies. Notice the `<chain name="chain-springosgi">` element nested inside the `<resolvers>` element.

Apache Ivy can define various `<chain>` elements. The whole purpose of a *chain* is to define a preference order for repositories. Under certain circumstances you might want to look up dependencies in Repository A, and then fall back on Repository B if a dependency is not found, and if a dependency is still not found, then try Repository C. For other circumstances, you might want to change the lookup order first to Repository C, and then A, and finally B. To simplify Apache Ivy's setup, however, the application will rely on a single chain.

Next, inside the <chain> element, you will find six repository definitions. The first one is a <filesystem> repository, used to look up a dependency on the file system of your workstation. On the first attempt to locate a dependency on your file system, it won't be available, of course, but it makes perfect sense thereafter to avoid pinging remote repositories to locate dependencies you've already downloaded. This is the reason why the <filesystem> repository is first.

Inside the <filesystem> element you will find both an <ivy> and <artifact> element with a pattern attribute. These last two elements along with the pattern values reflect how a repository archives dependencies. The pattern values might seem somewhat awkward, but these are conventions set forth by the early versions of Maven, a tool that pretty much sets the standard for dependency management tools.

For example, in Apache Ivy a bundle like persistence-api-1.0.jar would be archived in a directory structure of the form javax.persistence/persistence-api/jars/persistence-api-1.0.jar, with its corresponding Apache Ivy dependency file archived in a directory structure of the form javax.persistence/persistence-api/ivy-1.0.xml. The first location is the bundle (JAR) itself, and the second is the bundle's Apache Ivy file, which contains detailed information on its dependencies.

In this particular case, notice the patterns nested inside the <filesystem> element point toward the ${basedir}/ivylib directory, which is the ivylib directory of the Hello World "playground." If a pattern for a particular dependency cannot be matched in this last directory—which will always be the case on the first attempt—then Apache Ivy will fall back to the next resolver in the chain, which is an <url> element.

The <url> element is a remote site that contains bundle dependencies. Similar to the <filesystem> element, notice the nested <ivy> and <artifact> elements each with a pattern attribute. In this case the pattern values differ slightly, but this is due to how each repository owner opts to archive bundles.

Once Apache Ivy gets to a <url> element in the chain, it will attempt to download both the <ivy> and <artifact> element values from the remote site. For example, Apache Ivy will attempt to download a dependency on the persistence-api-1.0.jar bundle from a URL like http://repository.springsource.com/ivy/bundles/release/javax.persistence/persistence-api/1.0/persistence-api-1.0.jar, while looking for its corresponding Apache Ivy dependency file from a URL like http://repository.springsource.com/ivy/bundles/release/javax.persistence/persistence-api/1.0/ivy-1.0.xml. The first location is the bundle itself, and the second is the bundle's Apache Ivy file, which contains detailed information on its dependencies.

Since a <url> element represents a download, Apache Ivy doesn't just fetch dependencies, it also archives them locally for future use. This is a very important step to Apache Ivy's performance, for it would otherwise be necessary to constantly download dependencies each time Apache Ivy is invoked. So where are these dependencies archived? In the <caches> element.

Toward the top of Listing 7-17 is a statement in the form <caches defaultCacheDir="${basedir}/ivylib">. This tells Apache Ivy to archive every dependency it downloads in the ${basedir}/ivylib directory. If this value were not specified, by default all downloaded dependencies would be placed inside the `.ivy2/cache/<jar_package_familiy>` directory located inside the user's home directory that invoked Apache Ivy.

By overriding the default download location for dependencies, the first repository value or `<filesystem>` element makes more sense. Notice the `<ivy>` and `<artifact>` patterns for the `<filesystem>` element point toward the same directory defined in the `defaultCacheDir` attribute of the `<caches>` element. Thus if a dependency is requested on a second occasion and it was already retrieved from a remote repository, a local lookup will be sufficient to satisfy the dependency.

The second `<url>` element in the chain represents another repository. Here again, notice the slightly different `<ivy>` and `<artifact>pattern` values used to attempt to retrieve a dependency. It's important to note that an attempt to retrieve a dependency from this third repository will only take place if a dependency failed to be fulfilled locally (in the `<filesystem>` element) or be retrieved from the first `<url>` element.

The third `<url>` element is yet another repository with its own `<ivy>` and `<artifact>` patterns, serving as a fallback in case neither of the preceding repositories can fulfill a dependency.

At this point it is worth noting why these three `<url>` repositories were chosen first. Not only are they the primary repositories managed by the team behind the Spring Framework, but they are also ***the only ones that provide OSGi'fied versions of staple Java JARs. This is paramount.***

By default, Apache Ivy attempts to download dependencies from `http://repo1.maven.org/maven2/`, so what happens if you define a dependency on a common JAR like `persistence-api-1.0.jar`? If you don't give precedence to a repository that has OSGi'fied JARs, Apache Ivy will likely retrieve a version that has no OSGi information, making it inoperable in an OSGi environment.

OSGi aside, and to cover the possibility of dependencies that might not be present in one of the Spring team repositories, two more repositories are defined. These are the `<ibiblio>` element, which is a shortcut statement representing the repository maintained by `http://www.ibiblio.org/`, and another `<url>` element pointing toward the master `http://repo1.maven.org/maven2` repository.

Finally, it is worth noting the topmost element in Listing 7-17: `<settings defaultResolver="chain-springosgi"/>`. This indicates to use `chain-springosgi` as the default resolver.

Now that you've defined Apache Ivy's `ivysettings.xml` file, specifying where it will obtain its dependencies, you can define the dependencies themselves in Apache Ivy's `ivy.xml` file. Listing 7-18 illustrates the first iteration for this file.

Listing 7-18. *Apache Ivy `ivy.xml` File*

```
<ivy-module version="2.0">

    <info organisation="apache" module="hello-ivy"/>
    <configurations>
        <conf name="build"/>
```

```
        <conf name="logging"/>
        <conf name="db"/>
        <conf name="springcore"/>
        <conf name="tomcat" />
    </configurations>

    <dependencies>
        <!-- Download compile bundle dependencies for application build -->
        <dependency org="javax.persistence" name="persistence-api" ➥
rev="1.0" conf="build->*"/>
        <dependency org="org.springframework"➥
 name="org.springframework.web.servlet" rev="2.5.4.A" conf="build->*"/>
        <dependency org="org.springframework" name="org.springframework.jdbc"➥
 rev="2.5.4.A" conf="build->*"/>

        <!-- Download runtime bundle dependencies for application logging -->
        <dependency org="org.slf4j"➥
 name="com.springsource.slf4j.org.apache.commons.logging" ➥
rev="1.5.0" conf="logging->runtime"/>
        <dependency org="org.slf4j" ➥
name="com.springsource.slf4j.org.apache.log4j" rev="1.5.0" ➥
conf="logging->runtime"/>
        <dependency org="ch.qos.logback" ➥
name="com.springsource.ch.qos.logback.classic" rev="0.9.9" conf="logging->runtime"/>
    </dependencies>

</ivy-module>
```

The first declaration in this listing is the `<info>` element. It just contains descriptive information about the Ivy module, so there is not much to elaborate on. The second declaration in the form of the `<configurations>` element deserves closer attention. Each of the `<conf>` elements nested inside the `<configurations>` element represent dependency areas for the application.

Such areas serve to group dependent bundles into separate directories (e.g., Apache Tomcat bundles are grouped under `tomcat`, logging bundles are grouped under `logging`, etc.). The way these areas or `<conf>` elements are translated into directories is tied directly to the `<ivy:retrieve pattern="lib/[conf]/[artifact]-[revision].[ext]" >` element declared in the main Apache Ant file (Listing 7-16). Notice the `[conf]` value in the `pattern` attribute, which indicates to perform the retrieval process on directories based on `<conf>` element values.

Since `ivy.xml` declares five `<conf>` values, there will be five directories used to group dependencies: `lib/build`, `lib/logging`, `lib/db`, `lib/springcore`, and `lib/tomcat`, all present in the Hello World "playground." The remaining [artifact]-[revision].[ext] values in the <ivy:retrieve> pattern attribute represent the bundle's notation.

So now the interesting question is, what bundles get copied where? This is determined based on the conf attribute of each <dependency> element, which takes us to dependencies themselves.

First of all, notice each project <dependency> element needs to be nested inside the <dependencies> element. It's inside a <dependency> element that an application's dependencies are defined. Each dependency is defined on a bundle's organization, name, and revision values. Notice how the org, name, and rev conventions for defining a dependency are in line with the pattern values used to define repositories (Listing 7-17). Besides the org, name, and rev attributes, the <dependency> element also relies on the conf attribute, which is used to specify where to a copy a bundle's dependencies.

For example, a value like conf="build->*" tells Apache Ivy to copy a bundle and its dependencies to the build conf value (which maps to the physical directory lib/build of the Hello World "playground" on account of the <ivy:retrieve> pattern). The * assigned to the conf attribute is a wildcard notation indicating to copy every bundle related to the dependency.

Another variation of the conf attribute is a value like conf="logging->runtime". This tells Apache Ivy to copy a bundle's dependencies to the logging conf value (which maps to the physical directory lib/logging of the Hello World "playground"), but only those dependencies required for runtime level, as defined in its Ivy dependency file.

WHO DETERMINES WHAT A BUNDLE (JAR) DEPENDS ON?

The creator of the Ivy repository determines what a bundle (JAR) depends on. Notice that upon defining Apache Ivy repositories, besides the <artifact> pattern—which is the bundle itself—there is also an <ivy> pattern that points to a bundle's associated Ivy dependency file. Depending on the nature and popularity of a bundle, this Ivy dependency file can vary in nature.

Some JARs possess very elaborate dependency files with dependency levels (e.g., ->runtime), other JARs don't have dependencies or none have been defined for them (e.g., milestone release bundles), and yet other JARs can have dozens of unwarranted dependencies for your particular needs (e.g., you might require a single class in a JAR, but the entire JAR may depend on dozens of other JARs).

In short, you need to rely on an Ivy repository maintainer to correctly define a bundle's dependencies. The worst thing that can happen is the need to declare multiple <dependency> elements to satisfy dependencies that might have escaped an Ivy repository maintainer or be forced to download various bundles that aren't needed by your application but were defined by an Ivy repository maintainer as dependencies.

Before discussing the remaining section of the ivy.xml file to fulfill an application's dependencies, it is important that you don't confuse Apache Ivy's <conf> elements (directories) in ivy.xml with the cache directory <cache> element in ivysettings.xml. These values can be confusing at first since they both deal with physical directories and copying bundles (JARs). Figure 7-3 illustrates the entire retrieval and copying process for Apache Ivy.

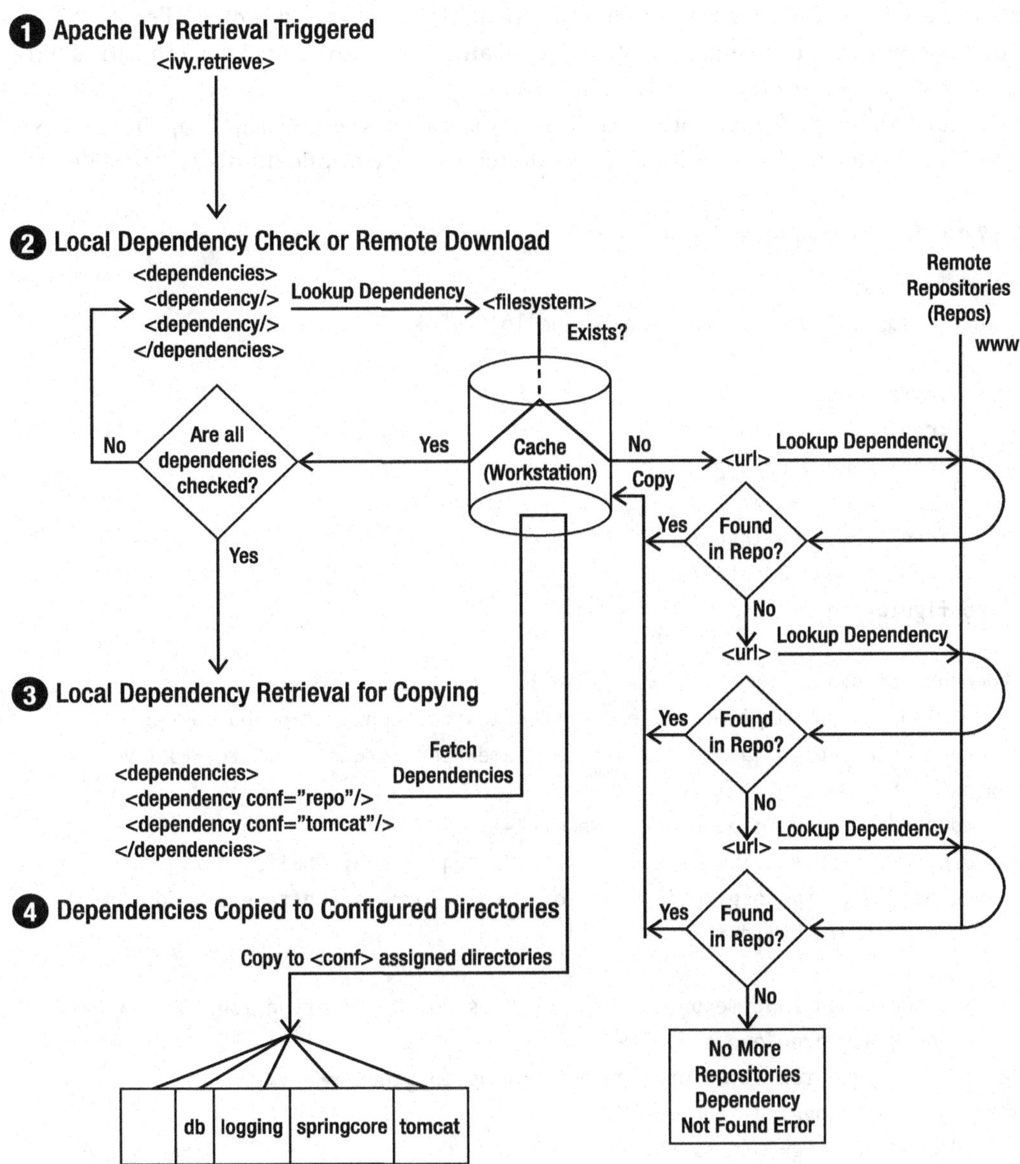

Figure 7-3. *Apache Ivy retrieval and copying process*

Notice that when the `<ivy:retrieve>` element is triggered, all dependencies are first checked against the cache directory. If the cache directory does not have them, a remote download is attempted from the repository *chain* configured in the `ivysettings.xml` file.

Once all `<dependency>` elements have been verified and are available locally, the `conf` attribute for each `<dependency>` element is inspected, and the corresponding dependencies are copied in accordance with the `conf` value. For example, `conf="build->*"` copies all dependencies to the `build` conf value (physical directory `lib/build`), and `conf="*"` copies all dependencies to every available `conf` value (physical directories `lib/build`, `lib/db`, `lib/logging`, `lib/springcore`, and `lib/tomcat`).

Now that you have a firmer understanding of Apache Ivy's retrieval and copying process, Listing 7-19 illustrates the remaining dependencies for the application's `ivy.xml` file.

Listing 7-19. *Apache Ivy `ivy.xml` File (Complete)*

```
<ivy-module version="2.0">
    <info organisation="apache" module="hello-ivy"/>

    <configurations>
         <conf name="build"/>
         <conf name="logging"/>
         <conf name="db"/>
         <conf name="springcore"/>
         <conf name="tomcat" />
    </configurations>

    <dependencies>
       <!-- Download compile bundle dependencies for application build -->
       <dependency org="javax.persistence" name="persistence-api" rev="1.0"➥
 conf="build->*"/>
       <dependency org="org.springframework"➥
 name="org.springframework.web.servlet" rev="2.5.4.A" conf="build->*"/>
       <dependency org="org.springframework" name="org.springframework.jdbc"➥
 rev="2.5.4.A" conf="build->*"/>

       <!-- Download runtime bundle dependencies for application logging -->
       <dependency org="org.slf4j"➥
 name="com.springsource.slf4j.org.apache.commons.logging" ➥
rev="1.5.0" conf="logging->runtime"/>
       <dependency org="org.slf4j" ➥
name="com.springsource.slf4j.org.apache.log4j" rev="1.5.0" conf="logging->runtime"/>
       <dependency org="ch.qos.logback" ➥
 name="com.springsource.ch.qos.logback.classic" rev="0.9.9" ➥
conf="logging->runtime"/>

     <!-- Download runtime bundle dependencies for application database -->
       <dependency org="com.mysql.jdbc" name="com.springsource.com.mysql.jdbc" ➥
rev="5.1.6" conf="db->runtime"/>
       <dependency org="org.springframework" name="org.springframework.orm" ➥
rev="2.5.4.A" conf="db->runtime"/>
```

```
        <dependency org="org.apache.commons"➥
 name="com.springsource.org.apache.commons.dbcp" rev="1.2.2.osgi" ➥
conf="db->runtime"/>
        <dependency org="javax.persistence"➥
 name="com.springsource.javax.persistence" rev="1.0.0" conf="db->runtime"/>
        <dependency org="javax.transaction"➥
 name="com.springsource.javax.transaction" rev="1.1.0" conf="db->runtime"/>

        <!-- Download runtime bundle dependencies for application springcore -->
        <dependency org="org.springframework" name="org.springframework.core" ➥
rev="2.5.4.A" conf="springcore->runtime"/>
        <dependency org="org.springframework" ➥
 name="org.springframework.web.servlet" rev="2.5.4.A" ➥
conf="springcore->runtime"/>
        <dependency org="org.springframework"➥
 name="org.springframework.context.support" rev="2.5.4.A" ➥
conf="springcore->runtime"/>
        <dependency org="org.apache.commons"➥
 name="com.springsource.org.apache.commons.collections" rev="3.2.0" ➥
conf="springcore->runtime"/>
        <dependency org="net.sourceforge.cglib"➥
 name="com.springsource.net.sf.cglib" rev="2.1.3" conf="springcore->runtime"/>
        <dependency org="edu.emory.mathcs.backport"➥
 name="com.springsource.edu.emory.mathcs.backport" rev="3.0.0" ➥
conf="springcore->runtime"/>

        <dependency org="javax.annotation"➥
 name="com.springsource.javax.annotation" rev="1.0.0" ➥
conf="springcore->runtime"/>
        <dependency org="org.springframework.osgi" ➥
name="spring-osgi-io" rev="1.2.0-m1" conf="springcore->*"/>
        <dependency org="org.springframework.osgi" ➥
name="spring-osgi-core" rev="1.2.0-m1" conf="springcore->*"/>
        <dependency org="org.springframework.osgi" ➥
name="spring-osgi-extender" rev="1.2.0-m1" conf="springcore->*"/>
        <dependency org="org.springframework.osgi" ➥
name="spring-osgi-web" rev="1.2.0-m1" conf="springcore->*"/>
        <dependency org="org.springframework.osgi" ➥
name="spring-osgi-web-extender" rev="1.2.0-m1" conf="springcore->*"/>

        <!-- Download runtime bundle dependencies for application tomcat -->
        <dependency org="javax.servlet"➥
```

```
 name="com.springsource.javax.servlet.jsp.jstl" rev="1.1.2" conf="tomcat->*"/>
       <dependency org="javax.el" ➥
name="com.springsource.javax.el" rev="1.0.0" conf="tomcat->*"/>
       <dependency org="org.apache.commons"➥
 name="com.springsource.org.apache.commons.el" rev="1.0.0" conf="tomcat->*"/>
       <dependency org="org.springframework" ➥
name="jasper-pholder" rev="5.5.23-20080305.122359-4" conf="tomcat->*">
         <artifact name="jasper.osgi" type="jar"➥
 url="http://s3.amazonaws.com/maven.springframework.org/osgi/org/springframework/➥
osgi/jasper.osgi/5.5.23-SNAPSHOT/jasper.osgi-5.5.23-20080305.122359-4.jar"/>
       </dependency>
       <dependency org="catalina.osgi" ➥
name="catalina-pholder" rev="5.5.23-SNAPSHOT" conf="tomcat->*">
         <artifact name="catalina.osgi" type="jar"➥
 url="http://s3.amazonaws.com/maven.springframework.org/osgi/org/springframework/➥
osgi/catalina.osgi/5.5.23-SNAPSHOT/catalina.osgi-5.5.23-20080425.154256-4.jar"/>
       </dependency>

       <dependency org="catalina.start.osgi" ➥
name="catalina.start-pholder" rev="1.0-20080425.161832-4" conf="tomcat->*">
         <artifact name="catalina.start.osgi" type="jar"➥
 url="http://s3.amazonaws.com/maven.springframework.org/osgi/org/➥
springframework/osgi/catalina.start.osgi/1.0-SNAPSHOT/➥
catalina.start.osgi-1.0-20080425.161832-4.jar"/>
       </dependency>

    </dependencies>
</ivy-module>
```

The first new section corresponds to the database dependencies that will be copied to the `lib/db` directory of the Hello World "playground." Notice these dependencies also rely on the `conf="db->runtime"` value, guaranteeing that only runtime dependencies be copied from Apache Ivy's cache.

In addition, notice that certain database bundles like `org.apache.commons.pool` are not declared even though they are used by the earlier versions of the application. This is precisely the purpose of a dependency management tool like Apache Ivy: it automatically figures out for you what you need to run a particular bundle.

Since a dependency on `org.apache.commons.dbcp` is declared, Apache Ivy will automatically download this bundle and its dependencies—which includes the `org.apache.commons.pool` bundle—along with any other dependent bundles.

The next section corresponds to the Spring libraries placed in the `lib/springcore` directory of the Hello World "playground." The `<dependency>` declarations are practically the same with the exception of those belonging to Spring-DM, which use the `conf="springcore->*"` qualifier.

Since the declared Spring-DM dependency versions are release candidates, the Ivy dependency file for each of these bundles does not have a `runtime`-level definition; therefore, it's necessary to use the wildcard (*) notation, which indicates to copy a bundle's full dependencies.

Finally come the Apache Tomcat library dependencies that will be placed in the `lib/tomcat` directory of the Hello World's playground. For Tomcat's dependencies, only those with a nested `<artifact>` element are different. The reason three of Apache Tomcat's dependencies rely on this notation is because the application relies on bundle snapshot versions.

Notice all bundle snapshot versions have a long string in the form of a date (e.g., `20080425.161832`). This type of bundle name does not match any particular pattern. So instead of trying to create a logical pattern, which doesn't exist for snapshot version naming, with a repository address in Apache Ivy's `ivysettings.xml`, an easier route is to include the exact location (URL) for a snapshot bundle.

By embedding the `<artifact>` element with the exact location (URL) of a bundle's location, Apache Ivy immediately attempts to download the bundle from this location, instead of relying on a repository chain.

Having reviewed the application's `ivy.xml` and `ivysettings.xml` file, you can now start the build process. If you place these two files in the root directory of the Hello World "playground" alongside Apache Ant's `build.xml` file and execute `ant ch7`, the entire build process will kick off with the retrieval of numerous bundles from remote repositories.

Each downloaded bundle will be placed inside the `ivylib` directory of the Hello World "playground." Once this download process is complete, all the application's dependencies will be prepped and colocated inside the subdirectories within the `lib` directory (`lib/build`, `lib/db`, `lib/logging`, `lib/springcore`, and `lib/tomcat*`).

Next, with the `build` bundles in place, Apache Ant will compile the application classes and create the application bundles.

Finally, it is only a matter of creating the necessary `config.ini` file for Eclipse Equinox to bootstrap the application, including `db`, `logging`, `spring`, and `tomcat` bundles, followed by the application itself. And since Apache Ivy aided in creating a layout structure for these dependency bundles, it is only a matter of placing the Eclipse Equinox file `config.ini` inside the appropriate directory of the Hello World "playground" to make the application work in a few simple steps.

Summary

In this chapter you learned how to create an OSGi bundle to access an RDBMS using JDBC, relying on the Spring Framework to ease the creation of a class based on this data access mechanism. In addition, you saw the requirements that need to be taken into account for deploying OSGi bundles using either JDBC or JPA without the aid of SpringSource dm Server.

You then explored BND, a tool that aids in the migration of standard JARs to OSGi-compliant bundles. You learned how to use BND functions like inspecting and determining a JARs dependency structure, automatically creating an OSGi-compliant bundle from a standard JAR, and more advanced transformation techniques relying on BND properties files containing regular expressions and macros.

Then you went on to rework the applications created in Chapter 2 and Chapter 5, only now to use an RDBMS in the context of OSGi and without the aid of the SpringSource dm Server. In the process you were introduced to Apache Ivy, a dependency management tool tightly integrated with Apache Ant to aid in fulfilling an application's dependencies.

Finally, you explored in detail how it is Apache Ivy performs its dependency management tasks, including how to define repositories and dependencies in its primary configuration files, `ivysetting.xml` and `ivy.xml`. You capped everything off by creating the necessary Apache Ivy configuration files to download the application's dependency bundles.

CHAPTER 8

Web Applications Using Spring and OSGi

Deploying an OSGi bundle to be enabled on the Web can be a little more demanding than deploying a standard OSGi bundle containing business services, because it has to be managed by an underlying OSGi'fied web container. Throughout the book you've explored many variations to do just this, starting off with a stand-alone OSGi web bundle in Chapter 1 and continuing on with an examination of the use of the standard Web Archive (WAR) format employed in Java web applications in Chapter 2.

In Chapter 3, you got your first glimpse of how Spring-DM tackles the issue of deploying web-bound bundles containing servlets and JSP files, through a special hybrid-WAR called a shared services WAR that takes advantage of OSGi's features. Then in Chapter 5, you learned how the SpringSource DM Server makes web enablement of Spring and OSGi applications more manageable through artifacts like Web Modules and Platform Archives (PARs).

So what could you be possibly missing out on? Well, all the available configuration options and the little subtleties that weren't mentioned in the earlier chapters for enabling web applications using Spring and OSGi. This chapter will concentrate exclusively on the following web access features available in Spring-DM:

- Using an alternate web container other than the default Apache Tomcat
- Using Transport Layer Security (TLS)—HTTPS
- Using Adobe's Flex in a web bundle

Web Bundle Concepts

Simply installing a bundle containing servlets and JSP files in an OSGi environment does not mean it will be enabled on the Web. You need to take certain steps to make the underlying OSGi environment and bundle operate with the same JSP files and servlets you would typically use in a non-OSGi environment.

In Chapter 1 you took the longest and most limited route, which was to manually register OSGi's `HttpService` backed by a Jetty Java web server, as well as manually registering a servlet with this service. Not only was this a *very tedious* process, but it also lacked support for more common artifacts used in Java web applications like JSP files and JSTL.

In order to simplify the whole process for web applications in OSGi, Spring-DM allows you to use Java's de facto web application format: WAR. As you explored in the introductory sample on Spring-DM in Chapter 3, a *WAR can be treated as an OSGi bundle* so long as it contains the necessary OSGi manifest.

The most important aspect of Spring-DM treating a WAR as an OSGi bundle is that it delegates the processing of a WAR to a web container that also needs to be present in the same OSGi environment. In more technical terms, the web application creation and thread management is delegated to the web container.

This raises an interesting question. If a WAR is treated as an OSGi bundle, how does Spring-DM determine whether it needs to be delegated to a web container? This is done through Spring-DM's extender mechanism.

Recall from Chapter 4 that each bundle installed after Spring-DM's extenders have been activated will be inspected for the presence of certain trigger points. *If a bundle is installed with a* `.war` *extension, it will automatically trigger Spring-DM's web extender to delegate the bundle for processing to the underlying web container.*

The bootstrapping process of a bundle (WAR) in a web container, however, is very different from that in a non-OSGi'fied web container. In a non-OSGi'fied web container, the web container operates under a single class loader, making a series of classes available to all installed WARs and at the same time loading classes from each WAR into a separate child class loader. In an OSGi'fied web container this is not the case, since a web container is split into different bundles, each having its own class loader.

The advantage to this approach is that you can pick and choose what bundles (JARs) make up your web container, as in Chapter 1 when we used a single bundle or in Chapter 3 when we added more bundles to support things like JSP files and JSTL. The disadvantage, though, is that bundles (WARs) deployed in an OSGi'fied container need to take this into account.

Spring-DM delegates a bundle (WAR) to the underlying OSGi'fied web container for processing, but this does not mean the bundle (WAR) will automatically have access to the same resources as in a non-OSGi'fied web container. These resources are the following:

- Java classes provided by the web container like `javax.servlet` and `javax.servlet.http`
- Java classes included in the bundle's own `/WEB-INF/classes/` directory
- Java libraries (JARs) included in the bundle's (WAR's) own `/WEB-INF/lib/` directory
- Java application classes containing business logic

This means that upon delegating a bundle (WAR) to an OSGi'fied container, the container will also need to contain the necessary OSGi headers to load these resources. Listing 8-1 illustrates what most bundles designed as web applications contain at a minimum.

Listing 8-1. *Import Java Servlet Packages*

```
Import-Package:  javax.servlet,
 javax.servlet.http,
 javax.servlet.resources
```

This last listing allows a bundle (WAR) access to Java's servlet packages that are available by default in non-OSGi'fied web containers, and which are by far the most common in web applications.

Additional packages available by default in a non-OSGi'fied web container can range from a JSP compiler, to JSTL libraries, to logging libraries. Adding these packages to a bundle's (WAR's) `MANIFEST.MF` file is dependent on the nature of the bundle itself (e.g., if a JSP file is used in a bundle, the page would require loading whatever JSP compiler classes/packages are used by the web container).

■ **Note** In addition to using the `Import-Package` header, you can also use the `Require-Bundle` header as a shorter route to accessing a web container's classes/packages. See Chapter 6, which contains a more extensive explanation on the use of this header.

Besides the classes/packages a bundle (WAR) is required to import explicitly and which are typically provided by a web container, it may also be necessary to load classes/packages that are contained in the bundle (WAR) itself.

In a standard WAR, the directories `/WEB-INF/classes` and `/WEB-INF/lib/` are inspected for the presence of classes and libraries, which are then loaded into its private class loader. This is part of the bootstrapping process for non-OSGi'fied web containers—see Chapter 3's "Application Servers: Classpath Loaders" section for more background on this topic.

In an OSGi'fied web container, this bootstrapping process does not take place. The reason it does not take place is because OSGi does not require special directories to load classes; it simply loads classes from the root directory of the bundle or from whatever `Import-Package` statements are made in a bundle's `MANIFEST.MF` file. Nevertheless, if you wish to support backward compatibility with these standard WAR directories, OSGi allows you to do so using the `Bundle-Classpath` header as illustrated in Listing 8-2.

Listing 8-2. *Alternative Classpath Locations in a Bundle Using* `Bundle-Classpath`

```
Bundle-Classpath: .,
 WEB-INF/classes,
 WEB-INF/lib/math.jar,
 WEB-INF/lib/spelling.jar
```

This listing illustrates how the `Bundle-Classpath` header expands a bundle's classpath to additional directories or JAR files. The first statement, `.` (dot), indicates to load classes from the root directory of the bundle—OSGi's default—while the second value indicates to load classes from the `WEB-INF/classes` directory.

The last two statements specify the loading of two *embedded JARs* into the bundle's classpath. It should be noted, however, that *embedding JARs* in a bundle (WAR) is discouraged. Consider OSGi'fying and deploying embedded JARs as stand-alone bundles themselves, since this allows a JAR's classes to be shared among more bundles and takes advantage of things like versioning.

The only exception to embedding a JAR in a bundle (WAR) is if the licensing of a JAR prohibits its modification, which is a necessary step to OSGi'fying a JAR. Otherwise, embedded JARs should be avoided. See the section "Introducing the BND Tool" in Chapter 7 for instructions on OSGi'fying JARs, and review Chapter 6, which discusses versioning, in case you're embedding JARs to avoid class clashes.

Finally, we come to the application classes containing business logic. In a standard WAR, it's common practice to package *everything* an application requires in directories like `/WEB-INF/classes` and `/WEB-INF/lib/` due to the sandbox class-loader nature of WARs. In an OSGi environment, though, application classes containing business logic are spread out across numerous bundles, not to mention application logic can also be available as OSGi services. So how does a bundle (WAR) access this application logic contained in other bundles?

Accessing classes in other bundles is very straightforward; it's simply a matter of using either `Import-Package` or `Require-Bundle` headers in a bundle's (WAR's) `MANIFEST.MF` file. However, accessing OSGi services also requires taking into account the delegation process of a bundle (WAR) to a web container.

Spring-DM always attempts to create an OSGi context—the `OsgiBundleXmlApplicationContext` kind—on every bundle it inspects that contains Spring artifacts, something that is used to access and register services (Chapter 4 discuss this topic). In a bundle (WAR), though, given that thread management is delegated to the web container, this context is not visible unless explicitly specified.

Spring-DM solves this issue through a special context class named `OsgiBundleXmlWebApplicationContext`—note the `Web` keyword in between `Xml` and `Application`—that hooks into a bundle's OSGi context (the `OsgiBundleXmlApplicationContext` kind) and which is configured in a web application's `web.xml` file. You've already used this approach earlier in the book, but Listing 8-3 illustrates the approach once more.

Listing 8-3. OSGiBundleXMLWebApplicationContext *Used in a* web.xml *File*

```
<context-param>
   <param-name>contextClass</param-name>
      <param-value>
org.springframework.osgi.web.context.support.OsgiBundleXmlWebApplicationContext
      </param-value>
</context-param>

<listener>
    <listener-class>
       org.springframework.web.context.ContextLoaderListener
    </listener-class>
</listener>
```

Note the use of the contextClass parameter with a value of OsgiBundleXmlWebApplicationContext, as well as Spring's context configuration bootstrap listener org.springframework.web.context.ContextLoaderListener.

The <listener> declaration is typical of web.xml files used to configure Spring web applications. However, the contextClass value is Spring-DM (OSGi) specific. By using this special contextClass class, a bundle (WAR) can access OSGi services from other bundles, even though its thread management is delegated to the web container.

Once this context class is defined in a bundle's (WAR's) web.xml file, it would then be assigned to whatever web artifact requires use of OSGi services. For example, assuming you had a servlet in this same application, you would use a statement like the one in Listing 8-4 to make the servlet OSGi aware.

Listing 8-4. *OSGi-Aware Servlet Using* OSGiBundleXMLWebApplicationContext *in a* web.xml *File*

```
<servlet>

    <description>
         Pro Spring-OSGi MVC Dispatch Servlet
     </description>

     <display-name>DispatcherServlet</display-name>
      <servlet-name>helloworld</servlet-name>
           <servlet-class>
              org.springframework.web.servlet.DispatcherServlet
           </servlet-class>
            <load-on-startup>1</load-on-startup>
            <init-param>
             <param-name>contextClass</param-name>
             <param-value>org.springframework.osgi.web.context.support.➥
OsgiBundleXmlWebApplicationContext</param-value>
            </init-param>
        </servlet>
```

Note the servlet is assigned an <init-param> value pointing to the specially provided Spring-DM OsgiBundleXmlWebApplicationContext class. Once a servlet is initialized in this form, access to OSGi's context—the OsgiBundleXmlApplicationContext kind—is performed using the servlet's own configuration file.

For example, given this last servlet is named helloworld, it's left to the servlet's configuration file, which by default would named helloworld-servlet.xml, to access OSGi's context. Listing 8-5 illustrates this servlet's configuration file.

Listing 8-5. *Servlet Configuration File Accessing OSGi Resources via Spring-DM*

```
<?xml version="1.0" encoding="UTF-8"?>

<beans xmlns="http://www.springframework.org/schema/beans"
       xmlns:xsi="http://www.w3.org/2001/XMLSchema-instance"
       xmlns:osgi="http://www.springframework.org/schema/osgi"
       xmlns:context="http://www.springframework.org/schema/context"
       xsi:schemaLocation="http://www.springframework.org/schema/beans

                                http://www.springframework.org/schema/beans/➥
spring-beans.xsd
                              http://www.springframework.org/schema/context

                                http://www.springframework.org/schema/context/➥
spring-context-2.5.xsd
                                http://www.springframework.org/schema/osgi

                                http://www.springframework.org/schema/osgi/Â
spring-osgi.xsd">

    <osgi:reference id="helloWorldService"Â
 interface="com.apress.springosgi.ch3.service.HelloWorldService"/>

   <bean id="helloWorldController"
             class="com.apress.springosgi.ch3.web.HelloWorldController">
       <property name="helloWorldService" ref="helloWorldService"/>
   </bean>
</beans>
```

Note the use of Spring-DM's osgi namespace, as well as the use of Spring-DM's <reference> element, which imports an OSGi service that is later injected into the servlet. *Were it not for the* OsgiBundleXmlWebApplicationContext *context class, it would not be possible for a bundle (WAR) to access any OSGi services.*

One more configuration option available for web bundles (WARs) is the Spring-DM header Web-ContextPath. This header is used to indicate the web context—URL subdirectory—under which a bundle (WAR) should be deployed. Listing 8-6 illustrates the use of this header.

Listing 8-6. `Web-ContextPath` *for a Web Bundle (WAR)*

```
Web-ContextPath: /chapter8app/
```

By placing this statement in a bundle (WAR), you are telling the underlying OSGi'fied web container to deploy this bundle under the web container's `/chapter8app/` subdirectory (e.g., `http://localhost:8080/chapter8app/`).

If this value is not specified in a bundle (WAR), the same conventions as those for non-OSGi'fied web containers are applied: the web context is defined by the bundle's (WAR's) name (e.g., a bundle [WAR] named `helloworld.war` would be deployed under the URL `http://localhost:8080/helloworld/`).

Now that you are aware of the various concepts that need to be taken into account in order to deploy OSGi web bundles (WARs), I will move on to more specific topics related to web applications and how they need to be tackled in the context of Spring and OSGi.

Using Different Web Containers

The market offers various web containers that can be used to deploy web applications. In Chapter 1 you leveraged the Jetty web server (a.k.a. web container), and in the remainder of the book you've used the Apache Tomcat web container. Both of these web containers are fully supported by Spring-DM, which is to say Spring-DM can delegate the installation of bundles (WARs) to either of these web containers. By default, however, Spring-DM is configured to delegate bundles (WARs) to an instance of Apache Tomcat.

So how do you change Spring-DM to delegate to another web container? To better answer this question, I will describe the entire process related to Spring-DM using a web container.

Spring-DM's `spring-osgi-web-extender.jar` bundle starts the entire process. When this bundle is *activated*, it will attempt to locate an OSGi'fied Apache Tomcat instance. If it cannot find one, you will receive an error:

```
Exception in thread "WebExtender-Init"`java.lang.NoClassDefFoundError:
org/apache/CatalinaLoader
```

If an Apache Tomcat instance is found and all its class dependencies are resolved, Spring-DM will then attempt to locate an *OSGi service* registered as `org.apache.catalina.Service`. If it cannot find such a service, you will receive an error message:

```
org.springframework.osgi.OsgiException: Cannot create Tomcat deployer
```

If the previous steps succeed, your OSGi'fied web container along with Spring-DM will be ready to accept web bundles (WARs) and delegate them to the underlying web container. As you will note, besides having an OSGi'fied web container on hand, there are two steps necessary to use a different web container with Spring-DM:

1. Override Spring-DM's default extender value to use another web container.

2. Have a service registration bundle to bootstrap the OSGi'fied web container.

Overriding the Default Extender Value

In order to override Spring-DM's default web container, it's necessary to use OSGi fragments. As outlined in Chapter 4's "OSGi Fragments with Spring-DM" section, Spring-DM extenders expose a series of values that can be overridden using fragments (see Table 4-6 in Chapter 4).

In the particular case of Spring-DM's web extender, it uses the web container specified as the value of the `warDeployer` bean. The current values supported by this bean are

- `TomcatWarDeployer`

- `JettyWarDeployer`

As their names imply, these support the Apache Tomcat and Jetty web containers, respectively.

Once a fragment overriding the `warDeployer` bean is installed, it will attach itself to Spring-DM's web extender bundle, so once *activation* occurs, an attempt to locate the explicitly configured OSGi'fied web container is performed.

Bootstrapping the Web Container

In addition to overriding Spring-DM's default web container using a fragment, it's also necessary to bootstrap the OSGi'fied web container and register its core functionality as a service. If you think about the way a non-OSGi'fied web container operates, this step becomes more obvious.

An OSGi'fied web container consists of various pieces, or bundles, making it more modular than its non-OSGi'fied counterpart. However, these modules still need to work in sync to provide the desired functionality. On what port will the web container run? How do you configure something like a SSL certificate? What if you want to use subdomains? And more importantly, how are applications (WARs) linked to a web container? All these questions are resolved at the time a web container is bootstrapped.

Both Apache Tomcat and the Jetty web container rely on configuration files—`server.xml` and `jetty.xml`—to deal with the issues raised by these questions. So we need to use a special bundle containing a web container's configuration files, one that upon deployment will *mimic* the bootstrapping process and later register the web container as a service for the benefit of web bundles (WARs).

Much like the Spring-DM `warDeployer` bean, the creators of Spring-DM offer a prebuilt starter bundle to achieve this bootstrap process for both Apache Tomcat and the Jetty web container. In the next section, I will provide a hands-on example for all the steps just outlined, migrating Chapter 7's application to use the Jetty web container instead of Apache Tomcat.

WHAT ABOUT ORACLE/BEA'S, SUN'S, AND IBM'S WEB CONTAINERS? HOW ARE THOSE USED WITH SPRING-DM?

Spring-DM's support for Apache Tomcat and Jetty web container raises an interesting question. Is it possible to use another web container with Spring-DM? The short answer is yes, but this inevitably leads to a question about the web container itself and two questions related to the process:

- Is the web container available as a set of OSGi'fied bundles?
- Spring-DM's `warDeployer` bean allows the `TomcatWarDeployer` and `JettyWarDeployer` values. How do you specify another web container?
- Are there starter OSGi bundles for other web containers like the ones provided for Apache Tomcat and Jetty web container?

Is the Web Container Available As a Set of OSGi'fied Bundles?

This is critical. If a web container's bundles are not OSGi'fied, you would need to modify each of the web container's bundles (JARs). This would not only be a painstaking task, but also likely violate the licenses that govern most Java binaries—not to mention this should be the web container vendor's job, not yours.

Fortunately, there has been a marked shift by *mostly every vendor* in the Java space to distribute a product's JARs with OSGi information. This in itself is part of a bigger trend by Java vendors, allowing customers to pick and choose separate product components (bundles) and run whichever bundles they require. For example, a product labeled as an SOA suite may in itself be composed of a Java web container's JARs (bundles, EJB implementation, BPEL JAR), among many other JARs (bundles), letting customers pick and choose as they see fit.

How Do You Specify Another Web Container?

This is probably the most elaborate step to using another web container with Spring-DM, since the `warDeployer` bean values are backed by Spring-DM-provided classes. Nevertheless, it should be straightforward to implement your own class and assign it to the `warDeployer` bean. You can see the documentation and source of these last classes at the following links:

- **Documentation (Tomcat)**: `http://static.springframework.org/osgi/docs/1.2.0-m1/api/org/springframework/osgi/web/deployer/tomcat/TomcatWarDeployer.html`
- **Source (Tomcat)**: `http://fisheye3.atlassian.com/qsearch/springframework/spring-osgi/trunk?q=TomcatWarDeployer`
- **Documentation (Jetty)**: `http://static.springframework.org/osgi/docs/1.2.0-m1/api/org/springframework/osgi/web/deployer/jetty/JettyWarDeployer.html`
- **Source (Jetty)**: `http://fisheye3.atlassian.com/qsearch/springframework/spring-osgi/trunk?q=JettyWarDeployer`

Are There Starter OSGi Bundles for Other Web Containers?

Currently, Spring-DM only provides starter bundles for Apache Tomcat and the Jetty web container. However, since a starter bundle contains a web container's default configuration file, *mimics* the bootstrapping of the web container, and registers it as a service, the steps are clear-cut. The bootstrapping process for a particular web container can be learned from its out-of-the-box startup script, since it contains the necessary configuration files, classes, and parameters to start up the web container. This process needs to be replicated in a Java class that then registers the web container as a service.

To get a better idea of the process, you can see the source code for both the Apache Tomcat and Jetty web container bundles in the directory of the Spring-DM distribution, with the names `jetty.start.osgi-1.0.0-sources.jar` and `catalina.start.osgi-1.0.0-sources.jar`.

Using the Jetty Web Container

The first step in using the Jetty web container for Spring-DM applications consists of creating a fragment that targets Spring-DM's web extender bundle and modifies the default value for the `warDeployer` bean. In Chapter 4 you learned to create precisely this fragment. Listings 4-30 and 4-31 illustrated the two files that make up the fragment, whereas Listing 4-32 illustrated the layout for the fragment bundle. You can refer to these listings for further explanation on the particular layout and syntax this fragment needs to use.

To avoid the trouble of building this fragment using an Apache Ant script or some other tool, you can use the Spring-DM fragment `jetty.web.extender.fragment.osgi-1.0.jar`, included in Spring-DM's distribution under the `lib` directory. This fragment overrides Spring-DM's default web container setting and tells Spring-DM to use Jetty—it of course contains the exact layout as in Listing 4-32 and contents from Listings 4-30 and 4-31.

Next, you will need to install an OSGi'fied version of the Jetty web container. Since Jetty was one of the web containers to adopt OSGi, its core bundles already come OSGi'fied in its standard download—unlike Apache Tomcat. You can download the Jetty web container from the following link: `http://dist.codehaus.org/jetty/`.

However, even though Jetty's core bundles (JARs) are OSGi'fied, some of the dependencies included in its download are not. Therefore, you will need to download the corresponding OSGi'fied versions from the SpringSource Enterprise Bundle Repository, some of which are already used by Apache Tomcat. The bundles required to run the Jetty web container are the following:

- **Core bundles:** `jetty-util-x.jar`, `jetty-x.jar`, `jetty-naming-x.jar`, `jetty-plus-x.jar`, `jetty-annotations.jar`, and `jetty-management-x.jar` (all included in Jetty's download `lib` directory)
- **Core dependency bundles:** `java.annotation-x.jar` and `javax.mail-x.jar` (available at the SpringSource Enterprise Bundle Repository)
- **JSP and servlet bundles:** `javax.servlet-2.5.0.jar`, `javax.el-1.0.0.jar`, `javax.servlet.jsp-2.1.0.jar`, `org.apache.commons.el-1.0.0.jar`, `jasper.osgi-5.15.25`, `org.apache.taglibs.standard-1.1.2.jar`, and `javax.servlet.jsp.jstl-1.1.2.jar` (already used by Apache Tomcat, and downloaded from the SpringSource Enterprise Bundle Repository)

■ **Note** Jetty uses the same JSP compiler, Jasper, as Tomcat.

In addition to the OSGi'fied Jetty web container, recall that you will also need a starter OSGi bundle to bootstrap the container and register it as a service. This bundle, named `jetty.start.osgi-1.0.0.jar`, can be found in the `lib` directory of the Spring-DM distribution. Once you have all these bundles, copy all of them to a subdirectory named `jetty` in the same deployment directory used to run the application created in Chapter 7. Next, you will need to modify the Eclipse Equinox configuration file `config.ini` inside the configuration directory, as reflected in Listing 8-7.

Listing 8-7. *Eclipse Equinox* `config.ini` *Using Jetty Web Server*

```
org.osgi.framework.system.package=javax.naming,javax.naming.directory,javax.naming
.spi,javax.management,javax.management.loading,javax.management.modelmbean,javax.man
agement.openmbean,javax.management.remote,javax.net,javax.rmi,javax.rmi.CORBA,org.om
g.CORBA,org.omg.CORBA.portable,org.omg.CORBA_2_3.portable,javax.net.ssl,javax.crypto
,javax.crypto.interfaces,javax.crypto.spec,javax.security.auth,javax.security.sasl,j
avax.security.auth.spi,javax.security.auth.callback,javax.security.auth.login,javax.
security.cert,javax.xml.parsers,javax.xml.xpath,javax.xml.transform.sax,javax.xml.tr
ansform.dom,javax.xml.namespace,javax.xml.transform,javax.xml.transform.stream,javax
.xml.validation,org.xml.sax,org.xml.sax.helpers,org.xml.sax.ext,com.sun.org.apache.x
alan.internal,com.sun.org.apache.xalan.internal.res,com.sun.org.apache.xml.internal.
utils,com.sun.org.apache.xpath.internal,com.sun.org.apache.xpath.internal.jaxp,com.s
```

```
un.org.apache.xpath.internal.objects,com.sun.org.apache.xml.internal,org.w3c.dom,org
.w3c.dom.traversal,org.w3c.dom.ls,javax.sql,javax.transaction,sun.misc
osgi.bundles=logging/com.springsource.ch.qos.logback.core-0.9.9.jar@start, \
logging/com.springsource.ch.qos.logback.classic-0.9.9.jar, \
logging/com.springsource.slf4j.api-1.5.0.jar@start, \
logging/com.springsource.slf4j.org.apache.commons.logging-1.5.0.jar@start, \
logging/com.springsource.slf4j.org.apache.log4j-1.5.0.jar@start, \
db/com.springsource.javax.persistence-1.0.0.jar@start, \
db/com.springsource.org.apache.commons.dbcp-1.2.2.osgi.jar@start, \
db/com.springsource.javax.transaction-1.1.0.jar@start, \
db/com.springsource.org.apache.commons.pool-1.3.0.jar@start, \
db/com.springsource.com.mysql.jdbc-5.1.6.jar@start, \
jetty/com.springsource.javax.servlet-2.5.0.jar@start, \
jetty/com.springsource.javax.el-1.0.0.jar@start, \
jetty/com.springsource.javax.servlet.jsp-2.1.0.jar@start, \
jetty/com.springsource.org.apache.commons.el-1.0.0.jar@start, \
jetty/jasper.osgi-5.5.23-20080305.122359-4.jar, \
jetty/com.springsource.org.apache.taglibs.standard-1.1.2.jar, \
jetty/com.springsource.javax.servlet.jsp.jstl-1.1.2.jar, \
jetty/jetty-util-6.1.11.jar@start, \
jetty/jetty-6.1.11.jar@start, \
jetty/com.springsource.javax.mail-1.4.1.jar@start, \
jetty/jetty-naming-6.1.11.jar@start, \
jetty/jetty-plus-6.1.11.jar@start, \
jetty/com.springsource.javax.annotation-1.0.0.jar@start, \
jetty/jetty-annotations-6.1.11.jar@start, \
jetty/jetty-management-6.1.11.jar@start, \
jetty/jetty.start.osgi-1.0.0.jar@start, \
jetty/jetty.web.extender.fragment.osgi-1.0.0.jar, \
springcore/com.springsource.edu.emory.mathcs.backport-3.0.0.jar@start, \
springcore/com.springsource.org.apache.commons.collections-3.2.0.jar@start, \
springcore/com.springsource.net.sf.cglib-2.1.3.jar@start, \
springcore/com.springsource.org.aopalliance-1.0.0.jar@start, \
springcore/org.springframework.core-2.5.4.A.jar@start, \
springcore/org.springframework.beans-2.5.4.A.jar@start, \
< Followed by more Spring bundle >
```

Note the various bundle statements and those that are to be installed from the `jetty` subdirectory. The installation order for each bundle is relevant—just like for Apache Tomcat—but notice the two bundles in bold. The `jetty.start.osgi-1.0.0.jar` bundle is the one used to bootstrap the Jetty web container, whereas the `jetty.web.extender.fragment.osgi-1.0.0.jar` bundle is the fragment used to override Spring-DM's default web container, Apache Tomcat.

It's critical that this last fragment be installed prior to Spring-DM's web extender. In this manner, once Spring-DM's web extender is installed, the fragment will be attached immediately, and upon activation the extender will in turn delegate to a Jetty web container instance.

Further note the line at the top of the file that starts with `org.osgi.framework.system.packages`. This is a special requirement for running the Jetty web container, which further illustrates OSGi's more stringent class-loading approach.

The Jetty web container relies on some classes that, even though they are included in Java SE, are optional to the architecture set forth by the Eclipse Equinox OSGi implementation. These classes/packages are included in the `rt.jar` JAR inside Java SE's `jre/lib` directory. In Eclipse Equinox it's necessary to explicitly import such classes/packages using this configuration parameter.

With this new configuration file in place, starting an Eclipse Equinox instance with the application designed in the previous chapter would deliver pages served by the Jetty web container. At first sight it won't be evident, but if you attempt to access a nonexistent URL, you will see a "404 Page Not Found" error with the legend "*Powered by Jetty://*."

Next, I will describe SSL/TLS, which is one of the most common security features used by web applications in general, as it relates to OSGi.

Using SSL/TLS with OSGi

Transport Layer Security and its predecessor, Secure Sockets Layer (SSL),[1] set forth the mechanisms to access applications in a secure fashion over the Web. Though SSL is the predecessor to TLS, you will more often hear the term SSL used interchangeably with TLS to describe the process of securing web application. Given this fact, and considering this is not a security book exploring the subtleties between SSL and TLS, I will also just use the term SSL from this point forward.

For end users, SSL translates into an `https://` site—note the `s` for security—that allows them to access the application in a secure fashion. For application developers, this entails installing a security certificate, as well as configuring a web container to support SSL.

Given the different installation processes for OSGi'fied and non-OSGi'fied containers, using SSL with an OSGi'fied web container also requires taking different steps from those used for non-OSGi'fied containers. Next, I will describe these steps, which use Apache Tomcat, as they relate to the application you created in Chapter 7.

Setting Up SSL in Apache Tomcat

The first thing you need to do is create a web container configuration file, just like you would for a non-OSGi'fied web container, to support SSL. In the case of Apache Tomcat, this process consists of adding a new `<Connector>` element to enable SSL to the `server.xml` configuration file. Listing 8-8 illustrates this.

1. Wikipedia, "Transport Layer Security," `http://en.wikipedia.org/wiki/Transport_Layer_Security`

Listing 8-8. *Apache Tomcat* `server.xml` *Using SSL*

```
<Server port="8005" shutdown="SHUTDOWN">
  <Service name="Catalina">

    <Connector port="8080"/>

    <Connector port="8443" minProcessors="5" maxProcessors="75"
         enableLookups="true" disableUploadTimeout="true"
         acceptCount="100" debug="0" scheme="https" secure="true"
         clientAuth="false" sslProtocol="TLS"/>

    <Engine name="Catalina" defaultHost="localhost">
      <Host name="localhost" unpackWARs="false" autoDeploy="false"
       liveDeploy="false" deployOnStartup="false"
       xmlValidation="false" xmlNamespaceAware="false"/>
    </Engine>

  </Service>
</Server>
```

Note this last listing has two `<Connector>` elements, one with the `port` attribute value of `8080`, which corresponds to the nonsecure address on which the web container will run, and another with the `port` attribute value of `8443`, which corresponds to the secure address on which the web container will run. The remainder of the listing represents the most basic configuration file for an Apache Tomcat web container.

Creating a JKS Keystore

The next thing you need to do is create a JKS keystore. A *keystore* is a Java SE security concept that is central to operating SSL, since the keystore is where Apache Tomcat will look up all the required credentials to enable SSL.

To expedite the setup process, I will illustrate how to use the `keytool` utility—part of Java SE—to create a keystore value directly (known as a dummy SSL certificate). Normally, in order to use SSL on a production site, you need to create a Certificate Signing Request (CSR) containing your company's information and site domain, send this information to a signing authority—a commercial service—for authentication, and upon approval convert it into a JKS keystore.

Listing 8-9 illustrates the simplest steps you need to take to create a JKS keystore using the `keytool` utility.

■ **Note** The `keytool` utility is available in the `bin` directory of every Java SE JDK.

Listing 8-9. *JKS Keystore-Generating Sequence Using the* `keytool` *Utility*

```
[web@localhost ~]$ keytool -genkey -alias tomcat -keyalg RSA
Enter keystore password:  changeit
What is your first and last name?

  [Unknown]:  Daniel Rubio
What is the name of your organizational unit?
  [Unknown]:  Editorial
What is the name of your organization?
  [Unknown]:  Apress
What is the name of your City or Locality?
  [Unknown]:  Berkeley
What is the name of your State or Province?
  [Unknown]:  CA
What is the two-letter country code for this unit?
  [Unknown]:  US
Is CN=Daniel Rubio, OU=Unknown, O=Apress, L=Berkley, ST=CA, C=US correct?
  [no]:  yes
Enter key password for <tomcat>
        (RETURN if same as keystore password):  changeit
[web@localhost ~]$
```

This listing will generate a JKS keystore for Apache Tomcat—note the flag `alias tomcat` upon invocation. The series of questions represent information that would otherwise be used to generate a CSR to obtain a certificate. Also note the use of the password value `changeit`, which is the default password used by Apache Tomcat to access a JKS keystore.

This process will generate a file named `.keystore`—in binary format—under the home directory of the user performing the operation.

■ **Note** Apache Tomcat will always look for a `.keystore` file in the home directory of the owner running the web container, as well as attempt to access it using the `changeit` password. If you use a different location and password, you need to configure SSL (Listing 8-8's `<Connector>` element) with the additional attributes `keystoreFile` and `keystorePass` to specify an alternative location for a `.keystore` file and password, respectively.

GENERATING A JKS KEYSTORE WITH A REAL CERTIFICATE

If you have a signed certificate on hand, a `.keystore` file can be generated using `openssl`, like so:

```
openssl pkcs12 -export -in mycert.crt -inkey mykey.key
   -out mycert.p12 -name tomcat -CAfile myCA.crt  -caname root -chain
```

Note the `-name tomcat` target.

Fulfilling Apache Tomcat's SSL Dependencies

Once you have the `.keystore` file in place, you just need to fulfill a dependency for using SSL with Apache Tomcat. The `tomcat-util.jar` file includes a series of classes used by Apache Tomcat SSL, but we haven't had a need for this bundle (JAR) yet. Unfortunately, this bundle is not available from the SpringSource Enterprise Bundle Repository where you downloaded other Apache Tomcat files.

In order to fulfill this dependency, you will need to download a non-OSGi'fied Apache Tomcat distribution from `http://archive.apache.org/dist/tomcat/tomcat-5/` and OSGi'fy this JAR yourself using BND.

The `tomcat-util.jar` file is located under the `server/lib` directory of the Apache Tomcat download. Listing 8-10 illustrates the instruction to convert this file to an OSGi'fied JAR using the BND utility. Chapter 7 contains a more detailed look at BND.

Listing 8-10. *OSGi'fying* `tomcat-util.jar` *Using BND*

```
java -jar bnd-0.0.249.jar wrap -output tomcat-util-osgi.jar tomcat-util.jar
```

This last statement invokes BND on the `tomcat-util.jar` JAR and outputs a bundle named `tomcat-util-osgi.jar` with the necessary `MANIFEST.MF` file needed to operate under an OSGi environment.

You now have all the parts necessary to use SSL with Apache Tomcat, but you still need to take one additional step to enable SSL on an OSGi'fied version of the web container. The Apache Tomcat configuration using SSL (Listing 8-8) needs to be packaged in a bundle, though not just any bundle. It needs to be a fragment targeting Apache Tomcat's starter bundle.

Creating the SSL Configuration Fragment

Recall that OSGi'fied web containers in Spring-DM are started by special bundles containing default configurations that later register the web containers as services. By using a fragment, a new SSL-enabled configuration can be attached to a starter bundle that effectively overrides the default configuration.

Listing 8-11 illustrates the layout for this fragment bundle, and Listing 8-12 shows the accompanying `MANIFEST.MF` file for the fragment bundle.

Listing 8-11. *Fragment Structure Used to Install SSL*

```
+META-INF-+
                  |
                  +-MANIFEST.MF
+conf-+
           |
           +-server.xml
```

Listing 8-12. `MANIFEST.MF` *for Fragment Used to Install SSL*

```
Bundle-Version: 1.0
Bundle-SymbolicName: com.apress.springosgi.ch8.ssl
Fragment-Host: org.springframework.osgi.catalina.start.osgi
Bundle-Name: HelloWorld Spring-OSGi SSL Certificate Configuration
Bundle-Vendor: Pro Spring-OSGi
Bundle-ManifestVersion: 2
```

The layout consists of two directories:

- The standard `META-INF` directory containing a bundle's `MANIFEST.MF` file.
- The `conf` directory containing the new `server.xml` configuration file for Apache Tomcat (Listing 8-8). Note the `conf` directory is the same directory as the one used by a non-OSGi'fied Apache Tomcat web container to locate its configuration file.

The `MANIFEST.MF` file used by the fragment targets a bundle with symbolic name value of `org.springframework.osgi.catalina.start.osgi`. This last bundle is precisely the starter bundle provided by Spring-DM that bootstraps an OSGi'fied version of Apache Tomcat. Therefore, once the Spring-DM server attaches this fragment to this host bundle, it will use the new configuration file employing SSL (Listing 8-8) to bootstrap the OSGi'fied web container. However, it will now also start an `https://` version of the same server.

Installing the Fragment

Finally, you need to take care of the installation for the SSL fragment. Since this fragment will override the default configuration files in the startup bundle, it needs to be installed prior to this bundle, so that upon activation the new configuration has already been attached. Listing 8-13 illustrates the relevant section for the Eclipse Equinox `config.ini` file as it pertains to Chapter 7's sample application, but now using SSL.

Listing 8-13. *Eclipse Equinox* `config.ini` *Using SSL*

```
tomcat/com.springsource.javax.servlet.jsp.jstl-1.1.2.jar@start, \
tomcat/catalina.osgi-5.5.23-SNAPSHOT.jar@start, \
tomcat/tomcat-util-osgi.jar@start, \
tomcat/tomcat-ssl-osgi.jar, \
tomcat/catalina.start.osgi-1.0-20080425.161832-4.jar@start, \
springcore/com.springsource.edu.emory.mathcs.backport-3.0.0.jar@start, \
springcore/com.springsource.org.apache.commons.collections-3.2.0.jar@start, \
< Followed by more Spring bundles >
```

In this last listing, the `tomcat-util-osgi.jar` file represents the OSGi'fied version of `tomcat-util.jar`—the output from Listing 8-10 and a dependency for using SSL—whereas `tomcat-ssl-osgi.jar` is the fragment represented in Listing 8-11. Note that both are installed prior to the starter bundle `catalina.start.osgi-1.0.0.jar`, and therefore the SSL `server.xml` configuration file is used at the time the web container is bootstrapped.

If you run this new configuration with the provided application, you would need to visit the URL `https://localhost:8443/` in order to access the secure version of the application. Upon visiting this address, be advised you will be presented with ominous warnings from all browsers, indicating you are about to enter an insecure site even though you are using `https://`. Ignore such warnings and proceed.

These last warnings are because the backing JKS keystore was created via a dummy SSL certificate using `keytool`. To avoid these warnings, the JKS keystore would have to be created using a signed certificate that coincided with the domain being accessed.

In addition, you may see a few errors or warnings not related to OSGi. If you see the error message "Keystore was tampered with, or password was incorrect," this indicates Apache Tomcat was not able to access the keystore using the default or provided password value and location. You will need to erase and re-create the JKS keystore file appropriately in order for Apache Tomcat to enable SSL access.

Another non-OSGi related warning you may observe is a `ClassNotFoundException` for the classes `PureTLSImplementation` and `JSSE15Factory`. These are known warnings even for non-OSGi versions of Apache Tomcat[2] and can be ignored since they have no effect on accessing an application using SSL.

This concludes looking at the steps needed to enable SSL on an OSGi'fied version of Apache Tomcat. Next, I will discuss another topic that has enjoyed recent success alongside Java web applications: the presentation format Flash generated through Flex.

Using Flex with OSGi

Web interfaces are generally designed around a mix of languages that include HTML, JavaScript, and Cascading Style Sheets (CSS), just to name a few. These languages are what most JSP files and servlets generate once they are processed on the server side. Other approaches like Flash were created to deal with some of the limitations imposed by these languages and deliver what are now known as Rich Internet Applications (RIAs).The appeal for using technologies like Flash stems from both its unique feature set and outright deficiencies in the staple languages—HTML, JavaScript, and CSS—used by most web applications. Some of these areas include the following:

---

2. `http://mail-archives.apache.org/mod_mbox/tomcat-users/200512.mbox/%3C000a01c5f753$cb6cab50$1a04a8c0@nsrp1.syrres.com%3E`

- **Fragmented support for HTML, JavaScript, and CSS across browsers**: This can cause problems ranging from layout discrepancies to browser crashes. Creating a single web interface that will *behave equally* across different browser vendors and versions is nearly impossible. Flash uses its own runtime across all browsers guaranteeing streamlined behavior.

- **Better support for manipulating large amounts of data in a browser**: Browsers and with it languages like HTML and JavaScript were never intended to manipulate or process data in large amounts, and doing so often leads to unresponsive applications. Flash uses its own runtime, which is more robust for these purposes.

- **Greater feature set of display elements**: Flash was designed to provide more visual effects than a combination like HTML and CSS. Its feature set has long been the basis for animations and game-like behaviors for applications on the Web.

- **Real-time communication between browser and server**: The stateless nature of web applications has never made time-sensitive applications easy to design. And though techniques like AJAX and Comet have given a lift to the classic trio of HTML, JavaScript, and CSS, Flash's runtime has long been designed to solve this type of problem.

Until recently though, Flash, which is perhaps synonymous with the RIA acronym, has lacked a programmatic approach, much like JSP's programmatic approach to creating HTML, JavaScript, and CSS interfaces. This has changed, however, with the appearance of Flex.

The following list summarizes some key points about Flex:[3]

- Flex applications are Flash applications:
  - Flex is a programmer-centric way to create Flash-based RIAs.
  - Flex applications are rendered using Flash Player 10.
  - Like all Flash RIAs, Flex SWF files are processed by the client, rather than the server.

3. http://www.adobe.com/products/flex/overview/

- The Flex framework contains the predefined class libraries and application services necessary to create Flex applications:
  - The framework is available in a free SDK and the Eclipse-based IDE named Flex Builder.
  - The framework includes a compiler that is available as a stand-alone tool or as part of Flex Builder.
  - The class libraries and application services provide developers with standard components and tools for quick application development. Standard UI components can be extended and customized.
- Flex applications are written using MXML and/or ActionScript:
  - MXML is an XML-based markup language that is primarily used to lay out application display elements.
  - ActionScript is an ECMAScript-compliant object-oriented programming language that is primarily used for application logic.
  - MXML and ActionScript code are compiled into binary SWF files.

From this brief summary, you will probably realize Flex is a pretty extensive topic, and there are indeed entire books written on the subject alone. So be advised that even though the following example is a very basic Flex-based interface designed to integrate with Spring and OSGi, you may need to consult other resources to get a stronger grasp for its concepts.

Laying Out a Flex User Interface

Flex applications start off as MXML files containing markup language. These MXML files are always transformed (compiled) into SWF files—Flash files—that represent the final delivery format, which is executed on end users' browsers. The process for compiling an MXML file into a SWF file can be done either manually, using a compiler provided by the Flex SDK, or automatically once the first request is made to a particular MXML file—a process that is strikingly similar to JSP files, which are compiled on the first request. No matter the approach used, SWF (Flash) files will always be delivered to end users' browsers and never MXML (Flex) files.

Figure 8-1 shows a rendered version of a Flash interface (generated by Flex) used by this chapter's application—the same application as in Chapters 5 and 7.

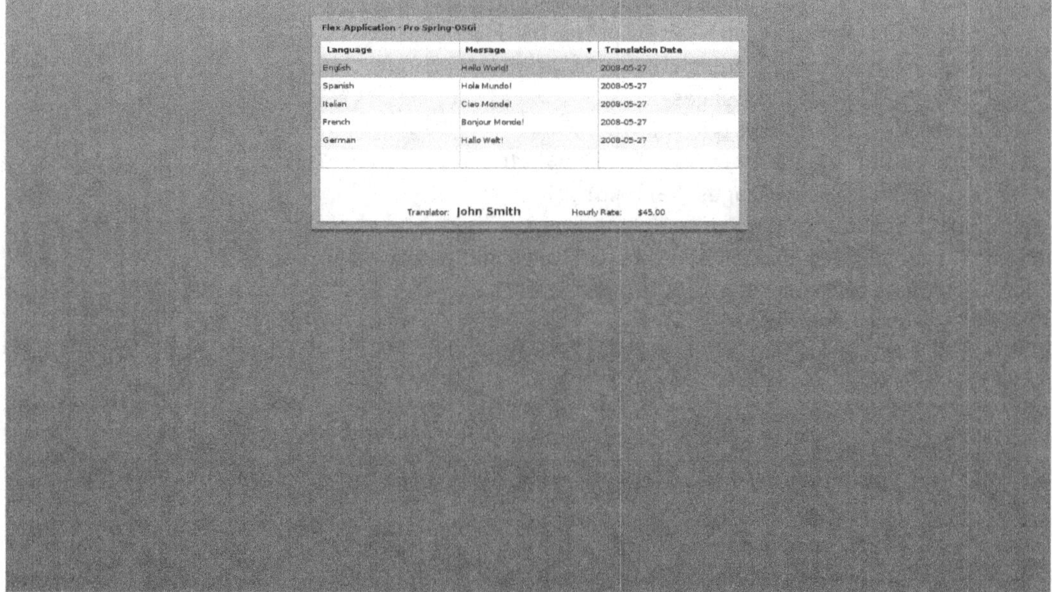

Figure 8-1. *Rendered Flash interface*

Notice how the layout looks sharper than a standard HTML and CSS interface. Additionally, notice how the column headers contain small arrows; if a user clicks any of these arrows, the data is sorted according to the column values. In addition, each time a user selects a line, it's automatically demarcated with another color.

This last sorting feature illustrates a powerful mechanism that is embedded in Flash's runtime engine. Incorporating this sorting behavior in an HTML and JavaScript interface would not only require a lot more work, but also be more error prone given the discrepancies between browser versions. This also applies to the coloring scheme, which can be troublesome to design using something like HTML and CSS.

But let's not digress on Flash's strong points, rather let's analyze how this interface is made up using MXML markup. Listing 8-14 illustrates the markup that makes up Figure 8-1.

Listing 8-14. *Flex* `statichome.mxml` *Using XML Data Sources*

```
<?xml version="1.0" encoding="utf-8"?>

<mx:Application xmlns:mx="http://www.adobe.com/2006/mxml"
  layout="vertical" horizontalAlign="center">

    <mx:CurrencyFormatter id="cFormat" precision="2" currencySymbol="$"➥
 useThousandsSeparator="true"/>
  <mx:Model id="messages" source="/data/messages.xml"/>
  <mx:XML id="translators" source="/data/translators.xml"/>
```

```
  <mx:Panel width="530" layout="absolute"
    title="Flex Application - Pro Spring-OSGi">
    <mx:Label horizontalCenter="0" y="1"
      text="HelloWorld Messages"
      fontSize="16" fontWeight="bold"/>
    <mx:DataGrid id="hwSpringFlex" width="510"
      dataProvider="{messages.helloworld}">
      <mx:columns>
        <mx:DataGridColumn headerText="Language" width="75">
          <mx:itemRenderer>
            <mx:Component>
                <mx:Label text="{data.language}"/>
            </mx:Component>
          </mx:itemRenderer>
        </mx:DataGridColumn>
        <mx:DataGridColumn headerText="Message" width="75">
          <mx:itemRenderer>
            <mx:Component>
                <mx:Label text="{data.message}"/>
            </mx:Component>
          </mx:itemRenderer>
        </mx:DataGridColumn>
        <mx:DataGridColumn headerText="Translation Date" width="75">
          <mx:itemRenderer>
            <mx:Component>
                <mx:Label text="{data.translationDate}"/>
            </mx:Component>
          </mx:itemRenderer>
        </mx:DataGridColumn>
      </mx:columns>
    </mx:DataGrid>
    <mx:Label x="105" y="210" text="Translator:"/>
    <mx:Label x="165" y="207"
      fontWeight="bold" fontSize="13" id="lblTranslator"
      text="{translators.translator.(@id ==
        hwSpringFlex.selectedItem.translatorID).name}"/>
    <mx:Label x="305" y="210" text="Hourly Rate:"/>
  <mx:Label x="385" y="210" id="lblHourlyRate"
      text="{cFormat.format(translators.translator.(@id ==
        hwSpringFlex.selectedItem.translatorID).hourlyRate)}"/>
  </mx:Panel>
</mx:Application>
```

The first thing to note is how this MXML file obtains its initial data. Notice how the elements <mx:Model> and <mx:XML> point toward XML files that are further referenced by ID inside the <mx:DataGrid> element. These XML files represent the initial data set for the application and are located alongside the MXML file in either a development environment or server-side space.

Calling Back to the Server

Once compilation of the MXML file takes place, creating a SWF (Flash) file, the XML files or any other resources referenced inside the MXML will be attached to the SWF file, creating a *self-contained application* that will be sent to a user's browser. This is a critical step to understanding the Flash/Flex architecture.

On the initial response by the server to a browser, much, if not all, of the application's logic and data are sent to a user. Depending on a user's interaction, the (now) Flash application might call back to obtain more data, which is where the integration aspect with Spring comes into the picture.

But before elaborating on the particularities of Flex and Spring integration, it's important to provide more background on this call-back mechanism. The call-back mechanism initially starts off as MXML snippets declared on the main interface, which once compiled and sent to the browser (as a SWF file) will then perform the necessary calls to a server's endpoint.

The call-back snippets along with the server-side endpoints that process these requests can be of various types. A Flash application can call back using any of the following methods:[4]

- It can use the `HttpService` component to send HTTP requests to a server and consume the response. Although the `HTTPService` is typically used to consume XML, it can be used to consume other types of responses. The Flex `HTTPService` is similar to the `XMLHttpRequest` component available in AJAX.

- It can use the `WebService` component to invoke SOAP-based web services.

- It can use the `RemoteObject` component to directly invoke methods of Java objects deployed in your application server, and consume the return value. The return value can be a value of a primitive data type, an object, a collection of objects, an object graph, etc. In distributed computing terminology, this approach is generally referred to as remoting. This is also the terminology used in Spring to describe how different clients can access Spring beans remotely.

- In addition to the RPC-type services described previously, the Flex Data Management Services provide an innovative and virtually code-free approach to synchronizing data between the client application and the middle tier.

The first two approaches operate on server endpoints that are not directly related to the use of Spring. Under these circumstances, Spring components or Spring-DM services need to be wrapped as REST or SOAP services. Furthermore, using any of these two XML-based callback approaches lacks the more sophisticated Flash capabilities like real-time communication and synchronization.

4. Christophe Coenraets, "Using Flex with Spring," `http://coenraets.org/flex-spring/`

The remaining two methods take full advantage of Flash's capabilities. However, this also requires the deployment of Flex data services. Flex data services is a group of JARs and configuration files especially designed to attend callback methods performed by Flash clients—and in fact, Flash data services are often quoted as a server itself (Flash server).

The use of Flex data services or Flash server leads us to the first integration issues with Spring. If a Flex data service processes callback methods from Flash clients, how does a Flex data service access a Spring component or Spring-DM service? This consists of multiple steps.

The first thing that needs to be done is configure Flex data services to access Spring components. For this purpose, a special Spring factory[5] is used to instantiate Spring components and integrate them with Flex data services. This factory is configured in Flex's data services `services-config.xml` configuration file, as illustrated in Listing 8-15.

Listing 8-15. *Flex Data Services Configured with Spring Factory in* `services-config.xml`

```
<factories>
<factory id="spring" class="flex.samples.factories.SpringFactory">
</factories>
```

This last statement prepares Flex data services to access Spring components. Next, it's necessary to indicate the specific Spring components that will be accessible from Flex data services and at what endpoint they will be accessible. This is achieved in Flex's data services' `remoting-config.xml` configuration file. Listing 8-16 illustrates the `remoting-config.xml` configuration file for a bean named `HelloWorld`.

Listing 8-16. *Spring Bean Configured to Be Accessed As a Flex Data Service in* `remote-config.xml`

```
<destination id="helloWorldEndpoint">
      <properties>
          <factory>spring</factory>
          <source>helloWorldBean</source>
      </properties>
</destination>
```

This last listing defines the destination `helloWorldEndpoint`. Notice how the endpoint declares the `<factory>` element pointing to the factory ID defined in Listing 8-15, and the `<source>` element points to a `helloWorldBean` value. The `helloWorldBean` value represents an actual bean configured in a web application's Spring context inside the `applicationContext.xml` file.

Once the Spring factory and individual Spring components are configured in Flex data services, any callback method can be invoked *directly* on a Spring component from Flex

---

5. http://www.adobe.com/cfusion/exchange/index.cfm?event=extensionDetail&loc=en_us&extid=1035406

clients. The actual MXML snippet performing the callback to a Spring-bound Flex data service component would look like the one in Listing 8-17.

Listing 8-17. *Flex MXML Snippet Remoting Call on a Spring-Backed Flex Data Service*

```
<mx:RemoteObject id="hw" destination="helloWorldEndpoint"/>
<mx:Button label="Say HelloWorld" click="hw.hello()"/>
<mx:TextInput id="SayingHello" text="{hw.message}"/>
```

Notice how the call is made to the destination helloWorldEndpoint, which is where a Flex data service backed by a Spring bean was configured. Upon a request to this endpoint, which is triggered by a user clicking a button (<mx:Button>), Flex data services would invoke the hello() method belonging to the Spring bean, which given the previous configuration would obtain its data directly from a Spring component or Spring-DM service. Finally, the resulting value is displayed through the RemoteObject ID hw using the <mx:TextInput> element.

Configuring OSGi and Flex

Knowing the steps needed to integrate Spring and Flex, we can now move on to OSGi's specific configuration as it relates to Flex. For the purpose of this chapter's application, the web bundle (WAR) will have Flex's data services embedded in its structure. Listing 8-18 illustrates the layout for this bundle.

Listing 8-18. *Flex Data Services Embedded in a Web Bundle (WAR)*

```
+META-INF-+
                 |
                 +-MANIFEST.MF

+WEB-INF-+
                |
                +-web.xml
                |
                +-server.xml
                |
                 +-flex-+
                        |
                        |-services-confix.xml
                        |
                        |-remoting-config.xml
                        |
                        |-(More Flex data services configuration files and JAR)
```

Notice how the WEB-INF directory contains a flex directory; it's this directory which holds Flex data services' configuration files and JARs. This same approach is typically used for deploying Flex data services in a non-OSGi environment. Another alternative can be to deploy Flex data services in their own WAR, but this setup would go beyond the scope of this book.

Next, it's necessary to take into account class/package visibility. Flex data services relies on several classes/packages for its proper operation. In order for them to be accessible in an OSGi environment, it's necessary to explicitly declare them in a web bundle's (WAR's) MANIFEST.MF file. Listing 8-19 illustrates this MANIFEST.MF file for a web bundle (WAR) using Flex/Flash.

Listing 8-19. MANIFEST.MF *File for a Web Bundle (WAR) Using Flex/Flash*

```
Bundle-Version: 1.0
Bundle-SymbolicName: com.apress.springosgi.ch8.web
Bundle-Name: HelloWorld Spring-OSGi Web
Bundle-Vendor: Pro Spring-OSGi
Bundle-Classpath: .,
 WEB-INF/classes,
 WEB-INF/flexlibs/flex-messaging-common.jar,
 WEB-INF/flexlibs/flex-messaging.jar,
 WEB-INF/flexlibs/flex-messaging-opt.jar,
 WEB-INF/flexlibs/flex-messaging-req.jar,
 WEB-INF/flexlibs/flex-spring-factory.jar,
 WEB-INF/flexlibs/flex-bootstrap.jar,
Import-Package: com.apress.springosgi.ch8.model;version="1.0.0",
 com.apress.springosgi.ch8.service;version="1.0.0",
 javax.management,
 javax.naming,
 javax.xml.parsers,
 javax.xml.transform,
 javax.xml.transform.stream,
 javax.xml.transform.dom,
 org.xml.sax,
 org.xml.sax.helpers,
 org.xml.sax.ext,
 org.w3c.dom,
 org.w3c.dom.traversal,
 org.springframework.core.io,
 org.springframework.beans,
 org.springframework.beans.factory,
 org.springframework.context,
 org.springframework.beans.factory.xml,
 org.springframework.beans.factory.support,
 javax.servlet;version="2.5.0",
```

```
 javax.servlet.http;version="2.5.0",
 javax.servlet.resources;version="2.5.0",
 org.springframework.aop;version="2.5.4",
 org.springframework.core;version="2.5.4",
 org.springframework.ui;version="2.5.4",
 org.springframework.stereotype;version="2.5.4",
 org.springframework.context.support;version="2.5.4",
 org.springframework.web.context;version="2.5.4",
 org.springframework.web.context.support;version="2.5.4",
 org.springframework.web.servlet;version="2.5.4",
 org.springframework.web.servlet.handler;version="2.5.4",
 org.springframework.web.servlet.mvc;version="2.5.4",
 org.springframework.web.servlet.view;version="2.5.4",
 org.springframework.web.bind.annotation;version="2.5.4",
 org.springframework.osgi.service.importer;version="1.2.0",
 org.springframework.osgi.web.context.support;version="1.2.0",
 org.springframework.osgi.service.importer.support;version="1.2.0"
Web-ContextPath: /
```

Notice this last listing relies on the `Bundle-Classpath` header and has values pointing toward various Flex-provided JAR files. This allows the bootstrapping of Flex data services to take place without `ClassNotFoundException` errors. Further note how the `Import-Package` values differ from other web bundles (WARs) used in the book; the lack of JSP and JSTL packages and the addition of `javax.management` and `javax.naming` are particularities due to the Flex/Flash-based nature of the bundle.

Recall from the start of the chapter that I mentioned *embedding JARs* in a web bundle (WAR) was discouraged, but this last listing illustrates the exception to this rule: licensing. The JARs on which Flex data services depend are proprietary, therefore it's against their licensing scheme to modify them. This concludes coverage of the topic of Flex with Spring and OSGi, as well as the overall topic of web applications using Spring and OSGi.

FOR THE OSGI PURIST: FLASH OPEN SOURCE FLASH SERVER—ROJO

For those looking to avoid embedding Flex's data services JARs in a web bundle (WAR), an alternative route would be to use a Flash server named Red 5 (`http://osflash.org/red5`). Given this project's open source licensing scheme, its JARs can be modified to include OSGi headers.

Be advised that even though the purpose behind Red 5 is to offer an alternative to the official Flex server, configuration and the application itself also require changes. An excellent post on using Red 5 with Spring written by Paco Hernandez Gomez can be found here: `http://www.hernandezgomez.com/index.php/calling-java-methods-from-flex-using-mxremoteobject-and-red5/`.

Summary

In this chapter you started by learning how Spring-DM determines whether a bundle is web bound and needs to be delegated to an OSGi'fied web container. Next, you learned the necessary provisions a web bundle (WAR) needs to take into account for it to be successfully deployed in an OSGi'fied web container.

You then explored how Spring-DM delegates web bundles (WAR) to an underlying OSGi'fied web container for processing and how this influences the brand selected to deploy web bundles into. Immediately after, you took to the task of switching Spring-DM's default web container—Apache Tomcat—in favor of the Jetty web container.

Next, you learned how to enable SSL on an OSGi'fied web container, seeing how it's possible to create secure access for Spring/OSGi applications. This last step also illustrated how both Spring-DM's out-of-the-box supported web containers—Apache Tomcat and Jetty—can be configured to support more sophisticated features like their non-OSGi'fied versions through the use of OSGi fragments.

Finally, you learned about Flex in the context of Spring and OSGi. You explored how to use this technology inside web bundles (WAR) by embedding Flex data services, allowing remote Flash clients to access Spring components backed by OSGi services.

CHAPTER 9

■ ■ ■

Testing with Spring and OSGi

The importance of application testing was briefly addressed back in Chapter 2, where you learned to perform both unit and integration testing in the context of the Spring Framework. In doing so, you saw how Spring's POJO-based approach favors unit testing, as well as explored Spring's facilities to perform integration testing against RDBMSs.

Testing OSGi applications presents its own set of challenges. Among these are replicating an OSGi environment to verify that bundles work as expected once installed in an OSGi production environment and creating tests that use OSGi services.

Using Spring-DM simplifies this process. As it's been illustrated numerous times throughout the book, Spring-DM allows OSGi logic to be decoupled from application classes. This favors the use of POJOs in OSGi applications, which in turn facilitates the creation of tests.

This chapter will take you through all the testing facilities offered by Spring-DM.

Testing with OSGi and Spring-DM

In the introductory chapter on OSGi (Chapter 1), you might recall it was classes that needed to include the registration and lookup sequences for OSGi services using the framework's API.

Under such circumstances, testing can get complicated. With a class's code intertwined with OSGi calls, it can be difficult to create the necessary tests to guarantee the integrity of a class's OSGi and business logic. In addition, it requires thinking about tests in broader terms, such as how OSGi services need to interact with business logic, which militates against one of the basic principles of testing: simplicity.

Since Spring-DM relies on the use of descriptors to register and look up OSGi services on behalf of classes, a class's code normally doesn't contain this type of logic. This separation allows a class's business logic to be tested using very simple cases, as done in Chapter 2, while OSGi logic is also tested using separate and simple cases.

This approach is one of the cornerstones to using the Spring Framework—allowing classes to remain POJOs and define a class's dependencies elsewhere, thus facilitating the creation of tests.

Still, this type of testing done at the class level—unit testing—can become very different when OSGi comes into the picture. In a typical unit test (the business logic kind) consisting of proving the integrity of getter-setter methods, a workflow, or a mathematical operation, a testing framework has a one-on-one interaction with the class it is testing.

By "one-on-one interaction," I mean that a test sequence consists of applying an input to a class's method, holding its state, and verifying whether the return value is the desired output. It is a back-and-forth process between class and testing framework. But what happens when a class needs to get ahold of an outside resource to perform a test?

This type of testing—integration testing—is unavoidable when testing OSGi and Spring-DM applications. Since even OSGi services used in single classes need to be registered and/or looked up in an OSGi environment, this requires the presence of an OSGi environment to fulfill tests—just as an RDBMS is an outside resource required to perform integration tests, as illustrated in Chapter 2.

This implies that there is little scope for unit testing in OSGi, since *all testing involving OSGi and Spring-DM is considered integration testing, due to this reliance on an outside resource (OSGi framework).*

Still you may be wondering, what does testing an application using OSGi and Spring-DM really accomplish? The purpose behind integration testing in an environment like OSGi is to verify the correctness of behavior such as the following:

- Are a bundle's packages being exported with the correct version?
- Is a service registered with the correct interface and properties?
- Is a service that is looked up and consumed producing the expected outcome?
- Are a bundle's imported packages available from other bundles in the application?

All these questions revolve around OSGi and are best answered in a testing environment, where their potential for disruption is limited. In addition, OSGi testing also ensures that once an OSGi and Spring-DM code base start to evolve, a minimum benchmark or "safety net" is kept so as to not break older and relied-upon OSGi logic. In essence, the same benefits as non-OSGi testing apply to OSGi and Spring-DM testing.

After this brief overview of testing with OSGi and Spring-DM, let's revisit the same unit and integration techniques presented in Chapter 2, only this time applied to the OSGi application created in Chapter 7.

Unit and Integration Revisited: Testing OSGi Applications Without OSGi

The title to this section might sound strange, but there are non-OSGi tests that can be performed on OSGi applications. How so? This type of testing refers to unit testing an

OSGi application's non-OSGi logic, as well as performing the corresponding integration tests to ensure an application works correctly with something like an RDBMS.

Chapter 7's application, even though designed around OSGi (being composed of five bundles and operating on the basis of multiple OSGi services), still contains logic that can and should be tested outside the context of OSGi. Since Chapter 7's application is an OSGi version ported from Chapter 2's stand-alone Spring application, you've already created some of these tests.

Listing 2-11 in Chapter 2 illustrates a unit test that can be applied equally to a code base designed around OSGi principles. This unit test ensures the classes belonging to the application's model bundle have the correct behavior in terms of their getter-setter methods, which of course has nothing to do with OSGi.

Another aspect of testing that requires attention and is outside the scope of OSGi is related to the business logic executed against an RDBMS. Listing 2-12 in Chapter 2 illustrates the integration test applicable to the application's DAO class. This integration test ensures the class belonging to the service DAO bundle has the correct behavior when it interacts with an RDBMS.

In the case of the integration test in Listing 2-12, it should be noted that it is designed to test a DAO class using the JPA, unlike Chapter 7's application, which introduced a JDBC-backed DAO class. As already outlined in Chapter 7, OSGi's modularity allows you to easily swap bundles using either RDBMS access strategy (JPA or JDBC).

However, for the sake of completeness and to illustrate how an RDBMS integration test can be performed against a DAO class based on JDBC, Listing 9-1 shows this test.

Listing 9-1. *(Non-OSGi) RDBMS Integration Test for a DAO Class Based on JDBC*

```
package com.apress.springosgi.ch9.tests;

import java.util.Date;
import java.util.List;

import com.apress.springosgi.ch9.model.HelloWorld;
import com.apress.springosgi.ch9.model.Person;
import com.apress.springosgi.ch9.service.HelloWorldService;

import org.springframework.test.AbstractTransactionalDataSourceSpringContextTests;

import static org.junit.Assert.assertEquals;
import static org.junit.Assert.assertTrue;
import org.junit.Test;

import org.springframework.dao.EmptyResultDataAccessException;
import org.springframework.orm.ObjectRetrievalFailureException;

public class HelloWorldServiceIntegrationTests extends➥
 AbstractTransactionalDataSourceSpringContextTests {
```

```
    protected HelloWorldService helloWorldService;

    public void setHelloWorldService(HelloWorldService helloWorldService) {
        this.helloWorldService = helloWorldService;
    }

    private static long EnglishId;
    private static long SpanishId;
    private static long FrenchId;
    private static boolean databasePopulated = false;

    protected void populateDatabase() {
       ("classpath:/com/apress/springosgi/ch9/tests/helloworld-hsqldb.sql", false);
        databasePopulated = true;
    }

    protected String[] getConfigLocations() {
        return new String[] { "classpath:/com/apress/springosgi/ch9/tests/➥
helloworld-service.xml" };
    }

    protected void onSetUpBeforeTransaction() throws Exception {
        // This method is executed before each test method
        // Database tables and data only inserted once
        if (!databasePopulated) {
            populateDatabase();
            HelloWorld hw1 = new HelloWorld("English",
                                            "Hello World!", new Date(),
                                            new Person("John","Smith",45.00));
            HelloWorld hw2 = new HelloWorld("Spanish",
                                            "Hola Mundo!", new Date(),
                                            new Person("Carlos","Perez",40.00));
            HelloWorld hw3 = new HelloWorld("French",
                                            "Bonjour Monde!", new Date(),
                                            new Person("Pierre","LeClair",40.00));
            helloWorldService.save(hw1);
            helloWorldService.save(hw2);
            helloWorldService.save(hw3);

            EnglishId = helloWorldService.findByLanguage("English").get(0).getId();
            SpanishId = helloWorldService.findByLanguage("Spanish").get(0).getId();
            FrenchId = helloWorldService.findByLanguage("French").get(0).getId();
        }

    }
```

```
    public void testFindById() {
        HelloWorld hw = helloWorldService.findById(EnglishId);
        assertNotNull(hw);
        assertEquals("English", hw.getLanguage());
    }

    try {
            HelloWorld hw = helloWorldService.findById(10000);
        } catch(EmptyResultDataAccessException expected) {
            assertTrue(true);
        }
    }

    public void testFindByLanguage() {
        List<HelloWorld> hws = helloWorldService.findByLanguage("Spanish");
        assertEquals(1, hws.size());
        HelloWorld hw = hws.get(0);
        assertEquals("Hola Mundo!", hw.getMessage());
    }

    public void testFindByBadLanguage() {
        List<HelloWorld> hws = helloWorldService.findByLanguage("Catalan");
        assertEquals(0, hws.size());
    }

    public void testFindByTranslatorFirstName() {
        List<HelloWorld> hws = helloWorldService.findByTranslatorFirstName("John");
        assertEquals(1, hws.size());
        HelloWorld hw = hws.get(0);
        assertEquals(EnglishId, hw.getId());
    }

    public void testFindByTranslatorLastName() {
        List<HelloWorld> hws = helloWorldService.findByTranslatorLastName➥
("LeClair");
        assertEquals(1, hws.size());
        HelloWorld hw = hws.get(0);
        assertEquals(FrenchId, hw.getId());
    }

 public void testFindByTranslatorFirstNameDoesNotExist() {
        try{
            List<HelloWorld> hws = helloWorldService.findByTranslatorFirstName➥
("Bill");
        } catch(EmptyResultDataAccessException expected) {
            assertTrue(true);
        }
    }
```

```
    public void testFindByTranslatorLastNameDoesNotExist() {
        try {
            List<HelloWorld> hws = helloWorldService.findByTranslatorLastName➥
("Matsusaka");
        } catch(EmptyResultDataAccessException expected) {
            assertTrue(true);
        }
    }

    public void testFindByTranslatorHourlyRateOver() {
        List<HelloWorld> hws = helloWorldService.findByTranslatorHourlyRateOver➥
(42.00);
        assertEquals(1, hws.size());
    }

    public void testModifyHelloWorldMessage() {
        String oldHelloMessage = "Bonjour Monde!";
        String newHelloMessage = "Bonjour Le Monde!";
        HelloWorld hw = helloWorldService.findByLanguage("French").get(0);
        hw.setMessage(newHelloMessage);
        HelloWorld hw2 = helloWorldService.update(hw);
        assertEquals(newHelloMessage, hw2.getMessage());
        List<HelloWorld> hw3 = helloWorldService.findByMessage(oldHelloMessage);
        assertEquals(0, hw3.size());
        hw3 = helloWorldService.findByMessage(newHelloMessage);
        assertEquals(1, hw3.size());
        HelloWorld newhw3 = hw3.get(0);
        assertEquals(newHelloMessage, newhw3.getMessage());
    }

     public void testDeleteHelloWorldCascade() {
        String transFirstName = "Carlos";
        HelloWorld hw = helloWorldService.findByTranslatorFirstName➥
(transFirstName).get(0);
        int transCountBefore = countRowsInTable("person");
        int helloCountBefore = countRowsInTable("helloworld");
        helloWorldService.delete(hw);
        try {
            List<HelloWorld>  hws = helloWorldService.findByTranslatorFirstName➥
(transFirstName);
        } catch(EmptyResultDataAccessException expected) {
            assertTrue(true);
        }

        int transCountAfter = countRowsInTable("person");
        int helloCountAfter = countRowsInTable("helloworld");
        assertEquals(transCountBefore -1, transCountAfter);
```

```
        assertEquals(helloCountBefore -1, helloCountAfter);
    }

    public void testFindAll() {
        List<HelloWorld> hws = helloWorldService.findAll();
        assertEquals(3, hws.size());
    }

}
```

The first thing you should note about this listing is that it defines the same test methods as its JPA counterpart in Listing 2-12. However, the logic used to perform each test is different in that the test is being performed against a DAO class based on JDBC.

Notice how this test class extends `AbstractTransactionalDataSourceSpringContextTests`. This class provided by the Spring Framework facilitates the testing of JDBC-backed classes, just as the `AbstractJpaTests` class provided by the Spring Framework is used to facilitate testing of JPA-backed classes.

Though the mechanisms provided by these last two Spring helper classes is fairly similar, there are some differences you need to be aware of. First is the `getConfigLocations` method, which contains the configuration parameters to set up a test RDBMS; this RDBMS will in turn be used to inject a `helloWorldService` reference into the test class. Listing 9-2 illustrates the `helloworld-service.xml` file declared in `getConfigLocations`.

Listing 9-2. *(Non-OSGi) `helloworld-service.xml` Context for Setting Up a Test RDBMS Based on JDBC*

```
<?xml version="1.0" encoding="UTF-8"?>
<beans xmlns="http://www.springframework.org/schema/beans"
      xmlns:xsi="http://www.w3.org/2001/XMLSchema-instance"
      xsi:schemaLocation="http://www.springframework.org/schema/beans
                          http://www.springframework.org/schema/beans/➥
spring-beans.xsd">

   <bean id="helloWorldService"
         class="com.apress.springosgi.ch9.servicedaojdbc.HelloWorldDAO">
     <property name="dataSource" ref="dataSource"/>
   </bean>

   <bean id="dataSource" class="org.springframework.jdbc.datasource.➥
DriverManagerDataSource">
      <property name="driverClassName" value="org.hsqldb.jdbcDriver"/>
      <property name="url" value="jdbc:hsqldb:mem:springosgi"/>
      <property name="username" value="sa" />
      <property name="password" value="" />
   </bean>
```

```
    <bean id="transactionManager" class="org.springframework.jdbc.datasource.➥
DataSourceTransactionManager">
        <property name="dataSource" ref="dataSource"/>
    </bean>

</beans>
```

Serving as basis for comparison, take a look at Listing 2-13 in Chapter 2, which illustrates the `helloworld-service.xml` file used for JPA testing. The only thing that is identical between these two modes of testing (JPA and JDBC) is the `dataSource` declaration, which corresponds to an in-memory HSQLDB RDBMS.

The `transactionManager` declaration in this case is only applied to the `dataSource` element. In Listing 2-13, note the `transactionManager` declaration, in addition to the `dataSource` element, is applied to the `entityManagerFactory` element, which is JPA specific.

Next you can observe the `helloWorldService` declaration, which is injected with the `dataSource` bean. This is in contrast with the JPA version, which is injected with an `entityManagerFactory` bean. This difference is due to how JPA- and JDBC-backing classes operate. A JPA class taps an RDBMS through an `entityManagerFactory` instance, whereas a JDBC class gets ahold of an RDBMS through a raw data source.

In addition, the presence of an `entityManagerFactory`—or lack thereof—influences how a test RDBMS is set up. If you look closely at the JPA version in Listing 2-13, you will note the `<property name="generateDdl" value="true"/>` statement inside the `entityManagerFactory` element.

This statement allows the JPA entity manager to execute Data Definition Language (DDL) against an RDBMS. As consequence, this permits a test to be started without any preexisting tables in an RDBMS. (Note that DDL corresponds to `CREATE TABLE` type statements to create data structures in an RDBMS.)

Since this is JPA-specific behavior, a JDBC test needs to take this into account, creating the necessary RDBMS tables (DDL) at the outset of a test, which is the purpose of the `populateDatabase` method in the JDBC test class (Listing 9-1).

This last method relies on the `executeSqlScript` method, which forms part of the Spring `AbstractTransactionalDataSourceSpringContextTests` class and is used to execute an SQL DDL script against the data source configured for the test class. Listing 9-3 illustrates this script.

Listing 9-3. *(Non-OSGi)* `helloworld-hsqldb.sql` *Script to Prepopulate RDBMS*

```
CREATE TABLE Person(ID IDENTITY, FNAME VARCHAR(200),LNAME VARCHAR(200),➥
hourlyRate DOUBLE);

CREATE TABLE HelloWorld(ID IDENTITY, language VARCHAR(200), ➥
message VARCHAR(200), transdate DATE, translator_id INTEGER NOT NULL, ➥
CONSTRAINT FK1 FOREIGN KEY (translator_id) REFERENCES Person(ID))
```

This listing contains the two DDL statements that will be executed against the in-memory HSQLDB RDBMS. It's important to note that this script is only executed once—the same number of times the `populateDatabase` method is called, which is controlled by the `databasePopulated` field. This is due to the sequence of steps in the testing process.

When the testing process starts, Spring will instantiate an in-memory HSQLDB that will last for the entire sequence of test methods (`testFindBy*`, `testModify`, `testDelete`, etc.). Prior to executing each of these test methods, which rely on the presence of data in the RDBMS, the `onSetUpBeforeTransaction` method will be invoked on each occasion.

This behavior of the `onSetUpBeforeTransaction` method allows each test method to start with a clean set of data in the RDBMS (if so required), but at the same time and given its recursive nature, also executes the SQL DDL script against the RDBMS on each occasion. This process leads to errors because tables (DDL) can only be created once against the same RDBMS instance. Hence the need for a protective clause based on the `databasePopulated` field in order to invoke the `populateDatabase` method—and with it the `executeSqlScript` method—only once.

The test, including its class, context file, and DDL script, can be started with JUnit using a tool like Apache Ant, just as you did for the JPA DAO version in Chapter 2. The book's accompanying download includes this test in a staged form ready to be executed with Apache Ant.

This concludes the discussion on non-OSGi testing performed on OSGi applications, as well as analysis of the parts needed to test a DAO JDBC class using Spring artifacts and an in-memory RDBMS. Next, I will shift focus to OSGi testing and how Spring-DM supports this process.

Spring-DM's Testing Framework

As mentioned at the outset of this chapter, the process of performing OSGi tests requires the presence of an OSGi environment in order to guarantee that the behavior of bundles is appropriate once in a production environment. This creates the first requirement for OSGi testing: a means to bootstrap an OSGi environment in which to run tests.

Since the tests themselves need to interact with an OSGi environment's registry and services, this creates a second requirement: a need to package test classes in an OSGi bundle. This may seem awkward, especially compared to non-OSGi unit and integration test classes that can be executed directly from the file system, but in OSGi classes need to be prepped and installed in OSGi's de facto deployment format—the bundle. They simply can't be run in isolation even if they are test classes.

In addition, a third requirement may arise in the form of provisioning the OSGi testing environment with additional bundle dependencies needed to run a test. For example, in order to perform a test on an OSGi web bundle, you would have to install an OSGi'fied web container like Tomcat or Jetty into the OSGi testing environment prior to running the test itself, since the target web bundle requires such a dependency to operate.

These requirements alone are a lot of work to be fulfilling on each test case involving OSGi, which is the reason behind Spring-DM's testing framework. The purpose of Spring-DM's testing framework is to streamline the following process:

1. Start an OSGi testing environment.
2. Install and start any specified bundles required for the test class.
3. Package the test class into a bundle—generating its `MANIFEST.MF` file if none is provided—and installing the bundle into the OSGi testing environment.
4. Execute the test class inside the OSGi environment.
5. Shut down the OSGi testing environment.
6. Pass the test results back to the originating test class instance that is running outside OSGi.

By doing so, the Spring-DM testing framework lets you concentrate on the primary task of creating tests. In order to use the Spring-DM testing framework, you will need to rely on a series of classes included in Spring-DM and on which all tests should be designed. Just as you've used other Spring classes—such as `AbstractTransactionalDataSourceSpringContextTests` and `AbstractJpaTests`—which aid in the creation of tests by allowing the placement of test methods in a class without your needing to worry about the setup process, so too are these Spring-DM test classes aimed at reducing the amount of "legwork" needed to create tests.

I will illustrate the use of these test classes shortly, but for the moment I want to continue with a few more important details you'll need to know on Spring-DM's testing framework.

Spring-DM's testing framework allows testing to be performed against any of the three major OSGi frameworks: Eclipse Equinox, Apache Felix, and Knopflerfish. This guarantees that any bundle's OSGi logic is compatible with any of these three implementations.

It's also important that you realize *Spring-DM's testing framework is tightly pegged against Apache Maven,* relying on this last dependency management tool for the invocation of tests and management of bundle dependencies that may be needed by the tests themselves.

Since I opted to stay away from Apache Maven due to its more demanding setup in favor of Apache Ivy in Chapter 7, all the tests presented in this chapter will be designed to operate with Apache Ivy as the dependency management tool and Apache Ant as the build tool.

Having covered this background on Spring-DM's testing framework, you may be wondering what the general process for creating tests in Spring-DM is. The following list presents this three-step sequence:

1. Create a test class based on one of Spring-DM's supporting test classes, containing several assertions in reference to a bundle's services, classes, versions, exports, or imports.

2. Have an OSGi framework on standby, prepped and downloaded by either Apache Maven or Apache Ivy.

3. Execute the test aided by Apache Maven or Apache Ant.

Knowing this three-step sequence, let's create one of the most basic Spring-DM tests possible with the help of Apache Ivy and Apache Ant.

Creating a Spring-DM Test Class

Spring-DM test classes are designed around a series of classes available in Spring-DM's `org.springframework.osgi.test` package prefixed with the `Abstract` keyword and ending with the `Tests` keyword. These classes are listed in Table 9-1.

Table 9-1. *Spring-DM Test Classes and Inheritance Hierarchy*

Test Class	Function	Subclasses
`AbstractOptionalDependency-InjectionTests`	JUnit superclass that creates an empty OSGi bundle appCtx when no configuration file is specified. Required for mixing Spring existing testing hierarchy with the OSGi testing framework functionality.	`AbstractOsgiTests`
`AbstractOsgiTests`	Base test for OSGi environments. Takes care of configuring the chosen OSGi platform, starting it, installing a number of bundles, and delegating the test execution to a test copy that runs inside OSGi.	`AbstractConfigurableOsgiTests`
`AbstractConfigurableOsgiTests`	Abstract JUnit superclass that configures an OSGi platform. This class offers more hooks for programmatic and declarative configuration of the underlying OSGi platform used when running a test suite.	`AbstractSynchronizedOsgiTests`

Table 9-1. *Spring-DM Test Classes and Inheritance Hierarchy (Continued)*

Test Class	Function	Subclasses
`AbstractSynchronizedOsgiTests`	JUnit superclass that offers synchronization for application context initialization. This class automatically determines Spring-powered bundles that are installed by the testing framework and (by default) will wait for their application context to fully start.	`AbstractDependencyManagerTests`
`AbstractDependencyManagerTests`	Dependency manager class that deals with locating various artifacts required by the OSGi test. The artifacts are considered to be OSGi bundles that will be installed during the OSGi platform startup. Additionally, this class installs the testing framework required bundles, such as Spring and Spring-DM.	`AbstractOnTheFlyBundleCreatorTests`
`AbstractOnTheFlyBundleCreatorTests`	Enhanced subclass of `AbstractDependencyManagerTests` that facilities OSGi testing by creating a JAR at runtime using the indicated `MANIFEST.MF` file and resource patterns.	`AbstractConfigurableBundleCreatorTests`
`AbstractConfigurableBundleCreatorTests`	Abstract JUnit base class that allows easy integration testing. This class follows the traditional Spring style of integration testing in which the test simply indicates the dependencies, leaving the rest of the work to be done by its superclasses.	

All these classes have the same purpose as other non-OSGi Spring testing classes you've met in this book: to provide a starting point with preconfigured testing behaviors that can be overridden on a case-by-case basis depending on the nature of the test.

For example, many of these Spring-DM test classes are designed to operate with some of the following behaviors, unless otherwise specified: use Eclipse Equinox as the OSGi testing environment, use an Apache Maven repository to load test dependencies, and generate a `MANIFEST.MF` file on the fly for the test bundle, among other things.

All these behaviors as you will see shortly can be overridden for a particular test class, so for example a test class may use Apache Felix as the OSGi testing environment, use an Apache Ivy repository to load test dependencies, or use a prebuilt `MANIFEST.MF` file for the test bundle.

Still with seven classes available to create Spring-DM tests, how do you decide which one is appropriate for a particular test? The short answer is it depends; however, the `AbstractConfigurableBundleCreatorTests` class is often the preferred choice. I will elaborate why.

As illustrated in Table 9-1, each of the Spring-DM test classes is a subclass to another (e.g., `AbstractConfigurableOsgiTests` is a subclass of `AbstractOsgiTests`, and `AbstractOsgiTests` is a subclass of `AbstractOptionalDependencyInjectionTests`). This inheritance hierarchy allows each test class access to its parent class methods.

For example, a method like `getTestBundles`, which is part of the `AbstractDependencyManagerTests` class, will be accessible and can be overridden in tests based on the `AbstractOnTheFlyBundleCreatorTests` and `AbstractConfigurableBundleCreatorTests` classes. Whether you need access to such a method or any other testing behavior will be dependent on what a test is designed to accomplish, which in turn will determine what class in the Spring-DM test hierarchy is the best option.

Inclusively, the top-level Spring-DM test class, `AbstractOptionalDependencyInjectionTests`, is a subclass tied to the Spring Framework's test class hierarchy. This allows Spring-DM test classes access to methods like `getConfigLocations`, `onSetUp`, `addContext`, and a series of `assert*` methods, which you've already been exposed to in non-OSGi Spring tests.

Therefore, because `AbstractConfigurableBundleCreatorTests` is a subclass of all the other Spring-DM testing classes, it's often the preferred choice for creating OSGi tests.

Let's create a Spring-DM test class using the `AbstractConfigurableBundleCreatorTests` class, designed to simply print the OSGi testing environment vendor and version, as well as the operating system used to run the test. Listing 9-4 shows this test class.

Listing 9-4. *Spring-DM Test Class Designed to Return the OSGi Environment Vendor and Version*

```
package com.apress.springosgi.ch9.testsosgi;

import org.springframework.osgi.test.AbstractConfigurableBundleCreatorTests;
import org.springframework.osgi.test.provisioning.ArtifactLocator;

import org.osgi.framework.Constants;

import com.apress.springosgi.ch9.testsosgi.testivyprovisions.➥
LocalFileSystemIvyRepository;

public class BootstrapTest extends AbstractConfigurableBundleCreatorTests {

    public String getRootPath() {
        return"file:./classes/";
    }
```

```
    public ArtifactLocator getLocator() {
        return new LocalFileSystemIvyRepository();
    }

    public void testOsgiPlatformStarts() throws Exception {
        System.out.println("OSGi Framework Vendor : " + bundleContext.➥
getProperty(Constants.FRAMEWORK_VENDOR));
        System.out.println("OSGi Framework Vendor Version : " + bundleContext.➥
getProperty(Constants.FRAMEWORK_VERSION));
        System.out.println("OS Name and Version :  " + bundleContext.➥
getProperty(Constants.FRAMEWORK_OS_NAME) + "-" + bundleContext.➥
getProperty(Constants.FRAMEWORK_OS_VERSION));
    }
}
```

The test class is short, but the meaning behind each of its statements is critical. The first thing to note is that the test class inherits its behavior from the `AbstractConfigurableBundleCreatorTests` class. This will in turn give the test class the capacity to override Spring-DM's various testing methods.

Note that since this test relies on the `getRootPath` method, it's necessary to use the `AbstractConfigurableBundleCreatorTests` class, since only this Spring-DM test class provides this method. Were it not for this requirement, the test could be designed using a test class in the Spring-DM hierarchy as high as `AbstractDependencyManagerTests`, because this class provides access to the `getLocator` method. And barring the need for these last two methods, the test could be designed with the top-level Spring-DM test class `AbstractOptionalDependencyInjectionTests`, since the only remaining method, `testOSGiPlatformsStarts`, is a test method agnostic to the Spring-DM testing framework.

The first overridden method is `getRootMethod`, which is used by the Spring-DM testing framework to locate the test class. In this case, it's indicating to search for the test class under the `classes` directory of the present working directory. But why is it necessary to indicate where the test class is located in the file system? Especially in the test class itself?

When the test class is executed by a tool like Apache Maven or Apache Ivy via JUnit, the location of the test class is known beforehand. However, since this same test class needs to be packaged inside an OSGi bundle and deployed to an OSGi testing environment, it is necessary to provide the directory in which the test class can be located by the Spring-DM testing framework. If this method is not overridden, Spring-DM's testing framework attempts to locate the test class inside a directory named `target/test-classes`.

Needless to say, if the test class cannot be located in the indicated directory, the test will fail. This error can be especially misleading, since initially it is not obvious why the test class fails if it cannot find itself in a certain directory, even though you are able to execute the test class from a tool like Apache Maven or Apache Ivy.

The second overridden method is `getLocator`, which is used by the Spring-DM testing framework to define an `ArtifactLocator`. In this case, the test class is using a custom-made `ArtifactLocator` named `LocalFileSystemIvyRepository` with the purpose of using Apache Ivy as the repository to locate bundle dependencies for the test class.

An `ArtifactLocator` is important because it tells the Spring-DM testing framework where to locate bundle dependencies for executing the test class, such as the OSGi testing framework (Equinox, Felix, or Knopflerfish), JUnit bundles, Spring core bundles, Spring-DM bundles, and any other bundle like Apache Commons or Apache Tomcat needed to run a test.

If the `getLocator` method is not overridden, Spring-DM's testing framework attempts to locate bundle dependencies in an Apache Maven type repository located by default in `.m2/repository` of a user's home directory.

Since we relied on Apache Ivy instead of Apache Maven in Chapter 7 to fulfill dependencies, we will do the same to perform Spring-DM tests. The custom-made `ArtifactLocator` named `LocalFileSystemIvyRepository` configures the Spring-DM testing framework to load bundle dependencies from an Apache Ivy repository that by default would be located in `.ivy2/cache` of a user's home directory. See the book's accompanying download for this custom-made `ArtifactLocator` source code.

If the test class cannot locate the minimal set of dependencies needed to run a Spring-DM test in the declared `ArtifactLocator`, the test will fail. The minimum set of bundles that need to be present in an `ArtifactLocator` (Apache Maven or Apache Ivy) to run a test are shown in Listing 9-5.

Listing 9-5. *Minimum Set of Bundles Needed to Be Present in `ArtifactLocator` (Apache Maven or Apache Ivy) to Perform the Spring-DM Test*

```
com.springsource.org.aopalliance.1.0.0,
com.springsource.junit,3.8.2,
com.springsource.org.objectweb.asm.2.2.3,
com.springsource.slf4j.api,1.5.0,
com.springsource.slf4j.log4j.1.5.0,
com.springsource.slf4j.org.apache.commons.logging,1.5.0,
org.springframework.spring-aop.2.5.5,
org.springframework.spring-beans,2.5.5,
org.springframework.spring-context,2.5.5,
org.springframework.spring-core.2.5.5,
org.springframework.spring-test.2.5.5,
org.springframework.osgi.log4j.osgi.1.2.15-SNAPSHOT,
org.springframework.osgi.spring-osgi-annotation.1.2.0-m1,
org.springframework.osgi.spring-osgi-core.1.2.0-m1,
org.springframework.osgi.spring-osgi-extender.1.2.0-m1,
org.springframework.osgi.spring-osgi-io.1.2.0-m1,
org.springframework.osgi.spring-osgi-test.1.2.0-m1
```

Note This minimum set of bundles is in addition to the OSGi testing environment (Eclipse, Felix, or Knopflerfish) used to execute the tests, which also needs to be available in the `ArtifactLocator`.

Finally, the test class declares the `testOsgiPlatformStarts` method, which is executed at the outset of a test. This particular method prints out various constants belonging to the `org.osgi.framework.Constants` class, namely `FRAMEWORK_VENDOR`, `FRAMEWORK_VERSION`, `FRAMEWORK_OS_NAME`, and `FRAMEWORK_OS_VERSION`.

In regards to this last method, it is important to note that this method is executed once the OSGi testing framework has been bootstrapped. Therefore, the test results will print out whichever OSGi implementation is used to run the test.

The next step consists of downloading and prepping the necessary bundle dependencies needed to run the test—those in Listing 9-5.

Downloading Spring-DM Test Dependencies with Apache Ivy

Chapter 7 provides a formal introduction to the benefits and configuration parameters of Apache Ivy, so if you're not familiar with how Apache Ivy works, you may want to go back to that chapter and look at the section "Hello World Application Revisited Without the SpringSource dm Server: Data Access and Apache Ivy." Next, I will illustrate Apache Ivy's main configuration files needed to run Spring-DM tests.

Listing 9-6 shows Apache Ivy's `ivy.xml` file with the necessary `<dependency>` elements to download the minimal set of Spring-DM test dependencies.

Listing 9-6. *Apache Ivy `ivy.xml` File with Minimal Spring-DM Test Dependencies*

```
<ivy-module version="2.0">
    <info organisation="apache" module="hello-ivy"/>
    <configurations>
         <conf name="build"/>
    </configurations>
   <!-- Download bundle dependencies for application testing (Non-OSGi and OSGi)-->
       <dependency org="org.junit" name="com.springsource.org.junit" rev="4.5.0"/>
       <dependency org="org.hsqldb" name="com.springsource.org.hsqldb" ➥
rev="1.8.0.9" />
       <dependency org="org.objectweb.asm"➥
 name="com.springsource.org.objectweb.asm" rev="2.2.3"/>
       <dependency org="org.aopalliance" name="com.springsource.org.aopalliance" ➥
rev="1.0.0"/>
        <dependency org="org.slf4j" name="com.springsource.slf4j.log4j" ➥
rev="1.5.0"/>
       <dependency org="org.springframework" name="spring-aop" rev="2.5.5.A"/>
       <dependency org="org.springframework" name="spring-beans" rev="2.5.5.A"/>
       <dependency org="org.springframework" name="spring-context" rev="2.5.5.A"/>
       <dependency org="org.springframework" name="spring-core" rev="2.5.5.A"/>
       <dependency org="org.springframework" name="spring-test" rev="2.5.5.A"/>
       <dependency org="org.springframework.osgi" name="log4j.osgi" ➥
rev="1.2.15-SNAPSHOT">
```

```
        <artifact name="log4j.osgi" type="jar" ➥
url="http://s3.amazonaws.com/maven.springframework.org/osgi/org/springframework/➥
osgi/log4j.osgi/1.2.15-SNAPSHOT/log4j.osgi-1.2.15-20080314.153110-17.jar"/>
      </dependency>
      <dependency org="org.springframework.osgi" name="spring-osgi-annotation"➥
 rev="1.2.0-m1"/>
      <dependency org="org.springframework.osgi" name="spring-osgi-test"➥
 rev="1.2.0-m1"/>
      <dependency org="org.eclipse.osgi" name="org.eclipse.osgi"➥
 rev="3.5.0.200811061137"/>
      <dependency org="org.apache.felix" name="org.apache.felix.main" rev="1.0.4"/>
      <dependency org="knopflerfish" name="framework" rev="2.1.0"/>
 </dependencies>
</ivy-module>
```

This last Apache Ivy configuration file takes care of downloading all the bundles enumerated in Listing 9-5, in addition to the three OSGi implementations that can be used to perform Spring-DM tests (Eclipse Equinox, Apache Felix, and Knopflerfish).

Besides the `ivy.xml` file, it is also necessary to define an `ivysettings.xml` file indicating the repositories from which these bundles can be downloaded. Listing 9-7 shows this file.

Listing 9-7. *Apache Ivy `ivysettings.xml` File for Spring-DM Test Dependencies*

```
<ivysettings>

  <settings defaultResolver="chain-springosgi"/>

  <caches defaultCacheDir="${basedir}/ivylib">
  </caches>

  <resolvers>
    <chain name="chain-springosgi">
        <filesystem name="my-repository">
          <ivy pattern="${basedir}/ivylib/[organisation]/[module]/[revision]/➥
[artifact]-[revision].[ext]"/>
          <artifact pattern="${basedir}/ivylib/[organisation]/[module]/[revision]/➥
[artifact]-[revision].[ext]"/>
        </filesystem>

      <url name="spring-release-repo">
              <ivy pattern="http://repository.springsource.com/ivy/bundles/➥
release/[organisation]/[module]/[revision]/[artifact]-[revision].[ext]" />
              <artifact pattern="http://repository.springsource.com/ivy/bundles/➥
release/[organisation]/[module]/[revision]/[artifact]-[revision].[ext]" />
      </url>
```

```
        <url name="spring-external-repo">
                  <ivy pattern="http://repository.springsource.com/ivy/bundles/➥
external/[organisation]/[module]/[revision]/[artifact]-[revision].[ext]" />
                  <artifact pattern="http://repository.springsource.com/ivy/bundles/➥
external/[organisation]/[module]/[revision]/[artifact]-[revision].[ext]" />
        </url>

        <url name="spring-milestone-repo" m2compatible="true">
                  <artifact pattern="http://s3.amazonaws.com/➥
maven.springframework.org/milestone/[organisation]/[module]/➥
[revision]/[artifact]-[revision].[ext]"/>
        </url>

        <ibiblio name="ibiblio"/>

        <url name="default-repo" m2compatible="true">
                  <artifact pattern="http://repo1.maven.org/maven2/[organisation]/➥
[module]/[revision]/[artifact]-[revision].[ext]"/>
        </url>

        <url name="knoper-repo" m2compatible="true">
                  <artifact pattern="http://springframework.svn.sourceforge.net/➥
svnroot/springframework/repos/repo-ext/[organisation]/[module]/[revision]/➥
[artifact]-[revision].[ext]"/>
        </url>
     </chain>

  </resolvers>

</ivysettings>
```

This `ivysettings.xml` file is very similar to the one used in Chapter 7, with two areas worth emphasizing. A new repository, `http://springframework.svn.sourceforge.net/`, is added to the list, since the OSGi Knopflerfish implementation—one of the three options for performing Spring-DM tests—is only available in this repository. And the default `defaultCacheDir` value is assigned an `ivylib` value, meaning dependencies will be downloaded to a subdirectory by this name in the current working directory.

Having defined the Apache Ivy configuration files needed to download dependencies to run Spring-DM tests, it is necessary to create an Apache Ant configuration file to trigger this task. In addition, since Apache Ant will also be used to execute the Spring-DM test via JUnit, the next section will show the configuration file needed to perform these two tasks.

Executing a Spring-DM Test with Apache Ant

The Apache Ant configuration file needed to perform Spring-DM tests will consist of two parts: one related to downloading and prepping bundle dependencies using Apache Ivy and the other to using JUnit to execute the test class illustrated in Listing 9-4.

The directory layout used by this Apache Ant file—such as where it locates source files and where it places compiled classes—follows the same Hello World "playground" conventions used in other examples in the book. Listing 9-8 illustrates the Apache Ant configuration needed to perform Spring-DM tests.

Listing 9-8. *Apache Ant `build.xml` File for Spring-DM Tests*

```
<?xml version="1.0"?>
<project xmlns:ivy="antlib:org.apache.ivy.ant" default="init" basedir=".">

<target name="init" description="Apress - Pro Spring-OSGi">
  <tstamp/>
  <property name="projectname" value="Pro Spring-OSGi"/>

  <echo message="-------${projectname}------"/>
  <property name="debug"           value="on"/>
  <property name="optimize"        value="off"/>
  <property name="deprication"     value="off"/>
 <property name="build.compiler" value="modern"/>
 <property name="target.vm"      value="1.5"/>
 <property name="build.dir"      value="classes"/>
 <property name="dist.dir"       value="dist"/>
 <property name="src.dir"        value="src"/>
 <property name="lib.dir"        value="lib/build"/>

 <!-- Load JARs onto the classpath, taken from lib/build sub-dir -->

 <path id="classpath">
  <fileset dir="${lib.dir}">
   <include name="*.jar"/>
  </fileset>
  <pathelement location="${build.dir}"/>
 </path>
</target>

<target name="compile" depends="init" description="Compile code">
```

```
  <ivy:retrieve pattern="lib/[conf]/[artifact]-[revision].[ext]" />

  <echo message="-------Compiling code for Pro-Spring OSGi------"/>

  <mkdir dir="${build.dir}"/>
  <mkdir dir="${dist.dir}"/>

  <javac srcdir="${src.dir}"
         destdir="${build.dir}"
         debug="${debug}"
         optimize="${optimize}"
         deprecation="${deprecation}"
         target="${target.vm}">
     <classpath refid="classpath"/>
  </javac>

 <copy todir="${build.dir}">
           <fileset dir="${src.dir}">
<!-- Some of the following statements are relevant to Ch2 -->
<!-- They are present here because the same compile task is used -->
               <include name="**/*.properties"/>
               <include name="**/*.xml"/>
               <include name="**/*.sql"/>
               <include name="**/*.MF"/>
               <exclude name="**/*.java"/>
               <exclude name="META-INF/**"/>
               <exclude name="WEB-INF/**"/>
               <exclude name="GUI/**"/>
            </fileset>
  </copy>
</target>

<target name="ch9" depends="compile" description="Build Chapter 9 ➥
Spring-OSGi Application">

  <echo message="------------- Building Chapter 9 Spring-OSGi Application ➥
for Pro Spring-OSGi -------------"/>
     <property name="ch9.dir"          value="${dist.dir}/ch9/"/>
     <mkdir dir="${ch9.dir}"/>
     <property name="test.dir"        value="${ch9.dir}/tests"/>
     <mkdir dir="${test.dir}"/>
      <echo message="------------- Starting Unit and Integration Testing ➥
(OSGi) -------------"/>
        <junit printsummary="yes" fork="yes">
        <sysproperty key="localRepository" value="ivylib"/>
        <sysproperty key="org.springframework.osgi.test.framework" ➥
value="org.springframework.osgi.test.platform.KnopflerfishPlatform"/>
```

```
62 <!--        <sysproperty key="org.springframework.osgi.test.framework" ➥
value="org.springframework.osgi.test.platform.FelixPlatform"/> -->
63 <!--        <sysproperty key="org.springframework.osgi.test.framework" ➥
value="org.springframework.osgi.test.platform.EquinoxPlatform"/>  -->
64         <classpath refid="classpath"/>
65         <formatter type="brief"/>
66         <batchtest todir="${test.dir}">
67            <fileset dir="${build.dir}">
68              <include name="com/apress/springosgi/ch9/testsosgi/*"/>
69            </fileset>
70         </batchtest>
71        </junit>
72        <echo message="-------------- Ending Unit and Integration Testing ➥
(OSGi) --------------"/>
73 </target>
74 </project>
```

I will explain the Apache Ivy–related configuration first. Notice how the top-level <project> element (Line 2) declares the Apache Ivy namespace needed to execute Ivy tasks. Next, you will find various properties used for compiling classes, chief among them the <path> element (Lines 17 to 22) with a value of lib/build, which will be the directory containing JARs needed to compile a project's classes.

Next, you will find the compile target (Line 24) used for compiling classes. Notice how the first statement in this target is <ivy:retrieve pattern="lib/[conf]/[artifact]-[revision].[ext]" /> (Line 25); this is used to trigger the retrieval of Ivy dependencies—those defined in ivy.xml (Listing 9-6).

In accordance with this last Apache Ivy configuration file, this will initiate the download of bundles into the ivylib directory (the defaultCacheDir value). Once the downloading of bundles is complete, and this time in accordance with the <ivy:retrieve> element defined in the Apache Ant configuration file, copies of downloaded bundles will be made on the basis of the pattern value lib/[conf]/[artifact]-[revision].[ext].

In this value, the [conf] snippet represents <configurations>/<conf> values in ivy.xml (Listing 9-6). Since there is only one value—<conf name="build"/>—and neither <dependency> element has a conf attribute, this means *all* dependencies in ivylib will be copied over to lib/build/, which is precisely where the Apache Ant <path> element will attempt to load JARs needed to compile a project's classes. Chapter 7 contains a more elaborate scenario on this copying process, including a visual description of the entire process in Figure 7-3.

With all dependencies downloaded by Apache Ivy—for both compiling and executing Spring-DM tests—the compilation of classes takes place with Apache Ant's <javac>element (Lines 29 to 36). Here it's worth noting that the <javac>element places compiled classes inside destdir="${build.dir}" where {build.dir} has a value of classes. This location is where the Spring-DM test class was configured to locate the compiled test class—the getRootPath() method in Listing 9-4.

Next, we come to the Apache Ant `ch9` target (Line 52), which triggers the actual Spring-DM test using the `<junit>` task (Lines 59 to 71). This task is the same one you employed in Chapter 2 to perform non-OSGi tests using Apache Ant, except this time it's equipped with a few additional parameters needed to run Spring-DM tests.

The first difference comes in the form of the attribute `fork="yes"`(Line 59).This attribute allows the test to run in a separate Java Virtual Machine (JVM), which is important since all tests require bootstrapping an OSGi environment. If this attribute is not used, the OSGi testing environment is bootstrapped in the same JVM as Apache Ant, a process that can cause security access errors in some OSGi environments; therefore, it's recommended to run tests in their own JVM.

Next, observe the `<sysproperty key="localRepository" value="ivylib"/>` element (Line 60), which is used to pass a variable named `localRepository` to the `ArtifactLocator` defined in the Spring-DM test.

By default, the custom-made `ArtifactLocator` defined for the test class attempts to locate bundle dependencies to run the test in `.ivy2/cache` of a user's home directory. However, since this class's bundle dependencies have already been downloaded into a directory named `ivylib`, this property overrides the location where the `ArtifactLocator` attempts to locate bundle dependencies.

■ **Note** This same `localRepository` value can be used to override Spring-DM's default Apache Maven `ArtifactLocator`. So instead of attempting to locate bundle dependencies to run a test in `.m2/repository` of a user's home directory, an alternative directory containing a Maven repository can be used.

The second `<sysproperty>` element (Line 61) is used to define the OSGi environment on which to perform the test. For this purpose, the `org.springframework.osgi.test.framework` key value is used, with a value of either `org.springframework.osgi.test.platform.EquinoxPlatform`, `org.springframework.osgi.test.platform.FelixPlatform`, or `org.springframework.osgi.test.platform.KnopflerfishPlatform`, indicating Eclipse Equinox, Apache Felix, or Knopflerfish, respectively.

If this value is omitted, the Spring-DM testing framework will attempt to run the test with Eclipse Equinox. It should also be pointed out that the Spring-DM testing framework will attempt to locate whatever OSGi environment is specified in the `ArtifactLocator`.

■ **Note** An alternative to specifying the OSGi testing environment using this last system property is to hard-code the desired OSGi testing environment in the test class itself by overriding the method `getPlatformName()`.

Next, you will find the `<classpath>` element (Line 64), used by JUnit to load the necessary runtime libraries, that points toward the `classpath <path>` or `lib/build` directory. This is followed by the `<formatter>` element (Line 65), which generates `brief` test reports.

Finishing off the `<junit>` task, you will encounter the `<batchtest>` element (Lines 66 to 70), which is used to indicate where to place test reports—in this case `${test.dir}`, which corresponds to `dist/ch9/tests`—and where to load tests classes from—in this case `classes/com/apress/springosgi/ch9/testsosgi/`, which is where the compiled Spring-DM test class is placed.

Upon invoking this Ant task, `ch9`, the `<junit>` task (Lines 59 to 71) will trigger the Spring-DM test, placing the test results in a text file inside the `dist/ch9/tests/` directory. Listing 9-9 illustrates the results of running the test using Eclipse Equinox on a Linux operating system.

Listing 9-9. *Test Results of Running Spring-DM Test Class* `BootstrapTest`

```
Testsuite: com.apress.springosgi.ch9.testsosgi.BootstrapTest

Tests run: 1, Failures: 0, Errors: 0, Time elapsed: 2.197 sec

------------- Standard Output ---------------

18:25:48.708 [main] DEBUG c.a.s.ch9.testsosgi.BootstrapTest - About to start➥
 Equinox OSGi Platform

18:25:49.614 [main] INFO  c.a.s.ch9.testsosgi.BootstrapTest - Equinox OSGi➥
 Platform [3.5.0.200811061137] started

18:25:49.641 [main] DEBUG c.a.s.ch9.testsosgi.BootstrapTest - Default framework ➥
bundles :{org.aopalliance,com.springsource.org.aopalliance,1.0.0,
org.junit,com.springsource.junit,3.8.2,
org.objectweb.asm,com.springsource.org.objectweb.asm,2.2.3,
org.slf4j,com.springsource.slf4j.api,1.5.0,
org.slf4j,com.springsource.slf4j.log4j,1.5.0,
org.slf4j,com.springsource.slf4j.org.apache.commons.logging,1.5.0,
org.springframework,spring-aop,2.5.5, org.springframework,spring-beans,2.5.5,
org.springframework,spring-context,2.5.5, org.springframework,spring-core,2.5.5,
org.springframework,spring-test,2.5.5, org.springframework.osgi,log4j.osgi,1.2.15-
SNAPSHOT, org.springframework.osgi,spring-osgi-annotation,1.2.0-m1,
org.springframework.osgi,spring-osgi-core,1.2.0-m1,
org.springframework.osgi,spring-osgi-extender,1.2.0-m1,
org.springframework.osgi,spring-osgi-io,1.2.0-m1, org.springframework.osgi,spring-
osgi-test,1.2.0-m1}
18:25:49.646 [main] INFO  c.a.s.c.t.t.LocalFileSystemIvyRepository - Local Ivy2 ➥
```

```
repository used: [ivylib]
<OTHER INFO AND DEBUG OUTPUT OMITTED FOR BREVITY>
18:25:50.566 [main] DEBUG c.a.s.ch9.testsosgi.BootstrapTest - Looking for ➥
Spring/OSGi powered bundles to wait for...
OSGi Framework Vendor : Eclipse
OSGi Framework Vendor Version : 1.5.0
OS Name and Version :  Linux-2.6.27
```

The initial lines of the test results will reflect a very long sequence of bundle installations performed by the Spring-DM testing framework, similar to the output generated by manually installing bundles in an OSGi shell.

Once all the required bundles for the Spring-DM testing framework and the test bundle containing the test class are installed, the test class is executed, outputting in this case the values of the OSGi implementation vendor and version, as well as the operating system used to run the test.

Now that you are familiar with how the different parts needed to run a Spring-DM test work together, I will show you how to create more elaborate Spring-DM test classes.

Hello World Application Spring-DM Test

Your first Spring-DM test didn't do all that much, except obtain values from the underlying OSGi testing environment and operating system used to run the test. A more interesting Spring-DM test would consist of guaranteeing a bundle publishes an OSGi service correctly, or the consumption of an OSGi service produces its expected outcome.

As it turns out, from Chapter 7 we have five bundles we can put to the test in order to avoid any surprises once they enter a production environment. So let's get started creating a Spring-DM test class with one of these bundles.

The test will consist of guaranteeing the integrity of the `helloworld-db.jar` bundle. This particular bundle is charged with providing a connection to a MySQL RDBMS and making it available as an OSGi service for other bundles in the application. Given this purpose, the following test will assert the OSGi service is published correctly and that the service can be used to perform a query against the RDBMS. Listing 9-10 shows the test class for the `helloworld-db.jar` bundle.

Listing 9-10. *Spring-DM `DataSourceBundleTest` for the `helloworld-db.jar` Bundle*

```
package com.apress.springosgi.ch9.testsosgi;

import org.springframework.osgi.test.AbstractConfigurableBundleCreatorTests;
import org.springframework.osgi.test.provisioning.ArtifactLocator;

import java.util.List;
import java.util.ArrayList;
import java.util.Collections;
```

```
import org.springframework.core.io.Resource;
import org.springframework.core.io.FileSystemResource;

import org.osgi.framework.BundleContext;
import org.osgi.framework.ServiceReference;

import javax.sql.DataSource;
import org.apache.commons.dbcp.BasicDataSource;
import java.sql.Connection;
import java.sql.Statement;
import java.sql.ResultSet;

import com.apress.springosgi.ch9.testsosgi.testivyprovisions.➥
LocalFileSystemIvyRepository;

public class DataSourceBundleTest extends➥
 AbstractConfigurableBundleCreatorTests {

    protected String getRootPath() {
        return"file:./classes/";
    }

    protected ArtifactLocator getLocator() {
        return new LocalFileSystemIvyRepository();
    }

    protected String[] getTestBundlesNames() {
        List col = new ArrayList();
        col.add("com.mysql.jdbc, com.springsource.com.mysql.jdbc, 5.1.6");
        col.add("org.apache.commons, com.springsource.org.apache.commons.dbcp,➥
 1.2.2.osgi");
        col.add("org.apache.commons, com.springsource.org.apache.commons.pool,➥
 1.3.0");
        return (String[]) col.toArray(new String[col.size()]);
    }

    protected Resource[] getTestBundles() {
        Resource[] repoBundles = locateBundles(getTestBundlesNames());
        Resource[] testBundles = new Resource[] {
            new FileSystemResource("dist/ch9/helloworld-db.jar")
        };
        List<Resource> allBundles = new ArrayList<Resource>();
        Collections.addAll(allBundles, repoBundles);
        Collections.addAll(allBundles, testBundles);
        return allBundles.toArray(new Resource[] {});
    }
```

```
41      public void testDataSourceService() {
42          waitOnContextCreation("com.apress.springosgi.ch9.db");
43          //The superclass provides access to the testing bundle's context, ➥
which can then get ahold of published services
44          ServiceReference ref = bundleContext.getServiceReference(DataSource.➥
class.getName());
45          assertNotNull("Service Reference is null", ref);
46          try {
47              DataSource dataSourceService = (DataSource) bundleContext.➥
getService(ref);
48              assertNotNull("Cannot find the service", dataSourceService);
49              // Start connection and query sequence to the DB using➥
 OSGi-backed service
50              Connection dataSourceConnection = dataSourceService.getConnection();
51              Statement statement = dataSourceConnection.createStatement();
52              ResultSet result = statement.executeQuery("select * from➥
 HelloWorld where language = 'Spanish'");
53              boolean rs = result.next();
54              if (rs) {
55                  assertEquals("Hola Mundo!",result.getString("message"));
56              } else {
57            throw new Exception("No record in DB belonging to Spanish➥
 tranlsation");
58              }
59              result.close();
60              statement.close();
61              dataSourceConnection.close();
62          } catch (Exception exc) {
63              exc.printStackTrace();
64          } finally {
65              bundleContext.ungetService(ref);
66          }
67      }
68  }
```

Just like the earlier test, this class inherits its behavior from Spring-DM's AbstractConfigurableBundleCreatorTests class (Line 17). This test class also overrides the getRootPath (Lines 18 to 20) and getLocator (Lines 21 to 23) methods to suit the particular needs of the project, which is to locate the test class inside the classes directory and locate bundle dependencies in an Apache Ivy repository.

Besides these two methods, which you are already familiar with, there are two new methods, getTestBundlesNames (Lines 24 to 30) and getTestBundles (Lines 31 to 40). These methods are used to load additional bundle dependencies needed to run tests in the Spring-DM testing framework.

The getTestBundlesNames method loads bundles from the ArtifactLocator defined in the test class, which in this case corresponds to a custom ArtifactLocator designed to use an Apache Ivy repository. The format used to define dependencies in the getTestBundlesNames method consists of a String array, with each string following a group, ID, and version notation, where the group, ID, and version are values in line with the conventions used to define dependencies in Apache Ivy and Apache Maven. In Apache Ivy the values for group, ID, and version map to the ivy.xml <dependency> element attributes org, name, and rev, respectively.

The getTestBundlesNames method for this particular test declares org.apache.commons.dbcp, org.apache.commons.pool, and com.mysql.jdbc as prerequisite bundles. This is because all three bundles are needed by the helloworld-db.jar bundle and as a consequence need be installed in order to perform a test on this last bundle.

■ **Note** Upon defining dependencies in a test class's getTestBundlesNames method, you will also need to ensure the ArtifactLocator is updated to download such dependencies. In such cases, you need to add the necessary <dependency> statements to Ivy's ivy.xml configuration file.

Since not every bundle needed to run a test will be located in a repository like Apache Ivy or Apache Maven, the getTestBundles method is used to load bundles using a file system route—via the FileSystemResource class. As a consequence, this method fits perfectly for loading the application helloworld-db.jar bundle.

This particular instance of getTestBundles, in addition to loading the helloworld-db.jar bundle using a FileSystemResource instance, also appends the bundles declared in the getTestBundlesNames method. This is due to Spring-DM's testing framework design. In order to use both the getTestBundles and getTestBundlesNames in a test class, the former method needs to explicitly call the latter; otherwise, the bundles declared in getTestBundlesNames are not installed in the OSGi testing environment.

Once all the required bundles for running the test are installed, the first and only test method, testDataSourceService, is executed. This test method will assert that an OSGi DataSource service is available and perform a query against the RDBMS.

The first declaration (Line 42) inside the test method is waitOnContextCreation("com.apress.springosgi.ch9.db"). The use of this statement tells the Spring-DM testing framework to hold the test until the context of a bundle with a symbolic name com.apress.springosgi.ch9.db is created; in this case, the symbolic name corresponds to the helloworld-db.jar bundle.

The waitOnContextCreation method is an important safeguard for performing tests, since it guarantees a test will have access to the bundle context on which the test will be performed. On tests consisting of multiple bundles, this can be especially important since it ensures that certain bundles providing services to other test bundles have their context created first.

The next line in the test class (Line 44) attempts to retrieve a service reference of the type `DataSource.class.getName()`, which is also equal to `javax.sql.DataSource`. Note that this service reference is located using the `bundleContext.getServiceReference` call, which is a standard OSGi method belonging to the `org.osgi.framework` package. The `bundleContext` in this case refers to the test bundle created on the fly by the Spring-DM testing framework to execute the test.

Next, you can see the `assertNotNull` statement (Line 45), which is used to guarantee the prior service reference is not null. By design, the `helloworld-db.jar` bundle is configured to publish a `javax.sql.DataSource` service reference, so if this application bundle installed using the `getTestBundles` method is designed correctly, the assertion will pass; otherwise the assertion and test will fail.

Following this first assertion is a `try/catch` block (Lines to 46 to 66) that will perform a query on the RDBMS. The first step consists of obtaining the OSGi service for the `javax.sql.DataSource` service reference (Line 47). The service reference is obtained using the statement `bundleContext.getService(ref)`, which also corresponds to a standard OSGi method.

Immediately after the service reference is obtained, another assertion statement is made to guarantee that the service is not null (Line 48). Here again, if for some reason the service published by the `helloworld-db.jar` bundle is not working correctly, the assertion and test will fail.

At this point the test guarantees the OSGi service is published by `helloworld-db.jar`, but the test can go a step further, executing a query against the RDBMS using this same service. Since the `dataSourceService` is a `javax.sql.DataSource`, this test can be performed using the regular JDBC query process: create a `Connection` object, followed by a `Statement` object and a `ResultSet` object.

Since we know beforehand the dataset held in the RDBMS, we also know the query performed against the RDBMS, `select * from HelloWorld where language = 'Spanish'`, should return a certain set of values. In this case, we expect the specified query to return an `Hola Mundo!` value for the `message` column. The final assertion in the form of `assertEquals` (Line 55) guarantees the data obtained from the RDBMS via an OSGi service is the correct data.

Given that this test class belongs to the same package, `com.apress.springosgi.ch9.testsosgi`, as the earlier test class, by placing it in the same source directory, the same Apache Ivy and Apache Ant configuration files can be used to trigger the execution of the test.

The mechanism for creating test classes for the remaining Hello World application bundles follows this same pattern, with the most variable step being the installation of dependency bundles needed to run the test from either a repository—like Apache Maven or Apache Ivy—or the file system, via the `getTestBundlesNames` and `getTestBundles` methods. For example, a test class for the Hello World application web bundle (WAR) would require the installation of Tomcat and a series of additional Spring bundles, as well as the other application bundles, since they are all dependencies for the web bundle (WAR).

As far as the test methods are concerned, the logic in such tests is open ended. As illustrated in this last test class, a test method can use APIs ranging from the OSGi framework to get ahold of services provided by other bundles in the test environment, to JDBC calls that interact with an RDBMS, to any other API required to assert a bundle's logic.

Finally, it's worth mentioning that the `AbstractConfigurableBundleCreatorTests` class has a few more methods that can be overridden. These range from the `getManifestLocation` method, used to provide a prebuilt `MANIEST.MF` file for the test bundle (instead of letting the Spring-DM testing framework generate one for you), to the `getConfigLocations` method, used to provide a prebuilt application context for the test bundle. Such methods, however, are rarely required to be overridden. You can consult the `AbstractConfigurableBundleCreatorTests` class's Java docs for more information on these and other methods.

This concludes our exploration into testing bundles using the Spring-DM testing framework, and with it the overall subject of testing Spring and OSGi applications.

Summary

In this chapter you learned how testing plays an important role in the overall life cycle of application development, ensuring a class's logic works as expected once in a production environment. In this same context, you explored why Spring-DM eases the creation of tests when an application leverages OSGi.

You then explored how non-OSGi tests—unit and integration with an RDBMS—can be equally applied to a code base that uses OSGi, thanks in part to the decoupling of OSGi logic achieved by using Spring-DM.

Then you continued on to explore the Spring-DM testing framework. You learned how it reduces the amount of work needed to perform tests on OSGi bundles, aiding in the bootstrapping of an OSGi testing environment and packaging test classes into bundles, as well as providing a series of base classes on which to construct tests.

You then created a test class that illustrated the basic procedure for all Spring-DM test classes. You saw how to override a test class's methods to accommodate the needs of a particular project and use an Apache Ivy repository to satisfy the bundle dependencies needed by a test, as well as use Apache Ant to execute Spring-DM tests.

Finally, you created one more test class designed around the application created in Chapter 7. This test class illustrated how a Spring-DM–powered bundle could be loaded into an OSGi testing environment, verifying that its OSGi services were published correctly and that such services were providing logical results.

Index

X